LUTHER'S WORKS

American Edition

VOLUME 46

Published by Concordia Publishing House

and Fortress Press in 55 volumes.

General Editors are Jaroslav Pelikan (for vols. 1-30)

and Helmut T. Lehmann (for vols. 31-55)

LUTHER'S WORKS

VOLUME 46

The Christian in Society

III

EDITED BY

ROBERT C. SCHULTZ

GENERAL EDITOR

HELMUT T. LEHMANN

FORTRESS PRESS/PHILADELPHIA

© 1967 by Fortress Press

Library of Congress Catalogue Number 55-9893

Printed in the United States of America 1-346

GENERAL EDITORS'
PREFACE

The first editions of Luther's collected works appeared in the sixteenth century, and so did the first efforts to make him "speak English." In America serious attempts in these directions were made for the first time in the nineteenth century. The Saint Louis edition of Luther was the first endeavor on American soil to publish a collected edition of his works, and the Henkel Press in Newmarket, Virginia, was the first to publish some of Luther's writings in an English translation. During the first decade of the twentieth century, J. N. Lenker produced translations of Luther's sermons and commentaries in thirteen volumes. A few years later the first of the six volumes in the Philadelphia (or Holman) edition of the *Works of Martin Luther* appeared. But a growing recognition of the need for more of Luther's works in English has resulted in this American edition of Luther's works.

The edition is intended primarily for the reader whose knowledge of late medieval Latin and sixteenth-century German is too small to permit him to work with Luther in the original languages. Those who can will continue to read Luther in his original words as these have been assembled in the monumental Weimar edition (*D. Martin Luthers Werke.* Kritische Gesamtausgabe, Weimar, 1883-   ). Its texts and helps have formed a basis for this edition, though in certain places we have felt constrained to depart from its readings and findings. We have tried throughout to translate Luther as he thought translating should be done. That is, we have striven for faithfulness on the basis of the best lexicographical materials available. But where literal accuracy and clarity have conflicted, it is clarity that we have preferred, so that sometimes paraphrase seemed more faithful than literal fidelity. We have proceeded in a similar way in the matter of Bible versions, translating Luther's translations. Where this could be done by the use of an existing

v

English version—King James, Douay, or Revised Standard—we have done so. Where it could not, we have supplied our own. To indicate this in each specific instance would have been pedantic; to adopt a uniform procedure would have been artificial—especially in view of Luther's own inconsistency in this regard. In each volume the translator will be responsible primarily for matters of text and language, while the responsibility of the editor will extend principally to the historical and theological matters reflected in the introductions and notes.

Although the edition as planned will include fifty-five volumes, Luther's writings are not being translated in their entirety. Nor should they be. As he was the first to insist, much of what he wrote and said was not that important. Thus the edition is a selection of works that have proved their importance for the faith, life, and history of the Christian church. The first thirty volumes contain Luther's expositions of various biblical books, while the remaining volumes include what are usually called his "Reformation writings" and other occasional pieces. The final volume of the set will be an index volume; in addition to an index of quotations, proper names, and topics, and a list of corrections and changes, it will contain a glossary of many of the technical terms that recur in Luther's works and that cannot be defined each time they appear. Obviously Luther cannot be forced into any neat set of rubrics. He can provide his reader with bits of autobiography or with political observations as he expounds a psalm, and he can speak tenderly about the meaning of the faith in the midst of polemics against his opponents. It is the hope of publishers, editors, and translators that through this edition the message of Luther's faith will speak more clearly to the modern church.

J. P.
H. T. L.

CONTENTS

General Editors' Preface   v

Abbreviations   IX

Introduction to Volume 46   XI

Admonition to Peace, A Reply to the Twelve
    Articles of the Peasants in Swabia, 1525   3
    Translated by Charles M. Jacobs
    Revised by Robert C. Schultz

Against the Robbing and Murdering Hordes of
    Peasants, 1525   45
    Translated by Charles M. Jacobs
    Revised by Robert C. Schultz

An Open Letter on the Harsh Book Against
    the Peasants, 1525   57
    Translated by Charles M. Jacobs
    Revised by Robert C. Schultz

Whether Soldiers, Too, Can Be Saved, 1526   87
    Translated by Charles M. Jacobs
    Revised by Robert C. Schultz

An Answer to Several Questions on Monastic Vows, 1526   139
    Translated by Robert C. Schultz

On War Against the Turk, 1529   155
    Translated by Charles M. Jacobs
    Revised by Robert C. Schultz

A Sermon on Keeping Children in School, 1530   207
    Translated by Charles M. Jacobs
    Revised by Robert C. Schultz

On Marriage Matters, 1530   259
    Translated by Frederick C. Ahrens

Indexes   321

ANF   — *The Ante-Nicene Fathers*, edited by Alexander Roberts and James Donaldson (Buffalo and New York, 1885-1896, American reprint of the Edinburgh edition).

BG   — *Luthers Werke für das christliche Haus*, edited by Georg Buchwald, *et al.* (Braunschweig, 1889-1892).

CIC   — *Corpus Iuris Canonici*, edited by E. Friedberg (Graz, 1955).

CL   — *Luthers Werkes in Auswahl*, edited by Otto Clemen, *et al.* (Bonn, 1912-1933; Berlin, 1955-1956).

C.R.   — *Corpus Reformatorum*, edited by C. G. Bretschneider and H. E. Bindseil (Halle/Saale, 1834-1860).

DRTA. JR   — *Deutsche Reichstagsakten unter Kaiser Karl V*, edited by Historische Kommission bei der Bayrischen Akademie der Wissenschaften (Gotha, 1893-).

EA   — *D. Martin Luthers sämmtliche Werke* (Frankfurt and Erlangen, 1826-1857).

FC   — *Fathers of the Church*, edited by Ludwig Schopp (New York, 1947-).

LW   — American Edition of *Luther's Works* (Philadelphia and St. Louis, 1955-).

LWZ   — *The Latin Works of Huldreich Zwingli*, 3 vols., translated and edited by S. M. Jackson, *et al.* (New York, 1912; Philadelphia, 1922, 1929).

MA[3]   — *Martin Luther. Ausgewählte Werke*, edited by H. H. Borcherdt and Georg Merz (3rd ed., München, 1948-).

MPG	— *Patrologia, Series Graeca,* 161 vols., edited by J. P. Migne (Paris, 1857-1866).
MPL	— *Patrologia, Series Latina,* 221 vols., edited by J. P. Migne (Paris, 1844-1904).
O.C.D.	— *The Oxford Classical Dictionary,* edited by M. Cary, *et al.* (2nd ed., Oxford University Press, 1950).
O.D.C.C.	— *The Oxford Dictionary of the Christian Church,* edited by F. L. Cross (2nd ed., Oxford University Press, 1958).
PE	— *Works of Martin Luther.* Philadelphia Edition (Philadelphia, 1915-1943).
PNF[1]	— *The Nicene and Post-Nicene Fathers of the Christian Church.* First Series, edited by Philip Schaff (New York, 1886-1900).
St. L.	— *D. Martin Luthers sämmtliche Schriften,* edited by Johann Georg Walch. Edited and published in modern German, 23 vols. in 25 (2nd ed., St. Louis, 1880-1910).
WA	— *D. Martin Luthers Werke.* Kritische Gesamtausgabe (Weimar, 1883-).
WA, Br	— *D. Martin Luthers Werke.* Briefwechsel (Weimar, 1930-).
WA, DB	— *D. Martin Luthers Werke.* Deutsche Bibel (Weimar, 1906-1961).
WA, TR	— *D. Martin Luthers Werke.* Tischreden (Weimar, 1912-1921).

INTRODUCTION TO VOLUME 46

For seven years after the posting of the *Ninety-five Theses*[1] in 1517 the tide had been running strongly in favor of the Wittenberg Reformation. Pope Leo X, who had excommunicated Luther, died in December, 1521, and was followed on the papal throne by Adrian VI. The new pontiff was quite conscious of the need to reform the church and regarded the rapidly spreading reformation inaugurated by Luther as a punishment divinely inflicted upon the church. Nonetheless, he was as adamant and unyielding in his determination to crush the Reformation as his predecessor had been. In a communication addressed to the imperial diet assembled at Nürnberg in November, 1522, Adrian demanded that the Edict of Worms be enforced against Luther.[2] The diet replied that enforcement was impossible, and renewed earlier demands for a general council to meet in Germany within a year. Pending such a council the diet called for the preaching of the "true, pure, genuine, holy gospel."[3] With the emperor involved in wars which kept him from German soil from 1521 to 1530 and with a stalemate over enforcement of the Edict of Worms, the Reformation movement continued its rapid spread and Luther became the symbol of a possible German national front against the papacy.

But in 1524 the tide began to ebb. In that year Erasmus published his *Freedom of the Will,* to which Luther replied the following year with *On the Bondage of the Will.* The break between Luther and the renowned Dutch scholar deprived the Reformation of the support of many humanists in Germany and elsewhere.

Another current in the ebbing tide was the dissatisfaction with Luther of such men as Andrew Karlstadt and Thomas Münzer. For them Luther was but a half-way reformer. They carried their message of radical reform to the less intellectual and lower classes, who received it with warmth and enthusiasm if not always with

---

[1] *LW* 31, 25-33.

[2] See B. J. Kidd (ed.), *Documents Illustrative of the Continental Reformation* (Oxford: Clarendon Press, 1911), pp. 107-109.

[3] *Ibid.,* pp. 110-113.

understanding. Furthermore, the Zwinglian Reformation in the German cantons of Switzerland was attracting many adherents among the Evangelicals of southern Germany, and attempts to effect a rapprochement between the Lutherans and the Zwinglians were frustrated at Marburg in 1529.

On the Catholic side there was still another change on the papal throne. The reign of Adrian VI lasted but twenty months. His successor, Clement VII,[4] appointed Cardinal Lorenzo Campeggio as his legate and commissioned him to capitalize on the misgivings of a number of German rulers who feared that the Lutheran movement would issue in a rebellion like that of the Hussites a century before. These misgivings were shared not only by Luther's foes but also by his friends and by the uncommitted German sovereigns. Through clever and appealing concessions, Campeggio effected an alliance of German Catholic rulers, thereby dividing the German nobility into three parties: Catholic, Lutheran, and undecided.[5] Despite these divisions Luther's own sovereign, Frederick the Wise of Electoral Saxony, expected a peaceful solution to the perplexing and explosive problem confronting church and state. This expectation was shattered by the outbreak of the brief but bloody Peasants' War, after which the spread of the Lutheran Reformation among the common people was severely curtailed.

All of the writings in this volume come from the five-year ebb tide between 1525 and 1530. Four of these treatises are related to the uprising of the peasants. In *Admonition to Peace* Luther replied to the published grievances of the peasants and sought to forestall insurrection and violence as well as to achieve an amelioration of the peasants' burdens. Before this little book could be published, however, the uprising had begun. Convinced that the peasants were bent upon nothing but revolution and anarchy, Luther called upon the authorities to crush the rebellion in *Against the Robbing and Murdering Hordes of Peasants*.

The insurrection was suppressed with such brutality that in *An Open Letter on the Harsh Book Against the Peasants* Luther

---

[4] Giulio de Medici reigned as Pope Clement VII from 1523 to 1534.
[5] Cf. Thomas M. Lindsay, *The Reformation in Germany from Its Beginning to the Religious Peace of Augsburg* ("A History of the Reformation," Vol. I [New York: Charles Scribner's Sons, 1922]), pp. 324-325.

had to defend the position he had taken toward the rebels, not only against his foes, but even against staunch supporters. In *An Answer to Several Questions on Monastic Vows* Luther advised a Catholic ruler, already deeply in debt from suppressing the rebellious peasants and confronted by the demands of monastics that he restore their rebellion-ravaged properties, that in the light of the gospel monastic vows are not binding.

During the half-decade covered by the writings in this volume an old threat to Christendom began to revive. The Muslim Turks, bent upon the conquest of a Europe now divided into Catholic and Protestant counteralliances, were on the march. Sincere Christians were questioning whether it was right to bear arms. Others were calling for a crusade against the infidel Turk, while still others simply did not know what to do in the face of the Turkish menace and the opposing Catholic and Protestant leagues which were then being formed. In *Whether Soldiers, Too, Can Be Saved* the pastor-professor of Wittenberg took the position that soldiery is a legitimate vocation which belongs to the God-given office of the sword. In this book Luther endorses and expounds the principle of defense as the divinely appointed duty of every government. In the treatise *On War Against the Turk* Luther denied the right of the church to lead any kind of military crusade. The defense of the empire and of its imperiled subjects belonged by divine order solely to the emperor, Luther declared.

The inability of the German realms to enforce the Edict of Worms led the 1526 Diet of Spires, acting in the emperor's absence, to declare that each territorial ruler was to "live, govern, and carry himself as he hopes and trusts to answer it to God and his imperial majesty."[6] The Protestant princes concluded from this declaration that they had the legal right to organize territorial churches based on evangelical teaching and practices.[7] The organization of territorial churches was a *de facto* ecclesiastical break with the papal church and raised a host of practical, theological, and legal problems to which Luther was called upon to address himself.

To this category of writings belong *A Sermon on Keeping*

---

[6] Kidd (ed.), *op. cit.*, p. 185.
[7] Cf. Lindsay, *op. cit.*, pp. 343-344.

Children in School and *On Marriage Matters.* In the latter Luther had to deal with problems pertaining to marriage, which previously had been regulated by canon law, now discarded by the Protestants. The interests of society, the troubled consciences of believers, and the confusion of magistrates and pastors demanded guidance, and Luther sought to give it. In the former treatise he sought to persuade reluctant parents to give their children an education to serve God in church, state, and society.

The Indexes were prepared by Dr. Frederick C. Ahrens, who also translated *On Marriage Matters.*

R. C. S.

LUTHER'S WORKS

VOLUME 46

ADMONITION TO PEACE
A REPLY TO
THE TWELVE ARTICLES OF
THE PEASANTS IN SWABIA

1525

Translated by Charles M. Jacobs

Revised by Robert C. Schultz

INTRODUCTION

For at least a century before the Reformation the increased burdens and demands of a crumbling feudal society had been causing widespread unrest among the peasants of Europe. This unrest embodied not a little resentment and hostility toward the institutional church whose bishops and abbots were among the chief landlords. Proposals for church reform—especially those which advocated apostolic poverty—found ready adherents among the peasants, as did heretical ideas, with overtones of the millennium.[1]

Throughout the fifteenth century peasant insurrections had been frequent occurrences.[2] Usually these uprisings had their inception in the visions and revelations received by their leaders. The Peasants' War of 1525 was the last and the most violent of these revolts. More significantly, however, it was the first armed conflict after the beginning of the Reformation in which the doctrines of Luther were laid hold of and misused to justify a political and social cause. To the peasants it seemed that Luther's teachings pointed out a way whereby the vested financial institutions of the church might be overthrown without forfeiting the spiritual benefits the church claimed to confer.

But the peasants did not stop at appropriating and misconstruing Luther's teachings. They were urged on by popular reformers such as Thomas Münzer[3] and Balthasar Hübmaier,[4] who

---

[1] For a summary presentation of German peasantry from the twelfth century to the Reformation era, see E. G. Schwiebert, *Luther and His Times* (St. Louis: Concordia Publishing House, 1950), pp. 556-570.

[2] Cf. Eileen Power (trans.), P. Boissonnade's *Life and Work in Medieval Europe* (New York: Alfred A. Knopf, 1950), pp. 327-331.

[3] Thomas Münzer (*ca.* 1490-1525) was a native of Stolberg in the Harz Mountains. After a rather unsettled career including duty as confessor in a convent, he became a preacher of radical religious and social reform. His incitement of the peasants and workers of Mühlhausen (Thuringia) led to their severe defeat in the battle of Frankenhausen. Münzer was subsequently executed for his role in the uprising.

[4] Hübmaier (*ca.* 1485-1528) had been a student of John Eck at Freiburg and Ingolstadt. At Waldshut (1523) he allied himself openly with Zwingli but soon embraced Anabaptist views. He later settled in Moravia and promoted the Anabaptist cause until Austrian authorities burned him at the stake in Vienna.

believed that the reformation of the church could be achieved only through the abolition of existing ecclesiastical institutions and the creation of new and pure ones. Their idea of society was a theocracy based on God's word written in Scripture or revealed by the Spirit to chosen prophets. It was the incitement by men such as these, whom Luther called "prophets of murder,"[5] which led to the bloody war of 1525.

In 1524 and 1525 the three main centers of peasant revolutionary activity were Swabia, Franconia, and Thuringia. Uprisings had broken out in these territories and violence spread rapidly.[6] In various places the peasants formulated their demands in the form of manifestos or articles. One of these documents, called *The Twelve Articles,* became quite prominent. They were adopted by the peasants of Memmingen in January or February, 1525. They appeared in print sometime before March 19 and were so widely circulated that they were reprinted two dozen times before May of that year.[7] Because of Luther's frequent reference to these articles, they are reprinted here.

When Luther first saw these articles is not known, but it was certainly before April 16, 1525, when Melanchthon wrote to Joachim Camerarius[8] that Luther intended to reply to them. The actual writing of *Admonition to Peace* took place during a journey by Luther into Thuringia,[9] one of the centers of discontent.

---

[5] Cf. p. 20.

[6] Cf. Schwiebert, *op. cit.,* p. 562.

[7] The authorship of these articles has not been established despite many intense and exhaustive efforts to do so. C. M. Jacobs cites Wilhelm Stolze's conclusion that it was either Hübmaier or one of his disciples (cf. *PE* 4, 207, and *O.D.C.C.,* p. 661). George Hunston Williams speaks of Sebastian Lotzer of Memmingen as responsible for the publication of the *Articles* and notes that most modern scholars feel that Hübmaier's literary association with this manifesto was of a secondary nature (cf. Williams, *The Radical Reformation* [Philadelphia: Westminster Press, 1962], p. 67, n. 8). Veit Valentin identifies Ulrich Schmid, a Swabian craftsman, as the author, but cites no evidence (Valentin, *The German People: Their History and Civilization from the Holy Roman Empire to the Third Reich* [New York: Alfred A. Knopf, 1952], pp. 160-161).

[8] The renowned German classical scholar and reformer (1500-1574) took part in drawing up the *Augsburg Confession.* The text of Melanchthon's letter is found in *C. R.* 1, 739.

[9] Cf. *WA* 18, 281.

There were several reasons Luther wrote the *Admonition*. First, although the peasants were in arms, Luther hoped that his appeal would help to avert widespread bloodshed and strife. Second, in *The Twelve Articles* the peasants repeatedly identified their cause as Christian, and they offered to submit to correction on the basis of Scripture if any article or articles proved to be contrary to God's word. Luther took this offer at face value.

But there was yet a third reason for writing the *Admonition*, which Luther indicates when he refers to an unidentified document[10] in which the peasants appealed to him by name for counsel. We know of two such documents. One was a set of instructions[11] given to representatives of the peasants as a guide for negotiations with the Swabian League.[12] Among other things, they are to ask for the appointment of a commission to interpret the "divine law." Luther was one of the men suggested for appointment to such a commission. The second document,[13] which later became the constitution of the "Christian Association,"[14] was adopted by the Swabian peasants on March 7, 1525. Appended to this document is a list of the names of fourteen men, Luther at the head, regarded as acceptable expounders of the "divine law."

The first part of the *Admonition* is an address to the princes and lords in which Luther urges them to take the threatened rebellion seriously, to try conciliation, to moderate their demands upon the peasants, and to reform their way of living. Luther tells the princes quite frankly that they alone are to blame for the present state of affairs.

In the second part, addressed to the peasants, Luther admits that many of the demands set forth in *The Twelve Articles* are just. Nonetheless, Luther says, the peasants are wrong to employ force in rectifying injustice, and doubly wrong in claiming that the

---

[10] Cf. p. 17.

[11] *WA* 18, 280.

[12] The Swabian League was an Austrian-sponsored alliance of towns.

[13] The text is given in Heinrich Boehmer, *Urkunden zur Geschichte des Bauernkrieges und der Wiedertäufer* (Bonn, 1910), pp. 22-24.

[14] The *Christliche Vereinigung* or Christian Association of Peasants was organized on May 7, 1525, under the leadership of Sebastian Lotzer. The association allied the peasant bands of Allgäu, Lake Constance, and Baltringen. Cf. Williams, *op. cit.*, p. 68.

gospel justifies such action. The Christian law requires submission to authority, not violence and insurrection. Then Luther deals at length with the preface and the first three articles of the peasants. The rest of the articles, he maintains, are matters for legal experts.

In the third part Luther addresses both princes and peasants. Neither of them has acted in a Christian way. If war should come, they will lose their souls and Germany will be ruined. This disaster can be averted only by appointing an arbitration commission whose proposals will be accepted by both parties. But before the *Admonition to Peace* could be published, the land was flooded with insurrection, arson, pillage, and murder.

The translation is a revision of that by Charles M. Jacobs in *PE* 4, 219-244, based on the German text *Ermahnung zum Frieden auf die zwölf Artikel der Bauernschaft in Schwaben* in WA 18, (279) 291-334.

C. M. J.
R. C. S.

The Twelve Articles[15]

The basic and chief articles of all the peasants and subjects of spiritual and temporal lords, concerning the matters in which they feel they are being denied their rights.

To the Christian reader: Peace and the grace of God through Christ.

Many antichrists [I John 2:18] have recently taken advantage of the assembling of the peasants and used it as an excuse to speak scornfully about the gospel. They say, "Is this the fruit of the new gospel? Will no one be obedient anymore? Will the people rebel everywhere, revolt against their lords, gather and organize in crowds, and use their power to reform or even to overthrow their spiritual and temporal authorities? Indeed, they may even

---

[15] The translation is that by Charles M. Jacobs (*PE* 4, 210-216), revised on the basis of the German text in Boehmer, *op. cit.*, pp. 3-10.

kill them." The following articles are our answer to these godless and blasphemous critics. Our intention is twofold: first, to remove this calumny from the word of God and, second, to excuse in a Christian way the disobedience and even the rebellion of the peasants.

First, the gospel does not cause rebellion and disturbance, because it is a message about Christ, the promised Messiah, whose words and life teach nothing but love, peace, patience, and unity. And all who believe in this Christ become loving, peaceful, patient, and agreeable. This is the basis of all the articles of the peasants (as will clearly appear), and they are basically concerned with hearing the word of God and living according to it. On what basis, then, can these antichrists call the gospel a cause of revolt and violence? That some antichrists and enemies of the gospel resist these demands and requests is not the fault of the gospel, but of the devil, the gospel's deadliest enemy, who by means of unbelief arouses opposition in his own. Through this opposition the word of God, which teaches love, peace, and unity, is suppressed and taken away.[16]

Romans 1

Romans 11
Isaiah 40
Romans 8
Exodus 3 and 14
Luke 18

Second, on this basis the conclusion is obvious that the peasants cannot properly be called disobedient and rebellious. For, as these articles indicate, they desire this gospel [to be the basis of] their teaching and life.[17] Now if God wills to hear the peasants' earnest and fervent prayer that they may live according to his word, who will criticize the will of God? Who will meddle in his judgment? Who indeed will resist his majesty? Did he not hear the children of Israel when they cried to him and release them out of the hand of Pharaoh [Exod. 3:7-8]; and can he not today deliver his own? Yes, he will deliver them, and will

---

[16] Cf. Mark 4:15.

[17] The implicit demand is that the laws of the community be based on divine right, that is, on the gospel.

do so quickly [Ps. 46:5]! Therefore, Christian reader, read the following articles carefully and then decide.

Here Follow the Articles

The First Article

I Timothy 3
Titus 1
Acts 14
Deuteronomy 17
Exodus 31
Deuteronomy 10
John 6
Galatians 2

First, we humbly ask and request—in accordance with our unanimous will and desire—that in the future the entire community have the power and authority to choose and appoint a pastor. We also desire the power to depose him, should he conduct himself improperly. The pastor whom we thus choose for ourselves shall preach the holy gospel to us clearly and purely. He is to add no teaching or commandment of men to the gospel, but rather is always to proclaim the true faith and encourage us to ask God for his grace. He is to instill and strengthen this true faith in us. For if the grace of God is not instilled in us, we remain mere flesh and blood. And mere flesh and blood is useless, as Scripture clearly says, for we can come to God only through true faith and can be saved only through his mercy. That is why we need such a leader and pastor; and thus our demand is grounded in Scripture.[18]

As the whole
Epistle to
the Hebrews says.

Psalm 109
Genesis 14
Deuteronomy 18
Deuteronomy 12

Second, since the tithe[19] is prescribed in the Old Testament, although it is fulfilled in the New, we are willing to pay the just tithe of grain, but it must be done in a proper way. Since men ought to give it to God and distribute it to those who are his, it belongs to the pastor who clearly proclaims the word of God, and we desire that in the future this tithe be

---

[18] The marginal reference to Exodus 31 is based on an allegorical interpretation of that passage.

[19] The tax for the support of the parish priest, usually paid in kind, not in money.

10

Deuteronomy 25
1 Timothy 5
Matthew 10
I Corinthians 9

gathered and received by our church provost, appointed by the community.[20] With the consent of the whole community the pastor, who shall be chosen by an entire community, shall receive out of this tithe a modest, sufficient maintenance for him and his; the remainder shall be distributed to the poor and needy in the same village, according to the circumstances and with the consent of the community. Anything that then remains shall be kept, so that if the needs of the land require the laying of a war tax, no general tax may be laid upon the poor, but it shall be paid out of this surplus.[21]

Luke 6
Matthew 5

If it should happen that there were one or more villages that had sold their tithes to meet certain needs, they are to be informed that he who has [bought] the tithes from a whole village is not to be deprived of them without compensation; for we will negotiate with him, in the proper way, form, and manner, to buy them back from him on suitable terms and at a suitable time.[22] But in case anyone has not bought the tithes from any village, and his forbears have simply appropriated them to themselves, we will not, we ought not, nor do we intend to pay him anything further, but will keep them for the support of the aforesaid, our chosen pastor, and for distribution to the needy, as the Holy Scriptures [command]. It does not matter whether the holders of the tithes be spiritual or temporal lords. The small tithe[23] we will not pay at all,

Genesis 1

for God the Lord created cattle for the free use of men, and we regard this tithe as an im-

---

[20] The lay officer who administered the property of the parish. He was known by many names. Cf. Boehmer, *op. cit.*, p. 5, n. 5.

[21] The wars against the Turks required a series of special taxes to meet the expense. These taxes were an especially heavy burden for the poor and the peasants. Cf. the listing of Luther's possessions subject to this tax in Schwiebert, *op. cit.*, p. 268.

[22] It would have been almost impossible to prove that the right to receive the tithes had actually been bought.

[23] Also known as the "blood-tithe" and the "cattle-tithe."

11

proper one which men have invented; therefore we will not give it any longer.

Third, it has been the custom for men to hold us as their own property. This situation is pitiable, for Christ has redeemed and bought us all with the precious shedding of his blood, the lowly[24] as well as the great, excepting no one. Therefore, it agrees with Scripture that we be free and will to be so. It is not our intention to be entirely free.[25] God does not teach us that we should desire no rulers. We are to live according to the commandments, not the free self-will of the flesh; but we are to love God, recognize him in our neighbor as our Lord,[26] and do all (as we gladly would do) that God has commanded in the Lord's Supper; therefore, we ought to live according to his commandment. This commandment does not teach us to disobey our rulers; rather to humble ourselves, not before the rulers only, but before everyone. Thus we willingly obey our chosen and appointed rulers (whom God has appointed over us) in all Christian and appropriate matters. And we have no doubt that since they are true and genuine Christians, they will gladly release us from serfdom, or show us in the gospel that we are serfs.

Fourth, it has been the custom that no poor man has been allowed to catch game, wild fowl, or fresh-water fish, which seems to us altogether improper and unbrotherly, selfish, and not according to the word of God. In some places the rulers keep the game to our vexation and great loss, because the unreasoning animals wantonly devour our crops which God causes to grow for man's use; and we have to put up with this and keep quiet about it, though it is against God and neighbor. When God the Lord created man, he gave him

Isaiah 53
I Peter 1
I Corinthians 7
Romans 13
Wisdom of
    Solomon 6
I Peter 2
Deuteronomy 6
Matthew 4
Luke 4
Matthew 5
John 13
Romans 13
Acts 5

Genesis 1
Acts 10
I Timothy 7
I Corinthians 10
Colossians 2

---

[24] Literally, "shepherds."

[25] The demand to be released from serfdom was introduced when the peasants began to formulate their demands on the basis of divine right.

[26] Cf. Matt. 25:31-45.

authority over all animals, over the birds of the air, and over the fish in the water. Therefore it is our request that if anyone has waters, he offer satisfactory documentary evidence that the waters have been intentionally sold to him. In that case we do not wish to take them from him by force; on the contrary, for the sake of brotherly love, Christian consideration must be shown. But whoever cannot offer sufficient proof shall surrender these waters to the community in a proper manner.

As is shown in the first chapter of Genesis.

Fifth, we also have a grievance about wood cutting, for our lords have appropriated all the forests solely to themselves, and when the poor man needs any wood, he must buy it at a double price. In our opinion the forests held by spiritual or temporal lords who have not bought them should revert to the entire community. This community should be free, in an orderly way, to allow anyone to take home what he needs for firewood without payment, and also to take for nothing any that he needs for wood-working; this is to be done with the approval of a supervisor appointed by the community. If there are any forests which have not been thus honestly purchased, a brotherly and Christian agreement should be reached about them; but if the property had first been expropriated[27] and afterward sold, an agreement shall be made in accordance with the facts of the case, and according to brotherly love and the Holy Scriptures.

Romans 10

Sixth, we are grievously oppressed by the free labor which we are required to provide for our lords.[28] The amount of labor required increases from day to day and [the variety of services required] increases from day to day. We ask that an appropriate investigation be

---

[27] The ordinary situation.

[28] The extent of the corvee was fixed by custom, but the limits were not always observed. Often these services required so much of the peasant's time that he could till his own land only by moonlight. Cf. Schwiebert, *op. cit.*, p. 556.

made of this matter and that the burdens laid upon us not be too heavy. We ask that we be dealt with graciously, just as our ancestors were, who provided these services according to the word of God.

Seventh, in the future we will not allow ourselves to be further oppressed by the lords. Rather, a man shall possess his holding according to the terms on which it has been granted, that is, according to the agreement between the lord and the peasants. The lord shall not in any way put pressure on the peasant, or force him to render more services, or demand anything else from him without payment, so that the peasant may use and enjoy his property unburdened and in peace; but if the lord needs more services, the peasant shall be obedient, and willing to perform them. However, he is to do so at a time when the peasant's own affairs do not suffer, and he shall receive a fair wage for this labor.

The Eighth Article

Matthew 10

We are greatly aggrieved because many of us have holdings that do not produce enough to enable us to pay the rents due on them. As a result, the peasants bear the loss and are ruined. We ask that the lords have honorable men inspect the said holdings, and fix a fair rent, so that the peasant shall not labor for nothing; for every laborer is worthy of his hire.

The Ninth Article

Isaiah 10
Ephesians 6
Luke 3
Jeremiah 26

We are aggrieved by the great wrong of continually making new laws. Punishment is inflicted on us, not according to the facts in the case, but at times by great ill-will, at times by great partiality. In our opinion we should be punished by the ancient written law, and the

14

cases dealt with according to the facts, and not according to partiality.[29]

The Tenth Article

Luke 6

We are aggrieved because some have expropriated meadows from the common fields which once belonged to a community. We would take these back again into the hands of our communities, unless they have been honestly purchased. If they have been improperly purchased, we should come to a kindly and brotherly agreement about them, according to the facts of the case.

The Eleventh Article

Deuteronomy 18
Matthew 8
Matthew 23
Isaiah 11

We would have the custom called death tax[30] entirely abolished. We will not tolerate it or allow widows and orphans to be so shamefully robbed by those who ought to guard and protect them, as now happens in many places and under many forms, contrary to God and honor. They have disgraced and cheated us, and although they had little authority, they have taken what was left after that. God will no longer permit it; it shall be entirely done away with. Henceforth no man shall be required to pay any of this tax, whether large or small.

Conclusion

Twelfth, it is our conclusion and final opinion that if one or more of the articles set forth here is not in agreement with the word of God (though we think this is not the case), and this disagreement is shown to us on the

---

[29] Primarily this protest is against the introduction of the Roman law, which replaced traditional practices and customs. Cf. Williams, *op. cit.*, pp. 61-62.
[30] A fee paid to the lord upon the death of a tenant. The nature of the payment was fixed by custom. Cf. the English heriot.

15

basis of Scripture, we shall withdraw such an article—after the matter is explained to us on the basis of Scripture. If some of our demands are granted and it is afterward found that they were unjust, they shall be null and void from that hour. Similarly, if additional articles are found to be properly based on Scripture and more offenses against God and our neighbor be revealed thereby, [they will be added to these articles]. We, for our part, will and have determined to use forbearance, and will discipline ourselves in all Christian doctrine and practice. We will pray to God the Lord for this; for he, and no one else, can give it to us. The peace of Christ be with us all.

ADMONITION TO PEACE
A REPLY TO
THE TWELVE ARTICLES OF
THE PEASANTS IN SWABIA

The peasants who have now banded together in Swabia have formulated their intolerable grievances against the rulers in twelve articles,[1] and have undertaken to support them with certain passages of Scripture. Now they have published them in printed form. The thing about them that pleases me most is that, in the twelfth article,[2] they offer to accept instruction gladly and willingly, if there is need or necessity for it, and are willing to be corrected, to the extent that it can be done by clear, plain, undeniable passages of Scripture. And it is indeed right and proper that no one's conscience should be instructed or corrected except by Holy Scripture.

Now if that is their serious and sincere meaning—and it would not be right for me to interpret it otherwise, because in these articles they come out into the open and do not shy away from the light— then there is good reason to hope that things will be well. Since I have a reputation for being one of those who deal with the Holy Scriptures here on earth, and especially as one whom they mention and call upon by name in the second document, I have all the more courage and confidence in openly publishing my instruction. I do this in a friendly and Christian spirit, as a duty of brotherly love, so that if any misfortune or disaster comes out of this matter, it may not be attributed to me, nor will I be blamed before God and men because of my silence. But if this offer of theirs is only pretense and show (without a doubt there are some people like that among them for it is impossible for so big a crowd all to be true Christians and

---

[1] See the text of *The Twelve Articles*, in this volume, pp. 8-16.
[2] See pp. 15-16.

have good intentions; a large part of them must be using the good intentions of the rest for their own selfish purposes and seeking their own advantage) then without doubt it will accomplish very little, or, in fact, it will contribute to their great injury and eternal ruin.

This, then, is a great and dangerous matter. It concerns both the kingdom of God and the kingdom of the world. If this rebellion were to continue and get the upper hand, both kingdoms would be destroyed and there would be neither worldly government nor word of God, which would ultimately result in the permanent destruction of all Germany. Therefore it is necessary for us to speak boldly and to give advice without regard to anyone. It is also necessary that we be willing to listen and allow things to be said to us, so that we do not now—as we have done before—harden our hearts and stop our ears, and so that God's wrath not run its full course. For the many terrible signs[3] that are seen both in heaven and earth point

---

[3] Luther felt that the apocalyptic signs of the end of the world described in Matthew 24, Mark 13, and Luke 21, were being fulfilled in his time. The events of 1524-1525 seemed to have brought disaster to the Reformation. It was clear at this time that Erasmus and the humanists were breaking with Luther on the question of the bondage of the will. And the disturbances among the peasants were establishing an association between the Reformation and revolution that was alienating many of Luther's supporters. At the same time, Luther's refusal to identify the Reformation with the program of *The Twelve Articles* antagonized many of the common people. All of this, together with the constant threat of invasion by the Turks and the continual opposition of the pope and the emperor to the gospel, seemed to be signs of the approaching end of the world. Luther interpreted these events, as well as unnatural and monstrous occurrences in the world of nature, as evidence that the devil was increasing his opposition to God's will. The intensity of that opposition pointed to the imminence of the conflict. His letters reflect this mood. Cf. Preserved Smith and Charles M. Jacobs (eds.), *Luther's Correspondence and Other Contemporary Letters* (Philadelphia: The Lutheran Publication Society, 1918), II, 125, 318, 432, 470, 512. Precisely for this reason, Luther felt that no particular event was of decisive significance. The real problem was to defeat the devil. That victory could not be gained before the end of the world, but in the meantime the devil could be confronted and opposed wherever he was at work in opposition to the gospel and to law and order. Since he might be at work in the emperor as well as in the Turk, in the peasants as well as in the lords, and even in the church, Luther was unable to identify himself with any particular side in a conflict as though the victory of that group would establish the kingdom of God on earth. However, since the devil was fighting on so many fronts, Luther thought, the surest way to lose the battle would be to side with him by using his weapons and strategy. This consciousness that he was living in the last times made it all the more important to Luther that law and order be maintained and the gospel preached.

to a great disaster and a mighty change in Germany. Sad to say, however, we care little about it. Nevertheless, God goes on his way, and someday he will soften our hardheadedness.

To the Princes and Lords

We have no one on earth to thank for this disastrous rebellion, except you princes and lords, and especially you blind bishops and mad priests and monks, whose hearts are hardened, even to the present day. You do not cease to rant and rave against the holy gospel, even though you know that it is true and that you cannot refute it. In addition, as temporal rulers you do nothing but cheat and rob the people so that you may lead a life of luxury and extravagance. The poor common people cannot bear it any longer. The sword is already at your throats, but you think that you sit so firm in the saddle that no one can unhorse you. This false security and stubborn perversity will break your necks, as you will discover. I have often told you before to beware of the saying, in Psalm 107 [:40], "*Effundit contemptum super principes*," "He pours contempt upon princes."[4] You, however, keep on asking for trouble and want to be hit over the head. And no warning or exhortation will keep you from getting what you want.

Well, then, since you are the cause of this wrath of God, it will undoubtedly come upon you, unless you mend your ways in time. The signs in heaven and the wonders on earth are meant for you, dear lords; they bode no good for you, and no good will come to you. A great part of God's wrath has already come, for God is sending many false teachers and prophets among us,[5] so that through our error and blasphemy we may richly deserve hell and

---

[4] Cf. also Job 12:21.

[5] In addition to Thomas Münzer (cf. p. 5, n. 3), Luther is thinking of Nicholas Storch, leader of the Zwickau prophets, who were responsible for fomenting the Wittenberg riots of 1522 when Luther was in exile at the Wartburg (cf. *LW* 51, 67-100), and Andrew Bodenstein Karlstadt. Karlstadt had been Luther's colleague at the University of Wittenberg, but like Münzer represented a completely independent direction of thought. He supported the Wittenberg riots and was banished by Luther after the disturbances had been quieted. Karlstadt generally was held responsible for the unrest among the Franconian peasants.

everlasting damnation. The rest of it is now here, for the peasants are banding together, and, unless our repentance moves God to prevent it, this must result in the ruin, destruction, and desolation of Germany by cruel murder and bloodshed.

For you ought to know, dear lords, that God is doing this because this raging of yours cannot, will not, and ought not be endured for long. You must become different men and yield to God's word. If you do not do this amicably and willingly, then you will be compelled to do it by force and destruction. If these peasants do not compel you, others will. Even though you were to defeat them all, they would still not be defeated, for God will raise up others. It is his will to defeat you, and you will be defeated. It is not the peasants, dear lords, who are resisting you; it is God himself, to visit your raging upon you. Some of you have said that you will stake land and people on exterminating the Lutheran teaching.[6] What would you think if you were to turn out to be your own prophets, and your land and people were already at stake? Do not joke with God, dear lords! The Jews, too, said, "We have no king" [John 19:15], and they meant it so seriously that they must be without a king forever.

To make your sin still greater, and guarantee your merciless destruction, some of you are beginning to blame this affair on the gospel and say that it is the fruit of my teaching. Well, well, slander away, dear lords! You did not want to know what I taught or what the gospel is; now the one who will soon teach you is at the door, unless you change your ways. You, and everyone else, must bear witness that I have taught with all quietness,[7] have striven earnestly against rebellion, and have energetically encouraged and exhorted people to obey and respect even you wild and dictatorial tyrants. This rebellion cannot be coming from me. Rather the murder-prophets,[8] who hate me as they hate you, have come among these

---

[6] Duke George of Saxony, a bitter foe of Luther, wrote a letter on February 10, 1522, to his officials urging them to imprison any Lutherans known to them. He said, ". . . in these un-Christian matters we will not hesitate, as a Christian prince, to stake our life and goods. . . ." Smith and Jacobs, *op. cit.*, p. 89.

[7] I.e., without inciting rebellion.

[8] Luther means the religious revolutionaries who were inciting the people to revolt and were using the gospel to support their position. Cf. p. 19, n. 5.

people and have gone about among them for more than three years, and no one has resisted and fought against them except me.[9]

Therefore, if God intends to punish you and allows the devil through his false prophets to stir up the people against you, and if it is, perhaps, God's will that I shall not be able to prevent it any longer, what can I or my gospel do? Not only have we suffered your persecution and murdering and raging; we have also prayed for you and helped to protect and maintain your rule over the common people. If I desired revenge, I could laugh up my sleeve and simply watch what the peasants are doing or even join in with them and help make matters worse; may God keep me from this in the future as he has in the past.

Therefore my dear lords—whether you are my enemies or friends—as a loyal subject I humbly beg you not to despise my faithfulness, though I am a poor man. I beseech you not to make light of this rebellion. It is not that I think or fear that the rebels will be too strong for you or that I want you to be afraid of them for that reason. Rather fear God and respect his wrath! If he wills to punish you as you have deserved (and I am afraid that he does), then he will punish you, even though the peasants were a hundred times fewer than they are. He can make peasants out of stones[10] and slay a hundred of you by one peasant, so that all your armor and your strength will be too weak to save you.

If it is still possible to give you advice, my lords, give way a little to the will and wrath of God. A cartload of hay must give way to a drunken man[11]—how much more ought you to stop your raging and obstinate tyranny and not deal unreasonably with the peasants, as though they were drunk or out of their minds! Do not start a fight with them, for you do not know how it will end. Try kindness first, for you do not know what God will do to prevent the spark that will kindle all Germany and start a fire that no one can

---

[9] The three year period dates from the Wittenberg riots at the beginning of 1522 and the activity of the Zwickau prophets preceding them. Luther took firm and decisive action against them, as he did against Münzer and Karlstadt, while the civil authorities were still uncertain about what to do.

[10] Cf. Matt. 3:9.

[11] Cf. Karl F. W. Wander (ed.), *Deutsches Sprichwörter Lexikon* (5 vols.; Leipzig, 1867-1880), III, *"Mann,"* No. 942, and I, *"Betrunkener,"* No. 4.

extinguish. Our sins are before God [Ps. 90:8]; therefore we have to fear his wrath when even a leaf rustles [Lev. 26:36], let alone when such a multitude sets itself in motion. You will lose nothing by kindness; and even if you did lose something, the preservation of peace will pay you back ten times. But if there is open conflict you may lose both your property and your life. Why risk danger when you can achieve more by following a different way that is also the better way?

The peasants have just published twelve articles, some of which are so fair and just as to take away your reputation in the eyes of God and the world and fulfil what the Psalm [107:40] says about God pouring contempt upon princes. Nevertheless, almost all of the articles are framed in their own interest and for their own good, though not for their best good. Of course, I would have formulated other articles against you that would have dealt with all Germany and its government.

I did this in my book *To the German Nobility,*[12] when more was at stake; but because you made light of that, you must now listen to and put up with these selfish articles. It serves you right for being a people to whom nothing can be told.

In the first article[13] they ask the right to hear the gospel and choose their pastors. You cannot reject this request with any show of right, even though this article does indeed make some selfish demands, for they allege that these pastors are to be supported by the tithes, and these do not belong to the peasants. Nevertheless, the basic sense of the article is that the preaching of the gospel should be permitted, and no ruler can or ought to oppose this. Indeed, no ruler ought to prevent anyone from teaching or believing what he pleases, whether it is the gospel or lies. It is enough if he prevents the teaching of sedition and rebellion.

The other articles protest economic injustices, such as the death tax.[14] These protests are also right and just, for rulers are not appointed to exploit their subjects for their own profit and advan-

---

[12] See *To the Christian Nobility of the German Nation Concerning the Reform of the Christian Estate* (1520). *LW* 44, 115-217.
[13] See p. 10.
[14] See p. 15, n. 30.

tage, but to be concerned about the welfare of their subjects. And the people cannot tolerate it very long if their rulers set confiscatory tax rates and tax them out of their very skins. What good would it do a peasant if his field bore as many gulden as stalks of wheat if the rulers only taxed him all the more and then wasted it as though it were chaff to increase their luxury, and squandered his money on their own clothes, food, drink, and buildings? Would not the luxury and the extravagant spending have to be checked so that a poor man could keep something for himself? You have undoubtedly received further information from the peasants' tracts,[15] so that you are adequately aware of their grievances.

To the Peasants

So far, dear friends, you have learned only that I agree that it is unfortunately all too true that the princes and lords who forbid the preaching of the gospel and oppress the people unbearably deserve to have God put them down from their thrones [Luke 1:52] because they have sinned so greatly against both God and man. And they have no excuse. Nevertheless, you, too, must be careful that you take up your cause justly and with a good conscience. If you have a good conscience, you have the comforting advantage that God will be with you, and will help you. Even though you did not succeed for a while, or even suffered death, you would win in the end, and you would preserve your souls eternally with all the saints. But if you act unjustly and have a bad conscience, you will be defeated. And even though you might win for a while and even kill all the princes, you would suffer the eternal loss of your body and soul in the end. For you, therefore, this is no laughing matter. The eternal fate of your body and soul is involved. And you must most seriously consider not merely how strong you are and how wrong the princes are, but whether you act justly and with a good conscience.

Therefore, dear brethren, I beg you in a kindly and brotherly way to look carefully at what you are doing and not to believe all

---

15 Cf. p. 6.

23

kinds of spirits and preachers [I John 4:1]. For Satan has now raised up many evil spirits of disorder and of murder, and filled the world with them. Just listen attentively, as you offer many times to do.[16] I will not spare you the earnest warning that I owe you, even though some of you have been so poisoned by the murderous spirits that you will hate me for it and call me a hypocrite. That does not worry me; it is enough for me if I save some of the goodhearted and upright men among you from the danger of God's wrath. The rest I fear as little as they despise me much; and they shall not harm me. I know One who is greater and mightier than they are, and he teaches me in Psalm 3 [:6], "I am not afraid of ten thousands of people who have set themselves against me round about." My confidence shall outlast their confidence; that I know for sure.

In the first place, dear brethren, you bear the name of God and call yourselves a "Christian association"[17] or union, and you allege that you want to live and act according to divine law.[18] Now you know that the name, word, and titles of God are not to be assumed idly or in vain, as he says in the second commandment, "Thou shalt not take the name of the Lord your God in vain," and adds, "for the Lord will not hold him guiltless who takes his name in vain" [Deut. 5:11]. Here is a clear, plain text, which applies to you, as to all men. It threatens you, as well as us and all others, with God's wrath without regard to your great numbers, rights, and terror. God is mighty enough and strong enough to punish you as he here threatens if his name is taken in vain, and you know it. So if you take his name in vain, you may expect no good fortune but only trouble. Learn from this how to judge yourselves and accept this friendly warning. It would be a simple thing for God, who once drowned the whole world with a flood [Gen. 7:17-24] and destroyed Sodom with fire [Gen. 19:24-28], to kill or defeat so many thousands of peasants. He is an almighty and terrible God.

Second, it is easy to prove that you are taking God's name in vain and putting it to shame; nor is there any doubt that you will, in the end, encounter all misfortune, unless God is not true. For here

---

[16] See pp. 15-16.
[17] See p. 7, n. 14.
[18] See p. 9.

is God's word, spoken through the mouth of Christ, "All who take the sword will perish by the sword" [Matt. 26:52]. That means nothing else than that no one, by his own violence, shall arrogate authority to himself; but as Paul says, "Let every person be subject to the governing authorities with fear and reverence" [Rom. 13:1].

How can you get around these passages and laws of God when you boast that you are acting according to divine law, and yet take the sword in your own hands, and revolt against "the governing authorities that are instituted by God?" Do you think that Paul's judgment in Romans 13 [:2] will not strike you, "He who resists the authorities will incur judgment"? You take God's name in vain when you pretend to be seeking divine right, and under the pretense of his name work contrary to divine right. Be careful, dear sirs. It will not turn out that way in the end.

Third, you say that the rulers are wicked and intolerable, for they will not allow us to have the gospel; they oppress us too hard with the burdens they lay on our property, and they are ruining us in body and soul.[19] I answer: The fact that the rulers are wicked and unjust does not excuse disorder and rebellion, for the punishing of wickedness is not the responsibility of everyone, but of the worldly rulers who bear the sword. Thus Paul says in Romans 13 [:4] and Peter, in I Peter 3 [2:14], that the rulers are instituted by God for the punishment of the wicked. Then, too, there is the natural law of all the world, which says that no one may sit as judge in his own case or take his own revenge. The proverb is true, "Whoever hits back is in the wrong."[20] Or as it is said, "It takes two to start a fight."[21] The divine law agrees with this, and says, in Deuteronomy 32 [:35], "Vengeance is mine; I will repay, says the Lord."[22] Now you cannot deny that your rebellion actually involves you in such a way that you make yourselves your own judges and avenge yourselves. You are quite unwilling to suffer any wrong. That is contrary not only to Christian law and the gospel, but also to natural law and all equity.

---

[19] See pp. 10-15.
[20] *Wer widder schlegt, der ist unrecht.* See Wander (ed.), *Deutsches Sprichwörter Lexikon*, V, "Schlagen," No. 2.
[21] *Wer widder schlegt macht hadder.*
[22] Luther quotes the Pauline wording of the passage in Rom. 12:19.

If your cause is to prosper when the divine and Christian law of the Old and New Testaments and even the natural law are all against you, you must produce a new and special command of God, confirmed by signs and wonders, which commands you to do these things. Otherwise God will not allow his word and ordinance to be broken by your violence. On the contrary, because you boast of the divine law and yet act against it, he will let you fall and be punished terribly, as men who dishonor his name. Then he will condemn you eternally, as was said above. For the word of Christ in Matthew 7 [:3] applies to you; you see the speck in the eye of the rulers, but do not see the log in your own eye. The word of Paul in Romans 3 [:8] also applies, "Why not do evil that good may come? Their condemnation is just." It is true that the rulers do wrong when they suppress the gospel and oppress you in temporal matters. But you do far greater wrong when you not only suppress God's word, but tread it underfoot, invade his authority and law, and put yourselves above God. Besides, you take from the rulers their authority and right, indeed, everything they have. What do they have left when they have lost their authority?

I make you the judges and leave it to you to decide who is the worse robber, the man who takes a large part of another's goods, but leaves him something, or the man who takes everything that he has, and takes his life besides. The rulers unjustly take your property; that is the one side. On the other hand, you take from them their authority, in which their whole property and life and being consist. Therefore you are far greater robbers than they, and you intend to do worse things than they have done. "Indeed not," you say, "We are going to leave them enough to live on." If anyone wants to believe that, let him! I do not believe it. Anyone who dares go so far as to use force to take away authority, which is the main thing, will not stop at that, but will take the other, smaller thing that depends upon it. The wolf that eats a whole sheep will also eat its ear.[23] And even if you permitted them to keep their life and some property, nevertheless, you would take the best thing they have, namely, their authority, and make yourselves lords over

---

[23] Cf. Wander (ed.), *Deutsches Sprichwörter Lexikon*, III, *"Ohr,"* No. 258.

them. That would be too great a robbery and wrong. God will declare you to be the greatest robbers.

Can you not think it through, dear friends? If your enterprise were right, then any man might become judge over another. Then authority, government, law, and order would disappear from the world; there would be nothing but murder and bloodshed. As soon as anyone saw that someone was wronging him, he would begin to judge and punish him. Now if that is unjust and intolerable when done by an individual, we cannot allow a mob or a crowd to do it. However, if we do permit a mob or a crowd to do it, then we cannot rightly and fairly forbid an individual to do it. For in both cases the cause is the same, that is, an injustice. What would you yourselves do if disorder broke out in your ranks and one man set himself against another and took vengeance on him? Would you put up with that? Would you not say that he must let others, whom you appointed, do the judging and avenging? What do you expect God and the world to think when you pass judgment and avenge yourselves on those who have injured you and even upon your rulers, whom God has appointed?

Now in all this I have been speaking of the common, divine, and natural law which even the heathen, Turks, and Jews have to keep if there is to be any peace or order in the world. Even though you were to keep this whole law, you would do no better and no more than the heathen and the Turks do. For no one is a Christian merely because he does not undertake to function as his own judge and avenger but leaves this to the authorities and the rulers. You would eventually have to do this whether you wanted to or not. But because you are acting against this law, you see plainly that you are worse than heathen or Turks, to say nothing of the fact that you are not Christians. What do you think that Christ will say about this? You bear his name, and call yourselves a "Christian association," and yet you are so far from being Christian, and your actions and lives are so horribly contrary to his law, that you are not worthy to be called even heathen or Turks. You are much worse than these, because you rage and struggle against the divine and natural law, which all the heathen keep.

27

See, dear friends, what kind of preachers you have and what they think of your souls. I fear that some prophets of murder[24] have come among you, who would like to use you so they can become lords in the world, and they do not care that they are endangering your life, property, honor, and soul, in time and eternity. If, now, you really want to keep the divine law, as you boast, then do it. There it stands! God says, "Vengeance is mine; I will repay" [Rom. 12:19], and, "Be subject not only to good lords, but also to the wicked" [I Pet. 2:18]. If you do this, well and good; if not, you may, indeed, cause a calamity, but it will finally come upon you. Let no one have any doubts about this! God is just, and will not endure it. Be careful, therefore, with your liberty, that you do not run away from the rain and fall in the water.[25] Beware of the illusion that you are winning freedom for your body when you are really losing your body, property, and soul for all eternity. God's wrath is there; fear it, I advise you! The devil has sent false prophets among you; beware of them!

And now we want to move on and speak of the law of Christ, and of the gospel, which is not binding on the heathen, as the other law[26] is. For if you claim that you are Christians and like to be called Christians and want to be known as Christians, then you must also allow your law to be held up before you rightly. Listen, then, dear Christians, to your Christian law! Your Supreme Lord Christ, whose name you bear, says, in Matthew 6 [5:39-41], "Do not resist one who is evil. If anyone forces you to go one mile, go with him two miles. If anyone wants to take your coat, let him have your cloak too. If anyone strikes you on one cheek, offer him the other too." Do you hear this, O Christian association? How does your program stand in light of this law? You do not want to endure evil or suffering, but rather want to be free and to experience only goodness and justice. However, Christ says that we should not resist evil or injustice but always yield, suffer, and let things be taken from us. If you will not bear this law, then lay aside the name of Christian and claim another name that accords with your actions,

---

24 See p. 19, n. 5.
25 Cf. Wander (ed.), *Deutsches Sprichwörter Lexikon*, III, "Regen," No. 150.
26 I.e., the divine natural law of which Luther speaks above.

or else Christ himself will tear his name away from you, and that will be too hard for you.

In Romans 12 [:19] Paul says, "Beloved, never avenge yourselves, but leave it to the wrath of God." In this same sense he praises the Corinthians for gladly suffering if someone hits or robs them, II Corinthians 11 [:20]. And in I Corinthians 6 [:1-2] he condemns them for going to court for the sake of property rather than suffering injustice. Indeed, our leader,[27] Jesus Christ, says in Matthew 7 [5:44] that we should bless those who insult us, pray for our persecutors, love our enemies, and do good to those who do evil to us. These, dear friends, are our Christian laws.

Now you can see how far these false prophets have led you astray. They still call you Christians, although they have made you worse than heathen. On the basis of these passages even a child can understand that the Christian law tells us not to strive against injustice, not to grasp the sword, not to protect ourselves, not to avenge ourselves, but to give up life and property, and let whoever takes it have it. We have all we need in our Lord, who will not leave us, as he has promised [Heb. 13:5]. Suffering! suffering! Cross! cross! This and nothing else is the Christian law! But now you are fighting for temporal goods and will not let the coat go after the cloak,[28] but want to recover the cloak. How then will you die and give up your life, or love your enemies and do good to them? O worthless Christians! Dear friends, Christians are not so commonplace that so many can assemble in one group. A Christian is a rare bird![29] Would to God that the majority of us were good, pious heathen, who kept the natural law, not to mention the Christian law!

I will give you some illustrations of Christian law so that you may see where the mad prophets have led you. Look at St. Peter in the garden. He wanted to defend his Lord Christ with the sword, and cut off Malchus' ear [John 18:10]. Tell me, did not Peter have great right on his side? Was it not an intolerable injustice that they were going to take from Christ not only his property, but also his

---

[27] *Unser Hertzog,* literally, "our duke."
[28] Cf. Matt. 5:40.
[29] Cf. Wander (ed.), *Deutsches Sprichwörter Lexikon,* IV, "Vogel," No. 599.

life? Indeed, they not only took his life and property, but in so doing they entirely suppressed the gospel by which they were to be saved and thus robbed heaven. You have not yet suffered such a wrong, dear friends. But see what Christ does and teaches in this case. However great the injustice was, he nevertheless stopped St. Peter, bade him put up his sword, and would not allow him to avenge or prevent this injustice. In addition, he passed a sentence of death upon him, as though upon a murderer, and said, "He who takes the sword will perish by the sword" [Matt. 26:52]. This should help us understand that we do not have the right to use the sword simply because someone has done us an injustice and because the law and justice are on our side. We must also have received power and authority from God to use the sword and to punish wrong. Furthermore, a Christian should also suffer it if anyone desires to keep the gospel away from him by force. It may not even be possible to keep the gospel from anyone, as we shall hear.

A second example is Christ himself. What did he do when they took his life on the cross and thereby took away from him the work of preaching for which God himself had sent him as a blessing for the souls of men? He did just what St. Peter says. He committed the whole matter to him who judges justly, and he endured this intolerable wrong [I Pet. 2:23]. More than that, he prayed for his persecutors and said, "Father, forgive them, for they know not what they do" [Luke 23:34].

Now, if you are genuine Christians, you must certainly act in this same way and follow this example. If you do not do this, then give up the name of Christian and the claim that Christian law is on your side, for then you are certainly not Christians but are opposing Christ and his law, his doctrine, and his example. But if you do follow the example of Christ, you will soon see God's miracles and he will help you as he helped Christ, whom he avenged after the completion of his passion in such a way that his gospel and his kingdom won a powerful victory and gained the upper hand, in spite of all his enemies. He will help you in this same way so that his gospel will rise with power among you, if you first suffer to the end, leave the case to him, and await his vengeance.[30] But because

---

[30] Cf. I Pet. 5:10.

of what you are doing, and because you do not want to triumph by suffering, but by your fists, you are interfering with God's vengeance and you will keep neither the gospel nor your fists.

I must also give you an illustration from the present. Pope and emperor have opposed me and raged against me. Now what have I done that the more pope and emperor raged, the more my gospel spread? I have never drawn a sword or desired revenge. I began neither conspiracy nor rebellion, but so far as I was able, I have helped the worldly rulers—even those who persecuted the gospel and me—to preserve their power and honor.[31] I stopped with committing the matter to God and relying confidently at all times upon his hand. This is why God has not only preserved my life in spite of the pope and all the tyrants—and this many consider a really great miracle, as I myself must also confess—but he has made my gospel grow and spread. Now you interfere with what I am doing. You want to help the gospel and yet you do not see that what you are doing hinders and suppresses it most effectively.

I say all this, dear friends, as a faithful warning. In this case you should stop calling yourselves Christians and stop claiming that you have the Christian law on your side. For no matter how right you are, it is not right for a Christian to appeal to law, or to fight, but rather to suffer wrong and endure evil; and there is no other way (I Corinthians 6 [:1-8]). You yourselves confess in the preface to your articles that "all who believe in Christ become loving, peaceful, patient, and agreeable."[32] Your actions, however, reveal nothing but impatience, aggression, anger, and violence. Thus you contradict your own words. You want to be known as patient people, you who will endure neither injustice nor evil, but will endure only what is just and good. That is a fine kind of patience! Any rascal can practice it! It does not take a Christian to do that! So again I say, however good and just your cause may be, nevertheless, because you would defend yourselves and are unwilling to suffer either violence or injustice, you may do anything that God does not prevent. However, leave the name Christian out of it. Leave the name Christian

---

[31] See Luther's *Temporal Authority: To What Extent It Should Be Obeyed* (1523). *LW* 45, 81-129.
[32] See p. 9.

31

out, I say, and do not use it to cover up your impatient, disorderly, un-Christian undertaking.[33] I shall not let you have that name, but so long as there is a heartbeat in my body, I shall do all I can, through speaking and writing, to take that name away from you. You will not succeed, or will succeed only in ruining your bodies and souls.

In saying this it is not my intention to justify or defend the rulers in the intolerable injustices which you suffer from them. They are unjust, and commit heinous wrongs against you; that I admit. If, however, neither side accepts instruction and you start to fight with each other—may God prevent it!—I hope that neither side will be called Christian. Rather I hope that God will, as is usual in these situations, use one rascal to punish the other.[34] If it comes to a conflict—may God graciously prevent it!—I hope that your character and name will be so well known that the authorities will recognize that they are fighting not against Christians but against heathen; and that you, too, may know that you are not fighting Christian rulers but heathen. Christians do not fight for themselves with sword and musket, but with the cross and with suffering, just as Christ, our leader, does not bear a sword, but hangs on the cross. Your victory, therefore, does not consist in conquering and reigning, or in the use of force, but in defeat and in weakness, as St. Paul says in II Corinthians 1 [10:4], "The weapons of our warfare are not material, but are the strength which comes from God," and, "Power is made perfect in weakness" [II Cor. 12:9].

Your name and title ought therefore to indicate that you are people who fight because they will not, and ought not, endure injustice or evil, according to the teaching of nature. You should use that name, and let the name of Christ alone, for that is the kind of works that you are doing. If, however, you will not take that name, but keep the name of Christian, then I must accept the fact that I am also involved in this struggle and consider you as enemies who, under the name of the gospel, act contrary to it, and want to do more to suppress my gospel than anything the pope and emperor have done to suppress it.

---

[33] Cf. I Pet. 2:16.

[34] Cf. Wander (ed.), *Deutsches Sprichwörter Lexikon*, I, *"Bube,"* No. 14.

I will make no secret of what I intend to do. I will put the whole matter into God's hands, risk my neck by God's grace, and confidently trust in him—just as I have been doing against the pope and the emperor. I shall pray for you, that God may enlighten you, and resist your undertaking, and not let it succeed. For I see well that the devil, who has not been able to destroy me through the pope, now seeks to exterminate me and swallow me up by means of the bloodthirsty prophets of murder and spirits of rebellion that are among you.[35] Well, let him swallow me! I will give him a bellyful, I know. And even if you win, you will hardly enjoy it! I beg you, humbly and kindly, to think things over so that I will not have to trust in and pray to God against you.

For although I am a poor, sinful man, I know and am certain that my concern in this matter is right and just, for I fight in behalf of the name Christian and pray that it not be put to shame. I am sure, too, that my prayer is acceptable to God and will be heard, for he himself has taught us to pray, in the Lord's Prayer, "Hallowed be thy name" [Matt. 6:9], and in the second commandment he has forbidden that it be put to shame [Deut. 5:11]. Therefore I beg you not to despise my prayer and the prayer of those who pray along with me, for it will be too mighty for you and will arouse God against you, as St. James says, "The prayer of the righteous man who prays persistently has great effects, just as Elijah's prayer did" [Jas. 5:16-17]. We also have many other comforting promises of God that he will hear us, such as John, "If you ask anything in my name I will do it" [John 14:14], and, "If we ask anything according to his will he hears us" [I John 5:14]. You cannot have such confidence and assurance in prayer because your own conscience and the Scriptures testify that your enterprise is heathenish, and not Christian, and, under the name of the gospel, works against the gospel and brings contempt upon the name Christian. I know that none of you has ever once prayed to God or called upon him in behalf of this cause. You could not do it! You dare not lift up your eyes to him[36] in this case. You only defiantly shake your fist at him, the fist which you have clenched because of your impatience and unwillingness to suffer. This will not turn out well for you.

---

[35] See p. 20, n. 8.
[36] Cf. Ps. 121:1.

If you were Christians you would stop threatening and resisting with fist and sword. Instead, you would continually abide by the Lord's Prayer and say, "Thy will be done," and, "Deliver us from evil, Amen" [Matt. 6:10, 13]. The psalms show us many examples of genuine saints taking their needs to God and complaining to him about them. They seek help from God: they do not try to defend themselves or to resist evil. That kind of prayer would have been more help to you, in all your needs, than if the world were full of people on your side. This would be especially true if, besides that, you had a good conscience and the comforting assurance that your prayers were heard, as his promises declare: "God is the Savior of all men, especially of those who believe," I Timothy 4 [:10]; "Call upon me in the day of trouble, I will deliver you," Psalm 50 [:15]; "He called upon me in trouble, therefore I will help him," Psalm 91 [:15]. See! That is the Christian way to get rid of misfortune and evil, that is, to endure it and to call upon God. But because you neither call upon God nor patiently endure, but rather help yourselves by your own power and make yourselves your own god and savior, God cannot and must not be your God and Savior. By God's permission you might accomplish something as the heathen and blasphemers you are—and we pray that he will prevent that—but it will only be to your temporal and eternal destruction. However, as Christians, or Evangelicals, you will win nothing. I would stake my life a thousand times on that.

On this basis it is now easy to reply to all your articles. Even though they all were just and equitable in terms of natural law, you have still forgotten the Christian law. You have not been putting this program into effect and achieving your goals by patiently praying to God, as Christians ought to do, but have instead undertaken to compel the rulers to give you what you wanted by using force and violence. This is against the law of the land and against natural justice. The man who composed your articles is no godly and honest man.[37] His marginal notes refer to many chapters of Scripture on which the articles are supposed to be based.[38] But he talks with his mouth full of nothing,[39] and leaves out the passages which

---

[37] Cf. p. 6, n. 7.
[38] Cf. the marginal Scripture references, pp. 10-16.

would show his own wickedness and that of your cause. He has done this to deceive you, to incite you, and to bring you into danger. Anyone who reads through the chapters cited will realize that they speak very little in favor of what you are doing. On the contrary, they say that men should live and act like Christians. He who seeks to use you to destroy the gospel is a prophet of discord. May God prevent that and guard you against him!

In the preface you are conciliatory and claim that you do not want to be rebels. You even excuse your actions by claiming that you desire to teach and to live according to the gospel.[40] Your own words and actions condemn you. You confess that you are causing disturbances and revolting. And then you try to excuse this behavior with the gospel. You have heard above that the gospel teaches Christians to endure and suffer wrong and to pray to God in every need. You, however, are not willing to suffer, but like heathen, you want to force the rulers to conform to your impatient will. You cite the children of Israel as an example, saying that God heard their crying and delivered them [Exod. 6:5-7]. Why then do you not follow the example that you cite? Call upon God and wait until he sends you a Moses, who will prove by signs and wonders that he is sent from God. The children of Israel did not riot against Pharaoh, or help themselves, as you propose to do. This illustration, therefore, is completely against you, and condemns you. You boast of it, and yet you do the opposite of what it teaches.

Furthermore, your declaration that you teach and live according to the gospel is not true.[41] Not one of the articles teaches anything of the gospel. Rather, everything is aimed at obtaining freedom for your person and for your property. To sum it up, everything is concerned with worldly and temporal matters. You want power and wealth so that you will not suffer injustice. The gospel, however, does not become involved in the affairs of this world, but speaks of our life in the world in terms of suffering, injustice, the cross, patience, and contempt for this life and temporal wealth. How,

---

[39] *Und behellt doch den brey yn maule,* i.e., to withhold what is really important. Cf. Ernst Thiele, *Luthers Sprichwörtersammlung* (Weimar, 1900), No. 135.

[40] See pp. 8-9.

[41] See pp. 8-9.

then, does the gospel agree with you? You are only trying to give your unevangelical and un-Christian enterprise an evangelical appearance; and you do not see that in so doing you are bringing shame upon the holy gospel of Christ, and making it a cover for wickedness.[42] Therefore you must take a different attitude. If you want to be Christians and use the name Christian, then stop what you are doing and decide to suffer these injustices. If you want to keep on doing these things, then use another name and do not ask anyone to call you or think of you as Christians. There is no other possibility.

True enough, you are right in desiring the gospel, if you are really serious about it. Indeed, I am willing to make this article even sharper than you do, and say it is intolerable that anyone should be shut out of heaven and driven by force into hell. No one should suffer that; he ought rather lose his life a hundred times. But whoever keeps the gospel from me, closes heaven to me and drives me by force into hell; for the gospel is the only means of salvation for the soul. And on peril of losing my soul, I should not permit this. Tell me, is that not stated sharply enough? And yet it does not follow that I must rebel against the rulers who do me this wrong. "But," you say, "how am I supposed to suffer it and yet not suffer it at the same time?" The answer is easy. It is impossible to keep the gospel from anyone. No power in heaven or on earth can do this, for it is a public teaching that moves about freely under the heavens and is bound to no one place. It is like the star that went in the sky ahead of the Wise Men from the east and showed them where Christ was born [Matt. 2:9].

It is true, of course, that the rulers may suppress the gospel in cities or places where the gospel is, or where there are preachers; but you can leave these cities or places and follow the gospel to some other place. It is not necessary, for the gospel's sake, for you to capture or occupy the city or place; on the contrary, let the ruler have his city; you follow the gospel. Thus you permit men to wrong you and drive you away; and yet, at the same time, you do not permit men to take the gospel from you or keep it from you. Thus the two things, suffering and not suffering, turn out to be one. If

---

[42] Cf. I Pet. 2:16.

you occupy the city for the sake of the gospel, you rob the ruler of the city of what is his, and pretend that you are doing it for the gospel's sake. Dear friend, the gospel does not teach us to rob or to take things, even though the owner of the property abuses it by using it against God, wrongfully, and to your injury. The gospel needs no physical place or city in which to dwell; it will and must dwell in hearts.

This is what Christ taught in Matthew 10 [:23], "When they persecute you in one town, flee to the next." He does not say, "When they persecute you in one town, stay there and take over the town by force and rebel against the ruler of the town—all to the praise of the gospel," as men now want to do, and are teaching. However, Jesus says, "Flee, flee straightaway into another, until the Son of man shall come." And in Matthew 23 [:34] he says that godless men will drive his evangelists from town to town. And in II Corinthians 4 [I Cor. 4:11] Paul says that we are homeless. And if it does happen that a Christian must, for the sake of the gospel, constantly move from one place to another, and leave all his possessions behind him, or even if his situation is very uncertain and he expects to have to move at any moment, he is only experiencing what is appropriate for a Christian. For because he will not suffer the gospel to be taken or kept from him, he has to let his city, town, property, and everything that he is and has be taken and kept from him. Now how does your undertaking conform to this? You capture and hold cities and towns that are not yours, and you will not let them be taken or kept from you; though you take and keep them from their natural rulers. What kind of Christians are these, who, for the gospel's sake, become robbers, thieves, and scoundrels, and then say afterward that they are evangelicals?

On the First Article

"The entire community should have the power and authority to choose and appoint a pastor."[43] This article is just only if it is

---

[43] See p. 10. Cf. also Luther's treatise, *The Right and Power of a Christian Congregation or Community to Judge All Teaching, and to Call, Appoint, and Dismiss Teachers, Established and Proved from Scripture* (1523). PE 4, 75-85.

understood in a Christian sense, even though the chapters indicated in the margin do not support it. If the possessions of the parish come from the rulers and not from the community, then the community cannot give these possessions to one whom they choose, for that would be robbery and theft. If they desire a pastor, let them first humbly ask the rulers to give them one. If the rulers are unwilling, then let them choose their own pastor, and support him out of their own possessions; they should let the rulers keep their property, or else secure it from them in a lawful way. But if the rulers will not tolerate the pastor whom they chose and support, then let him flee to another city, and let any flee with him who want to do as Christ teaches. That is a Christian and evangelical way to choose and have one's own pastor. Whoever does otherwise, acts in an un-Christian manner, and is a robber and brawler.

On the Second Article

The pastor "shall receive out of this tithe . . .; the remainder shall be distributed to the poor and needy."[44] This article is nothing but theft and highway robbery. They want to appropriate for themselves the tithes, which are not theirs but the rulers', and want to use them to do what they please. Oh, no, dear friends! That is the same as deposing the rulers altogether. Your preface expressly says that no one is to be deprived of what is his.[45] If you want to give gifts and do good, use your own possessions, as the wise man says [Prov. 3:9]. And God says through Isaiah, "I hate the offering that is given out of stolen goods" [Isa. 61:8]. You speak in this article as though you were already lords in the land and had taken all the property of the rulers for your own and would be no one's subjects, and would give nothing. This shows what your intention really is. Stop it, dear sirs, stop it! It will not be you who puts an end to it! The chapters of Scripture which your lying preacher and false prophet has smeared on the margin do not help you at all; they are against you.[46]

---

[44] See p. 10.
[45] See p. 10. The reference is not to the preface but to the second article.
[46] See the marginal Scripture references, pp. 10-16.

On the Third Article

You assert that no one is to be the serf of anyone else, because Christ has made us all free.[47] That is making Christian freedom a completely physical matter. Did not Abraham [Gen. 17:23] and other patriarchs and prophets have slaves? Read what St. Paul teaches about servants, who, at that time, were all slaves.[48] This article, therefore, absolutely contradicts the gospel. It proposes robbery, for it suggests that every man should take his body away from his lord, even though his body is the lord's property. A slave can be a Christian, and have Christian freedom, in the same way that a prisoner or a sick man is a Christian, and yet not free. This article would make all men equal, and turn the spiritual kingdom of Christ into a worldly, external kingdom; and that is impossible. A worldly kingdom cannot exist without an inequality of persons, some being free, some imprisoned, some lords, some subjects, etc.; and St. Paul says in Galatians 5 that in Christ the lord and the servant are equal.[49] My good friend Urbanus Rhegius has written more adequately on this subject. If you want to know more, read his book.[50]

On the Other Eight Articles

The other articles, which discuss the freedom to hunt game animals and birds, to catch fish, to use wood from the forest, their obligation to provide free labor, the amount of their rents and taxes, the death tax, etc., are all matters for the lawyers to discuss. It is not fitting that I, an evangelist, should judge or make decisions in such matters. I am to instruct and teach men's consciences in things

---

[47] See p. 12.
[48] Cf. I Cor. 7:21-24; Eph. 6:5-9; Col. 3:22-25; I Tim. 6:1-2; Titus 2:9-10.
[49] Gal. 5:13; cf. Gal. 3:28.
[50] Urbanus Rhegius (1489-1541) was at this time the leader of the Lutheran Reformation in the city of Augsburg. The title of his book is *Serfdom and Slavery: A Discussion of the Christian Relationship between Lords and Serfs on the Basis of Divine Law. A Sermon Preached in Augsburg* (*Von Leibaygenschaft Oder Knechthait, wie sich Herren und aygen leut christlich halten sollend . . .*) (Rostock, 1530). Earlier editions have been lost; the first edition was printed in 1525.

that concern divine and Christian matters; there are books enough about the other things in the imperial laws. I said above that these things do not concern a Christian, and that he cares nothing about them. He lets anyone who will rob, take, cheat, scrape, devour, and rage—for the Christian is a martyr on earth. Therefore the peasants ought properly to stop using the name Christian and use some other name that would show that they are men who seek their human and natural rights rather than their rights as Christians. For obtaining their rights as Christians would mean they should keep quiet about all these matters and complain only to God when they suffer.

Dear friends, this is the instruction that you asked me to give you in the second document.[51] Please remember that you have gladly offered to receive instruction on the basis of Scripture. So when this reaches you, do not be so ready to scream, "Luther flatters the princes and speaks contrary to the gospel." First read and examine my arguments from Scripture. For this is your affair; I am excused in the sight of God and the world. I know well the false prophets who are among you. Do not listen to them. They are surely deceiving you. They do not think of your consciences; they want to make Galatians of you.[52] They want to use you to gain riches and honor for themselves. Afterward, both you and they will be damned eternally in hell.

Admonition to Both Rulers and Peasants

Now, dear sirs, there is nothing Christian on either side and nothing Christian is at issue between you; both lords and peasants are discussing questions of justice and injustice in heathen, or worldly, terms. Furthermore, both parties are acting against God and are under his wrath, as you have heard. For God's sake, then, take my advice! Take a hold of these matters properly, with justice and not with force or violence and do not start endless bloodshed in Germany. For because both of you are wrong, and both of you

---

[51] See p. 17.
[52] People who have lost their faith in the gospel; cf. Gal. 1:6.

want to avenge and defend yourselves, both of you will destroy yourselves and God will use one rascal to flog another.[53]

Both Scripture and history are against you lords, for both tell how tyrants are punished. Even the heathen poets say that tyrants seldom die a dry death, but are usually slain and perish in their own blood.[54] Because, then, it is an established fact that you rule tyranically and with rage, prohibit preaching of the gospel, and cheat and oppress the poor, you have no reason to be confident or to hope that you will perish in any other way than your kind have always perished.

Look at all the kingdoms that have come to their end by the sword—Assyria, Persia, Israel, Judah, and Rome. In the end they were all destroyed in the same way they destroyed others. Thus God shows that he is Judge upon earth and that he leaves no wrong unpunished. Therefore nothing is more certain than that this same judgment is breathing down your necks,[55] whether it comes now or later, unless you reform.

Scripture and experience are also against you peasants. They teach that rebellion has never had a good end and that God always keeps his word exactly, "He that takes the sword will perish by the sword" [Matt. 26:52]. You are certainly under the wrath of God, because you are doing wrong by judging your own case and avenging yourselves and are bearing the name Christian unworthily. Even though you win and destroy all the lords, you will finally start tearing the flesh from one another's bones, like wild beasts. For because flesh and blood, not spirit, prevails among you, God will soon send an evil spirit among you, as he did to the men of Shechem and to Abimelech [Judg. 9:22-57]. See the end that finally comes to rebellion in the story of Korah, Numbers 16 [:31-35], and of Absalom [II Sam. 18:14-15], of Sheba [II Sam. 20:22], Zimri [I Kings 16:18], and others like them. In short, God hates both tyrants and rebels; therefore he sets them against each other, so that both parties perish shamefully, and his wrath and judgment upon the godless are fulfilled.

---

[53] See p. 32, n. 34.

[54] Juvenal, *Satires*, X, 112-113.

[55] *Auff dem halse ligt.*

As I see it, the worst thing about this completely miserable affair is that both sides will sustain irreparable damage; and I would gladly risk my life and even die if I could prevent that from happening. Since neither side fights with a good conscience, but both fight to uphold injustice, it must follow, in the first place, that those who are slain are lost eternally, body and soul, as men who die in their sins, without penitence and without grace, under the wrath of God. Nothing can be done for them. The lords would be fighting to strengthen and maintain their tyranny, their persecution of the gospel, and their unjust oppression of the poor, or else to help that kind of ruler. That is a terrible injustice and is against God. He who commits such a sin must be lost eternally. The peasants, on the other hand, would fight to defend their rebellion and their abuse of the name Christian. Both these things are great sins against God, and he who dies in them or for them must also be lost eternally, and nothing can prevent it.

The second injury is that Germany will be laid waste, and if this bloodshed once starts, it will not stop until everything is destroyed. It is easy to start a fight, but we cannot stop the fighting whenever we want to. What have all these innocent women, children, and old people, whom you fools are drawing with you into such danger, ever done to you? Why do you insist on filling the land with blood and robbery, widows and orphans? Oh, the devil has wicked plans! And God is angry; he threatens to let the devil loose upon us and cool his rage in our blood and souls. Beware, dear sirs, and be wise! Both of you are equally involved! What good will it do you intentionally to damn yourselves for all eternity and, in addition, to bequeath a desolate, devastated, and bloody land to your descendants, when you still have time to find a better solution by repenting before God, by concluding a friendly agreement, or even by voluntarily suffering for the sake of humanity? You will accomplish nothing[56] through strife and violence.

I, therefore, sincerely advise you to choose certain counts and lords from among the nobility and certain councilmen from the cities and ask them to arbitrate and settle this dispute amicably.

---

[56] Luther's manuscript reads *nichts gutts* ("nothing good"); the printed text omits *gutts*.

You lords, stop being so stubborn! You will finally have to stop being such oppressive tyrants—whether you want to or not. Give these poor people room in which to live and air to breath. You peasants, let yourselves be instructed and give up the excessive demands of some of your articles. In this way it may be possible to reach a solution of this dispute through human laws and agreements, if not through Christian means.

If you do not follow this advice—God forbid!—I must let you come to blows. But I am innocent of your souls, your blood, or your property. The guilt is yours alone. I have told you that you are both wrong and that what you are fighting for is wrong. You lords are not fighting against Christians—Christians do nothing against you; they prefer to suffer all things—but against outright robbers and defamers of the Christian name. Those of them who die are already condemned eternally. On the other hand, you peasants are not fighting against Christians, but against tyrants, and persecutors of God and man, and murderers of the saints of Christ. Those of them who die are also condemned eternally. There you have God's sure verdict upon both parties. This I know. Do what you please to preserve your bodies and souls, if you will not accept my advice.

I, however, will pray to my God that he will either reconcile you both and bring about an agreement between you, or else graciously prevent things from turning out as you intend. Nonetheless, the terrible signs and wonders that have come to pass in these times[57] give me a heavy heart and make me fear that God's wrath has grown too great; as he says in Jeremiah, "Though Noah, Job, and Daniel stood before me, I would have no pleasure in the people.[58] Would to God that you might fear his wrath and amend your ways that this disaster might be delayed and postponed a while! In any case, my conscience assures me that I have faithfully given you my Christian and fraternal advice. God grant that it helps! Amen.

"His mischief returns upon his own head, and on his own
    pate his violence descends."[59]

---

[57] Cf. p. 18, n. 3.

[58] Luther conflates Jer. 15:1 with Ezek. 14:14.

[59] In the original text this quotation from Ps. 7:16 was in Latin. *CL* omits it, following editions that contain both the *Admonition to Peace* and *Against the Robbing and Murdering Hordes of Peasants*.

AGAINST THE
ROBBING AND MURDERING
HORDES OF PEASANTS

1525

Translated by Charles M. Jacobs
Revised by Robert C. Schultz

INTRODUCTION

At the invitation of Count Albrecht of Mansfeld, Luther, accompanied by Melanchthon, journeyed to Eisleben in Thuringia to establish a new Christian school. At that time Luther was not ignorant of growing unrest among the German peasantry, but he was unaware of the violent course events were taking in the south. There the peasants had launched full-scale attacks upon their landlords and rulers, plundering and destroying castles, monasteries, and churches.[1] Franconia was at the mercy of peasant brigades led by Florian Geyer[2] and Goetz von Berlichingen.[3] Just when Luther learned of these events is not certain, but it appears to have been during the course of his Thuringian journey.[4]

During his journey, however, Luther had occasion to see and hear at first hand just how acute the situation was in Thuringia. There the peasant bands were riding the crest of victory. By the end of April a great many castles and some forty convents and monasteries[5] had fallen to the agrarian rebels. The cities of Erfurt and Salzungen, among others, surrendered to the foe. Nor was there any effective resistance or suppression of the uprising, for the most powerful ruler, Elector Frederick of Saxony, did nothing. The fact of the matter was that Frederick, who was fatally ill, continued to cling to the hope that a peaceful solution could be negotiated with the peasants.[6] Furthermore, Luther's ears were no doubt filled with reports of peasant violence by relatives whom he

---

[1] Cf. Schwiebert, *Luther and His Times,* p. 562.

[2] Geyer (*ca.* 1490-1525), a Franconian noble, had been a professional soldier in the service of Albert of Prussia. An early convert to Protestantism, he commanded an army of peasants to which Würzburg, Rothenburg, and Margrave Casimir of Brandenburg submitted. It was his aim to establish a kingdom based on the gospel. He was murdered after the battle of Ingolstadt.

[3] A Swabian of noble background, von Berlichingen (1480-1562) wore an iron hand to replace one lost in battle. Against his will he commanded the Odenwald peasants. He was released from prison in 1530 and returned to professional soldiering.

[4] Cf. WA 18, 344-345 and PE 4, 247.

[5] Cf. BG 7, 342.

[6] Cf. MA³ 4, 387-388.

visited, among them his brother-in-law Johann Ruehel, a court counselor at Mansfeld.

Luther attempted to forestall further violence by preaching, but he finally realized that preaching was not the solution. At Nordhausen hecklers had interrupted his sermon.[7] Convinced that the rebellious peasants would stop at nothing short of complete revolution and overthrow of the existing social order, Luther decided to publish his opinion upon his return to Wittenberg.

The exact date when *Against the Robbing and Murdering Hordes of Peasants* was written cannot be fixed with any degree of certainty. Because of the similarity of ideas and language in a letter written to Ruehel[8] on May 4, 1525, it is assumed that Luther wrote this strongly worded treatise at or about the same time as the letter. There is a similar difficulty with the date of publication. It was certainly before the middle of May, but a more exact date of publication cannot be given.

In the treatise Luther arraigned the peasants on three charges: (1) they had violated their oaths of loyalty to their rulers and were therefore subject to temporal punishment; (2) they had robbed, plundered, and murdered, and were subject to death in body and soul; and (3) they had committed their crimes under the cover of Christ's name, thereby shamefully blaspheming God. The peasants were like a mad dog which had to be destroyed. The government, he argued, must use its God-given office to subdue the rebels with force, the only language they understood. Whoever lost his life in suppressing this rebellion, Luther argues, would be a martyr to the gospel.

The translation by Charles M. Jacobs was based on *CL* 3, 69-74. The revision presented here is based on the German text, *Wider die räuberischen und mörderischen Rotten der Bauern*, in *WA* 18, (344) 357-361.

R. C. S.

---

[7] Cf. *WA* 17^{I}, 195-196.

[8] *WA*, Br 3, 480-482.

AGAINST THE
ROBBING AND MURDERING
HORDES OF PEASANTS

Against the rioting peasants, Martin Luther.

In my earlier book on this matter,[1] I did not venture to judge the peasants, since they had offered to be corrected and to be instructed;[2] and Christ in Matthew 7 [:1] commands us not to judge. But before I could even inspect the situation,[3] they forgot their promise and violently took matters into their own hands and are robbing and raging like mad dogs. All this now makes it clear that they were trying to deceive us and that the assertions they made in their *Twelve Articles*[4] were nothing but lies presented under the name of the gospel. To put it briefly, they are doing the devil's work. This is particularly the work of that archdevil who rules at Mühlhausen,[5] and does nothing except stir up robbery, murder, and bloodshed; as Christ describes him in John 8 [:44], "He was a murderer from the beginning." Since these peasants and wretched people have now let themselves be misled and are acting differently than they promised, I, too, must write differently of them than I have written, and begin by setting their sin before them, as God commands Isaiah [58:1] and Ezekiel [2:7], on the chance that some of them may see themselves for what they are. Then I must instruct the rulers how they are to conduct themselves in these circumstances.

The peasants have taken upon themselves the burden of three terrible sins against God and man; by this they have abundantly merited death in body and soul. In the first place, they have

---

[1] *Admonition to Peace.* See pp. 17-43.

[2] Luther refers to the conclusion of *The Twelve Articles;* see pp. 15-16.

[3] Luther became more closely acquainted with the situation during a journey through Thuringia. See p. 47.

[4] For the text of *The Twelve Articles,* see pp. 8-16.

[5] Thomas Münzer. Cf. p. 5, n. 3.

sworn[6] to be true and faithful, submissive and obedient, to their rulers, as Christ commands when he says, "Render to Caesar the things that are Caesar's" [Luke 20:25]. And Romans 13 [:1] says, "Let every person be subject to the governing authorities." Since they are now deliberately and violently breaking this oath of obedience and setting themselves in opposition to their masters, they have forfeited body and soul, as faithless, perjured, lying, disobedient rascals and scoundrels usually do. St. Paul passed this judgment on them in Romans 13 [:2] when he said that those who resist the authorities will bring a judgment upon themselves. This saying will smite the peasants sooner or later, for God wants people to be loyal and to do their duty.

In the second place, they are starting a rebellion, and are violently robbing and plundering monasteries and castles which are not theirs; by this they have doubly deserved death in body and soul as highwaymen and murderers. Furthermore, anyone who can be proved to be a seditious person is an outlaw before God and the emperor; and whoever is the first to put him to death does right and well. For if a man is in open rebellion, everyone is both his judge and his executioner; just as when a fire starts, the first man who can put it out is the best man to do the job. For rebellion is not just simple murder; it is like a great fire, which attacks and devastates a whole land. Thus rebellion brings with it a land filled with murder and bloodshed; it makes widows and orphans, and turns everything upside down, like the worst disaster. Therefore let everyone who can, smite, slay, and stab, secretly or openly, remembering that nothing can be more poisonous, hurtful, or devilish than a rebel. It is just as when one must kill a mad dog; if you do not strike him, he will strike you, and a whole land with you.

In the third place, they cloak this terrible and horrible sin with the gospel, call themselves "Christian brethren,"[7] take oaths and submit to them, and compel people to go along with them in these abominations. Thus they become the worst blasphemers of God and slanderers of his holy name. Under the outward appear-

---

[6] All men took this oath under the feudal system.
[7] Cf. p. 7, n. 14.

ance of the gospel, they honor and serve the devil, thus deserving death in body and soul ten times over. I have never heard of a more hideous sin. I suspect that the devil feels that the Last Day is coming and therefore he undertakes such an unheard-of act, as though saying to himself, "This is the end, therefore it shall be the worst; I will stir up the dregs and knock out the bottom."[8] God will guard us against him! See what a mighty prince the devil is, how he has the world in his hands and can throw everything into confusion, when he can so quickly catch so many thousands of peasants, deceive them, blind them, harden them, and throw them into revolt, and do with them whatever his raging fury undertakes.

It does not help the peasants when they pretend that according to Genesis 1 and 2 all things were created free and common, and that all of us alike have been baptized.[9] For under the New Testament, Moses does not count; for there stands our Master, Christ, and subjects us, along with our bodies and our property, to the emperor and the law of this world, when he says, "Render to Caesar the things that are Caesar's" [Luke 20:25]. Paul, too, speaking in Romans 12 [13:1] to all baptized Christians, says, "Let every person be subject to the governing authorities." And Peter says, "Be subject to every ordinance of man" [I Pet. 2:13]. We are bound to live according to this teaching of Christ, as the Father commands from heaven, saying, "This is my beloved Son, listen to him" [Matt. 17:5].

For baptism does not make men free in body and property, but in soul; and the gospel does not make goods common, except in the case of those who, of their own free will, do what the apostles and disciples did in Acts 4 [:32-37]. They did not demand, as do our insane peasants in their raging, that the goods of others—of Pilate and Herod—should be common, but only their own goods. Our peasants, however, want to make the goods of other men common, and keep their own for themselves. Fine Christians they are! I think there is not a devil left in hell; they have all

---

[8] Cf. Thiele, *Luthers Sprichwörtersammlung*, No. 335.

[9] Cf. the claim of the peasants in the third of their twelve articles that serfdom is un-Christian, p. 12.

gone into the peasants. Their raving has gone beyond all measure.

Now since the peasants have brought [the wrath of] both God and man down upon themselves and are already many times guilty of death in body and soul, and since they submit to no court and wait for no verdict, but only rage on, I must instruct the temporal authorities on how they may act with a clear conscience in this matter.

First, I will not oppose a ruler who, even though he does not tolerate the gospel, will smite and punish these peasants without first offering to submit the case to judgment.[10] He is within his rights, since the peasants are not contending any longer for the gospel, but have become faithless, perjured, disobedient, rebellious murderers, robbers, and blasphemers, whom even a heathen ruler has the right and authority to punish. Indeed, it is his duty to punish such scoundrels, for this is why he bears the sword and is "the servant of God to execute his wrath on the wrongdoer," Romans 13 [:4].

But if the ruler is a Christian and tolerates the gospel,[11] so that the peasants have no appearance of a case against him, he should proceed with fear. First he must take the matter to God, confessing that we have deserved these things, and remembering that God may, perhaps, have thus aroused the devil as a punishment upon all Germany. Then he should humbly pray for help against the devil, for we are contending not only "against flesh and blood," but "against the spiritual hosts of wickedness in the air" [Eph. 6:12; 2:2], which must be attacked with prayer. Then, when our hearts are so turned to God that we are ready to let his divine will be done, whether he will or will not have us to be princes and lords, we must go beyond our duty, and offer the mad peasants an opportunity to come to terms, even though they are not worthy of it. Finally, if that does not help, then swiftly take to the sword.

For in this case a prince and lord must remember that according to Romans 13 [:4] he is God's minister and the servant of

---

[10] In other words, a ruler need not wait for a judicial verdict against the peasants.

[11] I.c., has evangelical sympathies.

his wrath and that the sword has been given him to use against such people. If he does not fulfil the duties of his office by punishing some and protecting others, he commits as great a sin before God as when someone who has not been given the sword commits murder. If he is able to punish and does not do it—even though he would have had to kill someone or shed blood—he becomes guilty of all the murder and evil that these people commit. For by deliberately disregarding God's command he permits such rascals to go about their wicked business, even though he was able to prevent it and it was his duty to do so. This is not a time to sleep. And there is no place for patience or mercy. This is the time of the sword, not the day of grace.

The rulers, then, should press on and take action in this matter with a good conscience as long as their hearts still beat. It is to the rulers' advantage that the peasants have a bad conscience and an unjust cause, and that any peasant who is killed is lost in body and soul and is eternally the devil's. But the rulers have a good conscience and a just cause; they can, therefore, say to God with all confidence of heart, "Behold, my God, you have appointed me prince or lord, of this I can have no doubt; and you have given me the sword to use against evildoers (Romans 13 [:4]). It is your word, and it cannot lie, so I must fulfil the duties of my office, or forfeit your grace. It is also plain that these peasants have deserved death many times over, in your eyes and in the eyes of the world, and have been committed to me for punishment. If you will me to be slain by them, and let my authority be taken from me and destroyed, so be it: let your will be done. I shall be defeated and die because of your divine command and word and shall die while obeying your command and fulfilling the duties of my office. Therefore I will punish and smite as long as my heart beats. You will be the judge and make things right."

Thus, anyone who is killed fighting on the side of the rulers may be a true martyr in the eyes of God, if he fights with the kind of conscience I have just described, for he acts in obedience to God's word. On the other hand, anyone who perishes on the peasants' side is an eternal firebrand of hell, for he bears the sword against God's word and is disobedient to him, and is a member of the devil. And even if the peasants happen to gain the upper hand (God forbid!)—for to God all things are possible, and we do not know whether it may be his will, through the devil, to destroy all rule and order and cast the world upon a desolate heap, as a prelude to the Last Day, which cannot be far off[12]—nevertheless, those who are found exercising the duties of their office can die without worry and go to the scaffold with a good conscience, and leave the kingdom of this world to the devil and take in exchange the everlasting kingdom. These are strange times, when a prince can win heaven with bloodshed better than other men with prayer!

Finally, there is another thing that ought to motivate the rulers. The peasants are not content with belonging to the devil themselves; they force and compel many good people to join their devilish league against their wills, and so make them partakers of all of their own wickedness and damnation. Anyone who consorts with them goes to the devil with them and is guilty of all the evil deeds that they commit, even though he has to do this because he is so weak in faith that he could not resist them. A pious Christian ought to suffer a hundred deaths rather than give a hairsbreadth of consent to the peasants' cause. O how many martyrs could now be made by the bloodthirsty peasants and the prophets of murder![13] Now the rulers ought to have mercy on these prisoners of the peasants, and if they had no other reason to use the sword with a good conscience against the peasants, and to risk their own lives and property in fighting them, this would be reason enough, and more than enough: they would be rescuing and helping these souls whom the peasants have forced into their devilish league and who, without willing it, are sinning so horribly and must be damned. For truly these souls are in purgatory; indeed, they are in the bonds of hell and the devil.

Therefore, dear lords, here is a place where you can release, rescue, help. Have mercy on these poor people! Let whoever can stab, smite, slay. If you die in doing it, good for you! A more blessed death can never be yours, for you die while obeying the

---

[12] Luther anticipated the imminent coming of the Last Day. Cf. p. 18, n. 3.
[13] Cf. p. 20, n. 8.

divine word and commandment in Romans 13 [:1, 2], and in loving service of your neighbor, whom you are rescuing from the bonds of hell and of the devil. And so I beg everyone who can to flee from the peasants as from the devil himself; those who do not flee, I pray that God will enlighten and convert. As for those who are not to be converted, God grant that they may have neither fortune nor success. To this let every pious Christian say, "Amen!" For this prayer is right and good, and pleases God; this I know. If anyone thinks this too harsh, let him remember that rebellion is intolerable and that the destruction of the world is to be expected every hour.

AN OPEN LETTER
ON THE HARSH BOOK
AGAINST THE PEASANTS

1525

Translated by Charles M. Jacobs
Revised by Robert C. Schultz

INTRODUCTION

The cause of the rebelling peasants was hopelessly lost before May 15, 1525, when Münzer's[1] forces were decisively defeated at the battle of Frankenhausen. The peasants had no leaders of real political and military ability, and when the rulers recovered from their shock and went into action, the result was a foregone conclusion. The professional soldiers of the Swabian League[2] moved quickly and effectively in the south and east. Hesse, Brunswick, and Saxony joined forces and suppressed the revolt in Thuringia. Münzer himself was seized, tortured, and finally beheaded. All in all, it is estimated that one hundred thousand peasants lost their lives in the revolt.[3]

The defeated peasants were at the mercy of their victorious rulers, who in the hour of triumph sated a lust for blood. Nor did the nobles appear to have any pangs of conscience about the severity of the punishments they meted out. Indeed, both Catholic and Protestant princes interpreted Luther's *Against the Robbing and Murdering Hordes of Peasants*,[4] which had gained wide circulation by the middle of May, as justification for their actions.[5]

As the memory of the peasants' atrocities faded and new atrocities were perpetrated by the victorious rulers, Luther came under widespread and stinging criticism for his strongly-worded book against the peasants. The rebels felt that he had betrayed them. His Catholic opponents charged that Luther had encouraged the peasants in *Admonition to Peace*.[6] But when the tide turned against the peasants, his opponents charged, Luther deserted them and

---

[1] Cf. p. 19, n. 5.

[2] Cf. p. 7, n. 12.

[3] Cf. G. R. Elton, *Reformation Europe, 1517-1559* (Cleveland and New York: Meridian Books, the World Publishing Company, 1964), p. 59.

[4] Cf. pp. 45-55.

[5] In a letter to Luther dated May 21, 1525, Ruehel reports that at the rate the authorities were meting out death penalties, he feared that the entire population would eventually be wiped out. Cf. WA 18, 376.

[6] Cf. pp. 17-43.

went crawling back to the princes.[7] They even charged that Luther had abandoned his teaching of justification by faith when he said that heaven could be earned by princes through suppressing the rebellion.[8]

But it was not only his religious adversaries who criticized Luther as being responsible for the brutal retaliatory acts of the princes. Even his friends and sympathizers could not understand or justify the harsh language of *Against the Robbing and Murdering Hordes of Peasants;* still less could they reconcile it with *Admonition to Peace.*[9] Luther's brother-in-law, Johann Ruehel, reported the rumor that Luther had written so harshly about the peasants because Elector Frederick had died and now Luther feared for his own skin.[10] Indeed, Luther was aware that many regarded him as a "flatterer of princes"[11] because of the position he had taken against the peasants.

Luther's friends urged him to make a retraction.[12] At first he steadfastly refused either to retract or explain his stand.[13] Gradually, however, he realized that he had to explain his stand, and he did so in his Pentecost sermons at Wittenberg.[14] Later he decided to make a more formal and public explanation. It took the form of an open letter to Caspar Müller, a chancellor to the counts of Mansfeld and a frequent correspondent of Luther, and bore the title *An Open Letter on the Harsh Book Against the Peasants.* The date of its composition is uncertain, but probability argues for a

---

[7] Cf. the list of John Cochlaeus' replies to *Against the Robbing and Murdering Hordes of Peasants* in WA 18, 348-349. Hartmann Grisar quotes Cochlaeus as charging, "Now that the poor, unhappy peasants have lost the wager, you [Luther] go over to the princes. But in the previous booklet, when there was still a good chance of their success, you wrote very differently." E. M. Lamond (trans.), Hartmann Grisar's *Luther* (St. Louis: B. Herder, 1916), II, 212.

[8] Cf. p. 54.

[9] See the report of Zwickau's mayor Hermann Mühlpfort cited in WA 18, 376.

[10] Cf. WA 18, 376. Ruehel's report is contained in a letter to Luther dated May 26, 1525. The text is given by Georg Buchwald in *Theologische Studien und Kritiken* (Gotha, 1896), pp. 148-150.

[11] Cf. WA, Br 3, 517.

[12] Cf. Schwiebert, *Luther and His Times*, p. 568.

[13] Cf. p. 63.

[14] The text of the sermon is in WA 17¹, 265-267.

date early in July.[15] By August 1 Spalatin was distributing copies that had just been published.[16]

In this treatise Luther defends at length the views he had advanced in *Admonition to Peace* and *Against the Robbing and Murdering Hordes of Peasants.* The peasants should not have rebelled, for the duty of a Christian is to suffer injustice, not to seize the sword and take to violence. His opponents, Luther says, can criticize him as they will, but they cannot change the fact that in the light of God's word the rebellious peasants deserved to be put to death and to have their insurrection suppressed by the full force of the governing authorities. Force was the only language the rebels understood. Furthermore, Luther argues, his critics' sudden surge of sympathy for the defeated peasants marks them as secret rebels against God and state.

But if there was no excuse for the peasants to rebel, neither was there any excuse for the rulers to indulge their lust for rebel blood. Here, however, Luther is not moved by any sense of "fair play." He disclaims responsibility for the wanton cruelty of the rulers, which, he says, is nothing but the flagrant abuse by the princes of their God-given office. Such cruelty is as reprehensible and sinful as insurrection. The princes, he says, will surely reap God's wrath for such conduct.

The translation by Charles M. Jacobs was based on *CL* 3, 75-93. The revision presented here is based on the German text, *Ein Sendbrief von dem harten Büchlein wider die Bauern,* in *WA* 18, (375) 384-401.

R. C. S.

---

[15] Cf. *WA* 18, 377, which reasons that Luther made the definite decision to publish his explanation during the course of conversations with friends (Müller among them) who had gathered for his wedding on June 27, 1525.

[16] *WA* 18, 377.

AN OPEN LETTER
ON THE HARSH BOOK
AGAINST THE PEASANTS

To the honorable and wise Caspar Müller, chancellor of Mansfeld, my good friend. Grace and peace in Christ.

I have been obliged to answer your letter[1] in a printed book because the little book that I published against the peasants has given rise to so many complaints and questions,[2] as though it were un-Christian and too hard. Indeed, I had intended to plug my ears and to let those blind, ungrateful creatures who seek nothing in me but causes of offense smother in their own vexation until they had to rot in it. It seems that reading my other books has not helped men to accept such a plain, simple judgment about earthly things. For I remembered the word of Christ in John 3 [:12], "If I have told you earthly things and you do not believe, how can you believe if I tell you heavenly things?" And when the disciples asked, "Do you know that the Pharisees were offended when they heard this saying?" he said, "Let them be offended. They are blind and blind leaders of the blind," Matthew 15 [:12-14].

They cry and boast, "There, there you see Luther's spirit! He teaches bloodshed without any mercy. The devil must speak through him." Oh, well, if I were not used to being judged and condemned, I might become excited; but nothing makes me prouder than when my work and teaching suffers reverses[3] and is crucified. No one is satisfied unless he can condemn Luther. Luther is the target of opposition. Everyone has to win his spurs against him[4] and carry off the honors of the tournament. In these matters everyone else has a higher spirit than I, and I must be altogether fleshly. Would to God that they had a higher spirit! Indeed, I would gladly

---

[1] This letter is lost.

[2] Cf. pp. 59-60.

[3] Reading *herhalten* (*CL* 3, 76) rather than *erhalten* (*WA* 18, 384).

[4] *Ritter werden.* The phrase appears often in Luther; cf. *WA* 18, 384, n. 2.

be a man of flesh[5] and say, as St. Paul said to his Corinthians, "You are rich. You are full. You rule without us" [I Cor. 4:8]. But I fear it is all too true that they have a high spirit, for I have not as yet seen them undertake very much that does not bring them to sin and shame.

But they do not see how they stumble when they thus pass judgment on me, and how their opposition reveals the thoughts of their hearts, as Simeon says of Christ in Luke 2 [:34-35]. They say that they note well what kind of a spirit I have; I, too, note how splendidly they have grasped and learned the gospel. They have, in fact, not a spark of knowledge of it, and yet they babble on and on about it. How can they know what heavenly righteousness in Christ may be, according to the gospel, when they do not know what earthly righteousness in rulers is, according to the law? Such people are not worthy to hear a single word or see a single work that might make them better; they ought to have nothing but offense, as the Jews had in Christ—because their hearts are so full of wicked wiles that they desire nothing more than to be offended—so that they may fare according to Psalm 18 [:26], "With the crooked, thou dost show thyself perverse," and Deuteronomy 32 [:21], "I will stir them to jealousy with those who are no people; I will provoke them with a foolish nation."

These were the reasons I wanted to keep silent and confidently let them stumble on and take offense: so that with heart hardened and eyes blinded by sheer offense, those people would go to destruction who have still learned nothing from the great, clear light of the gospel, which has shone[6] so lavishly everywhere, who have made so little of the fear of God that they think nothing is more "evangelical" than to despise and judge others, and to consider themselves great in spirit and high in understanding, and who—like the spider which sucks only poison from the rose[7]—draw only vain pride from the doctrine of humility. However, you have asked for

---

[5] Luther may be alluding to Thomas Münzer's book *Against the Soft-living Flesh at Wittenberg.*

[6] Literally, "The light . . . which has sounded so richly." *WA* 18, 385.

[7] A proverb; cf. Thiele, *Luthers Sprichwörtersammlung*, No. 49; Wander (ed.), *Deutsches Sprichwörter Lexikon*, IV, "*Spinne*," Nos. 6, 12, 19. The rose was a personal symbol for Luther, for example, in his coat of arms.

an explanation not for your own benefit, but to use to make these worthless fellows keep quiet. I suspect that you are undertaking a vain and impossible task; for who can stop the mouth of a fool?[8] His heart is crammed so full of nonsense and "out of the abundance of the heart, the mouth speaks" [Matt. 12:34]. Nevertheless, because you ask it, I will do you this vain and lost service.

First of all, then, I must warn those who criticize my book to hold their tongues and to be careful not to make a mistake and lose their own heads; for they are certainly rebels at heart, and Solomon says, "My son, fear the Lord and the king, and do not be a fellow-traveler with the rebels for their disaster will come suddenly and who can know what the ruin of both you and them will be?" Proverbs 24 [:21-22]. Thus we see that both rebels and those who join them are condemned. God does not want us to make a joke out of this but to fear the king and the government. Those who are fellow-travelers with rebels sympathize with them, feel sorry for them, justify them, and show mercy to those on whom God has no mercy, but whom he wishes to have punished and destroyed. For the man who thus sympathizes with the rebels makes it perfectly clear that he has decided in his heart that he will also cause disaster if he has the opportunity. The rulers, therefore, ought to shake these people up until they keep their mouths shut and realize that the rulers are serious.

If they think this answer is too harsh, and that this is talking violence and only shutting men's mouths,[9] I reply, "That is right." A rebel is not worth rational arguments, for he does not accept them. You have to answer people like that with a fist, until the sweat[10] drips off their noses. The peasants would not listen; they would not let anyone tell them anything, so their ears must now be unbuttoned with musket balls till their heads jump off their shoulders. Such pupils need such a rod.[11] He who will not hear God's word when it is spoken with kindness,[12] must listen to the

---

[8] Cf. Eccles. 10:14.

[9] I.e., that Luther is advocating the use of force rather than persuasion.

[10] Luther probably means blood. Cf. WA 18, 386, n. 2.

[11] Cf. Wander (ed.), *Deutsches Sprichwörter Lexikon,* II, "*Hören,*" No. 78.

[12] A reference to *Admonition to Peace.*

headsman, when he comes with his axe. If anyone says that I am being uncharitable and unmerciful about this, my reply is: This is not a question of mercy; we are talking of God's word. It is God's will that the king be honored and the rebels destroyed; and he is as merciful as we are.

Here I do not want to hear or know about mercy, but to be concerned only about what God's word requires. On this basis, my little book was and remains right, even though the whole world take offense at it. If it pleases God, I do not really care whether you like it or not. If he will have wrath, and not mercy, what business do you have being merciful? Did not Saul sin by showing mercy to Amalek [Agag] when he failed to execute God's wrath, as he had been commanded [I Sam. 15:4-24]? Did not Ahab sin by having mercy on the king of Syria and letting him live, contrary to God's word [I Kings 20:42]? If you want to have mercy, then do not consort with rebels, but respect authority and do good; "but if you do wrong, be afraid," Paul says, "for he does not bear the sword in vain" [Rom 13:4].

This ought to be answer enough to all who are offended by my book and make it useless. Should not a man keep quiet when he hears that God says this, and that this is God's will? Or does God have to give reasons to such empty babblers, and tell them why this is his will? I would think that the mere wink of his eye would be enough to silence every creature, to say nothing of what should happen when he speaks. God's word says, "My son, fear the Lord and the king; if you do not, disaster will suddenly come upon you" [Prov. 24:21-22]. And in Romans 12 [13:2], "Whoever resists God's authority will incur judgment." Why is not St. Paul merciful? If we are to preach God's word, we must preach the word that declares his wrath, as well as that which declares mercy. We must preach of hell as well as heaven, and help extend God's word and judgment and work over both the righteous and the wicked, so that the wicked may be punished and the good protected.

And yet, in order that the righteous God may hold his own against these his judges, and that his decree be found just and pure, we shall undertake to advocate his word against these blasphemers and show the reason for his divine will, and light two candles for the devil.[13] They cast it up to me that Christ teaches, "Be merciful, even as your Father is merciful" [Luke 6:36]; and again, "I desire mercy and not sacrifice" [Matt. 9:13]; and again, "The Son of man is come not to destroy souls, but to save them" [Luke 19:10], etc. And they think this hits the nail on the head. "Luther ought to have taught that we should have mercy on the peasants, and he teaches, instead, that we should kill them immediately. What do you think of that? Let us see whether Luther will get out of this![14] I think he is caught." Well now, I thank you, dear teachers. If these lofty spirits had not taught me, how would I ever have known this or found it out? How should I know that God demands mercy —I, who have taught and written more about mercy than any other man in a thousand years?

It is the very devil himself who wants to do all the evil that he can, and so he stirs up good and pious hearts and tempts them with things like this, so that they may not see how black he is, and he tries to deck himself out in a reputation for mercy. But it will not help him! My good friends, you praise mercy so highly because the peasants are beaten; why did you not praise it when the peasants were raging, smiting, robbing, burning, and plundering, in ways that are terrible to see or even to hear about? Why were they not merciful to the princes and lords, whom they wanted to exterminate completely? No one spoke of mercy then. Everything was "rights"; nothing was said of mercy, it was nothing. "Rights, rights, rights!" They were everything. Now that the peasants are beaten, and the stone that they threw at heaven is falling back on their own heads,[15] no one is to say anything of rights, but to speak only of mercy.

And yet they are stupid enough to think that no one notices the rascal behind it! Ah, no! We see you, you black, ugly devil! You praise mercy not because you are seriously concerned about mercy, or you would have praised it to the peasants; on the contrary, you are afraid for your own skin, and are trying to use the

---

[13] I.e., throw light on the subject.

[14] *Stucklin;* Clemen follows the emendation suggested in *WA* 18, 387, n. 2, and reads *stricklin* ("little snare") for *stucklin* ("little piece"). Jacobs translated the sentence as, "Let us see whether Luther will jump that ditch!" *PE* 4, 263.

[15] Ecclus. 27:25. Cf. Thiele, *Luthers Sprichwörtersammlung*, No. 29.

appearance and reputation of mercy to escape God's rod and punishment. That will not work dear fellow! You must take your turn, and die without mercy. St. Paul says, "If you do wrong, be afraid, for he does not bear the sword in vain; he is the servant of God to execute his wrath on the wrongdoer" [Rom. 13:4]. You, however, are trying to do wrong and yet escape wrath by praising mercy. Come back tomorrow and we shall bake you a cake.[16] Who cannot do this? Suppose I were to break into a man's house, rape his wife and daughters, break open his strong box, take his money, put a sword to his chest, and say, "If you will not put up with this, I shall run you through, for you are a godless wretch"; then if a crowd gathered and were about to kill me, or if the judge ordered my head off, suppose I were to cry out, "Hey, Christ teaches you to be merciful and not to kill me," what would people say?

That is exactly what these peasants and their sympathizers are now doing. Now that they have, like robbers, murderers, thieves, and scoundrels, done what they pleased to their masters, they want to put on a song and dance about mercy, and say, "Be merciful, as Christ teaches, and let us rage, as the devil teaches: do good to us, and let us do our worst to you; be satisfied with what we have done and call it right, and call what you are doing wrong." Who would not like to get away with that? If that is mercy, then we shall institute a pretty state of affairs; we shall have no sword, ruler, punishment, hangman, or prison, and let every scoundrel do as he pleases; then, when he is to be punished, we shall sing, "Hey, be merciful, as Christ teaches." That would be a fine way of doing things! Here you see the intention of those who condemn my book as though it forbade mercy. It is certain that they are either peasants, rebels, and bloodhounds themselves, or have been misled by such people; for they would like all wickedness to go unpunished. Thus under the name of mercy they would be—so far as it is in their power—the most merciless and cruel destroyers of the whole world.

"Not at all," they say, "we do not justify the peasants and would not prevent their punishment, but it seems wrong to us for you to teach that the poor peasants should be shown no mercy; for you

---

[16] *Wyr wollen dyr eyn kuchlin dazu backen.* Cf. Wander (ed.), *Deutsches Sprichwörter Lexikon*, II, "Küchlein," No. 2.

say that they ought to be slain without mercy."[17] I can only answer that if you really mean that, I am blameless.[18] That is just a cover for your bloodthirsty self-will and your secret pleasure with the peasants. Where have I ever taught that no mercy should be shown? Do I not in that very book beg the rulers to show grace to those who surrender?[19] Why do you not open your eyes and read it? Then it would not have been necessary for you to damn my book and take offense at it. But you are so full of poison that you seize upon the one part of it in which I say that those who will not surrender or listen ought to be killed without mercy; and you skip over the rest of it, in which I say that those who surrender are to be shown grace. Everybody can see that you are a spider that sucks poison from the rose.[20] It is not true that you condemn the peasants or love mercy—what you would really like to see is wickedness go free and unpunished, and the temporal sword made ineffective. Nevertheless, you will not accomplish it.

So much for the un-Christian and merciless bloodhounds who praise the sayings about mercy[21] so that sheer wickedness and mercilessness may rule in the world as they please! To the others, whom they have led astray, or who are so weak that they cannot reconcile my book with the words of Christ, I have this to say: There are two kingdoms, one the kingdom of God, the other the kingdom of the world. I have written this so often that I am surprised that there is anyone who does not know it or remember it.[22] Anyone who knows how to distinguish rightly between these two kingdoms will certainly not be offended by my little book, and he will also properly understand the passages about mercy. God's kingdom is a kingdom of grace and mercy, not of wrath and punishment. In it there is only forgiveness, consideration for one another, love, service, the doing of good, peace, joy, etc. But the kingdom of the world is a kingdom of wrath and severity. In it there is only

---

[17] See pp. 50-53.
[18] Literally, "I am golden." Cf. Wander (ed.), *Deutsches Sprichwörter Lexikon*, I, "*Golden*," No. 1.
[19] Cf. pp. 54-55.
[20] Cf. p. 64, n. 7.
[21] The sayings of Christ, quoted above.
[22] Cf. for example, *LW* 45, 75-129 *passim*, and 231-237 *passim*.

punishment, repression, judgment, and condemnation to restrain the wicked and protect the good.[23] For this reason it has the sword, and Scripture calls a prince or lord "God's wrath," or "God's rod" (Isaiah 14 [:5-6]).

The Scripture passages which speak of mercy apply to the kingdom of God and to Christians, not to the kingdom of the world, for it is a Christian's duty not only to be merciful, but also to endure every kind of suffering—robbery, arson, murder, devil, and hell. It goes without saying that he is not to strike, kill, or take revenge on anyone. But the kingdom of the world, which is nothing else than the servant of God's wrath upon the wicked and is a real precursor of hell and everlasting death, should not be merciful, but strict, severe, and wrathful in fulfilling its work and duty. Its tool is not a wreath of roses or a flower of love, but a naked sword; and a sword is a symbol of wrath, severity, and punishment. It is turned only against the wicked, to hold them in check and keep them at peace, and to protect and save the righteous [Rom. 13:3-4]. Therefore God decrees, in the law of Moses and in Exodus 22 [21:14] where he institutes the sword, "You shall take the murderer from my altar, and not have mercy on him." And the Epistle to the Hebrews [10:28] acknowledges that he who violates the law must die without mercy. This shows that in the exercise of their office, worldly rulers cannot and ought not be merciful—though out of grace, they may take a day off from their office.

Now he who would confuse these two kingdoms—as our false fanatics do—would put wrath into God's kingdom and mercy into the world's kingdom; and that is the same as putting the devil in heaven and God in hell. These sympathizers with the peasants would like to do both of these things. First they wanted to go to work with the sword, fight for the gospel as "Christian brethren,"[24] and kill other people, who were supposed to be merciful and patient. Now that the kingdom of the world has overcome them, they want to have mercy in it; that is to say, they are unwilling to endure the worldly kingdom, but will not grant God's kingdom to anyone. Can you imagine anything more perverse? Not so, dear friends! If

[23] Cf. I Pet. 2:14.
[24] See p. 7, n. 14.

one has deserved wrath in the kingdom of the world, let him submit, and either take his punishment, or humbly sue for pardon. Those who are in God's kingdom ought to have mercy on everyone and pray for everyone, and yet not hinder the kingdom of the world in the maintenance of its laws and the performance of its duty; rather they should assist it.

Although the severity and wrath of the world's kingdom seems unmerciful, nevertheless, when we see it rightly, it is not the least of God's mercies. Let everyone consider and decide the following case. Suppose I had a wife and children, a house, servants, and property, and a thief or murderer fell upon me, killed me in my own house, ravished my wife and children, took all that I had, and went unpunished so that he could do the same thing again, when he wished. Tell me, who would be more in need of mercy in such a case, I or the thief and murderer? Without doubt it would be I who would need most that people should have mercy on me. But how can this mercy be shown to me and my poor, miserable wife and children, except by restraining such a scoundrel, and by protecting me and maintaining my rights, or, if he will not be restrained and keeps it up, by giving him what he deserves and punishing him, so that he must stop it? What a fine mercy to me it would be, to have mercy on the thief and murderer, and let him kill, abuse, and rob me!

These advocates of the peasants do not consider this kind of mercy which rules and acts through the temporal sword. They see and talk only about the wrath and say that we are flattering the furious princes and lords when we teach that they are to punish the wicked. And yet they are themselves ten times worse flatterers of the murderous scoundrels and wicked peasants. Indeed, they are bloodthirsty murderers, rebels at heart, for they have no mercy on those whom the peasants overthrew, robbed, dishonored, and subjected to all kinds of injustice. For if the intentions of the peasants had been carried out, no honest man would have been safe from them, but whoever had one cent more than another would have had to suffer for it. They had already begun that, and it would not have stopped there; women and children would have been put to shame; they would have taken to killing each other, too, and there would have been no peace or safety anywhere. Has anything ever been

71

heard of that is more unrestrained than a mob of peasants when they are filled with food and have got power? As Solomon says, in Proverbs 30 [:21-22], "Such people the world cannot bear."

Are we now to have mercy on such people above others, and are we to let them rage on, doing as they please with everyone's body, life, wife, children, honor, and property? Are we to leave them unpunished, and allow the innocent to perish shamefully before our very eyes, without mercy, help, or comfort? I hear reliable reports that the Bamberg peasants were offered more than they asked, provided only that they would keep the peace, and they would not.[25] Margrave Casimir,[26] too, promised his peasants that whatever others won with strife and rebellion, he would give them out of free grace; but that did not help either. It is well known that the Franconian peasants, out of sheer wantonness, planned nothing else than robbing, burning, breaking, and destroying.[27] It is my own experience with the Thuringian peasants that the more they were exhorted and instructed, the more obstinate, the prouder, the madder they became.[28] Their attitude everywhere was so wanton and defiant that it seemed as though they really wanted to be slain without grace or mercy. They most scornfully defied God's wrath, and now it is coming upon them, as Psalm 109 [:17] says, "He did not like blessing; may it be far from him."

---

[25] Early in April, 1525, after lengthy, personal negotiations conducted by the bishop of Bamberg, an agreement was reached with the peasants whereby their grievances would be reviewed by a commission representing them, the city of Bamberg, and the bishop. The authorities even granted an amnesty. A few weeks later the peasants broke the truce which had prevailed since the agreement and violence flared anew. Cf. Wilhelm Stolze, Der deutsche Bauernkrieg (Halle, 1907), pp. 193-232.

[26] Margrave Casimir of Brandenburg (1481-1527) was at this time administrator of the Franconian princedoms. The community of Kitzingen, for example, disregarded the concessions made to it and joined the rebellion.

[27] For example, the leaders of the peasants from the Neckar Valley and the Odenwald tried to establish law and order among the peasants under conditions that met most of their demands, but the peasants repudiated their leadership. Günther Franz, Der deutsche Bauernkrieg (4th ed. rev.; Darmstadt: Hermann Gentner, 1956), p. 196.

[28] The peasants in Thuringia were influenced primarily by Thomas Münzer. Luther's visit to the peasants in the area of Weimar during the first days of May convinced him that they would not respond to him. On the basis of his experience, Luther wrote Against the Robbing and Murdering Hordes of Peasants. Cf. pp. 47-48.

The Scriptures, therefore, have good, clear eyes [Matt. 6:22-23] and see the temporal sword aright. They see that out of great mercy, it must be unmerciful, and from utter kindliness, it must exercise wrath and severity. As Peter and Paul say, it is God's servant for vengeance, wrath, and punishment upon the wicked, but for the protection, praise, and honor of the righteous [I Pet. 2:14; Rom. 13:4]. It looks upon the righteous with mercy, and so that they may not suffer, it guards, bites, stabs, cuts, hews, and slays, as God has commanded; and it knows that it serves God in doing even this. The merciless punishment of the wicked is not being carried out just to punish the wicked and make them atone for the evil desires that are in their blood, but to protect the righteous and to maintain peace and safety. And beyond all doubt, these are precious works of mercy, love, and kindness, since there is nothing on earth that is worse than disturbance, insecurity, oppression, violence, and injustice. Who could or would stay alive if such things were the rule? Therefore the wrath and severity of the sword is just as necessary to a people as eating and drinking, even as life itself.

"Not at all," they say. "We are not talking about the obdurate peasants who are unwilling to surrender, but of those who have been defeated or have surrendered. The princes ought to show them mercy, and not treat them so cruelly." I answer: You cannot be a good man if you slander my little book and say that in it I speak of such conquered peasants, or of those who have surrendered; I made it plain that I was speaking of those who were first approached in a friendly way, and would not respond. All my words were directed against the obdurate, hardened, blinded peasants, who would neither see nor hear, as anyone may see who reads them; and yet you say that I advocate the merciless slaughter of the poor captured peasants. If you are going to read books this way and interpret them as you please, what book will have any chance with you? Therefore, as I wrote then so I write now: Let no one have mercy on the obstinate, hardened, blinded peasants who refuse to listen to reason; but let everyone, as he is able, strike, hew, stab, and slay, as though among mad dogs, so that by so doing he may show mercy to those who are ruined, put to flight, and led astray by these peasants, so that peace and safety may be maintained. It is better to cut off one member without mercy than to have the

73

whole body perish by fire, or by disease [Matt. 5:29-30]. How do you like that? Am I still a preacher of the gospel who advocates grace and mercy? If you think I am not, it makes little difference, for you are a bloodhound, and a rebellious murderer and destroyer of the country, you and your rebellious peasants, whom you are flattering in their rebellion.

They say further that the peasants have slain no one in the way they themselves are being slain. What shall be said to that? What a splendid argument! They have slain no one! That was because people had to do what they wanted! They threatened to kill those who would not go along with them; they laid hold of the sword that did not belong to them; they attacked property, houses, and possessions. Arguing this way, a thief and murderer who took from me what he wanted by threatening to kill me would be no murderer. If they had done what they were asked in a kind way to do, they would not have been killed; but because they were not willing to do it, it was right to do to them what they themselves had done or threatened to do to those who did not agree with them. Besides, it is plain that they are faithless, perjured, disobedient, rebellious thieves, robbers, murderers, and blasphemers, and there is not one of them who has not deserved to be put to death ten times without mercy. People are not seeing straight in the matter.[29] They see only the punishment and the pain and not the crime and its guilt and the indescribable injury and ruin that would have resulted. If the punishment hurts, stop doing evil. Paul gives the same answer to this kind of people when he says in Romans 13 [:3-4], "Would you have no fear of him who is in authority? Then do what is good. . . . But if you do evil, be afraid."

They say, in the third place, that the lords are misusing their sword and slaying too cruelly. I answer: What has that to do with my book? Why lay others' guilt on me? If they are misusing their power, they have not learned it from me; and they will have their reward. For the Supreme Judge, who is using them to punish the self-willed peasants, has not forgotten them either, and they will not escape him. My book speaks not of what the lords deserve, but of what the peasants deserve and how they ought to be punished;

---

[29] Matt. 6:22-23; cf. pp. 49-52.

I have deceived no one about that. When I have time and occasion to do so, I shall attack the princes and lords, too, for in my office of teacher, a prince is the same to me as a peasant. I have already served them faithfully in ways that have not made me very popular with them; but I do not care about that. I have One who is greater than all of them, as St. John [Matt. 3:11] says.

If my first advice, given when the rebellion was just beginning,[30] had been followed, and a peasant or a hundred of them had been knocked down so that the rest would have tripped over them, and if they had not been allowed to get the upper hand, many thousands of them who now have to die would have been saved, for they would have stayed at home. That would have been a necessary act of mercy that could have been performed with little wrath; now it is necessary to use so much severity because there are so many of them to control.

But God's will has been done, in order to teach both sides a lesson. First, the peasants had to learn that things had been too easy for them and that they were not able to stand prosperity and peace.[31] They had to learn that hereafter they ought to thank God if they have to give up only one cow to enjoy the other cow in peace; for it is always better to possess the half of one's property in peace and safety than to have all of it and at every instant be in danger from thieves and murderers—and under those conditions not really have it at all. The peasants did not know what a precious thing it is to be in peace and safety and to enjoy one's food and drink in happiness and security, and so they did not thank God for it. He had to take this way to teach them, and relieve their itch.[32]

This was a profitable experience for the lords, too. They have learned what the rabble is like and how far they can be trusted, so they might learn to rule justly and to keep order in their territories and on their highways. There was no longer either government or order; it had all been abandoned.[33] There was no longer any fear or reverence among the people; everybody did just as he pleased;[34]

---

[30] In *Admonition to Peace* Luther had recommended arbitration.

[31] Cf. p. 79.

[32] Cf. *MA*[3] 4, 396, note to p. 168.

[33] *Es stund alles offen und mussig.* Cf. *MA*[3] 4, 396, note to p. 168.

[34] Cf. Judg. 21:25.

no one wanted to give anything, but everyone wanted to revel, drink, dress up, and be idle, as though every man were a lord. The donkey needs to feel the whip, and the people need to be ruled with force.[35] God knew that full well, and so he gave the rulers not a featherduster,[36] but a sword.

One of their more important distortions of the situation is this: They claim that many righteous people participated in the revolt innocently—because they were forced to do so. To execute them would be unjust in God's sight. I answer: They are talking like people who have never heard a single word of God, and therefore I must reply here as I would to heathen or to little children; for so little has been accomplished among the people by all the books and sermons!

I say, in the first place, that no injustice is done to those whom the peasants forced to participate. No Christian stayed among them, and these men did not get involved innocently, as they pretend. Indeed, it seems that they are suffering injustice, but it is not so. Tell me, my dear friend, if a man killed your father and mother, abused your wife and children, burned your house, and took your money and everything that you had, and then said that he had to do it because he had been forced to do it, what kind of an excuse would that be? Who ever heard of anyone being compelled to do good or evil? Who can compel a man's will? This argument does not hold water. Nor does it make sense for a man to say, "I have to do wrong; I am forced to do it." To deny Christ and the word of God is a great sin and wrong, and many are forced to do it, but do you think that that excuses them? Likewise, to start an insurrection, to become disobedient and faithless to rulers, to perjure oneself, to rob and burn—that is a great wrong, and some of the peasants were forced to do it; but how does that help them? Why do they let themselves be forced?

"No," they say, "but they threatened to take my life and my property." Come now, friend, are you willing to break God's commandments, to kill me, and to abuse my wife and children to keep

---

[35] Ecclus. 33:24. Cf. Wander (ed.), *Deutsches Sprichwörter Lexikon*, I, "*Esel*," Nos. 115-117.

[36] *Fuchsschwantz*, literally, "a foxtail."

your life and property? But how did God and I get involved in that? Would you be willing to suffer the same things at my hands? If the peasants had forced you to go along with them by tying you hand and foot, and carried you along by force, and you had defended yourself with your mouth, and rebuked them for doing it, and your heart had thus confessed and borne witness that it was unwilling and refused to consent, then your honor would have been preserved; you would have been compelled in body, but not in will. But as it is, you kept silent and did not rebuke them; you went along with the crowd and did not make your unwillingness known, and thus nothing helps you. This has gone on too long for you now to say that you were unwilling. You ought to have feared and heeded God's commandment more than men,[37] even at the risk of danger or of death. He would not have deserted you, but would have stood by you faithfully, rescued you, and helped you. Therefore, just as they are damned who deny God, even though they are forced to do it, so it is no excuse for the peasants that they have let themselves be forced.

If that excuse were accepted, there would be no more punishment of sin or crime; for where is there a sin to which the devil, the flesh, and the world do not drive us and, as it were, force us? Do you not think that there are times when a wicked lust drives men to adultery with a raging fever that may well be considered a greater compulsion than that which drove a peasant to revolt? Who is lord of his own heart? Who can resist the devil and the flesh? Indeed, it is not possible for us to ward off the lightest sin, for the Scriptures say that we are captives of the devil, as though he were our prince and god, so that we have to do what he wills and what he puts into our hearts [II Tim. 2:26]. There are some terrible stories to prove this. Ought such sins therefore go unpunished and be thought right? Indeed not! It is our duty to call upon God for help and to resist sin and wrong. If you die or suffer for it, good for you! Your soul is blessed before God and highly honored by the world! But if you yield and obey, you must die anyhow, and your death is shameful before God and the world because you have allowed yourself to be forced to do wrong. Thus it would be better

---

[37] Cf. Acts 5:29.

to die with honor and blessedness, in praise of God, than to have to die with shame, in punishment and pain.

"Good God!" you say. "If only we had known that!" Good God, I reply, how can I help it? Ignorance is no excuse.[38] Ought not a Christian to know what can be known? Why do they not learn? Why do they not support good preachers? They deliberately choose to remain ignorant. The gospel has come into Germany; many persecute it, few desire it—fewer accept it, and they are so lax and lazy that they let the schools go to ruin,[39] and the parishes and pulpits fall apart. No one gives any thought to maintaining the gospel and training the people, and everywhere it seems as though it hurts us to learn anything and as though we wanted to know nothing. Why be surprised, then, if God afflicts us and lets us see a bit of the punishment that comes from despising his gospel, a sin of which we all are guilty (for even though some of us are innocent of this rebellion, we have deserved worse things), in order to warn us and drive us to school, so that we may get some sense and some knowledge.

Isn't this what it is like in wartime, when the innocent must suffer with the guilty? Indeed, it seems that the innocent suffer most, for it is they who become the widows and the orphans. These are plagues that God sends; and they are always well deserved. And we must suffer them together if we want to live together at other times. The proverb says: You have to put up with it if a fire in your neighbor's house burns your house too.[40]

If you want to live in a community, you must share the community's burdens, dangers, and injuries, even though not you, but your neighbor has caused them. You must do this in the same way that you enjoy the peace, profit, protection, wealth, freedom, and security of the community, even though you have not won them or brought them into being. You must learn to take comfort and sing with Job, "Shall we receive good at the hand of the Lord, and shall we not also receive evil?" [Job 2:10]. So many good days are worth

---

[38] Wander (ed.), *Deutsches Sprichwörter Lexikon*, IV, "*Unwissend*," Nos. 5 and 6.

[39] Cf. pp. 209-211.

[40] *Eyn nachbar ist dem andern eyn brand schuldig;* literally, "one neighbor owes the other a fire." Cf. Thiele, *Luthers Sprichwörtersammlung*, No. 382.

a bad hour, and so many good years are worth a bad day, or year. For a long time we have had peace and good times, until we became presumptuous and self-confident, did not know what peace and good days meant, and did not once thank God for them; now we have to learn.

My advice is to stop complaining and murmuring and thank God that, by his grace and mercy, we have not experienced the greater misfortune which the devil intended to bring upon us through the peasants. That is what Jeremiah did when the Jews were driven out and captured and slain. He comforted himself and said, "It is of the Lord's grace and goodness that we are not entirely destroyed."[41] We Germans are much worse than the Jews, and yet we have not been driven out and slain, as they were; but we want to murmur and become impatient and justify ourselves. We are so unwilling to have a part of us slain that God's wrath against us may increase and he may let us go to destruction, remove his hand, and give us over entirely to the devil. We are acting as we mad Germans always do: we know nothing about God, and we talk about these things as though there were no God who does them and wills that they be done. We do not intend to suffer at all, but to be nobles, who can sit on cushions and do as they please.

You would really have seen something if this devil's business of the peasants had gone on and if God had not answered the prayers of godly Christians and restrained them with the sword. Throughout all Germany, people would have suffered exactly what those suffer who are now being killed and destroyed; only it would have been much worse. No one would have been safe from another; any man might have killed another, burned down his house and barn, and abused his wife and children. For this business did not start with God: there was no order in it; they had already reached the state where no one trusted or believed the other; they deposed one captain after another; and things were done, not as honest men would have had them done, but according to the wishes of the vilest scoundrels. The devil intended to lay all Germany to utter waste because there was no other way by which he could suppress the gospel. Who knows what will yet happen, if we keep on with our

---

[41] Cf. Lam. 3:22 and Job 2:10.

murmuring and ingratitude? God can let the peasants go mad again, or release some other plague upon us, so that things may become worse than they are now. I think that this has been a good strong warning and threat. If we disregard it, and neither repent nor fear God, let us beware of what may come to us, lest this shall prove to have been only a joke, and a really serious situation confronts us in the future.

Finally it may be said, "You yourself teach rebellion, for you say that everyone who can, should hew and stab among the rebels, and that, in this case, everyone is both supreme judge and executioner." I reply: My little book was not written against ordinary evildoers, but against rebels. You must make a very, very great distinction between a rebel and a thief, or a murderer, or any other kind of evildoer. A murderer or evildoer lets the head of the government alone and attacks only the members or their property; indeed, he fears the ruler. So long as the head remains, no one ought to attack such a murderer, because the head can punish. Everyone ought to await the judgment and command of the head, to whom God has committed the sword and the office of punishment. But a rebel attacks the head himself and interferes with the exercise of his sword and his office, and therefore his crime is not to be compared with that of a murderer. We cannot wait until the head gives commands and passes judgment, for the head himself is captured and beaten and cannot give them. Rather, everyone who can must run, uncalled and unbidden, and, as a true member, help to rescue his head by stabbing, hewing, and killing, and risk his life and goods for the sake of the head.

I must make that clear by a simple illustration. Suppose I were some lord's servant, and saw his enemy running at him with a drawn sword, and I were able to ward him off, but stood still and let my lord be shamefully slain. Tell me, what would God and the world say of me? Would they not rightly say that I was an absolute rogue and traitor, and must certainly be in league with the enemy?[42] But if I were to leap between my lord and his enemy, risk my body for my lord, and run his enemy through, would that not be an honor-

---

[42] *Kop und teyl mit dem feynde haben;* literally, "have head and tail with the enemy." Cf. Thiele, *Luthers Sprichwörtersammlung,* No. 307.

able and honest deed, and be praised and lauded before God and the world? Or, if I myself were to be run through in doing it, how could I die a more Christian death? I would be dying in the true service of God, as far as what I was doing is concerned; and if I had faith, I would be a true, holy martyr of God.

But suppose I tried to excuse myself by saying I did nothing because I was waiting for my lord to command me to defend him, what would that excuse do but condemn me twice as much and make me worthy to be cursed by everyone for making a joke out of it. Did not Christ himself praise this kind of thing in the gospel, and make it right for servants tò fight for their lords, when he stood before Pilate and said, "My kingship is not of this world; if my kingship were of this world, my servants would fight, that I might not be handed over to the Jews" [John 18:36]? There you see that before God and the world it is right for servants to fight for their lords; otherwise, what would worldly government be?

Now look! A rebel is a man who runs at his head and lord with a naked sword. No one should wait, then, until his lord commands him to defend him, but the first person who can, ought to take the initiative and run in and stab the rascal, and not worry about committing murder; for he is warding off an arch-murderer,[43] who wants to murder the whole land. Indeed, if he does not thrust and slay, but lets his lord be run through, he, too, is an arch-murderer; for he must then remember that because his lord suffers and is laid low, he is himself, in that case, lord, judge, and executioner. Rebellion is no joke, and there is no evil deed on earth that compares with it. Other wicked deeds are single acts; rebellion is a flood of all wickedness.

I am called a clergyman and am a minister of the word, but even if I served a Turk and saw my lord in danger, I would forget my spiritual office and stab and hew as long as my heart beat. If I were slain in so doing, I should go straight to heaven.[44] For rebellion is a crime that deserves neither a court trial nor mercy, whether it be among heathen, Jews, Turks, Christians, or any other people;

---

[43] Cf. John 8:44.

[44] *Von mund auf gen hymel faren;* literally, "straight out of my mouth to heaven." The picture is that of the soul leaving the body through the mouth at the time of death.

the rebel has already been tried, judged, condemned, and sentenced to death and everyone is authorized to execute him. Nothing more needs to be done than to give him his due and to execute him. No murderer does so much evil, and none deserves so much evil. For a murderer commits a punishable offense, and lets the penalty stand; but a rebel tries to make wickedness free and unpunishable, and attacks the punishment itself. Moreover, he now gives the gospel a bad reputation with its enemies, who blame the gospel for this rebellion and open their slanderous mouths wide enough in blaspheming against it, although this does not excuse them and they know better.[45] Christ will smite them, too, in his own time.

See, then, if I was not right when I said in my little book that we ought to slay the rebels without any mercy. I did not teach, however, that mercy ought not to be shown to the captives and those who have surrendered. They accuse me of having said it, but my book proves the opposite. Nor do I intend here to strengthen the raging tyrants, or to praise their raving, for I hear that some of my "knightlets"[46] are treating the poor people with unbounded cruelty, and are very bold and defiant, as though they had won the victory and were firmly in the saddle. They are not seeking to punish and stop the rebellion; rather are they satisfying their furious self-will and cooling a rage which they, perhaps, have long nursed, thinking that they now have an opportunity and excuse to do so. And they are also devoting more energy to their opposition of the gospel; they are trying to re-establish the monasteries and endowed ecclesiastical foundations. And to preserve the pope's crown, they deliberately confuse our cause with that of the rebels. But soon they will reap what they are now sowing [Gal. 6:7]. He who sits in heaven sees them, and he will come before they expect him. Their plans will fail, as they have failed before; this I know.

In the same book I said that these are strange times, when a man can earn heaven with slaughter and bloodshed.[47] "God help

---

[45] The peasants had formerly demanded that the old Germanic laws be reinstituted and the recently introduced Roman laws be set aside (cf. p. 15, n. 29). They had, however, begun to demand that laws based on "divine laws" be introduced and asserted that the "gospel" was the norm of such laws.

[46] *Junckerlin;* literally, "little landed proprietors," a term of contempt.

[47] See p. 54.

us. Luther forgot himself that time! Before he taught that a man must obtain grace and salvation by faith alone, and not by works, and here he ascribes salvation not only to works, but even to the heinous work of bloodshed! The Rhine is on fire at last!"[48]

Dear God, how thoroughly they investigate me! How they lie in wait for me! But it is of no use. I hope I may be allowed to use the words and expressions, not only of the common people, but also of the Scriptures. Does not Christ say in Matthew 5 [:3, 11-12], "Blessed are the poor, for theirs is the kingdom of heaven," and, "Blessed are you when you are persecuted, for great is your reward in heaven"? In Matthew 25 [:34-46] does he not reward works of mercy, etc.? And yet it remains true that works avail nothing before God, but only faith avails. I have told how that is in many of my writings, and especially in the *Sermon on the Unrighteous Mammon.*[49] If there is anyone who is not satisfied with that, let him keep on being offended as long as he lives.

As for the charge that I make bloodshed such a precious work, the passage in my book shows plainly that I was speaking of worldly rulers who are Christians and who are doing their duty in a Christian way, especially when they battle against the rebel bands. If they are not doing right in shedding blood and fulfilling the duty of their office, then Samuel, David, and Samson must have done wrong when they punished evildoers and shed blood. If that kind of bloodshed is not good and right, then we ought to let the sword alone, and be "free brethren," and do as we like.

I earnestly ask you, and everyone, to read my book fairly, and not run through it so hurriedly. Then you will see that I was advising only Christian and pious rulers, as befits a Christian preacher. I say it again and for the third time. I was writing only for rulers who might wish to deal in a Christian or otherwise honest way with their people, to instruct their consciences concerning this matter to the effect that they ought to take immediate action against the bands of rebels both innocent and guilty. And if they struck the innocent, they were not to let their consciences trouble them, since

---

[48] Cf. Wander (ed.), *Deutsches Sprichwörter Lexikon,* III, "Rhein," Nos. 28, 30, 33, 37, 38.
[49] *WA* 10III, 273-292.

they were by the very act confessing that they were bound to do their duty to God. Afterward, however, if they won, they were to show grace, not only to those whom they considered innocent, but to the guilty as well.

But these furious, raving, senseless tyrants, who even after the battle cannot get their fill of blood, and in all their lives ask scarcely a question about Christ—these I did not undertake to instruct. It makes no difference to these bloody dogs whether they slay the guilty or the innocent, whether they please God or the devil. They have the sword, but they use it to vent their lust and self-will. I leave them to the guidance of their master, the devil, who is indeed leading them. I have heard that at Mühlhausen one of these big shots summoned the poor wife of Thomas Münzer, now a pregnant widow, fell on one knee before her, and said, "Dear lady, let me * * * you." O a knightly, noble deed, done to a poor, helpless, pregnant little woman! That is a brave hero for you! He is worth three knights, at the very least! Why should I write for scoundrels and hogs like that? The Scriptures call such people "beasts" [Titus 1:12], that is, "wild animals," such as wolves, boars, bears, and lions, and I shall not make men of them; and yet we must put up with them, when God plagues us with them. I had two fears. If the peasants became lords,[50] the devil would become abbot; but if these tyrants became lords, the devil's mother would become abbess. Therefore I wanted to do two things: quiet the peasants, and instruct the pious lords. The peasants were unwilling to listen, and now they have their reward; the lords, too, will not hear, and they shall have their reward also. However, it would have been a shame if they had been killed by the peasants; that would have been too easy a punishment for them.[51] Hell-fire, trembling, and gnashing of teeth [Matt. 22:13] in hell will be their reward eternally, unless they repent.

This, dear sir and friend, is my answer to your letter. I hope that I have more than satisfied you. If anyone is not satisfied, let him remain, in God's name, wise and prudent, righteous and holy; and let me remain a fool and a sinner. I wish that they would leave

---

[50] Cf. Wander (ed.), *Deutsches Sprichwörter Lexikon*, I, "Bauer," No. 370.
[51] Literally, "a foxtail." See p. 76, n. 36.

me in peace; but they will not win, and what I teach and write will still be true, even though the whole world were to burst. If anyone wants to be peculiar, I, too, shall be peculiar, and we shall see who is right in the end.

God be with you! Tell Conrad to make no mistake, and to get in the right bed.[52] The printer should be careful hereafter not to call you "Chanclor."[53]

---

[52] The reference to "Conrad" has been interpreted in various ways. Conrad was a name commonly used to designate a character type—usually a peasant. The peasant movement in Württemberg thus gave itself the code name "the poor Conrad." Luther's remark could, therefore, be an indirect message to the peasants. It could also, however, like the next sentence, be a private joke between Luther and Müller. The various interpretations are summarized in WA 18, 401, n. 4.

[53] Either on the first page of this treatise or elsewhere, the printer may have given Müller the title of *Cantzeler,* instead of *Cantzler.*

WHETHER SOLDIERS, TOO, CAN BE SAVED

1526

Translated by Charles M. Jacobs

Revised by Robert C. Schultz

INTRODUCTION

The question of whether soldiers could be Christians and continue in their profession was the subject of a conversation between Luther and Assa von Kram in Wittenberg in July, 1525. The occasion of the conversation was related to the recent assumption of the throne of Electoral Saxony by Prince John.[1]

Von Kram, a counselor of Duke Ernst of Braunschweig-Lüneberg and a professional soldier,[2] appears to have been troubled in conscience and unable to reconcile his confession of the Christian faith with his profession. He and others urged Luther to publish the views the Reformer apparently had shared with them.[3] Luther consented,[4] but by January, 1526, he had not yet done so and had to be reminded of his promise by von Kram.[5] It is not clear when Luther began to write the treatise, but by October, 1526, *Whether Soldiers, Too, Can Be Saved* was being printed. Its publication, however, was inexplicably delayed,[6] and although copies were available before the last day of 1526,[7] the title page bore the date January 5, 1527.

The question of whether Christians might bear arms and be professional soldiers was not simply a conversational or theoretical matter. The Reformation, both in its intellectual and socio-political expression, had called the whole structure of medieval society, beliefs, and practices into question. It raised questions for which answers had to be found not in the solitude of meditation and re-

---

[1] Elector Frederick the Wise had died on May 5, 1525. From July 13 to 16 the new ruler was in Wittenberg to receive the homage of his subjects there. Cf. *Archiv für Reformationsgeschichte*, XXV (1928), 74.

[2] His last service was in the emperor's army during the Italian campaign of 1528. Cf. *BG* 7, 384.

[3] See p. 93.

[4] See p. 93.

[5] Perhaps at the baptism of Gabriel Zwilling's son, Luther's godchild, in Torgau. Cf. p. 137, and *WA* 19, 616.

[6] Cf. *MA*³ 5, 426.

[7] On January 1, 1527, Luther sent a copy of the book to Michael Stiefel. *WA*, Br 4, 152.

flection, but in the crucible of events. One of these practices was the matter of warfare.

Following the defeat of King Francis I of France[8] by Charles V in January, 1526, the emperor urged Catholic rulers to exterminate the Lutheran heresy.[9] In July of the previous year Duke George of Ducal Saxony[10] joined in an alliance with Albrecht of Mainz,[11] Joachim of Brandenburg, Eric of Braunschweig/Calenberg, and Henry of Braunschweig/Wolfenbüttel for this very purpose.[12] This alliance had its effect upon evangelical rulers, who joined the alliance formed between Electoral Saxony and Hesse at Torgau in 1526. In the meantime, however, these alliances were overshadowed by new threats from the Turks, who defeated King Louis II of Bohemia and Hungary at Mohacs on August 29, 1526.

The Anabaptists and others to the right of Luther took the position that a Christian could not bear arms under any circumstances.[13] Luther did not agree with this view, nor did the evangelical princes.

In *Whether Soldiers, Too, Can Be Saved* Luther affirms the legitimacy of the military profession. He identifies it with the divine institution of the sword to punish evil, protect the good, and preserve peace. Luther candidly admits that the military calling can be abused, but misuse by no means invalidates its legitimacy

---

[8] Emperor Charles forced Francis, who was his prisoner, to agree to aid the empire against Turks and heretics as a condition of his release. See Article XXVI of *The Treaty of Madrid, 14 January 1526* in B. J. Kidd (ed.), *Documents Illustrative of the Continental Reformation*, No. 86, p. 180.

[9] In March, 1526, Charles dispatched letters to Catholic princes of the empire in which he called for a prompt, thorough extermination of the "seductive, damnable, Lutheran doctrine which has caused so much murder, mayhem, blasphemy, and destruction." Cf. BG 7, 385. For the text of the letter to Duke Henry of Braunschweig/Wolfenbüttel, see C. Gotthold Neudecker (ed.), *Urkunden aus der Reformationszeit* (Cassel, 1836), I, 10-14.

[10] George, the brother of Frederick the Wise, was an implacable foe of Luther and of the Reformation.

[11] The same archbishop of Mainz whose sale of indulgences prompted Luther to post his *Ninety-five Theses* in 1517.

[12] This alliance was concluded on July 19, 1525, within a week of Luther's original conversation with von Kram. Cf. Kidd, *op. cit.*, p. 181.

[13] Typical of this position is the statement of Felix Mantz (*ca.* 1500-1527), the Zurich Anabaptist, "A Christian will not wield the sword, nor will he resist evil." BG 7, 384.

and function. In developing this basic thesis Luther discusses how a soldier must execute his God-given office.

First, Luther deals with the question of fighting against overlords, i.e., the legitimate government. To do this is to rebel against the order instituted by God. The Reformer is quite aware that there are rulers who distort, abuse, and debase their office, nonetheless, their misconduct cannot harm men's souls.

Second, Luther treats the question of whether a soldier may fight in a war in which equals war against equals. Here he enunciates the principle of self-defense. A ruler is charged by God to defend and protect his people when they are attacked, and to do this he needs soldiers who serve him because God has appointed him to be their ruler. At the same time, however, Luther cautions that a soldier must not trust in the justness of the cause for which he fights. Confidence and trust must be in God, who alone gives victory.

Finally, the question of whether soldiers may participate in wars waged by rulers against their subjects is treated. Here Luther elaborates upon his position that such action is justified in the event of rebellion—and it is obvious that the memory of the Peasants' War is still fresh in his mind. But Luther reminds his readers that lords and rulers, even the emperor himself, are, ultimately, subjects of God. He does not give, as it were, a military *carte blanche* to those in authority. In summary, then, the soldier's duty is to exercise his legitimate and divinely appointed office in the service of God.

The German text, *Ob Kriegesleute auch in seligem Stande sein können,* is given in WA 19, (616) 623-662. The translation is a revision of that by Charles M. Jacobs in *PE* 5, 32-74.

R. C. S.

WHETHER SOLDIERS,
TOO, CAN BE SAVED

To the worshipful and honorable Assa von Kram, knight, my gracious lord and friend, [from] Martin Luther.

Most honorable and dear sir and friend, grace and peace to you in Christ.

When you were in Wittenberg recently—at the time of the elector's entry into the city[1]—we talked about men in military service. In the course of the conversation we discussed many matters involving questions of conscience. As a consequence, you and several others asked me to put my opinion into writing and publish it because many soldiers are offended by their occupation itself. Some soldiers have doubts. Others have so completely given themselves up for lost that they no longer even ask questions about God and throw both their souls and their consciences to the winds. I myself have heard some of them say that if they thought too much about these problems, they would never be able to go to war again. One would think that war was such an absorbing matter that they were unable to think about God and their souls. Actually, however, we ought to think most about God and our souls when we are in danger of death.

I agreed to your request and promised to provide this book in order—to the best of my ability—to give the best advice to these weak, timid, and doubting consciences, and so that those who do not care may be better instructed. For whoever fights with a good and well-instructed conscience can also fight well. This is especially true since a good conscience fills a man's heart with courage and boldness. And if the heart is bold and courageous, the fist is more powerful, a man and even his horse are more energetic, everything turns out better, and every happening and deed contributes to the victory which God then gives. On the other hand, a timid and insecure conscience makes the heart fearful. It cannot possibly

---

[1] Cf. p. 89, n. 1.

be otherwise: a bad conscience can only make men cowardly and fearful. This is what Moses says to his Jews, "If you are disobedient, God will make your heart fearful; You shall go out one way against your enemies and flee seven ways before them, and you will have no good fortune" [Deut. 28:20, 25]. Then both man and horse are lazy and clumsy; they lack vigor for the attack, and in the end they are defeated. There are indeed some rough and cynical people in service—they are called daredevils and roughnecks—for whom everything happens accidentally, whether they win or lose. The outcome of the battle is the same for them as for those who have good or bad consciences. They are simply part of the army. They are only the shells and not the true core of the army.

Accordingly, I now send you this opinion of mine, given according to the ability that God has granted me, so that you and others who would like to go to war in such a way that you will not lose God's favor and eternal life may know how to prepare and instruct yourselves. God's grace be with you. Amen.

In the first place, we must distinguish between an occupation and the man who holds it, between a work and the man who does it. An occupation or a work can be good and right in itself and yet be bad and wrong if the man who does the work is evil or wrong or does not do his work properly. The occupation of a judge is a valuable divine office. This is true both of the office of the trial judge who declares the verdict and the executioner who carries out the sentence.[2] But when the office is assumed by one to whom it has not been committed or when one who holds it rightly uses it to gain riches or popularity, then it is no longer right or good. The married state is also precious and godly, but there are many rascals and scoundrels in it. It is the same way with the profession or work of the soldier; in itself it is right and godly, but we must see to it that the persons who are in this profession and who do the work are the right kind of persons, that is, godly and upright, as we shall hear.

---

[2] Both officials were called judges (*Richter*). The trial judge was *Mundrichter* ("mouth judge"); the executioner was the *Faust-* or *Scharfrichter* ("fist" or "axe judge").

In the second place, I want you to understand that here I am not speaking about the righteousness that makes men good in the sight of God. Only faith in Jesus Christ can do that; and it is granted and given us by the grace of God alone, without any works or merits of our own, as I have written and taught so often and so much in other places. Rather, I am speaking here about external righteousness which is to be sought in offices and works. In other words, to put it plainly, I am dealing here with such questions as these: whether the Christian faith, by which we are accounted righteous before God, is compatible with being a soldier, going to war, stabbing and killing, robbing and burning, as military law requires us to do to our enemies in wartime. Is this work sinful or unjust? Should it give us a bad conscience before God? Must a Christian only do good and love, and kill no one, nor do anyone any harm? I say that this office or work, even though it is godly and right, can nevertheless become evil and unjust if the person engaged in it is evil and unjust.

In the third place, it is not my intention to explain here at length how the occupation and work of a soldier is in itself right and godly because I have written quite enough about that in my book *Temporal Authority: To What Extent It Should Be Obeyed.*[3] Indeed, I might boast here that not since the time of the apostles have the temporal sword and temporal government been so clearly described or so highly praised as by me. Even my enemies must admit this, but the reward, honor, and thanks that I have earned by it are to have my doctrine called seditious and condemned as resistance to rulers.[4] God be praised for that! For the very fact that the sword has been instituted by God to punish the evil, protect the good, and preserve peace [Rom. 13:1-4; I Pet. 2:13-14] is powerful and sufficient proof that war and killing along with all the things that accompany wartime and martial law have been instituted by God. What else is war but the punishment of wrong and evil? Why does anyone go to war, except because he desires peace and obedience?

---

[3] *LW* 45, 81-129.

[4] Luther alludes to the frequent charge that the Peasants' War was largely incited by his teaching.

Now slaying and robbing do not seem to be works of love. A simple man therefore does not think it is a Christian thing to do. In truth, however, even this is a work of love. For example, a good doctor sometimes finds so serious and terrible a sickness that he must amputate or destroy a hand, foot, ear, eye, to save the body. Looking at it from the point of view of the organ that he amputates, he appears to be a cruel and merciless man; but looking at it from the point of view of the body, which the doctor wants to save, he is a fine and true man and does a good and Christian work, as far as the work itself is concerned. In the same way, when I think of a soldier fulfilling his office by punishing the wicked, killing the wicked, and creating so much misery, it seems an un-Christian work completely contrary to Christian love. But when I think of how it protects the good and keeps and preserves wife and child, house and farm, property, and honor and peace, then I see how precious and godly this work is; and I observe that it amputates a leg or a hand, so that the whole body may not perish. For if the sword were not on guard to preserve peace, everything in the world would be ruined because of lack of peace. Therefore, such a war is only a very brief lack of peace that prevents an everlasting and immeasurable lack of peace, a small misfortune that prevents a great misfortune.

What men write about war, saying that it is a great plague, is all true. But they should also consider how great the plague is that war prevents. If people were good and wanted to keep peace, war would be the greatest plague on earth. But what are you going to do about the fact that people will not keep the peace, but rob, steal, kill, outrage women and children, and take away property and honor? The small lack of peace called war or the sword must set a limit to this universal, worldwide lack of peace which would destroy everyone.

This is why God honors the sword so highly that he says that he himself has instituted it [Rom. 13:1] and does not want men to say or think that they have invented it or instituted it. For the hand that wields this sword and kills with it is not man's hand, but God's; and it is not man, but God, who hangs, tortures, beheads, kills, and fights. All these are God's works and judgments.

To sum it up, we must, in thinking about a soldier's office, not concentrate on the killing, burning, striking, hitting, seizing, etc. This is what children with their limited and restricted vision see when they regard a doctor as a sawbones who amputates, but do not see that he does this only to save the whole body. So, too, we must look at the office of the soldier, or the sword, with the eyes of an adult and see why this office slays and acts so cruelly. Then it will prove itself to be an office which, in itself, is godly and as needful and useful to the world as eating and drinking or any other work.

There are some who abuse this office, and strike and kill people needlessly simply because they want to. But that is the fault of the persons, not of the office, for where is there an office or a work or anything else so good that self-willed, wicked people do not abuse it? They are like mad physicians who would needlessly amputate a healthy hand just because they wanted to. Indeed, they themselves are a part of that universal lack of peace which must be prevented by just wars and the sword and be forced into peace. It always happens and always has happened that those who begin war unnecessarily are beaten. Ultimately, they cannot escape God's judgment and sword. In the end God's justice finds them and strikes, as happened to the peasants in the revolt.[5]

As proof, I quote John the Baptist, who, except for Christ, was the greatest teacher and preacher of all. When soldiers came to him and asked what they should do, he did not condemn their office or advise them to stop doing their work; rather, according to Luke 3 [:14], he approved it by saying, "Rob no one by violence or by false accusation, and be content with your wages." Thus he praised the military profession, but at the same time he forbade its abuse. Now the abuse does not affect the office. When Christ stood before Pilate he admitted that war was not wrong when he said, "If my kingship were of this world, then my servants would fight that I might not be handed over to the Jews" [John 18:36]. Here, too, belong all the stories of war in the Old Testament, the stories of Abraham, Moses, Joshua, the Judges, Samuel, David, and all the kings of Israel. If the waging of war

---

[5] Luther is referring to the defeat and punishment of the peasants in 1525.

and the military profession were in themselves wrong and displeasing to God, we should have to condemn Abraham, Moses, Joshua, David, and all the rest of the holy fathers, kings, and princes, who served God as soldiers and are highly praised in Scripture because of this service, as all of us who have read even a little in Holy Scripture know well, and there is no need to offer further proof of it here.

Perhaps someone will now say that the holy fathers[6] were in a different position because God had set them apart from the other nations by choosing them as his people, and had commanded them to fight, and that their example is therefore not relevant for a Christian under the New Testament because they had God's command and fought in obedience to God, while we have no command to fight, but rather to suffer, endure, and renounce everything. This objection is answered clearly enough by St. Peter and St. Paul, who both command obedience to worldly ordinances and to the commandments of worldly rulers even under the New Testament [Rom. 13:1-4; I Pet. 2:13-14]. And we have already pointed out that St. John the Baptist instructed soldiers as a Christian teacher and in a Christian manner and permitted them to remain soldiers, enjoining them only not to use their position to abuse people or to treat them unjustly, and to be satisfied with their wages. Therefore even under the New Testament the sword is established by God's word and commandment, and those who use it properly and fight obediently serve God and are obedient to his word.

Just think now! If we gave in on this point and admitted that war was wrong in itself, then we would have to give in on all other points and allow that the use of the sword was entirely wrong. For if it is wrong to use a sword in war, it is also wrong to use a sword to punish evildoers or to keep the peace. Briefly, every use of the sword would have to be wrong. For what is just war but the punishment of evildoers and the maintenance of peace? If one punishes a thief or a murderer or an adulterer, that is punishment inflicted on a single evildoer; but in a just war a whole crowd of evildoers, who are doing harm in proportion to the size

---

[6] I.e., the biblical patriarchs and rulers.

of the crowd, are punished at once. If, therefore, one work of the sword is good and right, they are all good and right, for the sword is a sword and not a foxtail[7] with which to tickle people. Romans 13 [:4] calls the sword "the wrath of God."

As for the objection that Christians have not been commanded to fight and that these examples are not enough, especially because Christ teaches us not to resist evil but rather suffer all things [Matt. 5:39-42], I have already said all that needs to be said on this matter in my book *Temporal Authority.*[8] Indeed, Christians do not fight and have no worldly rulers among them. Their government is a spiritual government, and, according to the Spirit, they are subjects of no one but Christ. Nevertheless, as far as body and property are concerned, they are subject to worldly rulers and owe them obedience. If worldly rulers call upon them to fight, then they ought to and must fight and be obedient, not as Christians, but as members of the state and obedient subjects. Christians therefore do not fight as individuals or for their own benefit, but as obedient servants of the authorities under whom they live. This is what St. Paul wrote to Titus when he said that Christians should obey the authorities [Titus 3:1]. You may read more about this in my book *Temporal Authority.*

That is the sum and substance of it. The office of the sword is in itself right and is a divine and useful ordinance, which God does not want us to despise, but to fear, honor, and obey, under penalty of punishment, as St. Paul says in Romans 13 [:1-5]. For God has established two kinds of government among men. The one is spiritual; it has no sword, but it has the word, by means of which men are to become good and righteous, so that with this righteousness they may attain eternal life. He administers this righteousness through the word, which he has committed to the preachers. The other kind is worldly government, which works through the sword so that those who do not want to be good and righteous to eternal life may be forced to become good and righteous in the eyes of the world. He administers this righteousness through the sword. And although God will not reward this kind of

---

[7] *Fuchsschwantz;* cf. p. 76, n. 36.
[8] Cf. p. 31, n. 31.

righteousness with eternal life, nonetheless, he still wishes peace to be maintained among men and rewards them with temporal blessings. He gives rulers much more property, honor, and power than he gives to others so that they may serve him by administering this temporal righteousness. Thus God himself is the founder, lord, master, protector, and rewarder of both kinds of righteousness. There is no human ordinance or authority in either, but each is a divine thing entirely.

Since, then, there is no doubt that the military profession is in itself a legitimate and godly calling and occupation, we will now discuss the persons who are in it and the use they make of their position, for it is most important to know who is to use this office and how he is to use it. And here we have to face the fact that it is impossible to establish hard and fast rules and laws in this matter. There are so many cases and so many exceptions to any rule that it is very difficult or even impossible to decide everything accurately and equitably. This is true of all laws; they can never be formulated so certainly and so justly that cases do not arise which deserve to be made exceptions. If we do not make exceptions and strictly follow the law we do the greatest injustice of all, as the heathen author Terence has said, "The strictest law is the greatest injustice."[9] And Solomon teaches in Ecclesiastes [7:16; 10:1] that we should not carry justice to an extreme and at times should not seek to be wise.[10]

Let me give an example. In the recent rebellion of the peasants there were some who were involved against their will.[11] These were especially people who were well-to-do, for the rebellion struck at the rich, as well as the rulers, and it may fairly be assumed that no rich man favored the rebellion. In any case, some were involved against their will. Some yielded under this pressure, thinking that they could restrain this mad mob and that their good advice would, to some extent, prevent the peasants from carrying out their evil purpose and doing so much evil. They thought that

---

[9] Cf. *Self-Tormentor* (*Heautontimorumenos*), scene 4, l. 48, and Cicero, *On Moral Obligation* (*de officiis*), I, 10.

[10] During 1526 Luther was doing extensive work in the book of Ecclesiastes. Cf. *MA*³ 5, 407, note to p. 178.

[11] Cf. pp. 54, 76-77.

they would be doing both themselves and the authorities a service. Still others became involved with the prior consent and approval of their lords, whom they consulted in advance. There may have been other similar cases.[12] For no one can imagine all of them, or take them all into account in the law.

Here is what the law says, "All rebels deserve death, and these three kinds of men were apprehended among the rebellious crowd, in the very act of rebellion." What shall we do to them? If we allow no exceptions and let the law take its strict course, they must die just like the others, who are guilty of deliberate and intentional rebellion, although some of the men of whom we speak were innocent in their hearts and honestly tried to serve the authorities. Some of our knightlets,[13] however, refused to make such exceptions, especially if the man involved was rich. They thought they could take their property by saying, "You also were in the mob. You must die." In this way they have committed a great injustice to many people and shed innocent blood, made widows and orphans, and taken their property besides.[14] And yet they call themselves "nobles." Nobles indeed! The excrement of the eagle can boast that it comes from the eagle's body even though it stinks and is useless; and so these men can also be of the nobility.[15] We Germans are and remain Germans, that is, swine and senseless beasts.

Now I say that in cases like the three kinds mentioned above, the law ought to yield and justice take its place. For the law matter of factly says, "Rebellion is punishable with death; it is the *crimen lese maiestatis*, a sin against the rulers."[16] But justice says, "Yes, dear law, it is as you say; but it can happen that two men do similar acts with differing motives in their hearts. Judas, for example, kissed Christ in the garden. Outwardly this was a good

---

[12] See pp. 54, 76-77.
[12] See pp. 54, 76-77.
[13] See p. 82, n. 46.
[14] For Luther's opinion on the way rulers dealt with defeated peasant rebels, see p. 84.
[15] An untranslatable play on the words *Adel* ("nobility") and *Adeler* ("eagle").
[16] Under the Roman and feudal law it was an offense against the person of the ruler.

work; but his heart was evil and he used a good work, which Christ and his disciples at other times did for one another with good hearts, to betray his Lord [Matt. 26:49]. Here is another example: Peter sat down by the fire with the servants of Annas and warmed himself with the godless, and that was not good [Luke 22:55]. Now if we were to apply the law strictly, Judas would have to be a good man and Peter a rascal; but Judas' heart was evil and Peter's was good; therefore justice in this case must correct the law.

Therefore justice not only acquits those who were among the rebels with good intentions, but considers them worthy of double grace. They are just like the godly man, Hushai the Archite, who, acting under David's orders, joined and served the rebellious Absalom with the intention of helping David and restraining Absalom, as it is all finely written in II Samuel 15 [:32-37] and 16 [:16-19]. Outwardly considered, Hushai, too, was a rebel with Absalom against David; but he earned great praise and everlasting honor before God and all the world. If David had allowed Hushai to be condemned as a rebel, it would have been just as praiseworthy a deed as those which our princes and knightlets are now doing to equally innocent people, yes, even to people who have deserved good.

In Greek this virtue, or wisdom, which can and must guide and moderate the severity of law according to cases, and which judges the same deed to be good or evil according to the difference of the motives and intentions of the heart, is called *epieikeia;* in Latin it is *aequitas,* and *Billichkeit*[17] in German. Now because law must be framed simply and briefly, it cannot possibly embrace all the cases and problems. This is why the judges and lords must be wise and pious in this matter and mete out reasonable justice, and let the law take its course, or set it aside, accordingly. The head of a household makes a law for his servants, telling them what they are to do on this day or that; that is the law, and the servant who does not keep it must take his punishment. But now one of them may be sick, or be otherwise hindered from keeping the law through no fault of his own; then the law is sus-

---

[17] *Billigkeit* in modern German.

pended, and anyone who would punish his servant for that kind of neglect of duty would have to be a mad lord of the house. Similarly, all laws that regulate men's actions must be subject to justice, their mistress, because of the innumerable and varied circumstances which no one can anticipate or set down.

So then, we have this to say about people who live under military law or who are involved in fighting a war. First, war may be made by three kinds of people. An equal may make war against his equal, that is, neither of the two persons is the vassal or subject of the other even though one may be less great or glorious or mighty than the other. Or an overlord may fight against his subject. Or a subject may fight against his overlord. Let us take the third case. Here is what the law says, "No one shall fight or make war against his overlord; for a man owes his overlord obedience, honor, and fear" (Romans 13 [:1-7]). If you chop over your head, the chips fall in your eyes.[18] And Solomon says, "If you throw a stone into the air, it will land on your own head."[19] That is the law in a nutshell. God himself has instituted it and men have accepted it, for it is not possible both to obey and resist, to be subject and not put up with their lords.

But we have already said that justice ought to be the mistress of law, and where circumstances demand it, guide the law, or even command and permit men to act against it. Therefore the question here is whether a situation can ever develop in which it is just for people to act against this law, to be disobedient to rulers and fight against them, depose them, or put them in bonds.

There is a vice in us men which is called fraud, that is, deception or trickery. If this vice of ours discovers that justice is superior to law, as has been said, then it becomes a foe of the law and spends day and night looking for some way to sell itself in the marketplace under the name and appearance of justice. When it succeeds, law comes to nothing and fraud becomes the sweet darling that does everything it ought to do. This is how we get the proverb which says, "*Inventa lege, inventa est fraus*

---

[18] Cf. Thiele, *Luthers Sprichwörtersammlung*, No. 29.
[19] Prov. 26:27.

legis," "As soon as a law goes into effect, Mistress Fraud finds a loophole."[20]

Because they knew nothing of God, the heathen did not know that temporal government is God's ordinance (they thought of it as the fortunate creation of men) and therefore they jumped right in and thought that it was not only right, but also praiseworthy, to depose, kill, and expel worthless and wicked rulers. This is why the Greeks, in public laws, promised jewels and gifts to tyrannicides, that is, to those who stab or otherwise murder a tyrant.[21] In the days of their empire the Romans followed this example very closely and themselves killed almost the majority of their emperors. As a result, in that great empire almost no emperor was ever killed by his enemies, and yet few of them died a natural death in bed. The people of Israel and Judah also killed and destroyed some of their kings.[22]

But these examples are not enough for us, for here we are not concerned with what the heathen or the Jews did, but what is the right and the just thing to do, not only before God in the Spirit, but also in the divine external ordinance of temporal government. Suppose that a people would rise up today or tomorrow and depose their lord or kill him. That certainly could happen if God decrees that it should, and the lords must expect it. But that does not mean that it is right and just for the people to do it. I have never known of a case in which this was a just action, and even now I cannot imagine any. The peasants who rebelled claimed that the lords would not allow the gospel to be preached and that they robbed the poor people[23] and, therefore, the lords had to be overthrown. I answered this by saying that although the lords did wrong in this, it would not therefore be just or right to do wrong in return, that is, to be disobedient and destroy God's ordinance, which is not ours to do.[24] On the con-

---

[20] Cf. Wander (ed.), *Deutsches Sprichwörter Lexikon*, III, "*List*," No. 287.

[21] August Pauly and Georg Wissowa, *Realencyclopädie der classischen Altertumswissenschaft* (2nd ed.), VII (1890), 1810.

[22] Cf. I Kings 15:25-29; 16:8-10; and II Kings 9:27-28.

[23] See the complaints presented by the peasants in *The Twelve Articles*, pp. 10-16.

[24] See p. 25.

trary, we ought to suffer wrong, and if a prince or lord will not tolerate the gospel, then we ought to go into another realm where the gospel is preached, as Christ says in Matthew 10 [:23], "When they persecute you in one town, flee to the next."[25]

It is only right that if a prince, king, or lord becomes insane, he should be deposed and put under restraint, for he is not to be considered a man since his reason is gone. "That is true," you say, "and a raving tyrant is also insane; he is to be considered as even worse than an insane man, for he does much more harm." It will be a little difficult for me to respond to that statement, for that argument seems very impressive and seems to be in agreement with justice and equity. Nevertheless, it is my opinion that madmen and tyrants are not the same. A madman can neither do nor tolerate anything reasonable, and there is no hope for him because the light of reason has gone out. A tyrant, however, may do things that are far worse than the insane man does, but he still knows that he is doing wrong. He still has a conscience and his faculties. There is also hope that he may improve and permit someone to talk to him and instruct him and follow this advice. We can never hope that an insane man will do this for he is like a clod or a stone. Furthermore, such conduct has bad results or sets a bad example. If it is considered right to murder or depose tyrants, the practice spreads and it becomes a commonplace thing arbitrarily to call men tyrants who are not tyrants, and even to kill them if the mob takes a notion to do so. The history of the Roman people shows us how this can happen. They killed many a fine emperor simply because they did not like him or he did not do what they wanted, that is, let them be lords and make him their fool. This happened to Galba, Pertinax, Gordian, Alexander, and others.[26]

We dare not encourage the mob very much. It goes mad too quickly; and it is better to take ten ells[27] from it than to allow it a handsbreadth, or even a fingersbreadth in such a case. And it is better for the tyrants to wrong them a hundred times than for the

---

[25] For Luther's discussion on this point, see p. 37.
[26] These emperors were deposed in revolutions by the army; Galba in A.D. 69; Pertinax, 193; Gordian, 244; and Alexander, 235.
[27] The ell, used chiefly for measuring cloth, varied in length from thirty-seven to forty-eight inches.

mob to treat the tyrant unjustly but once. If injustice is to be suffered, then it is better for subjects to suffer it from their rulers than for the rulers to suffer it from their subjects. The mob neither has any moderation nor even knows what moderation is. And every person in it has more than five tyrants hiding in him. Now it is better to suffer wrong from one tyrant, that is, from the ruler, than from unnumbered tyrants, that is, from the mob.

It is said that years ago the Swiss slew their overlords and made themselves free,[28] and the Danes have recently driven out their king.[29] In both cases their subjects were driven to do this by the intolerable tyranny which they suffered at the hands of these rulers. However, as I said above, I am not discussing here what the heathen do or have done, or anything that resembles their examples and history, but what one ought to do and can do with a good conscience. That is the course of action that makes us certain that what we are doing is not wrong in God's sight. I know

---

[28] The struggles of the Swiss to gain their freedom began with their protest in 1291 against the lords' violation of the traditional laws. This protest became a war against the Hapsburgs of Austria, in which the Swiss—who lived in a small part of present-day Switzerland—won their freedom. In 1401 the people of Appenzell and the city of St. Gallen banded together to oppose what they considered as the attempt of the abbot of the St. Gallen monastery to impose new duties and taxes beyond those traditionally required. They were defeated in 1408. In 1489 the peasants of the city of Zurich revolted and the peasants of St. Gallen again joined the revolt. The peasant wars of the sixteenth century first broke out in Switzerland in 1513 and spread from there to southern Germany. In defending the legality of their struggle the peasants appealed to the original war of freedom at the close of the thirteenth century. See Franz, *Der deutsche Bauernkrieg*, pp. 3-9.

[29] King Christian II of Denmark, who ruled Scandinavia from 1513 to 1523, made efforts to introduce the Reformation there as early as 1520. Karlstadt spent some time there in 1521, and the king apparently even sought to have Luther come to Denmark at that time. In 1523, however, Christian was driven out and fled to Germany. He spent some time in Wittenberg with the elector, who was his uncle, before settling permanently in his imperial court; Charles V was his brother-in-law. During his stay in Wittenberg he showed great enthusiasm for the Reformation, apparently in the hope of gaining the support of the Protestant princes for his attempt to regain the throne. In any case, he renounced the Reformation when it seemed that this step would help him gain the emperor's support. Luther was apparently unaware of his duplicity. It is interesting that although the opposition to Christian II was led by clergy who were loyal to Rome, his successor, King Frederick I, was a supporter of the Reformation and established it in Denmark. See Julius Köstlin, *Martin Luther. Sein Leben und Schriften*, ed. and rev. by Gustav Kawerau (5th ed.; 2 vols.; Berlin: Alexander Duncker, 1903), I, 625-627.

well enough and I have read in not a few history books of subjects deposing and exiling or killing their rulers. The Jews, the Greeks, and the Romans all did this and God permitted it and even let these nations grow and prosper in spite of it. However, the final outcome was always tragic. The Jews were finally conquered and their nation destroyed by the Assyrians.[30] The Greeks were defeated by King Philip.[31] And the Roman nation was conquered by the Goths and the Lombards.[32] As a matter of fact, the Swiss have paid and are still paying for their own rebellion with great bloodshed, and one can easily predict what the final outcome will be.[33] The Danes, too, have not yet survived their rebellion.[34] I feel that there can be no stable government unless a nation respects and honors its rulers. The Persians, the Tartars, and others like them are good examples of this. They were not only able to preserve their independence against the full power of the Romans, but they ultimately destroyed the Romans and many other nations.[35]

My reason for saying this is that God says, "Vengeance is mine, I will repay" [Rom. 12:19]. He also says, "Judge not" [Matt. 7:1]. And the Old Testament strictly and frequently forbids cursing rulers or speaking evil about them. Exodus 23 [:22:28] says, "You shall not curse the prince of your people." Paul, in I Timothy 2 [:1-2], teaches Christians to pray for their rulers, etc. Solomon in Proverbs and Ecclesiastes[36] repeatedly teaches us to obey the king and be subject to him. Now no one can deny that when subjects set themselves against their rulers, they avenge themselves and make themselves judges. This is not only against the

---

[30] Luther apparently is referring to the destruction of Samaria by the Assyrians in 722-721 B.C. (II Kings 17:6).

[31] The Macedonians under Philip, the father of Alexander the Great, defeated the Greeks in the battle of Chaeronea in 338 B.C.

[32] The Lombard invasion of Italy began in the second half of the sixth century A.D.

[33] Protestant forces were defeated by the Catholics at the battle of Kappel, October 11, 1531. The result was a division among the Swiss.

[34] Christian II had written Luther as late as May 20, 1525, that he expected a popular movement to restore him to the throne. WA, Br 3, 503-504.

[35] Cf. p. 105.

[36] E.g., Prov. 24:21 and Eccles. 10:20.

ordinance and command of God, who reserves to himself the authority to pass judgment and administer punishment in these matters, but such actions are also contrary to all natural law and justice. This is the meaning of the proverbs, "No man ought to judge his own case,"[37] and, "The man who hits back is in the wrong."[38]

Now perhaps you will say, "How can anyone possibly endure all the injustice that these tyrants inflict on us? You allow them too much opportunity to be unjust, and thus your teaching only makes them worse and worse. Are we supposed to permit everyone's wife and child, body and property to be so shamefully treated and always to be in danger? If we have to live under these conditions, how can we ever begin to live a decent life?" My reply is this: My teaching is not intended for people like you who want to do whatever you think is good and will please you. Go ahead! Do whatever you want! Kill all your lords! See what good is does you! My teaching is intended only for those who would like to do what is right. To these I say that rulers are not to be opposed with violence and rebellion, as the Romans, the Greeks, the Swiss, and the Danes have done; rather, there are other ways of dealing with them.

In the first place, if you see that the rulers think so little of their soul's salvation that they rage and do wrong, what does it matter to you if they ruin your property, body, wife, and child? They cannot hurt your soul, and they do themselves more harm than they do you because they damn their own souls and that must result in the ruin of body and property. Do you think that you are not already sufficiently avenged?

In the second place, what would you do if your rulers were at war and not only your goods and wives and children, but you yourself were broken, imprisoned, burned, and killed for your lord's sake? Would you slay your lord for that reason? Think of all the good people that Emperor Maximilian[39] lost in the wars that he waged in his lifetime. No one did anything to him because of it.

---

[37] Cf. Wander (ed.), *Deutsches Sprichwörter Lexikon,* III, *"Niemand,"* No. 55.
[38] Cf. p. 25, n. 20.

[39] Maximilian I, Holy Roman emperor from 1493 to 1519, was extensively occupied with military undertakings during his reign.

And yet, if he had destroyed them by tyranny no more cruel deed would ever have been heard of. Nevertheless, he was the cause of their death, for they were killed for his sake. What is the difference, then, between such a raging tyrant and a dangerous war as far as the many good and innocent people who perish in it are concerned? Indeed, a wicked tyrant is more tolerable than a bad war, as you must admit from your own reason and experience.

I can easily believe that you would like to have peace and good times, but suppose God prevents this by war or tyrants! Now, make up your mind whether you would rather have war or tyrants, for you are guilty enough to have deserved both from God. However, we are the kind of people who want to be scoundrels and live in sin and yet we want to avoid the punishment of sin, and even resist punishment and defend our skin. We shall have about as much success at that as a dog has when he tries to bite through steel.[40]

In the third place, if the rulers are wicked, what of it? God is still around, and he has fire, water, iron, stone, and countless ways of killing. How quickly he can kill a tyrant! He would do it, too, but our sins do not permit it, for he says in Job [34:30], "He permits a knave to rule because of the people's sins." We have no trouble seeing that a scoundrel is ruling. However, no one wants to see that he is ruling not because he is a scoundrel, but because of the people's sin. The people do not look at their own sin; they think that the tyrant rules because he is such a scoundrel—that is how blind, perverse, and mad the world is! That is why things happened the way they did when the peasants revolted. They wanted to punish the sins of the rulers, as though they themselves were pure and guiltless; therefore God had to show them the log in their eye so they would forget about the speck in another man's eye [Matt. 7:3-5].

---

[40] *Das wird uns gelingen wie dem hunde der ynn die stachel beysset.* Our translation is quite literal and interprets *stachel* as "steel." Luther could be alluding to a dog's attempting to bite someone in armor. *Stachel* could also mean a spiked dog-collar, and the passage would then be understood in the sense of "chewing nails." *Stachel* may, however, also mean the quills of a porcupine. In that case, there is a related proverb, "The dog who bites the porcupine gets a bloody mouth." Cf. Thiele, *Luthers Sprichwörtersammlung*, No. 426.

In the fourth place, the tyrants run the risk that, by God's decree, their subjects may rise up, as has been said, and kill them or expel them. For here we are giving instruction to those who want to do what is right, and they are very few. The great multitude remain heathen, godless, and un-Christian; and these, if God so decrees, wrongfully rise up against the rulers and create disaster, as the Jews and Greeks and Romans often did. Therefore you have no right to complain that our doctrine gives the tyrants and rulers security to do evil; on the contrary, they are certainly not secure. We teach, to be sure, that they ought to be secure, whether they do good or evil. However, we can neither give them this security nor guarantee it for them, for we cannot compel the multitude to follow our teaching if God does not give us grace. We teach what we will, and the world does what it wills. God must help, and we must teach those who are willing to do what is good and right so that they may help hold the multitude in check. The lords are just as secure because of our teaching as they would be without it. Unfortunately, your complaint is unnecessary, since most of the crowd does not listen to us. The preservation of the rulers whom God has appointed is a matter that rests with God and in his hands alone. We experienced this in the peasants' rebellion. Therefore do not be misled by the wickedness of the rulers; their punishment and disaster are nearer than you might wish. Dionysius, the tyrant of Syracuse,[41] confessed that his life was like the life of a man over whose head a sword hung by a silken thread and under whom a glowing fire was burning.[42]

In the fifth place, God has still another way to punish rulers, so that there is no need for you to avenge yourselves. He can raise up foreign rulers, as he raised up the Goths against the Romans, the Assyrians against the Jews, etc. Thus there is vengeance, punishment, and danger enough hanging over tyrants and rulers, and God does not allow them to be wicked and have peace and joy. He is right behind them; indeed, he surrounds them and has them between spurs and under bridle. This also agrees with

---

[41] Dionysius (*ca.* 432-367 B.C.) was renowned for conquests which made Syracuse the most powerful of the western Greek cities.

[42] Cicero, *Tuscullan Orations* (*Tusculanae*), V, 21.

the natural law that Christ teaches in Matthew 7 [:12], "Whatever you wish that men would do to you, do so to them." Obviously, no father would want his own family to drive him out of the house, kill him, or ruin him because he had done things that were wrong, especially if his family did it maliciously and used force to avenge themselves without previously having brought charges against him before a higher authority. It ought to be just as wrong for any subject to treat his tyrant in such a way.

I must give an example or two of this. Note them well, for you will profit from them. We read of a widow who stood and prayed for her tyrant most devoutly, asking God to give him long life, etc. The tyrant heard it and was astonished because he knew very well that he had done her much harm, and that this was not the usual prayer for tyrants. People do not ordinarily pray such prayers for tyrants, so he asked her why she prayed thus for him. She answered, "I had ten cows when your grandfather lived and ruled. He took two of them and I prayed that he might die and that your father might become lord. This is what happened, and your father took three cows. I prayed again that you might become lord, and that your father might die. Now you have taken four cows, and so I am praying for you, for now I am afraid that your successor will take the last cow and everything that I have."[43] The scholars, too, have a parable about a beggar who was full of wounds. Flies got into them and sucked his blood and stung him. Then a merciful man came along and tried to help him by shooing all the flies away from him. But the beggar cried out and said, "What are you doing? Those flies were almost full and did not worry me so much; now the hungry flies will come in their place and will plague me far worse."[44]

Do you understand these fables? There is as great a differ-

---

[43] WA 19, 666, reports that this story, without the reference to the cows, is found in John Agricola, *Proverbs* (later than this text), No. 128, and elsewhere.

[44] Although Luther's version does not correspond in every detail to Aesop's fable of *The Fox and the Hedgehog*, this story is undoubtedly the source of the illustration. Aristotle, with whose works Luther was well acquainted, quotes the story in *Rhetoric* 2, 20. Cf. also Josephus, *Antiquities of the Jewish People*, 18, 174-175 (VI, 5).

ence between changing a government and improving it as the distance from heaven to earth. It is easy to change a government, but it is difficult to get one that is better, and the danger is that you will not. Why? Because it is not in our will or power, but only in the will and the hand of God. The mad mob, however, is not so much interested in how things can be improved, but only that things be changed. Then if things are worse, they will want something still different. Thus they get bumblebees instead of flies, and in the end they get hornets instead of bumblebees. They are like the frogs of old who could not put up with a log for lord; instead they got a stork that pecked their heads and devoured them.[45] A mad mob is a desperate, accursed thing. No one can rule it as well as tyrants, who are like the leash tied to a dog's neck.[46] If there were a better way to rule over a mob, God would have established some other form of government for them than the sword and tyrants. The presence of the sword shows the nature of the children under it: people who, if they dared, would be desperate scoundrels.

Therefore I advise everyone who wants to act with a good conscience in this matter to be satisfied with the worldly rulers and not to attack them. For worldly rulers cannot harm the soul, as clergy and false teachers do. He should follow the example of the good David, who suffered as much violence from King Saul as you can ever suffer, and yet would not lay a hand upon his king, as he could often have done.[47] Rather, he commended the matter to God, let things go as long as God would have them so, and endured to the end. If war or strife arise against your overlord, leave the fighting and struggling to those who want it. For as we have said, if God does not hold back the crowd, we cannot restrain them. But if you want to do what is right and have a secure conscience, let your weapons and armor lie and do not fight against

---

[45] The story is told by Aesop (*The Frogs and the Stork*) and in Phaedrus, *Fables*, I, 2. Luther was very fond of fables and translated some into German. The text of his translation of this fable, which was published after his death, is found in *WA* 50, 440-460.

[46] Cf. Thiele, *Luthers Sprichwörtersammlung*, No. 236.

[47] Cf. I Sam. 24:1-7; 26:6-12.

your lord or tyrant. Rather suffer everything that can happen to you. The crowd that does the fighting, however, will be brought to justice.

"But," you say, "suppose that a king or lord has given an oath to his subjects to rule according to articles that have been agreed upon and then does not keep the agreement.[48] He thereby forfeits his right to rule. It is said that the king of France must rule according to the parlements, and that the king of Denmark must also swear to certain articles, etc."[49] Here is my answer: It is right and proper for rulers to govern according to laws and administer them and not to rule arbitrarily. I add, however, that a king does not only promise to keep the law of his land or the articles of election, but God himself commands him to be righteous, and he promises to do so. Well, then, if this king keeps neither God's law nor the law of the land, ought you to attack him, judge him, and take vengeance on him? Who commanded you to do that? Another ruler would have to come between you, hear both sides, and condemn the guilty party; otherwise you will not escape the judgment of God, who says, "Vengeance is mine" [Rom. 12:19], and again, "Judge not" (Matthew 7 [:1]).

The case of the king of Denmark is an example.[50] Lübeck and the cities of the sea towns[51] joined with the Danes to depose him.[52] I shall express my opinion in this matter for the benefit of those who might have a bad conscience about this matter and for those who might want to reconsider and better understand what they have done. Let us assume that the kings really were unjust before God and the world and that law and justice were entirely on the side of the Danes and the Lübeckers. That is one thing. But there is another thing, that is, that the Danes and Lübeckers have acted as judges and overlords of the king, and have punished

---

[48] Such an agreement was implicit in the giving and receiving of the feudal oath. Sometimes these conditions were placed in writing, and thus became the primal form of a written constitution.

[49] For example, Frederick I, who ruled Denmark from 1523 to 1533, had to promise to protect the rights of the nobility.

[50] Luther is discussing the deposition and exile of Christian II. See p. 106, n. 29.

[51] Luther is referring to the alliance known as the Hanseatic League.

[52] For details about this alliance, see BG 7, 408, n. 1.

and avenged the wrong, and thus assumed the right of judgment and vengeance. This raises questions for the conscience. When the case comes before God, he will not ask if the king was unjust and you just, for that has become clear. He will however ask, "You citizens of Denmark and Lübeck, who commanded you to do these acts of punishment and vengeance? Did I command you, or did the emperor, or overlord? If so, prove it by sealed documents." If they can do so, then they have a good case. If not, God will judge thus, "You rebellious thieves have stolen what belongs to God. You have assumed my office and have maliciously assumed to yourselves the administration of divine vengeance. You are guilty of treason against God.[53] You have invoked my judgment upon yourselves."

For two completely different things are involved in being unjust and condemning injustice, in law and the execution of law, in justice and the administration of justice. Every man is involved in justice and injustice. However, God alone is lord over justice and injustice, and God alone passes judgment and administers justice. It is God who commits this responsibility to rulers to act in his stead in these matters. Therefore let no one presume to do this, unless he is sure that he has a command from God, or from God's servants the rulers.

What would become of the world if everyone who was in the right punished everyone who did wrong? The servant would strike his master, the maid her mistress, the children the parents, the pupils the teacher. That would be a fine state of affairs! What need would there be, then, for judges and temporal rulers appointed by God? Let the Danes and Lübeckers consider whether they would think it right for their servants, citizens, and subjects to rebel against them whenever they treated them unjustly. Why, then, do they not do to others as they wish that others would do to them, and not treat others in a way they do not wish to be treated themselves? This is what Christ teaches in Matthew 7 [:12], and the natural law teaches it too.

To be sure, the Lübeckers and the other cities might excuse themselves by saying that they were not the king's subjects but

---

[53] Cf. p. 101, n. 16.

had dealt with him as enemies dealing with an enemy, as equals dealing with their equal. The poor Danes, however, were his subjects and they rebelled against their ruler without any command from God. And the Lübeckers advised and helped them. Thus they burdened themselves with other men's sins and have become involved, entangled, and caught in this rebellious disobedience toward both God and man. I will not mention the fact that they also disregarded the emperor's commands.

I mention this as an example because we are considering the doctrine that a subject ought not rebel against his ruler. The story of the deposition of the king of Denmark is very significant and serves here as a warning to all others to beware of this example. I hope that the consciences of those who did it may be touched and that some of them may reform and leave their iniquity before God comes and avenges himself on his enemies and those who have robbed him. Not that all of them will care about this! The great multitude, as has been said, does not care about God's word; it is an abandoned crowd and is being made ready for God's wrath and punishment. But I will be satisfied if some take it to heart and do not involve themselves in the deeds of the Danes and Lübeckers; and if they have been involved, I hope they will get out of it and not be a party to the sins of others. Each of us has more than enough of his own sins to answer for.

At this point I shall have to pause and listen to my critics, who cry, "See here, in my opinion you are flattering the princes. Are you now creeping to the cross and seeking pardon? Are you afraid? etc." I just let these bumblebees buzz and fly away. If anyone can do better, let him. I have not undertaken here to preach to the princes and lords. I think, too, that they will not be very happy to receive this flattery and that I will not have ingratiated myself with them, because it jeopardizes their whole class, as you have heard.[54] Besides, I have said often enough elsewhere, and it is all too true, that the majority of the princes and lords are godless tyrants and enemies of God, who persecute the gospel.[55]

---

[54] Cf. pp. 105-107.

[55] Cf. *Temporal Authority: To What Extent It Should Be Obeyed* (1523). LW 45, 84, 109-110; cf. also in this volume, p. 19.

They are my ungracious lords and sirs, and I am not very concerned about that. But I do teach that everyone should know how to conduct himself in this matter of how he ought to act toward his overlord, and should do what God has commanded him. Let the lords look out for themselves and stand on their own feet. God will not forget the tyrants and men of high rank. God is able to deal with them, and he has done so since the beginning of the world.

Moreover, I do not want anyone to think that what I have written here applies only to peasants, as though they were the only ones of lower rank and the nobles were not also subjects. Not at all! What I say about "subjects" is intended for peasants, citizens of the cities, nobles, counts, and princes as well. For all of these have overlords and are the subjects of someone else. A rebellious noble, count, or prince should have his head cut off the same as a rebellious peasant. The one should be treated like the other, and no one will be treated unjustly.

I believe Emperor Maximilian could have sung a pretty little song about rebellious princes and nobles who put their heads together to start a rebellion. And the nobles! How often have they complained and conspired and sought to defy the princes and rebel? Think of the furor the Franconian nobles alone have made about how little they care for the emperor or for their bishops. However, we are not supposed to call these knightlets[56] rebels or troublemakers, although that is exactly what they were. The peasant, on the other hand, is supposed to stand for it and keep quiet. But unless my mind deceives me, God has punished the rebellious lords and nobles through the rebellious peasants, one scoundrel with another.[57] Maximilian had to put up with these nobles and could not punish them, though he had to restrain the peasants as long as he lived. The situation in Germany was so critical that I would be willing to wager that if the peasants had not revolted, a rebellion would have broken out among the nobles against the princes and perhaps against the emperor. But now the peasants are the ones who have revolted and they alone have become the

---

[56] Cf. p. 82, n. 46.
[57] Cf. p. 41, n. 53.

villains.[58] As a result the nobles and the princes get off easy and can wipe their mouths as though they had done nothing wrong.[59] But God is not deceived [Gal. 6:7]; he has used these events to warn the nobles that they, too, should learn to obey their rulers. Let this be my flattery of princes and lords!

Here you say, "Are we, then, to put up with a ruler who would be such a scoundrel that he lets land and people go to ruin?" To say it as the nobles would, "Devil! St. Vitus' Dance! Pestilence! St. Anthony! St. Quirinus![60] I am a nobleman and am I supposed to allow my wife and children and body and property to be so shamefully ruined?" I reply: Listen here! I am not trying to teach you anything. Go ahead and do what you please! You are smart enough. You do not need me! I do not have to worry about anything except watching while you sing this proud little song to the bitter end.[61]

To the others, who would like to keep their conscience clear, we have this to say: God has thrown us into the world, under the power of the devil. As a result, we have no paradise here. Rather, at any time we can expect all kinds of misfortune to body, wife, child, property, and honor. And if there is one hour in which there are less than ten disasters or an hour in which we can even survive, we ought to say, "How good God is to me! He has not sent every disaster to me in this one hour." How is that possible? Indeed, as long as I live under the devil's power, I should not have one happy hour. That is what we teach our people. Of course, you may do something else. You may build yourself a paradise where the devil cannot get in so that you need not expect the rage of any tyrant. We will watch you! Actually things go too well for us. We are too happy and content.[62] We do not know how good God is to us and we believe neither that God takes care of us nor

---

[58] Literally, "the only black ones."

[59] Cf. Thiele, *Luthers Sprichwörtersammlung*, No. 315. Cf. Prov. 21:20.

[60] These expletive invocations of the saints call upon them to afflict with the malady whose cure popular piety attributed to them: St. Vitus, epilepsy; St. Anthony, an inflamed condition of the skin; and St. Quirinus, the plague. Cf. Helen Roeder, *Saints and Their Attributes* (London, New York, Toronto, 1955), pp. 32, 62, 102, 115, 221.

[61] Cf. Thiele, *Luthers Sprichwörtersammlung*, Nos. 158-159.

[62] *Ibid.*, No. 323.

that the devil is so evil. We want to be nothing but wicked scoundrels and yet receive nothing but good from God.

That is enough on the first point, that is, that war and uprisings against our superiors cannot be right. However, people do and are in danger of doing this every day, just as they do everything else that is evil and unjust. But when it comes from God and he does not prevent it, the final outcome is not good and the people involved suffer, even though such rebels seem to have good fortune for a while.

Now we will move on to the second point and discuss the question whether equals may wage war against equals. I would have this understood as follows: It is not right to start a war just because some silly lord has gotten the idea into his head. At the very outset I want to say that whoever starts a war is in the wrong. And it is only right and proper that he who first draws his sword is defeated, or even punished, in the end. This is what has usually happened in history. Those who have started wars have lost them, and those who fought in self-defense have only seldom been defeated. Worldly government has not been instituted by God to break the peace and start war, but to maintain peace and to avoid war. Paul says in Romans 13 [:4] that it is the duty of the sword to protect and punish, to protect the good in peace and to punish the wicked with war. God tolerates no injustice and he has so ordered things that warmongers must be defeated in war. As the proverb says, "No one has ever been so evil that he does not meet someone more evil than he is."[63] And in Psalm 68 [:30] God has the psalmist sing of him, *"Dissipat gentes, quae bella volunt,"* that is, "He scatters the peoples who delight in war."

Beware, therefore; God does not lie! Take my advice. Make the broadest possible distinction between what you want to do and what you ought to do, between desire and necessity, between lust for war and willingness to fight. Do not be tempted to think of yourself as though you were the Turkish sultan. Wait until the situation compels you to fight when you have no desire to do so. You will still have more than enough wars to fight and will be able to say with heartfelt sincerity, "How I would like to have peace.

---

[63] Cf. Thiele, *Luthers Sprichwörtersammlung*, No. 51.

If only my neighbors wanted it too!" Then you can defend yourself with a good conscience, for God's word says, "He scatters the peoples who delight in war." Look at the real soldiers, those who have played the game of war. They are not quick to draw their sword, they are not contentious; they have no desire to fight. But when someone forces them to fight, watch out! They are not playing games. Their sword is tight in the sheath, but if they have to draw, it does not return bloodless to the scabbard. Those fools who are the first to fight in their thoughts and even make a good start by devouring the world with words and are the first to flash their blades, are also the first to run away and sheathe their swords. The mighty Roman Empire won most of its victories because the Romans were forced to fight; that is, everyone wanted a chance at the Romans to win his spurs at their expense. When the Romans were forced to defend themselves, they set about it vigorously enough! Hannibal, the prince from Africa, hurt them so badly that he almost destroyed them.[64] But how shall I say it? He started it; he also had to stop it. Courage (from God!) remained with the Romans even when they were losing, and where courage stays, deeds surely follow.[65] For it is God who does the deeds; he desires peace and is the enemy of those who start wars and break the peace.

I must mention here the example of Duke Frederick, elector of Saxony, for it would be a shame if that wise prince's sayings were to die with his body.[66] He had to endure many wicked plots on the part of his neighbors and many others. He had so many reasons to start a war that if some mad prince who loved war had been in his position, he would have started ten wars. But Frederick did not draw his sword. He always responded with reasonable words and almost gave the impression that he was afraid and was running away from a fight. He let the others boast and threaten and yet he held his ground against them. When he was asked why he let them threaten him so, he replied, "I shall not start anything; but if

---

[64] He inflicted severe losses upon the Romans at Lake Trasimeno in the spring of 217 B.C.

[65] *Wo aber mut bleibt, da folget auch die that gewislich.* WA 19, 646.

[66] Frederick the Wise, Luther's sovereign, had died the year before Luther wrote these words. Luther and many others held Frederick in esteem as a man of peace. Cf. *MA*³ 5, 429, note to p. 192.

I have to fight, you will see that I shall be the one who decides when it is time to stop." So although many dogs bared their fangs at him, he was never bitten. He saw that the others were foolish and that he could be indulgent with them. If the king of France had not started the war against Emperor Charles, he would not have been so shamefully defeated and captured.[67] And now that the Venetians and Italians are setting themselves against the Emperor and starting trouble,[68] God grant that they must also be the first to have to stop. (Although the emperor is my enemy, I still do not like this kind of injustice.) Let the saying remain true, "God scatters the peoples who delight in war" [Ps. 68:30].

God confirms all this with many excellent examples in the Scriptures. He had his people first offer peace to the kingdoms of the Amorites and Canaanites and would not permit his people to start a war with them. He thereby confirmed this as his principle. But when those kingdoms started the war and forced God's people to defend themselves, they were completely destroyed [Num. 21:21-30; Deut. 2:26-37]. Self-defense is a proper ground for fighting and therefore all laws agree that self-defense shall go unpunished; and he who kills another in self-defense is innocent in the eyes of all men. But when the people of Israel wanted to start an unnecessary war with the Canaanites, the Israelites were defeated, Numbers 14 [:40-45]. And when Joseph and Azariah wanted to fight to gain honor for themselves, they were beaten [I Mac. 5:55-60]. And Amaziah, king of Judah, wanted to start a war against the king of Israel; but read II Kings 14 [:8-14] and see what happened to him. King Ahab started a war against the Syrians at Ramoth, but lost both the war and his own life, I Kings 22 [:2-40]. And the men of Ephraim intended to devour Jephthah and lost forty-two thousand men [Judg. 12:1-6], and so on. You find that the losers were almost always those who started the war. Even good King Josiah had to be slain because he started a war against the king of Egypt [II Kings 23:29] so that the saying would hold true, "He scatters

---

[67] At the battle of Pavia, February 25, 1525, King Francis I was taken captive by the emperor's forces. Cf. p. 90, n. 8.

[68] The trouble which Luther speaks of resulted in the sack of Rome by the imperial army in May, 1527, less than a year after the publication of this treatise.

the peoples who delight in war." Therefore my countrymen in the Harz Mountains[69] have a saying, "It is truly said that whoever strikes anyone else will be struck in return."[70] Why? Because God rules the world powerfully and leaves no wrong unpunished. He who does wrong will be punished by God, as sure as he lives, unless he repents and makes amends to his neighbor. I believe that even Münzer and his peasants would have to admit this.[71]

Let this be, then, the first thing to be said in this matter: No war is just, even if it is a war between equals, unless one has such a good reason for fighting and such a good conscience that he can say, "My neighbor compels and forces me to fight, though I would rather avoid it." In that case, it can be called not only war, but lawful self-defense, for we must distinguish between wars that someone begins because that is what he wants to do and does before anyone else attacks him, and those wars that are provoked when an attack is made by someone else. The first kind can be called wars of desire; the second, wars of necessity. The first kind are of the devil; God does not give good fortune to the man who wages that kind of war. The second kind are human disasters; God help in them!

Take my advice, dear lords. Stay out of war unless you have to defend and protect yourselves and your office compels you to fight. Then let war come. Be men, and test your armor. Then you will not have to think about war to fight. The situation itself will be serious enough, and the teeth of the wrathful, boasting, proud men who chew nails[72] will be so blunt that they will scarcely be able to bite into fresh butter.

The reason is that every lord and prince is bound to protect his people and to preserve the peace for them. That is his office; that is why he has the sword, Romans 13 [:4]. This should be a matter of conscience for him. And he should on this basis be certain that this work is right in the eyes of God and is commanded by him. I

---

[69] Mansfeld, which Luther regarded as his hometown, is situated in the Harz Mountains.

[70] Cf. Wander (ed.), *Deutsches Sprichwörter Lexikon*, IV, "*Schlagen*," No. 60.

[71] Münzer and many peasants were executed at the end of the Peasants' War; see pp. 59-60.

[72] *Eissenfresser*, literally, "iron-eater."

am not now teaching what Christians are to do, for your government does not concern us Christians; but we are rendering you a service and telling you what you are to do before God, in your office of ruler. A Christian is a person to himself; he believes for himself and for no one else. But a lord and prince is not a person to himself, but on behalf of others. It is his duty to serve them, that is, to protect and defend them. It would indeed be good if he were also a Christian and believed in God, for then he would be saved. However, being a Christian is not princely, and therefore few princes can be Christians; as they say, "A prince is a rare bird in heaven."[73] But even if princes are not Christians, they nevertheless ought to do what is right and good according to God's outward ordinance. God wants them to do this.

But if a lord or prince does not recognize this duty and God's commandment and allows himself to think that he is prince, not for his subjects' sake, but because of his handsome, blond hair as though God had made him a prince to rejoice in his power and wealth and honor, take pleasure in these things, and rely on them. If he is that kind of prince, he belongs among the heathen; indeed, he is a fool. That kind of prince would start a war over an empty nut[74] and think of nothing but satisfying his own will. God restrains such princes by giving fists to other people, too. There are also people on the other side of the mountain.[75] Thus one sword keeps the other in the scabbard. However, a sensible prince does not seek his own advantage. He is satisfied if his subjects are obedient. Though his enemies and neighbors boast and threaten and spew out many bad words, he thinks, "Fools always chatter more than wise men;[76] an empty sack holds many words;[77] silence is often the best answer."[78] Therefore he does not concern himself much about them until he sees that his subjects are attacked or finds the sword actually drawn. Then he defends himself as well as he can, ought, and must. For anyone who is such a coward that he tries to catch every

[73] Cf. ibid., I, "Fürst," No. 61; cf. also LW 45, 113.
[74] Cf. ibid., III, "Nuss," No. 137.
[75] Ibid., I, "Berg," No. 8.
[76] Ibid., III, "Narr," No. 879.
[77] Ibid., V, "Wort," Nos. 223-224.
[78] Ibid., IV, "Schweigen," Nos. 38, 42.

word and evaluate it is like a man who tries to trap the wind in his coat.[79] And if you want to know what peace or profit he gets out of that, ask him and you will soon find out.

This is the first thing to be said in this matter. The second should be just as carefully observed. Even though you are absolutely certain that you are not starting a war but are being forced into one, you should still fear God and remember him. You should not march out to war saying, "Ah, now I have been forced to fight and have good cause for going to war." You ought not to think that that justifies anything you do and plunge headlong into battle. It is indeed true that you have a really good reason to go to war and to defend yourself, but that does not give you God's guarantee that you will win. Indeed, such confidence may result in your defeat—even though you have a just cause for fighting the war— for God cannot endure such pride and confidence except in a man who humbles himself before him and fears him. He is pleased with the man who fears neither man nor devil and is bold and confident, brave and firm against both, if they began the war and are in the wrong. But there is nothing to the idea that this will produce a victory, as though it were our deeds or power that did it. Rather, God wants to be feared and he wants to hear us sing from our hearts a song like this, "Dear Lord, you see that I have to go to war, though I would rather not. I do not trust, however, in the justice of my cause, but in your grace and mercy, for I know that if I were to rely on the justness of my cause and were confident because of it, you would rightly let me fall as one whose fall was just, because I relied upon my being right and not upon your sheer grace and kindness."

Just listen now to what the heathen say about this, the Greeks and Romans, who knew nothing of God and the fear of God. They thought that it was they who made war and won victories all by themselves. But by experience over a long period of time in which a great and well-armed people was often beaten by a small number of poorly armed people, they had to learn and freely admitted that nothing is more dangerous in war than to be secure and confident. So they concluded that one should never underestimate the enemy,

---

[79] *Ibid.,* V, *"Wind,"* Nos. 347-348.

no matter how small he may be; that one should surrender no advantage, no matter how small it may be; that one should neglect no precaution, vigilance, or concern, no matter how small it may be. One should be as careful with everything as one would be if one were weighing gold. Foolish, confident, heedless people accomplish nothing in war, except to do harm. They regarded the words *"non putassem"*—"I did not think of it"—as the most shameful words a soldier could speak. These words indicate that he was one of those secure, confident, careless men, who in one moment, by one step, with one word, can do more damage than ten like him can repair, and then he will say, "Indeed, I did not think of it."[80] Prince Hannibal badly defeated the Romans as long as they were confident and secure against him. And history is full of innumerable examples of this kind, just as we see them happening with our own eyes every day.

The heathen learned this by experience and taught it, but they did not know how to account for it other than to blame it on Fortune. They felt that they had to be afraid of Fortune. However, as I have said, the actual cause of this is that God wants to demonstrate through such histories that he wants men to fear him, and that he will not tolerate confidence, contempt, temerity, or security in such things until we learn to receive from his hands all that we can and want to have, as a gift of pure grace and mercy. It is therefore remarkable for a soldier who has a good cause to be confident and discouraged at the same time. How can he fight if he is discouraged? But if he goes into battle with complete confidence, the danger is even greater. This, then, is what he should do: Before God he should be discouraged, fearful, and humble, and commit his cause to him that he may dispose things, not according to our understanding of what is right and just, but according to his kindness and grace. In this way he wins God to his side with a humble, fearful heart. Toward men he should be bold, free, and confident because they are in the wrong, and smite them with a confident and untroubled spirit. Why should we not do for our God what the Romans, the greatest fighters on earth, did for their false god, For-

---

[80] Cicero, *On Moral Obligation* (*de officiis*), I, 23.

tune, whom they feared? Whenever they did not do this, they fought in great danger and even were badly beaten.

Our conclusion on this point, then, is that war against equals should be waged only when it is forced upon us and then it should be fought in the fear of God. Such a war is forced upon us when an enemy or neighbor attacks and starts the war, and refuses to cooperate in settling the matter according to law or through arbitration and common agreement, or when one overlooks and puts up with the enemy's evil words and tricks, but he still insists on having his own way. I am assuming throughout that I am preaching to those who want to do what is right in God's sight. Those who will neither offer nor consent to do what is right do not concern me. Fearing God means that we do not rely on the justness of our cause, but that we are careful, diligent, and cautious, even in the very smallest details, in so small a thing as a whistle.[81] With all this, however, God's hands are not bound so that he cannot bid us make war against those who have not given us just cause, as he did when he commanded the children of Israel to go to war against the Canaanites. In such a case God's command is necessity enough. However, even such a war should not be fought without fear and care, as God shows in Joshua 3 [7:1-5] when the children of Israel marched confidently against the men of Ai, and were beaten. The same kind of necessity arises if subjects fight at the command of their rulers; for God commands us to obey our rulers [Rom. 13:1], and his command requires that we fight, though this too must be done with fear and humility. We shall discuss this further below.

The third question is whether overlords have the right to go to war with their subjects. We have, indeed, heard above that subjects are to be obedient and are even to suffer wrong from their tyrants. Thus, if things go well, the rulers have nothing to do with their subjects except to cultivate fairness, righteousness, and judgment. However, if the subjects rise up and rebel, as the peasants did recently, then it is right and proper to fight against them. That, too, is what a prince should do to his nobles and an emperor to his princes if they are rebellious and start a war. Only it must be done in the fear of God, and too much reliance must not be placed on

---

[81] Cf. Wander (ed.), *Deutsches Sprichwörter Lexikon*, III, *"Pfeife,"* No. 1260.

being in the right, lest God determine that the lords are to be punished by their subjects, even though the subjects are in the wrong. This has often happened, as we have heard above. For to be right and to do right do not always go together. Indeed, they never go together unless God joins them. Therefore, although it is right that subjects patiently suffer everything and do not revolt, nevertheless, it is not for men to decide whether they shall do so. For God has appointed subjects to care for themselves as individuals, has taken the sword from them, and has put it into the hands of another. If they rebel against this, get others to join them and break loose, and take the sword, then before God they are worthy of condemnation and death.

Overlords, on the other hand, are appointed to be persons who exist for the sake of the community,[82] and not for themselves alone. They are to have the support of their subjects and are to bear the sword. Compared to his overlord the emperor, a prince is not a prince, but an individual who owes obedience to the emperor, as do all others, each for himself. But when he is seen in relationship to his own subjects he is as many persons as he has people under him and attached to him. So the emperor, too, when compared with God, is not an emperor, but an individual person like all others; compared with his subjects, however, he is as many times emperor as he has people under him. The same thing can be said of all other rulers. When compared to their overlord, they are not rulers at all and are stripped of all authority. When compared with their subjects, they are adorned with all authority.

Thus, in the end, all authority comes from God, whose alone it is; for he is emperor, prince, count, noble, judge, and all else, and he assigns these offices to his subjects as he wills, and takes them back again for himself. Now no individual ought to set himself against the community or attract the support of the community to himself, for in so doing he is chopping over his head, and the chips will surely fall in his eyes.[83] From this you see that those who resist their rulers resist the ordinance of God, as St. Paul teaches in Ro-

---

[82] *Eine gemeine person;* i.e., one whose person symbolizes the community as a whole.

[83] See p. 103, n. 18.

mans 13 [:2]. In I Corinthians 15 [:24] Paul also says that God will abolish all authority when he himself shall reign and return all things to himself.

So much on these three points; now come the questions. Now since no king can go to war alone (any more than he can administer the law courts alone—he must have people who serve him in war just as he must have counselors, judges, lawyers, jailers, executioners, and whatever else is necessary for the administration of justice), the question arises whether a man ought to hire himself out for wages, *dienstgelt* or *mangelt* as they call it, and commit himself to serve the prince as the occasion may demand, as is customary.[84] To answer this question we must distinguish various types of soldiers.

In the first place, there are some subjects who, even without such an arrangement, are under obligation to aid their overlords with their body and property and to obey their lord's summons. This is especially true of the nobles and of those who hold property granted by charter from the authorities. For the properties held by counts, lords, and nobles were parceled out in ancient times by the Romans and the Roman emperors and were given in fief on the condition that those who possess them should always be armed and ready—the one with this many horses and men, the other with that many, according to the size of their holdings. These fiefs were the wages with which they were hired. This is why they are called fiefs and why these incumbrances still rest upon them. The emperor permits these holdings to be inherited; and this is right and fine in the Roman Empire.[85] The Turk, it is said, does not allow such inheritances and tolerates no hereditary principality, county, or knights' fee or fief, but assigns and distributes them as, when, and to whom he will. This is why he has such immeasurable wealth and is absolute lord in the land, or rather a tyrant.

The nobles, therefore, should not think that they have their property for nothing, as though they had found it or won it by

---

[84] The employment of mercenaries was a common practice. Many such soldiers were Germans. *BG* 7, 427, n. 2.

[85] Luther's understanding of the origins of feudal structures appears to be based on such writings as Peter Andlau's *Libellus de Caesarea Monarchia*, Title 13, first published in 1460 and republished by Joseph Hürbin in *Zeitschrift der Savignystiftung für Rechtsgeschichte, Germanische Abteilung,* Vol. XII (1890).

gambling. The encumbrance on it and the feudal rents show whence and why they have it, namely, as a loan from the emperor or the prince. Therefore they ought not use it to finance their own ostentatious display and riotous conduct, but be armed and prepared for war to defend the land and to maintain the peace. Now if they complain that they must keep horses and serve the princes and lords while others have peace and quiet, I reply: Dear sirs, let me tell you something. You have your pay and your fief, and you are appointed to this office and are well paid for it. But do not others also have to work hard enough to maintain their little properties? Or are you the only ones who have work to do? And your office[86] is seldom called for, but others must do their duty every day. If you are not willing to do this or think it burdensome or unjust, then give up your fief. It will be easy to find others who will be glad to accept it and do in return what it requires of them.

Therefore, wise men have divided the work of all men into two categories, *Agriculturam* and *Militiam,* that is, agricultural and military occupations. And this is the natural division. The farmers feed us and the soldiers defend us. Those who have the responsibility of defending are to receive their income and their food from those who have the responsibility of feeding, so that they will be able to defend. Those who have the responsibility of feeding are to be defended by those who have the responsibility of defending, so that they will be able to provide food. The emperor or prince in the land is to supervise both groups and see to it that those who have the responsibility of defending are armed and have mounts, and that those who have the responsibility of feeding honestly try to increase the supply of food. However, he should not tolerate useless people, who neither feed nor defend, but only consume, are lazy, and live in idleness, and drive them out of the land, as do the bees, which sting the drones to death because they do not work and only eat up the honey of the other bees. This is why Solomon, in Ecclesiastes [5:8-9], calls the kings builders who build the land, for that should be their responsibility. But God preserve us Germans! We are not getting any wiser or doing this the right way, but are continuing for a while to be consumers, and we let those be feeders

---

[86] I.e., the responsibility of military service.

and defenders who have the desire for it or cannot evade it.[87]

In Luke 2 [3:14] St. John the Baptist confirms the right of this first class to their pay and to hold fiefs, and says that they rightly do their duty when they help their lord make war and serve him. When the soldiers asked him what they were to do, he answered, "Be content with your wages." Now if it were wrong for them to take wages, or if their occupation were against God, he could not have let it continue, permitted it, and confirmed it, but, as a godly, Christian teacher, he would have had to condemn it and deter them from it. This is the answer to those who, because of tenderness of conscience—though this is now rare among these people—profess that it is dangerous to take up this occupation for the sake of temporal goods, since it is nothing but bloodshed, murder, and the inflicting of all kinds of suffering upon one's neighbor, as happens in wartime. These men should inform their consciences that they do not do this from choice, desire, or ill-will, but that this is God's work and that it is their duty to their prince and their God. Therefore, since it is a legitimate office, ordained by God, they should be paid and compensated for doing it, as Christ says in Matthew 10 [:10], "A laborer deserves his wage."[88]

Of course, it is true that if a man serves as a soldier with a heart that neither seeks nor thinks of anything but acquiring wealth, and if temporal wealth is his only reason for doing it, he is not happy when there is peace and not war. Such a man strays from the path and belongs to the devil, even though he fights out of obedience to his lord and at his call. He takes a work that is good in itself and makes it bad for himself by not being very concerned about serving out of obedience and duty, but only about seeking his own profit. For this reason he does not have a good conscience which can say, "Well, for my part, I would like to stay at home, but because my lord calls me and needs me, I come in God's name and know that I am serving God by doing so, and that I will earn or accept the pay that is given me for it." A soldier ought to have the knowledge and

---

[87] The literature of the period raised frequent complaints about the number of persons who were supported without working. Sebastian Frank expressed the opinion that scarcely a third of the German populace actually worked for a living. Cf. BG 7, 424, n. 1, and MA³ 5, 430, note to p. 199.

[88] Cf. Luke 10:7.

confidence that he is doing and must do his duty to be certain that he is serving God and can say, "It is not I that smite, stab, and slay, but God and my prince, for my hand and my body are now their servants." That is the meaning of the watchwords and battle cries, "Emperor!" "France!" "Lüneburg!" "Braunschweig!" This is how the Jews cried against the Midianites, "The sword of God and Gideon!" Judges 7 [:20].

Such a greedy man spoils all other good works, too. For example, a man who preaches for the sake of temporal wealth is lost, though Christ says that a preacher shall live from the gospel.[89] It is not wrong to do things for temporal wealth, for income, wages, and pay are also temporal wealth. If it were wrong, no one should work or do anything to support himself on the ground that it is done for temporal wealth. But to be greedy for temporal wealth and to make a Mammon[90] of it is always wrong in every office, position, and occupation. Leave out greed and other evil thoughts, and it is not sin to fight in a war. Take your wages for it, and whatever is given you. This is why I said above that the work, in itself, is just and godly, but that it becomes wrong if the person is unjust or uses it unjustly.

A second question: "Suppose my lord were wrong in going to war." I reply: If you know for sure that he is wrong, then you should fear God rather than men, Acts 4 [5:29], and you should neither fight nor serve, for you cannot have a good conscience before God. "Oh, no," you say, "my lord would force me to do it; he would take away my fief and would not give me my money, pay, and wages. Besides, I would be despised and put to shame as a coward, even worse, as a man who did not keep his word and deserted his lord in need." I answer: You must take that risk and, with God's help, let whatever happens, happen. He can restore it to you a hundredfold, as he promises in the gospel, "Whoever leaves house, farm, wife, and property, will receive a hundredfold," etc. [Matt. 19:29].

In every other occupation we are also exposed to the danger that the rulers will compel us to act wrongly; but since God will

---

[89] Matt. 10:10; cf. I Cor. 9:14.
[90] Cf. Matt. 6:24.

have us leave even father and mother for his sake, we must certainly leave lords for his sake. But if you do not know, or cannot find out, whether your lord is wrong, you ought not to weaken certain obedience for the sake of an uncertain justice; rather you should think the best of your lord, as is the way of love, for "love believes all things" and "does not think evil," I Corinthians 13 [:4-7]. So, then, you are secure and walk well before God. If they put you to shame or call you disloyal, it is better for God to call you loyal and honorable than for the world to call you loyal and honorable. What good would it do you if the world thought of you as a Solomon or a Moses, and in God's judgment you were considered as bad as Saul or Ahab?

The third question: "Can a soldier obligate himself to serve more than one lord and take wages or salary from each?" Answer: I said above that greed is wrong, whether in a good or an evil occupation. Agriculture is certainly one of the best occupations;[91] nonetheless, a greedy farmer is wrong and is condemned before God. So in this case to take wages is just and right, and to serve for wages is also right. But greed is not right, even though the wages for the whole year were less than a gulden.[92] Again, to take wages and serve for them is right in itself; it does not matter whether the wages come from one, or two, or three, or however many lords, so long as your hereditary lord or prince is not deprived of what is due him and your service to others is rendered with his will and consent. A craftsman may sell his skill to anyone who will have it, and thus serve the one to whom he sells it, so long as this is not against his ruler and his community. In the same way a soldier has his skill in fighting from God and can use it in the service of whoever desires to have it, exactly as though his skill were an art or trade, and he can take pay for it as he would for his work. For the soldier's vocation also springs from the law of love. If anyone needs me and calls for me, I am at his service, and for this I take my wage or whatever is given me. This is what St. Paul says in I Corinthians 9 [:7], "Who serves as a soldier at his own expense?"

---

[91] Luther regarded agriculture highly. Cf., e.g., Luther's *To the Christian Nobility of the German Nation* (1520). *LW* 44, 214.
[92] On the gulden, see Schwiebert, *Luther and His Times*, p. 258.

Thereby Paul approves the soldier's right to his salary. If a prince needs and requires another's subject for fighting, the subject, with his own prince's consent and knowledge, may serve and take pay for it.

"But suppose that one of the princes or lords were to make war against the other, and I were obligated to both, but preferred to serve the one who was in the wrong because he has showed me more grace or kindness than the one who was in the right and from whom I get less—what then?" Here is the quick, short answer: What is right, that is, what pleases God, should be more important than wealth, body, honor and friends, grace, and enjoyment; and in this case there is no respecting of persons, but only of God. In this case, too, a man must put up with it for God's sake if it is thought that he acts ungratefully and is despised for doing it. He has an honorable excuse because God and right will not tolerate our serving the people we like and forsaking those whom we do not like. Although the old Adam[93] does not listen willingly to this, nevertheless, this is what we must do if right is to be maintained. For there is no resisting God, and whoever resists what is right resists God, who gives, orders, and maintains all that is right.

The fourth question: "What is to be said about the man who goes to war not only for the sake of wealth, but also for the sake of temporal honor, to become a big man and be looked up to?" Answer: Greed for money and greed for honor are both greed; the one is as wrong as the other. Whoever goes to war because of this vice earns hell for himself. We should leave and give all honor to God alone and be satisfied with our wages and rations.

It is, therefore, a heathen and not a Christian custom to exhort soldiers before the battle with words like this, "Dear comrades, dear soldiers, be brave and confident; God willing, we shall this day win honor and become rich." On the contrary, they should be exhorted like this, "Dear comrades, we are gathered here to serve, obey, and do our duty to our prince, for according to God's will and ordinance we are bound to support our prince with our body and our possessions, even though in God's sight we are as poor sinners as our enemies are. Nevertheless, since we know that our prince is in the

---

[93] I.e., man's sinful nature.

right in this case, or at least do not know otherwise, we are therefore sure and certain that in serving and obeying him we are serving God. Let everyone, then, be brave and courageous and let no one think otherwise than that his fist is God's fist, his spear God's spear, and cry with heart and voice, 'For God and the emperor!' If God gives us victory, the honor and praise shall be his, not ours, for he wins it through us poor sinners. But we will take the booty and the wages as presents and gifts of God's goodness and grace to us, though we are unworthy, and sincerely thank him for them. Now God grant the victory! Forward with joy!"

There can be no doubt but that if one seeks the honor of God and lets him have it—as is just and right, and as it ought to be—then more honor will come than anyone could want, for in I Samuel 2 [:30] God promises, "Those who honor me I will honor, and those who despise me shall be lightly esteemed." Since God cannot fail to keep his promise, he must honor those who honor him. Seeking one's own honor is one of the greatest sins. It is nothing less than *crimen lese maiestatis divine,* that is, robbery of the divine majesty.[94] Let others, therefore, boast and seek honor; you be obedient and quiet, and your honor will find you. Many a battle has been lost that might have been won if honor alone could have done it. These honor-greedy warriors do not believe that God is in the war and gives the victory; therefore they do not fear God and are not joyful, but are foolhardy and mad, and in the end they are defeated.

But I think the "best comrades"[95] are those who encourage themselves and are encouraged before the battle by thinking about the women they love, and have this said to them, "Hey, now, let everyone think about the woman he loves best." I admit that if two credible men who are experienced in these matters had not told me this, I would never have believed that in a business of this kind, where the danger of death stares men in the face, the human heart could so forget itself and be so light. Of course, no one does this when he fights alone with death. But when the company is assembled one stirs up the other, and no one gives a thought to what affects him, because it affects many. But to a Christian heart it is

---

[94] Cf. p. 101, n. 16.
[95] Luther is speaking ironically.

terrible to think and hear that at a time when he is confronted by God's judgment and the peril of death, a man arouses and encourages himself with fleshly love; for those who are killed or die thus certainly send their souls straight to hell without delay.

"Indeed," they say, "if I were to think of hell, I could never again go to war." It is still worse to put God and his judgment wilfully out of mind and neither know nor think nor hear anything about them. For this reason a great many soldiers belong to the devil. And some of them are so full of the devil that they know no better way to prove their joy than by speaking contemptuously of God and his judgment, as if their boasting made them really tough;[96] they also dare to swear shamefully by Christ's Passion, and curse and defy God in heaven. It is a lost crowd; it is chaff, and, as in other classes, there is much chaff and little wheat.

It follows that those mercenaries who wander about the country seeking war, although they might work and ply a trade till they were called for and thus from laziness or roughness and wildness of spirit waste their time, cannot be on good terms with God. They can neither give God any good explanation for this nor have a good conscience about their wandering. All they have is a foolhardy desire or eagerness for war or to lead the free, wild life which is typical of such people. Ultimately some of them will become scoundrels and robbers. However, if they would labor or take up a trade and earn their bread, as God has commanded all men to do, until their prince summoned them for himself or permitted and asked them to serve someone else, then they could go to war with the good conscience of men who knew that they were serving at the pleasure of their overlord. Otherwise they could not have such a good conscience. Almighty God shows us a great grace when he appoints rulers for us as an outward sign of his will, so that we are sure we are pleasing his divine will and are doing right, whenever we do the will and pleasure of the ruler. For God has attached and bound his will to them when he says, "Render therefore to Caesar the things that are Caesar's" [Matt. 22:21], and in Romans 13 [:1], "Let every person be subject to the governing authorities." The

---

[96] *Die rechten eisenfresser,* literally, "real iron-eaters." Cf. p. 121, n. 72.

whole world ought to think of this as a great joy and comfort and even as a compelling reason to love and honor those who rule over us.

Finally, soldiers have many superstitions in battle. One commends himself to St. George,[97] another to St. Christopher;[98] one to this saint, another to that. Some cast magical spells on iron and bullets; some bless horse and rider; some carry St. John's Gospel,[99] or some other object on which they rely. All these soldiers are in a dangerous condition, for they do not believe in God. On the contrary, they sin through unbelief and false trust in God; and if they were to die, they could not avoid being lost.

This is what they ought to do. When the battle begins and the exhortation of which I spoke above[100] has been given, they should simply commend themselves to God's grace and adopt a Christian attitude. For the above exhortation is only a form for doing the external work of war with a good conscience; but since good works save no man, everyone should also say this exhortation in his heart or with his lips, "Heavenly Father, here I am, according to your divine will, in the external work and service of my lord, which I owe first to you and then to my lord for your sake. I thank your grace and mercy that you have put me into a work which I am sure is not sin, but right and pleasing obedience to your will. But because I know and have learned from your gracious word that none of our good works can help us and that no one is saved as a soldier but only as a Christian, therefore, I will not in any way rely on my obedience and work, but place myself freely at the service of your will. I believe with all my heart that only the innocent blood of your dear Son, my Lord Jesus Christ, redeems and saves me, which he shed for me in obedience to your holy will. This is the basis on which I stand before you. In this faith I will live and die, fight, and

---

[97] The fourth-century patron saint of England was venerated as the patron of calvarymen and soldiers.

[98] Christopher, whose legend tells how he bore the Christ child across a river, was the patron saint of navigators, sailors, and travelers. His aid was invoked for safe journeys and against storms.

[99] Some wore amulets containing the verses John 1:1-14, the last Gospel of the mass. WA 19, 660, n. 1.

[100] Cf. pp. 132-133.

do everything else. Dear Lord God the Father, preserve and strengthen this faith in me by your Spirit. Amen." If you then want to say the Creed and the Lord's Prayer, you may do so and let that be enough. In so doing commit body and soul into God's hands, draw your sword, and fight in God's name.

If there were many such soldiers in an army, do you think anyone could do anything to them? They would devour the world without lifting a sword. Indeed, if there were nine or ten such men in a company, or even three or four, who could say these things with a true heart, I would prefer them to all the muskets, spears, horses, and armor. Then I would be willing to let the Turk come on, with all his power; for the Christian faith is not a joke, nor is it a little thing, but as Christ says in the gospel, "It can do all things" [Mark 9:23]. But, my dear friend, where are those who believe thus and who can do such things? Nevertheless, although the great majority does not do this, we must teach it and know it for the sake of those who will do it, however few they may be. As Isaiah 55 [:11] says, God's word does not return empty, but accomplishes his purpose. The others who despise this wholesome teaching which is given for their salvation have their judge to whom they must answer. We are excused; we have done our part.

Here I shall let this rest for this time. I wanted to say something about war against the Turk because it has come so close to us,[101] and some accused me of advising against war with the Turk.[102] I have long known that at last I would have to become a Turk, and it does not help me that I have written so plainly about this and have said, especially in my book *Temporal Authority: To What Extent It Should Be Obeyed,* that equal may well go to war with equal.[103] But since the Turk is back home again and our Ger-

---

[101] In the spring of 1526 the Turks conquered Hungary and threatened to invade Austria and Germany. The situation was so critical that the emperor did not take military action against the Lutheran princes because he needed their support. Cf. p. 90.

[102] The papal bull excommunicating Luther made this point. For Luther's reply to the accusation, see *LW* 32, 89-90.

[103] *LW* 45, 125.

mans are no longer asking about this, it is not yet time to write about it.[104]

I should have completed this instruction, dear Assa, long ago; but it has been delayed so long that meanwhile, by God's grace, you and I have become godfathers.[105] And yet I hope that the delay has not been fruitless and that the cause has been furthered by it. I commend you to God.

---

[104] Luther did write about war with the Turks: in 1529 he published *On War Against the Turk* (see pp. 155-205) and wrote his *Army Sermon Against the Turk* (*Heerpredigt wider den Türken;* WA 30ᴵᴵ, 160-197); in 1541 he wrote *Admonition to Pray Against the Turk* (*Vermähnung zum Gebet wider den Türken;* WA 51, 585-625).

[105] See p. 89, n. 5.

AN ANSWER TO SEVERAL QUESTIONS ON MONASTIC VOWS

1526

Translated by Robert C. Schultz

INTRODUCTION

In 1521 Luther had written his lengthy and exhaustive book, *The Judgment of Martin Luther on Monastic Vows.*[1] In that book he took the position that the taking of perpetual vows was a denial of salvation through Christ in favor of salvation through works. Perpetual vows, he argued, violated the God-given freedom of a Christian. Throughout that book Luther contended that the cloistered life must be freely chosen, not compelled by false ideas of salvation and of the perpetually binding character of vows. Whether in cloistered community or in the secular world a God-pleasing life is one which is devoted to the service and welfare of one's neighbor and obedience to God's word. As Luther saw it, "The only difference between the 'religious' life and the 'secular' life is the form, not the content."[2]

In the present work, *An Answer to Several Questions on Monastic Vows,* Luther does not deal as thoroughly with vows as he did in his earlier systematic refutation of the monastic system. The present work confines itself to the validity of the interpretation of Scripture passages cited as authority for the binding nature of vows, and was written in response to a problem faced by the Count of Henneberg.[3]

The territory of Henneberg was an example of medieval piety at its extreme. A friend of Luther described it as a land whose populace was totally given over to devotion to Mary and the saints, to religious celebrations and festivals, the veneration of relics, and particularly to a host of monastic and conventual orders. Parents could not prevent their children from taking orders.[4] Husbands and wives often deserted each other and their families to secure their salvation in monastery or convent. Indeed, the taking of vows

---

[1] *LW* 44, 243-400.

[2] *LW* 44, 249.

[3] Luther's family had its roots in Möhra, which belonged to the realm of Henneberg. Many of his relatives were living in the territory.

[4] On this point, see Luther's letter to his father in *LW* 48, 330-336.

was regarded as a greater work than the passion of Christ, and those who were under vows were regarded as living saints.[5]

Such an account, of course, reflects the partisanship of Luther's friend. But the fact remains that Henneberg had an unusually large number of endowed churches, monastic institutions, shrines, and places of pilgrimage,[6] not to mention a host of monastic and conventual orders and religious societies for laymen.[7] Despite this attitude, however, the Reformation movement did make inroads in the territory. Evangelical preaching was introduced at various places as early as 1524.[8] But the Reformation was not introduced on a large scale, primarily because of Count Wilhelm VI.[9]

The count had been present at the Diet of Worms in 1521 when Luther refused to recant. Although he may have been greatly impressed by the courage and conviction of the Saxon monk, he had a number of reasons for not endorsing Luther. The chief reason, however, was the Peasants' War,[10] for which Wilhelm and many others held Luther's teaching responsible.[11] Only with the aid of Electoral Saxony, of which Luther was a citizen, were the Henneberg peasants subdued. The devout Catholic count, heavily indebted to the Lutheran elector, set about reclaiming his realm from the ruin and havoc of the insurrection.

---

[5] Cf. W. Höhn, *Kurze Geschichte der Kirchenreformation in der gefürsteten Grafschaft Henneberg* (Halle/Salle: Verein für Reformationsgeschichte, 1894), pp. 10-12.

[6] Cf. *ibid.*, pp. 13-21, for a list and description.

[7] *Ibid.*, pp. 15-16.

[8] *Ibid.*, p. 22. For an extensive treatment of the Reformation in Henneberg, see W. Germann, *D. Johann Forster der hennebergische Reformator ein Mitarbeiter und Mitstreiter D. Martin Luthers* (Festschrift zum 350 jährigen hennebergischen Reformationsjubiläum, n.d.).

[9] The count (1478-1559) was only two years old when his father died. His training was, therefore, largely in the hands of his intensely devout mother, from whom he no doubt received much of his own piety. He was a lavish contributor to monastic institutions and made frequent pilgrimages and retreats. He was not, however, unaware of the need for reforming the church. Cf. Höhn, *op. cit.*, pp. 23-24; 29-30.

[10] Cf. pp. 3-85.

[11] Among the other reasons was Luther's denunciation of pilgrimages to places such as Grimmenthal, to which Count Wilhelm was especially attached. After 1521 the number of pilgrims declined steadily, and so did the financial receipts of the shrine. Cf. *LW* 44, 185, n. 179, and Höhn, *op. cit.*, p. 26.

During the uprising many monasteries, convents, and shrines had been attacked and pillaged and the monks and nuns had been forced to flee. With the restoration of civil order the expelled monks and nuns[12] called for the repair and restoration of their properties that they might resume the life to which they claimed their vows bound them. In support of this claim they cited a number of biblical passages.[13] Faced with this additional and heavy expense, the count, already heavily in debt, wrote to Prince John, elector of Saxony, on April 9, 1526, requesting that Luther reply to these biblical texts.[14] In compliance with this request Luther wrote the treatise presented here. Luther's letter[15] accompanying the treatise was dated May 18, 1526, and the treatise, with the passages cited by the Henneberg monastics, was published the same year. It is not likely, however, that Luther initiated its publication, for there is no evidence that the printing was done in Wittenberg.[16]

The translation presented here is based on the German text, *Antwort auf etliche Fragen, Klostergelübde belangend, allen den, die sich aus dem stand der Pfafferey, Moncherey odder Nunnerey wircken, vast tröstlich,* given in WA 19, (283) 287-293.

---

[12] One of the nuns was Count Wilhelm's daughter Margareta (1508-1546), who married in 1534.

[13] Cf. pp. 151-154.

[14] The text of the letter is given in WA 19, 283-284, and in Germann, *op. cit.,* Book IV, pp. 34-35. Cf. especially the comments in WA 19, 284, about the texts to which Luther was replying.

[15] The text is given in WA 19, 284, and in Germann, *op. cit.,* p. 35.

[16] Cf. WA 19, 285.

AN ANSWER TO
SEVERAL QUESTIONS
ON MONASTIC VOWS

*A Very Comforting Message to All Who Are
Leaving the Priesthood and Monastic and
Conventual Orders*

In my book about monastic vows[1] I have adequately discussed
this topic. There I show in a thoroughgoing way why the monastic life is to be condemned. Since, however, objections have
been raised on the basis of specific passages of Scripture,[2] I offer
my answer in Christian love.

First, everyone ought to know that Moses and his law have
been abrogated by Christ and are not binding on us Christians.
Paul says this, "I have died to the law and live to Christ," Galatians 1 [2:19]; "Christ is the end of the law," Romans 10 [:4]; "The
brightness of Moses faded," and, "The letter kills," II Corinthians
4 [3:7, 6]. Christ himself says, "The law and the prophets are
valid until the time of John," Matthew 11 [:13], and again, "I have
come to fulfil the law," Matthew 5 [:17]. Therefore anyone who
wants to keep a single law of Moses as though he were obligated
to do so must keep them all. He must have himself circumcised
and become a Jew. This is what Paul says in Galatians 6 [5:3],
"Every man who receives circumcision . . . is bound to keep the
whole law." Or on what basis could anyone say that one law is
binding and another law is not, for they have all been given by
the one God through one and the same Moses?

However, these laws do serve us through the verifying witness they bear to our law, that is, the gospel. This is what Paul

---

[1] *The Judgment of Martin Luther on Monastic Vows* (1521). LW 44, 243-400.
[2] Cf. pp. 151-154.

145

says in Romans 3 [:21], "But now the righteousness of God has been manifested apart from law, although the law and the prophets bear witness to it."

Therefore there is one answer that can be made to all attempts to cite passages from the Old Testament to support [monastic] vows. One need merely ask, "Do you Christians want to be Jews?" Prove your case from the New Testament! The Old Testament has been set aside through Christ and is no longer binding. If it is binding, then you do not have Christ and you must observe the entire law. The attempt to distinguish between judicial, ceremonial, and moral laws[3] does not support their case either. I pointed this out in my book *Against the Heavenly Prophets in the Matter of Images and Sacraments,*[4] which I wrote against Dr. Karlstadt. Furthermore, Moses' laws about vows are all ceremonial laws. Since, however, the ceremonial laws are not binding, as they themselves[5] confess, why do they cite these laws as an argument and thus contradict their own confession? Furthermore, even when Moses' laws were still binding on the Jewish people, it was stipulated that no vow is binding which is impossible or beyond our power and ability.[6] That is why Moses also says, "When a man vows a vow to the Lord, or swears an oath to bind his soul, etc."[7] Now when the Scriptures use the word "soul,"[8] they refer not to the conscience or the inner life, but to a man's living body.[9] Thus Christ says, "The good shepherd lay down his soul for his sheep" [John 10:11].

The vows that people[10] made, therefore, set aside and pledged a man's house, farm, cattle, or his life to service in the temple or

---

[3] I.e., of the Old Testament.

[4] *LW* 40, 93.

[5] Cf. *LW* 40, 94.

[6] Cf. Luther's conclusion on chastity, poverty, and obedience in *LW* 44, 337, 341-344.

[7] Num. 30:2; Luther is referring to the entire chapter, which stipulates that certain vows are not binding because those making the vows have no right to make them; for example, a married woman's vow is invalid if her husband disapproves.

[8] *Seele.*

[9] *Lebendige leib.*

[10] I.e., the people of the Old Testament.

for the support of the priests. Such service was promised for a limited period of time. Now since the cause of the vow was a temporal one, the vow was also temporal. It was even possible to substitute other things in place of what had been promised in the vow.[11] And no one could make an impossible vow or a vow for all eternity.[12] Only one thing corresponded to an eternal vow, that is, material that was devoted to the Lord as "anathema"[13] was to be destroyed. Whatever was thus devoted had to be killed and could not be redeemed. Read the last chapter [27] of Leviticus and you will see what I am talking about.

If our monks and nuns now wish to observe the law of Moses:

1. They must not pledge anything they do not have or that does not belong to them.

2. They must leave open the possibility of making a substitution or of redeeming what is pledged.[14]

3. It must be a temporal and not an eternal vow even though it is not immediately redeemed.[15]

4. If they insist on making an eternal vow, that is, on being anathema, then they must let themselves be put to death immediately; that is the law of Moses. They must either observe his laws or not make such vows. So then, monastic vows are contrary to Moses' law because the monastics make an eternal vow and then do not perform it according to Moses' stipulations.

Likewise, an eternal vow is an impossible thing. We do not have the power to be voluntarily poor, obedient, or chaste. God alone can make that possible. Therefore whoever makes this kind of a vow pledges things that do not belong to him.[16] In so doing, he blasphemes and despises God. Indeed, he steals and robs from God and then tries to give it back to God—if he could only get away with it.

---

[11] Luther refers to regulations such as those in Leviticus 27.

[12] Property dedicated to the Lord was returned in the year of the jubilee, Lev. 27:16-24.

[13] Luther here uses the Septuagint translation. The same word "anathema" is used in the New Testament (Gal. 1:9). Luther is obviously emphasizing the word because of the church's anathema resting upon him.

[14] Cf., e.g., Lev. 27:1-13.

[15] Cf. p. 146, n. 6.

[16] Cf. LW 44, 320.

This is my answer to their articles insofar as they quote the Old Testament. Even Samuel, whose mother dedicated him to God [I Sam. 1:22-28] did not always observe the vow, but, as I Samuel clearly indicates, became a ruler, traveled around the country, served the people, and did not always remain in the temple as had been vowed.[17] On the contrary, Samuel later lived in Ramah [I Sam. 15:34], and his example is a powerful argument against eternally binding monastic vows.

When they quote Proverbs 20 [:25] they do so with a bad conscience, for they quote half of it according to the Latin[18] translation and half of it according to my translation. Thus they quote, "It is a snare for a man to desecrate that which is holy and afterward to retract his vows." What is the use of such lies and deception? What this passage really says is, "It is a snare for a man to desecrate that which is holy and then to go around making vows." This means that there are hypocrites who neglect to hear God's word and to worship him in Jerusalem and then afterward want to make up for such blasphemy and disobedience by making vows. This is just what they do in the monasteries: they neglect the gospel and instead go around making vows. But even if this passage meant what they say it does, nothing that Moses says about vows would be changed. Ecclesiastes 5 [:4] also says, "When you vow a vow to God, do not delay paying it!" All of that repeats what Moses said.

The psalms speak of a special vow: to praise God, which results in a passage like Psalm 48 [50:14], "Offer to God a sacrifice of thanksgiving, and pay your vows to the most high." That whole psalm, however, rejects all sacrifices and vows and requires sacrifices and vows of praise. Thus it closes with the words that he who brings praise as his sacrifice honors God (that is the true worship of God), and that is the way to see God's salvation [Ps.

---

[17] Luther interprets Hannah's vow that Samuel would live in the "presence of the Lord" as stipulating that he would live in the temple. A broader interpretation would open the way for an interpretation of monastic vows that would permit their fulfilment outside the monastery. The reference to the "house of the Lord" as the "temple" rather than the tabernacle is an understandable anachronism, especially since this interpretation is that of those who cited Hannah's vow in support of monastic vows.

[18] I.e., the Vulgate.

50:23]. Read the psalm itself and see how it really attacks the monasteries. Yet they quote it as though it were on their side.

Now They Come to the New Testament

First they quote Matthew 19 [:12], "There are eunuchs who have made themselves eunuchs."[19] First they have to prove that the people in the monasteries are those who have been made eunuchs.[20] It is not enough that they simply assert it. Why didn't Christ, the apostles, and many holy bishops and martyrs not move into monasteries and become monks? Or didn't they castrate themselves? It is unfortunately all too easy to prove—and if they are willing to admit it, they would certainly also agree—how the monasteries have been castrated! Would to God that they did what they boast of having done. No one would prevent them. It is however dangerous before God to pretend that something is true when there is no truth behind it. We are well aware that voluntary chastity is a precious thing. But at the same place it also says, "He who is able to receive this, let him receive it" [Matt. 19:12]. I find ten "castrated" and chaste people outside the monasteries without being able to find a single one in the monasteries. For the outside is so full of work, trouble, worry, and temptation[21] that one soon loses the itch and is daily compelled to pray. In the monasteries they sit idle and brood day and night over their evil thoughts; and then they think that a woolen cloth or shirt will make them chaste.

Living in a monastery is really a lazy, secure, and good life.[22] They however boast that they are chastising themselves. I have seen and tried it for myself, to a degree that almost no one else has. But just let them engage in productive and creative work as the people outside have to do, and they will find that the situation is quite different. The monasteries are full of good living and not holy life—one's skin prickles at the thought—and they try to cover this up by quoting the Scriptures.

---

[19] Cf. *LW* 44, 261.

[20] I.e., castrated.

[21] *Anfechtung.*

[22] Cf. *LW* 44, 357-358.

Second, Paul does not say in I Timothy 5 [:11-12] that young widows "become wanton" against their rule or vows but rather that they "become wanton against Christ." He himself explains this by saying that they "break the faith" which they once had in Christ. They deny Christ for the sake of their wantonness so that they can get married more easily. Once they believed in Christ, but now they again associate with the heathen and the Jews so that they can find the kind of men they are looking for. Satan tempts them and they stray after him, as Paul says here [I Tim. 5:15]. And it is impossible to interpret "Christ" and "faith" in this passage as though they meant monastic rules and vows.[23]

The last passages—which they quote so frequently—deal with "killing the flesh with its lusts" [Rom. 8:12-13; Col. 3:5-6]. It is good to do that. But it is not right for them to interpret such passages as though they referred to monasteries. Did not St. Paul write this to all Christians at a time when there were no monasteries, or are only those people who live in monasteries Christians? Would to God that they would do what these passages teach. In Romans 8 [:13], however, Paul says, "If by the Spirit you put to death the deeds of the body you will live." He does not say "by vows or rules" but "by the Spirit." The Spirit must do it. And they try to do it with rules and vows! The final result is just what it has been up until now: nowhere under heaven are the flesh and unchastity so terribly strengthened as in the monasteries. All that results in the full, lazy, secure life, and they wallow in it like pigs in filth.

"Killing the flesh" must first be accomplished through the Spirit in faith. Then a man becomes the enemy of his flesh and its lusts. Then come work, suffering, trouble, worry, and interrupted sleep; but he eats and drinks with confidence. That is the way that married people can do it, who never have any peace from their children or servants, and are never without work day or night. It is among such people that you will find those who believe and have killed their flesh. But the man who sits all alone in the corner of the monastery serves no one and is of no use at all. He simply hands himself over to the devil so that he can

_____
[23] Cf. LW 44, 396-397.

arouse all his evil lusts and make his thoughts worse than all the lusts of the world. To serve God is to serve one's neighbor as Christ and the apostles did—they did not isolate and hide themselves forever in monasteries.

To sum it up, *"Fac hoc et vives,"* "Do this, and you will live," Luke [10:28]. If they only did what they say they do! But since they do not do it, they also ought to stop bragging about it.

The Above Answer Is in Response to These Articles

Numbers 30

Moses said to the heads of the tribes of the people of Israel, "This is what the Lord has commanded. When a man vows a vow to the Lord, or swears an oath to bind himself by a pledge, he shall not break his word; he shall do according to all that proceeds out of his mouth" [Num. 30:1-2].

"Or when a woman in her youth vows a vow to the Lord and binds herself by a pledge while within her father's house and her father hears of her vow and of her pledge by which she has bound herself, and says nothing to her—then all her vows shall stand, and every pledge by which she has bound herself shall stand. But if her father expresses disapproval to her on the day that he hears of it, no vow of hers, no pledge by which she has bound herself, shall stand; and the Lord will forgive her, because her father opposed her" [Num. 30:3-5].

"And if she is married to a husband while under her vows, a thoughtless vow of her lips by which she has bound herself, and her husband hears of it, but says nothing to her on the day that he hears, then her vows shall stand, and her pledges by which she has bound herself shall stand. But if, on the day that her husband comes to hear of it, he expresses disapproval, then he shall void the vow which was on her, and the thoughtless utterance of her lips by which she bound herself; and the Lord will forgive her" [Num. 30:6-8].

"But any vow of a widow or of a divorced woman, anything by which she has bound herself, shall stand against her" [Num. 30:9].

"And if she vowed in her husband's house, or bound herself

by a pledge with an oath, and her husband heard of it, and said nothing to her, and did not oppose her, then all her vows shall stand, and every pledge by which she bound herself shall stand. But if her husband makes them null and void on the day that he hears them, then whatever proceeds out of her lips concerning her vows, or concerning her pledge of herself, shall not stand: her husband has made them void, and the Lord will forgive her. Any vow and any binding oath to afflict herself, her husband may establish or her husband may make void. But if her husband says nothing to her from day to day, then he establishes all the vows or all the pledges that are upon her; he has established them because he said nothing to her on the day that he heard of them. But if he makes them null and void after he has heard of them, then he shall bear her iniquity" [Num. 30:10-15].

"These are the statutes which the Lord gave Moses governing a man and his wife, and a father and his daughter while in her youth within her father's house" [Num. 30:16].

The Articles of Certain Monks and Scholars

It is written in Numbers 30 [:2], "When a man vows a vow to the Lord, or swears an oath to bind himself by a pledge, he shall not break his word."

It is written in Deuteronomy 23 [:21-23], "When you make a vow to the Lord your God, you shall not be slack to pay it; for the Lord your God will surely require it of you, and it would be sin in you. But if you refrain from vowing, it shall be no sin in you. You shall be careful to perform what has passed your lips, for you have voluntarily vowed to the Lord your God what you have promised with your mouth."

Solomon writes in Proverbs 20 [:25], "It is a snare for a man to desecrate holy things and then to retract his vows."[24]

It is written in Ecclesiastes 5 [:4-5], "When you vow a vow to God, do not delay paying it; for he has no pleasure in fools. Pay what you vow. It is better that you should not vow than that

---

[24] The passage is translated here according to Luther's version. Cf. p. 148. The RSV reads, "It is a snare for a man to say rashly, 'It is holy,' and to reflect only after making his vows."

you should vow and not pay." Psalm 48 [50:14] says, "Offer to God a sacrifice of thanksgiving, and pay your vows to the Most High."

Psalm 76 [:11], "Make your vows to the Lord your God, and perform them."

In Psalm 66 [:13-14] it is written, "I will pay thee my vows, that which my lips uttered."

Christ says in Matthew 19 [:12], "There are eunuchs who have made themselves eunuchs for the sake of the kingdom of heaven."

Paul says in I Timothy 5 [:11-12], "But refuse to enrol younger widows; for when they grow wanton against Christ they desire to marry, and so they incur condemnation for having violated their first pledge."[25]

Likewise, Hannah, the mother of Samuel, made a vow to God to sacrifice her son to God and give him to live his whole life in the temple, I Samuel 1 [:22-28].

Furthermore, the Scriptures admonish us to resist our flesh and our passions. Sirach 18 [:30] says, "Do not follow your base desires, but restrain your appetites."

Likewise, Romans 6 [:12-13, 19], "Let not sin therefore reign in your mortal bodies, to make you obey their passions. Do not yield your members to sin as instruments of wickedness, but yield yourselves to God as men who have been brought from death to life, and your members to God as instruments of righteousness," etc. "For just as you once yielded your members to impurity and to greater and greater iniquity, so now yield your members to righteousness for sanctification," etc.

Romans 8 [:12-13], "So then, brethren, we are debtors, not to the flesh, to live according to the flesh—for if you live according to the flesh you will die, but if by the Spirit you put to death the deeds of the body you will live."

Colossians 3 [:5-6], "Put to death therefore what is earthly in you: immorality, impurity, passion, evil desire, and covetousness, which is idolatry. On account of these the wrath of God is coming upon the children of unbelief.

In I Thessalonians 4 [:3-5] it is written, "For this is the will

---

[25] Cf. LW 44, 396-398.

of God, for your sanctification: that you abstain from immorality; that each one of you know how to take a wife for himself in holiness and honor, not in the passion of lust like heathen who do not know God."

Likewise I Timothy 6 [:10] tells us to learn to flee desire, which is the root of all evil. Furthermore, I John 2 [:15-17], "Do not love the world or the things in the world. If any one loves the world, love for the Father is not in him. For all that is in the world, the lust of the flesh and the lust of the eyes and the pride of life, is not of the Father but is of the world. And the world passes away, and the lust of it; but he who does the will of God abides forever."

ON WAR
AGAINST THE TURK

1529

Translated by Charles M. Jacobs
Revised by Robert C. Schultz

INTRODUCTION

For more than three quarters of a century the Ottoman Turks had cast a menacing shadow over Europe. Constantinople had fallen to them in 1453, and by the end of the fifteenth century they had consolidated their power up to the Danube River. To the east and south, Persia, Syria, and Egypt fell under Turkish sway. Under the rule of Suleiman the Magnificent (1520-1566) the Turks turned their attention once more toward Christian Europe. In 1520 they captured Belgrade. The following year Rhodes fell to the Muslims. Then in 1526 King Louis II of Hungary was killed and his troops soundly defeated in the Battle of Mohacs on the Danube.[1] This defeat sent a wave of terror over Europe. Only pressing domestic problems which demanded undivided and immediate attention prevented Suleiman from pursuing his advantage.[2]

The Turkish menace produced a varied and voluminous literature in the West, particularly during the years coinciding with Luther's work of reform. Dark and foreboding prophecies warning of the bloodshed, violence, and terror which the Turks brought found their way into print.[3] One group of writings called for resistance and crusades against the Turks.[4] Another group urged resignation to Turkish conquest and even praised Turkish rule. The authors of these tracts, pamphlets, and books argued that if Europeans did not resist, they would find that the Turks were gentle masters.[5] Following the Turkish victory at Mohacs the literature on the subject mushroomed as books with woodcut illustrations of

---

[1] Cf. p. 202, n. 1.

[2] Cf. Schwiebert, *Luther and His Times*, p. 63, and E. Harris Harbison, *The Age of Reformation* (Ithaca, New York: Cornell University Press, 1955), p. 26.

[3] Cf. WA 30$^\mathrm{II}$, 83.

[4] Typical of this group was a pamphlet entitled *A Call for a Crusade Against the Turks and All who Are Opposed to the Christian Faith* (*Das ist ein Anschlag eins zugs wider die Türcken und alle die wider den christlichen glauben sindt*), which was first published in 1518 and then republished in enlarged form in 1522 and addressed to all of Christendom. See WA 30$^\mathrm{II}$, 84.

[5] See WA 30$^\mathrm{II}$, 85. This point of view was refuted by other publications which related tales of Turkish atrocities and duplicity. The outstanding example of such refutation was the *Turkish Book* (*Türckenbiechlin*), published in 1522.

Turkish atrocities and books by statesmen, popular poets, and humanist thinkers[6] began to be published.

Luther was by no means uninvolved with the Turkish menace.[7] In his *Explanations of the Ninety-five Theses* (1518) Luther had made the statement that "to fight against the Turk is the same as resisting God, who visits our sin upon us with this rod."[8] Now that the Turks were once more on their way westward, Luther's words were recalled and he was held responsible both for the Turkish advance itself as well as for the unwillingness of many to resist the foe of Christendom.[9]

For some time Luther's friends had been urging him to write on the question of war against the Turks,[10] but it was not until 1528 that he actually did so. Even then he wrote not in reply to critics but out of pastoral concern for those who looked to him for guidance.

In 1526 in *Whether Soldiers, Too, Can Be Saved*[11] Luther indicated that he wanted to deal with the Turkish question, but the first hint that such a book was in the offing came in a letter to Nicholas Hausmann[12] dated August 5, 1528.[13] Apparently the actual writing began early in October, but by February, 1529, the book still had

---

[6] See WA 30[II], 86-87.

[7] Luther was certainly aware of, if not influenced by, the mass of literature about the Turks, especially Ulrich von Hutten's *Exhortation to the German Princes* (*Ad principes Germaniae ut bellum inuehant. Exhortatoria*) (1518). See WA 30[II], 91, and Eduard Böcking (ed.), *Ulrichi Hutteni Opera* (Leipzig, 1861). Cf. also in this volume, pp. 136-137.

[8] *LW* 31, 91-92.

[9] Typical of such charges is *Why the Turks Defeated the Hungarians* (*Ein Sendbrief darinn angetzeigt wird vermeinte ursach warumb der Tuerck widder die Hungern triumphirt un oblegen hab. Antwurt und verlegung obgemelter ursach, durch das rechtgeschaffen wort Gotes und was oder wo dasselbig seye einem jtzlichen Christen zuuoran zu disen getzeiten lustig und nutzlich zu lesen*) (1526). This book attributes the defeat of the king of Hungary at Mohacs to Luther's leading people from the true faith. WA 30[II], 92.

[10] Cf. p. 161.

[11] Cf. pp. 87-137.

[12] Hausmann (*ca.* 1478-1538) was a close friend of Luther. As pastor in Zwickau he bore the brunt of the activities of the "Zwickau prophets" and of the city council, which attempted to interfere in the affairs of the church. From 1532 to 1538 he was court chaplain to the dukes of Anhalt. He died in 1538 of a stroke suffered during his inaugural sermon at Freiberg.

[13] *WA*, Br 4, 511.

not appeared. On February 13, 1529, Luther wrote to Hausmann explaining that a number of manuscript pages had been lost and that it had been difficult for him to rewrite the missing sections.[14] The printing was completed by April 23.

In the present treatise Luther does not attempt to lay down a universally binding law or principle. He deals with a specific problem within the context of the moment.[15] At the very outset he defends the position he had taken in 1518[16] on the ground that what he had said then was still essentially true, but that the political circumstances attending his statement were different. Luther makes it clear that a war against the Turks cannot and must not be a crusade or religiously motivated and led by the church. Emphatically he states that it is not the business of church and clergy to promote and wage warfare.[17]

Luther's concern throughout the book is to teach men how to fight with a clear conscience.[18] In so doing he develops two major points. There are, he says, only two men who may properly fight the Turk. The first of these is the Christian, who by prayer, repentance, and reform of life takes the rod of anger out of God's hand and compels the Turk to stand on his own strength.[19] The second man who may wage war is the emperor. The Turk has wrongfully attacked the emperor's subjects, and by virtue of the office to which God has appointed him, the emperor is duty-bound to protect and defend the subjects with whose care God has entrusted him.[20]

The translation is a revision of that by Charles M. Jacobs in *PE* 5, 79-123, based on the German text, *Vom Kriege wider den Türken*, in *WA* 30ᴵᴵ, (81) 107-148.

R. C. S.

---

[14] *WA, Br* 5, 17-18.
[15] Cf. Heinz Zahrnt, *Luther deutet Geschichte* (München: Verlag Paul Müller, 1952), p. 119.
[16] Cf. p. 162.
[17] Cf. pp. 167-168.
[18] Cf. p. 169.
[19] Cf. p. 170.
[20] Cf. p. 184.

ON WAR
AGAINST THE TURK

To the serene, highborn prince and lord, Philip, landgrave of Hesse,[1] count of Katzenellenbogen, Ziegenhain, and Nidda, my gracious lord.

Grace and peace in Christ Jesus our Lord and Savior.

Serene, highborn prince, gracious lord, for the past five years certain persons have been begging me to write about war against the Turks, and to arouse and encourage our people. Now that the Turk is actually approaching,[2] even my friends are urging me to do this, especially since there are some stupid preachers among us Germans (as I am sorry to hear) who are making the people believe that we ought not and must not fight against the Turks. Some are even so foolish as to say that it is not proper for Christians to bear the temporal sword or to be rulers. Furthermore, some actually want the Turk to come and rule because they think our German people are wild and uncivilized—indeed, that they are half-devil and half-man. The blame for this wicked error among the people is laid on Luther and must be called "the fruit of my gospel," just as I am blamed for the rebellion,[3] and for every bad thing that happens anywhere in the world. My accusers know better, but—God and his word to the contrary—they pretend not to know better, and they seek occasion to speak evil of the Holy Ghost and of the truth that is openly confessed, so that they may earn the reward of hell and never repent or receive the forgiveness of their sins.

Therefore it is necessary for me to write about these things for my own sake and that of the gospel to defend ourselves; not be-

---

[1] Philip (1504-1567) had introduced the Reformation into his realm at an early date and was a leader of the Protestant rulers. His bigamous marriage in 1540, to which Luther had consented, was a severe blow to the Protestant cause.

[2] Cf. p. 157. The Turkish advance resumed the spring of 1529 when Suleiman the Magnificent began his march to Vienna.

[3] The Peasants' War of 1525.

cause of the blasphemers, however. I do not think they are worth my saying a single word to them in my defense, for to them the gospel must always be a stench and savor of death to death [II Cor. 2:16], as they have deserved by their wilful blasphemy. But I must write so that innocent consciences may no longer be deceived by these slanderers and made suspicious of me or my doctrine, and so they may not be deceived into believing that we must not fight against the Turks. I have thought it best to publish this little book under the name of Your Grace, a famous and powerful prince, so that it may be better received and more diligently read. Thus, if it came to a discussion of a crusade against the Turks, the princes and lords would readily recall it. Indeed, I am perfectly willing to point out several passages which ought to be thought about and emphasized. I commend Your Grace to the merciful grace and favor of our God; may he keep Your Grace against all error and against the craft of the devil, and enlighten and strengthen Your Grace for a blessed reign.

Your Grace's devoted,
MARTIN LUTHER

Wittenberg, October 9, 1528[4]

Pope Leo X in the bull in which he put me under the ban[5] condemned, among other statements, the following one, "To fight against the Turk is the same as resisting God, who visits our sin upon us with this rod."[6] This may be why they say that I oppose and dissuade from war against the Turk. I do not hesitate to admit that this article is mine and that I stated and defended it at the time; and if things in the world were in the same state now that they were in then, I would still have to hold and defend it. But it is not fair to forget what the situation was then and what my grounds and reasons were, and to take my words and apply them to another situation where those grounds and reasons do not exist. With this kind of skill who could not make the gospel a pack of lies or pretend that it contradicted itself?

[4] See pp. 158-159.
[5] The bull *Exsurge, Domine* was issued on June 15, 1520.
[6] See *Explanations of the Ninety-five Theses* (1518). LW 31, 91-92.

This was the state of things at that time: no one had taught, no one had heard, and no one knew anything about temporal government, whence it came, what its office and work were, or how it ought to serve God. The most learned men (I shall not name them) regarded temporal government as a heathen, human, ungodly thing, as though it jeopardized salvation to be in the ranks of the rulers. This is how the priests and monks drove kings and princes into the corner and persuaded them that to serve God they must undertake other works, such as hearing mass, saying prayers, endowing masses,[7] etc. In a word, princes and lords who wanted to be pious men regarded their rank and office as of no value and did not consider it a service of God. They became real priests and monks, except that they did not wear tonsures and cowls. If they wanted to serve God, they had to go to church. All the lords living at that time would have to testify to this, for they knew it by experience. My gracious lord, Duke Frederick,[8] of blessed memory, was so glad when I first wrote *Temporal Authority*[9] that he had the little book copied and put in a special binding, and was happy that he could see what his position was in God's sight.

And so it was that at that time the pope and the clergy were all in all and through all, like God in the world [Eph. 4:6], and the temporal rulers were in darkness, oppressed and unknown. But the pope and his crowd wanted to be Christians, too, and therefore they pretended to make war on the Turk. It was over those two points that the discussion arose, for I was then working on doctrine that concerned Christians and the conscience,[10] and had as yet written nothing about temporal rulers. The papists called me a flatterer of princes because I was dealing only with the spiritual class,[11] and not with the temporal; just as they call me seditious now that I have written in such glorification of temporal government as no teacher has done since the days of the apostles, except, perhaps, St. Augus-

---

[7] Endowed masses were generally said for the benefit of deceased persons who had made testamentary provision for them.

[8] Cf. p. 89, n. 1.

[9] *Temporal Authority: To What Extent It Should Be Obeyed* (1523). LW 45, 81-129.

[10] Luther is speaking of the general nature of his work, not of a specific writing.

[11] I.e., the clerical estate or clergy.

tine.[12] I can boast of this with a good conscience, and the testimony of the world will support me.

Among the points of Christian doctrine, I discussed what Christ says in Matthew [5:39-41], namely, that a Christian shall not resist evil, but endure all things, let the coat go and the cloak, let them be taken from him, turn the other cheek, etc. The pope with his universities and cloister schools had made a counsel of this, something which was not commanded and which a Christian need not keep; thus they perverted Christ's word, taught false doctrine throughout the world, and deceived Christians. But since they wanted to be Christians—indeed, the best Christians in the world— and yet fight against the Turk, endure no evil, and suffer neither compulsion nor wrong, I opposed them with these words of Christ that Christians shall not resist evil, but suffer all things and surrender all things. I based the article condemned by Pope Leo upon this. He was eager to condemn it because I took away the cloak covering the Roman knavery.

The popes had never seriously intended to wage war against the Turk; instead they used the Turkish war as a cover for their game[13] and robbed Germany of money by means of indulgences whenever they took the notion.[14] The whole world knew it, but now it is forgotten. So they condemned my article not because it opposed the Turkish war, but because it tore away this cloak and blocked the path along which the money went to Rome. If they had seriously wished to fight the Turk, the pope and the cardinals would have had enough from the pallia,[15] annates,[16] and other unmentionable sources of income so that they would not have needed to practice such extortion and robbery in Germany. If there had

---

[12] Luther is probably speaking in general terms, rather than of a specific writing.

[13] Thiele, *Luthers Sprichwörtersammlung*, No. 88.

[14] Luther had dealt with this point at some length in *To the Christian Nobility* (1520). *LW* 44, 144.

[15] The pallium, or woolen shoulder cape, is the emblem of the archepiscopal office. It had to be secured from Rome. Luther charged that the pallium (and the office it symbolized) was for sale at exorbitant prices. Cf. *LW* 44, 148-149.

[16] Originally the annates were the income received by a bishop from vacant benefices in his diocese. The right to this income was subsequently claimed by the papacy. Cf. *LW* 44, 146-148.

been a general opinion that a serious war was at hand, I could have polished my article somewhat more and made some distinctions.

Nor did I like it that the Christians and the princes were driven, urged, and irritated into attacking the Turk, and making war on him, before they amended their own ways and lived as true Christians. These two points, or either one by itself, were enough reason to dissuade from war. I shall never advise a heathen or a Turk, let alone a Christian, to attack another or begin war. That is nothing else than advising bloodshed and destruction, and it brings no good fortune in the end, as I have written in the book *Whether Soldiers, Too, Can Be Saved;*[17] and it never does any good when one rascal punishes another[18] without first becoming good himself.

But what motivated me most of all was this: They undertook to fight against the Turk in the name of Christ, and taught and incited men to do this, as though our people were an army of Christians against the Turks, who were enemies of Christ. This is absolutely contrary to Christ's doctrine and name. It is against his doctrine because he says that Christians shall not resist evil, fight, or quarrel, nor take revenge or insist on rights [Matt. 5:39]. It is against his name because there are scarcely five Christians in such an army, and perhaps there are worse people in the eyes of God in that army than are the Turks; and yet they all want to bear the name of Christ. This is the greatest of all sins and is one that no Turk commits, for Christ's name is used for sin and shame and thus dishonored. This would be especially so if the pope and the bishops were involved in the war, for they would bring the greatest shame and dishonor to Christ's name because they are called to fight against the devil with the word of God and with prayer, and they would be deserting their calling and office to fight with the sword against flesh and blood. They are not commanded to do this; it is forbidden.

O how gladly Christ would receive me at the Last Judgment if, when summoned to the spiritual office to preach and care for souls, I had left it and busied myself with fighting and with the temporal sword! Why should Christ or his people have anything to do with

17 Cf. pp. 93-137.
18 Cf. p. 41, n. 53.

the sword and going to war, and kill men's bodies, when he declared that he has come to save the world, not to kill people [John 3:17]? His work is to deal with the gospel and to redeem men from sin and death by his Spirit to help them from this world to everlasting life. According to John 6 [:15] he fled and would not let himself be made king; before Pilate he confessed, "My kingship is not of this world" [John 18:36]; and in the garden he bade Peter to put up his sword and said, "All who take the sword will perish by the sword" [Matt. 26:52].

I say this not because I would teach that worldly rulers ought not be Christians, or that a Christian cannot bear the sword and serve God in temporal government. Would to God they were all Christians, or that no one could be a prince unless he were a Christian! Things would be better than they now are, and the Turk would not be so powerful. But what I want to do is to keep a distinction between the callings and offices, so that everyone can see to what God has called him and fulfil the duties of his office faithfully and sincerely in the service of God. I have written more than enough about this elsewhere, especially in the books *Whether Soldiers, Too, Can Be Saved*[19] and *Temporal Authority*.[20] In the church, where all should be Christians, Paul will not permit one person to assume another's office, Romans 12 [:4] and I Corinthians 12 [:14-26], but exhorts every member to do his own work so that there be no disorder, rather, that everything be done in an orderly way [I Cor. 14:40]. How much less, then, are we to tolerate the disorder that arises when a Christian abandons his office and assumes a temporal office, or when a bishop or pastor gives up his office and assumes the office of a prince or judge; or, on the other hand, when a prince takes up the office of a bishop and gives up his princely office? Even today this shameful disorder rages and rules in the whole papacy, contrary to their own canons and laws.

Experience shows how well we have succeeded with the Turkish war up to now, though we have fought as Christians until we have lost Rhodes;[21] almost all of Hungary, and much German soil

---

[19] Cf. pp. 87-137.
[20] Cf. *LW* 45, 81-129.
[21] The Isle of Rhodes had fallen to the Turks in December, 1521.

besides.[22] And to show us clearly that he is not with us in our war against the Turks, God has never put much courage or spirit into the minds of our princes to be able to deal seriously with the Turkish war even once. Though many of the diets,[23] almost all of them in fact, have been called and held on this account, the matter will neither be settled nor arranged, and it seems as though God were mocking our diets and letting the devil hinder them and get the better of them until the Turk comes ravaging on at his leisure and ruins Germany without effort or resistance. Why does this happen? Because my article,[24] which Pope Leo condemned, remains uncondemned[25] and valid. And because the papists reject it, arbitrarily and without Scripture, the Turk must take its side and prove its validity with fist and deeds. If we will not learn from the Scriptures, we must learn from the Turk's scabbard, until we learn from dreadful experience that Christians should not make war or resist evil. Fools should be beaten with rods.[26]

How many wars, do you think, have there been against the Turk in which we would not have suffered heavy losses if the bishops and clergy had not been there? How pitifully the fine king Lassla was beaten with his bishops by the Turk at Varna.[27] The Hungarians themselves blamed Cardinal Julian and killed him for it.[28] Recently King Louis[29] would perhaps have fought with more success if he had not lead a priests' army or, as they call it, a Christian army, against the Turks. If I were emperor, king, or prince and were in a campaign against the Turk, I would exhort my bishops and priests to stay at home and attend to the duties of their office, praying, fasting, saying mass, preaching, and caring for the

---

[22] Cf. p. 157.

[23] The diets of Nürnberg (1523 and 1524) and of Spires (1526 and 1529) discussed the Turkish war at length.

[24] Cf. p. 158, n. 8.

[25] So far as Luther is concerned, the article is not condemned by God.

[26] Cf. p. 65, n. 11.

[27] Ladislaus III, king of Poland and Hungary, was killed along with the bishops of Erlau and Grosswardein in the battle of Varna, November 10, 1444.

[28] Julian (Giuliano) Caesarini, papal legate in Hungary who had preached the crusade, was present at Varna and was murdered during the retreat which followed the battle.

[29] Louis II, king of Bohemia and Hungary, fell during the battle of Mohacs, August 29, 1526.

poor, as not only Holy Scripture, but their own canon law teaches and requires. If, however, they were to be disobedient to God and their own law and desire to go along to war, I would teach them by force to attend to their office and not, by their disobedience, put me and my army under the danger of God's wrath. It would be less harmful to have three devils in the army than one disobedient, apostate bishop who had given up his office and assumed the office of another. For there can be no good fortune with such people around, who go against God and their own law.

I have heard from fine soldiers who thought that the king of France,[30] when he was defeated and captured by the emperor before Pavia, had all of his bad fortune because he had the pope's, or, as they boastfully call them, the church's army with him. After they came to his camp with a great cry of "*Ecclesia, ecclesia!* Here is the church! Here is the church!" there was no more good fortune there. This is what the soldiers say, though perhaps they do not know the reason for it, namely, that it is not right for the pope, who wants to be a Christian, and the highest and best Christian preacher at that, to lead a church army, or army of Christians, for the church ought not to strive or fight with the sword. It has other enemies than flesh and blood; their name is the wicked devils in the air [Eph. 6:12]; therefore the church has other weapons and swords and other wars; it has enough to do and cannot get involved in the wars of the emperor or princes, for the Scriptures say that there shall be no good fortune where men are disobedient to God.[31]

And, too, if I were a soldier and saw a priest's banner in the field, or a banner of the cross, even though it was a crucifix, I should run as though the devil were chasing me; and even if they won a victory, by God's decree, I should not take any part in the booty or the rejoicing. Even the wicked iron-eater,[32] Pope Julius,[33] who was half-devil, did not succeed, but finally had to call on Emperor Maximilian and let him take charge of the game, despite the

---

[30] Cf. p. 90, n. 8.

[31] Cf. I Sam. 12:15.

[32] Cf. p. 101, n. 72.

[33] Julius II (1503-1513).

fact that Julius had more money, arms, and people. I think, too, that this present pope, Clement,[84] who people think is almost a god of war, succeeded well with his fighting until he lost Rome and all its wealth to a few ill-armed soldiers. The conclusion is this: Christ will teach them to understand my article that Christians shall not make war, and the condemned article must take its revenge,[85] for it refers to Christians and will stand uncondemned. It is right and true, although they do not care and do not believe it, but hardened and unrepentant rush headlong to destruction. To this I say Amen, Amen.

It is true, indeed, that since they have temporal lordship and wealth, they ought to make the same contributions to the emperor, kings, or princes that other possessors of holdings properly make, and render the same services that others are expected to render. Indeed, these "goods of the church," as they call them, ought to be used especially and first of all to serve and help in the protection of the needy and the welfare of all classes, for that is the purpose for which they were given, not for a bishop to give up his office and use these goods for war or battle. If the banner of Emperor Charles or of a prince is in the field, then let everyone run boldly and gladly to the banner to which his allegiance is sworn—more on this will be said later. But if the banner of a bishop, cardinal, or pope is there, then run the other way, and say, "I do not know this coin;[86] if it were a prayer book, or the Holy Scriptures preached in the church, I would rally to it."

Now before I exhort or urge war against the Turk, hear me, for God's sake. I want first to teach you how to fight with a good conscience. For although (if I wanted to give way to the old Adam) I could keep quiet and look on while the Turk avenged me upon the tyrants (who persecute the gospel and blame me for all kinds of misfortune) and paid them back for it, nevertheless, I shall not do this, but rather, shall serve both friends and enemies so that my sun may rise on both bad and good, and my rain fall on the thankful and unthankful [Matt. 5:45].

---

[84] Clement VII (1523-1534).

[85] Cf. p. 158, n. 8.

[86] Cf. Wander (ed.), *Deutsches Sprichwörter Lexikon*, III, "Münzen," No. 39.

In the first place, the Turk certainly has no right or command to begin war and to attack lands that are not his. Therefore his war is nothing but an outrage and robbery with which God is punishing the world, as he often does through wicked scoundrels, and sometimes through godly people. The Turk does not fight from necessity or to protect his land in peace, as the right kind of a ruler does; but, like a pirate or highwayman, he seeks to rob and ravage other lands which do and have done nothing to him. He is God's rod and the devil's servant [Isa. 10:5]; there is no doubt about that.

In the second place, we must know who the man is who is to make war against the Turk so that he may be certain that he has a commission from God and is doing right. He must not plunge in to avenge himself or have some other mad notion or reason. He must be sure of this so that, win or lose, he may be in a state of salvation and in a godly occupation. There are two of these men, and there ought to be only two: the one is named Christian,[37] the other, Emperor Charles.

Christian should be there first, with his army. Since the Turk is the rod of the wrath of the Lord our God and the servant of the raging devil, the first thing to be done is to smite the devil, his lord, and take the rod out of God's hand, so that the Turk may be found only, in his own strength, all by himself, without the devil's help and without God's hand. This should be done by Sir Christian, that is, by the pious, holy, precious body of Christians. They are the people who have the arms for this war and they know how to use them. If the Turk's god, the devil, is not beaten first, there is reason to fear that the Turk will not be so easy to beat. Now the devil is a spirit who cannot be beaten with armor, muskets, horses, and men, and God's wrath cannot be allayed by them, as it is written in Psalm 33 [147:10], "His delight is not in the strength of the horse, nor his pleasure in the legs of a man; but the Lord takes pleasure in those who fear him, in those who hope in his steadfast love." Christian weapons and power must do it.

Here you ask, "Who are the Christians and where does one find them?" Answer: There are not many of them, but they are everywhere, though they are spread thin and live far apart, under

---

[37] The name personifies Christian believers.

good and bad princes. Christendom must continue to the end, as the article of the creed says, "I believe one holy Christian church." So it must be possible to find them. Every pastor and preacher ought diligently to exhort his people to repentance and to prayer. They ought to drive men to repentance by showing our great and numberless sins and our ingratitude, by which we have earned God's wrath and disfavor, so that he justly gives us into the hands of the devil and the Turk. And so that this preaching may work the more strongly, they ought to cite examples and sayings from the Scriptures, such as the Flood [Gen. 7:1-24], Sodom and Gomorrah [Gen. 19:24-28], and the children of Israel, and show how cruelly and how often God punished the world and its lands and peoples. And they ought to make it plain that it is no wonder, since we sin more grievously than they did, if we are punished worse than they.

This fight must be begun with repentance, and we must reform our lives, or we shall fight in vain; as the prophet Jeremiah says in chapter 18 [:7-8], "If at anytime I declare concerning a nation or a kingdom that I will pluck up and break down and destroy it, and if that nation concerning which I have spoken turns from its evil, I will repent of the evil that I intended to do it." And again, "And if at any time I declare concerning a nation or a kingdom that I will build and plant it, and if it does evil in my sight, not listening to my voice, then I will repent of the good which I had intended to do it. Now, therefore, say to the men of Judah and to the inhabitants of Jerusalem, Behold I am shaping evil against you and devising a plan against you. Return, every one of you and amend your ways and your doings" [Jer. 18:9-11]. We may apply these words to ourselves, for God is devising evil against us because of our wickedness and is certainly preparing the Turk against us, as he says in Psalm 7 [:12-13], "If a man does not repent, God will whet his sword; he has bent and strung his bow; he has prepared his deadly weapons."

Along with these must be cited the words and illustrations of Scripture in which God makes known how well pleased he is with true repentance or amendment made in faith and reliance on his word—such as the examples of kings David,[38] Ahab,[39] and Manasseh[40] in the Old Testament, and the like; in the New Testament, of St. Peter,[41] the malefactor,[42] the publican in the Gospel,[43] and so forth. Although I know that to the scholars and saints who need no repentance this advice of mine will be laughable for they will consider it a simple and common thing which they have long since passed beyond, nevertheless, I have not been willing to omit it for the sake of myself and of sinners like myself, who need both repentance and exhortation to repentance every day. In spite of it, we remain all too lazy and lax, and have not, with those ninety and nine just persons,[44] got so far as they let themselves think they have.[45]

After people have thus been taught and exhorted to confess their sin and amend their ways they should then be most diligently exhorted to prayer and shown that such prayer pleases God, that he has commanded it and promised to hear it, and that no one ought to think lightly of his own praying or have doubts about it, but with firm faith be sure that it will be heard; all of which has been published by us in many tracts.[46] The man who doubts, or prays for good luck, would do better to let prayer alone because such prayer is merely tempting God and only makes things worse. Therefore I would advise against processions,[47] which are a heathenish and useless practice, for they are more pomp and show than prayer. I say the same thing about celebrating a lot of masses and calling upon the saints. It might, indeed, be of some use to have the people, especially the young people, sing the Litany at mass or vespers or in the church after the sermon, pro-

---

[38] II Sam. 24:10.

[39] I Kings 21:27-29.

[40] II Chron. 33:10-13.

[41] Cf. Mark 14:72; John 21:15-19.

[42] Luke 23:40-42.

[43] Luke 18:10-14.

[44] Luke 15:7.

[45] Wander (ed.), *Deutsches Sprichwörter Lexikon*, I, "Berg," Nos. 29, 65, 104, 109, 113.

[46] Cf. *WA*, 2, 57-65.

[47] Processions were regarded as especially solemn forms of prayer.

vided that everyone, even at home by himself, constantly raised to Christ at least a sigh of the heart for grace to lead a better life and for help against the Turk. I am not speaking of much and long praying, but of frequent brief sighs, in one or two words, such as, "O help us, dear God the Father; have mercy on us, dear Lord Jesus Christ!" or the like.

See, now, this kind of preaching will hit home with Christians and find them out, and there will be Christians who will accept it and act according to it; it does not matter if you do not know who they are. The tyrants and bishops may also be exhorted to stop their raging and persecution against the word of God and not to hinder our prayer; but if they do not stop, we must not cease to pray, but keep on and take the chance that they will have the benefit of our prayer and be preserved along with us, or that we shall pay for their raging and be ruined along with them. They are so perverse and blind that if God gave them good fortune against the Turk they would ascribe it to their holiness and merit and boast of it against us. On the other hand, if things turned out bad, they would ascribe it to no one but us, and lay the blame on us, disregarding the shameful, openly sinful, and wicked lives which they not only lead, but defend; for they cannot teach rightly a single point about the way to pray, and they are worse than the Turks. Oh, well, we must leave that to God's judgment.

In exhorting to prayer we must also introduce words and examples from the Scriptures which show how strong and mighty a man's prayer has sometimes been; for example, Elijah's prayer, which St. James praises [Jas. 5:17]; the prayers of Elisha[48] and other prophets; of kings David,[49] Solomon,[50] Asa,[51] Jehoshaphat,[52] Jesias,[53] Hezekiah,[54] etc.; the story of how God promised Abraham that he would spare the land of Sodom and Gomorrah for

---

[48] Perhaps Luther had in mind passages such as II Kings 4:1-7.
[49] Cf. II Sam. 24:10.
[50] Cf. I Kings 3:6-10.
[51] II Chron. 14:11-12.
[52] II Chron. 20:5-12.
[53] Perhaps Luther meant Josiah or Joash. Cf. II Chron. 34:33 and 24:2.
[54] II Kings 19:14-19.

the sake of five righteous men.[55] For the prayer of a righteous man can do much if it be persistent, St. James says in his Epistle [Jas. 5:16]. They are also to be warned to be careful not to anger God by not praying and not to fall under his judgment in Ezekiel 13 [:5], where God says, "You have not gone up into the breaches or built up a wall for the house of Israel, that it might stand in battle in the day of the Lord"; and in chapter 22 [:30-31], "I sought for a man among them who should build up the wall and stand in the breach before me for the land, that I should not destroy it; but I found none. Therefore I have poured out my indignation upon them; I have consumed them with the fire of my wrath; their way have I requited upon their heads, says the Lord God."

It is easy to see from this that God would have men set themselves in the way of his wrath and stave it off, and that he is greatly angered if this is not done. That is what I meant when I spoke above about taking the rod out of God's hand.[56] Let him fast who will. Let him go down on his knees and bow and fall to the ground if he is in earnest, for the bowing and kneeling that has been practiced up to now in the chapters and monasteries was not in earnest; it was, and still is, sheer nonsense. It is not for nothing that I exhort pastors and preachers to impress this upon the people, for I see plainly that it rests entirely with the preachers whether the people shall amend their ways and pray or not. Little will be accomplished by preaching in which men call Luther names and blaspheme, and do not touch upon repentance and prayer; but where God's word is spoken, it is not without fruit [Isa. 55:11]. They, however, must preach as though they were preaching to saints who had learned all that there was to know about repentance and faith, and they, therefore, have to talk about something higher.

The great need of our time should have moved us to this prayer against the Turk, for the Turk, as has been said, is the servant of the devil,[57] who not only devastates land and people with the sword, as we shall hear later, but also lays waste the

---

[55] Gen. 18:22-32.

[56] Cf. p. 170.

[57] Cf. p. 170.

Christian faith and our dear Lord Jesus Christ. For although some praise the Turk's government because he allows everyone to believe what he will so long as he remains the temporal lord, yet this reputation is not true, for he does not allow Christians to come together in public, and no one can openly confess Christ or preach or teach against Mohammed. What kind of freedom of belief is it when no one is allowed to preach or confess Christ, and yet our salvation depends on that confession, as Paul says in Romans 10 [:9], "To confess with the lips saves," and Christ has strictly commanded us to confess and teach his gospel.[58]

Since, therefore, faith must be stilled and held in secret among this wild and barbarous people and under this severe rule, how can it exist or remain alive in the long run, when it requires so much effort and labor in places where it is preached most faithfully and diligently?[59] Therefore it happens, and must happen, that those Christians who are captured or otherwise get into Turkey fall away and become altogether Turkish, and it is very seldom that one remains true to his faith, for they lack the living bread[60] of the soul and see the abandoned and carnal life of the Turks and are obliged to adapt themselves to it.

How can one injure Christ more than with these two things, namely, force and wiles? With force they prevent preaching and suppress the word. With wiles they put wicked and dangerous examples before men's eyes every day and draw men to them. So in order not to lose our Lord Jesus Christ, his word and faith, we must pray against the Turks as against other enemies of our salvation and of all good, indeed, as we pray against the devil himself.

In this connection the people should be told about the Turk's dissolute life and ways so that they may the better feel the need of prayer. To be sure, it has often disgusted me, and still does,

---

[58] Matt. 10:32. Christians under Turkish rule were not permitted to organize congregations. The use of bells was prohibited and conversion to Christianity was punishable by death. *BG* 7, 454, n. 2.

[59] Luther devoted the last part of his 1529 *Army Sermon Against the Turk* (*Heerpredigt wider den Türken*) to prisoners and other Christians in this situation. Cf. *WA* 30ᴵᴵ, 160-197.

[60] Cf. John 6:35.

that neither our great lords nor our scholars have taken any pains to give us any certain knowledge about the life of the Turks in the two estates, spiritual and temporal; and yet the Turk has come so near to us.[61] It is said that the Turks, too, have chapters and monasteries. Some, indeed, have invented outrageous lies about the Turks to incite us Germans against them, but there is no need for lies; there is enough truth. I will tell my dear Christians a few things, so far as I know the real truth, so that they may the better be moved and stirred to pray earnestly against the enemy of Christ our Lord.

I have some parts of Mohammed's Koran which in German might be called a book of sermons or doctrines of the kind that we call pope's decretals. When I have time I must translate it into German so that everyone may see what a foul and shameful book it is.[62]

In the first place, he greatly praises Christ and Mary as being the only ones without sin, and yet he believes nothing more of Christ than that he is a holy prophet, like Jeremiah or Jonah, and denies that he is God's Son and true God. Furthermore, he does not believe that Christ is the Savior of the world who died for our sins, but that he preached to his own time and completed his work before his death, just like any other prophet.

On the other hand, Mohammed highly exalts and praises himself and boasts that he has talked with God and the angels, and that since Christ's office of prophet is now complete, he has been commanded to bring the world to his faith, and if the world is not willing, to compel it or punish it with the sword; there is much glorification of the sword in it. Therefore the Turks think that their

---

[61] Cf. p. 157.

[62] In 1542 Luther published *Brother Richard's Refutation of the Koran, Translated into German by Dr. M. Luther* (*Widerlegung des Alkoran Bruder Richardi; verdeutscht durch Dr. M. Luther*) (WA 53, [261] 271-396). In the preface Luther expressed amazement that the Koran had not been translated into Latin. He went on to say that as recently as Shrove Tuesday 1542 he had seen such a translation for the first time, but that it was a very poor one. Later that year a new Latin version was published in Basel, but it was banned by the magistrate. Luther urged the lifting of this ban. Cf. Köstlin, *Martin Luther*, II, 603.

Mohammed is much higher and greater than Christ, for the office of Christ has come to an end and Mohammed's office is still in force.

From this anyone can easily see that Mohammed is a destroyer of our Lord Christ and his kingdom, and if anyone denies the articles concerning Christ, that he is God's Son, that he died for us and still lives and reigns at the right hand of God, what has he left of Christ? Father, Son, Holy Ghost, baptism, the sacrament, gospel, faith, and all Christian doctrine and life are gone, and instead of Christ only Mohammed with his doctrine of works and especially of the sword is left. That is the chief doctrine of the Turkish faith in which all abominations, all errors, all devils are piled up in one heap.

And yet the world acts as though it were snowing[63] pupils of the Turkish faith, for it is extraordinarily pleasing to reason that Christ is not God, as the Jews, too, believe, and especially is reason pleased with the thought that men are to rule and bear the sword and get ahead in the world. The devil is behind that. Thus the Turk's faith is a patchwork of Jewish, Christian, and heathen beliefs. He gets his praise of Christ, Mary, the apostles, and other saints from the Christians. From the Jews he gets abstinence from wine and fasting at certain times of the year, washing like the Nazirites [Num. 6:1-21], and eating off the ground. And the Turks perform the same holy works as some of our monks and hope for everlasting life at the Judgment Day, for, holy people that they are, they believe in the resurrection of the dead, though few of the papists believe in it.[64]

What pious Christian heart would not be horrified at this enemy of Christ when he sees that the Turk allows no article of our faith to stand, except the single one about the resurrection of the dead? Then Christ is no redeemer, savior, or king; there is no forgiveness of sins, no grace, no Holy Ghost. Why should I say

---

[63] Cf. Thiele, *Luthers Sprichwörtersammlung*, No. 71.

[64] See the text of the decree affirming the immortality of the soul, *Apostolici regiminis*, adopted by the Fifth Lateran Council (December 19, 1513) in H. J. Schroeder, *Disciplinary Decrees of the General Councils* (St. Louis: B. Herder Book Co., 1937), pp. 487-488 (English) and pp. 630-631 (Latin).

more? In the article that Christ is beneath Mohammed, and less than he, everything is destroyed. Who would not rather be dead than live under such a government, where he must say nothing about his Christ, and hear and see such blasphemy and abomination against him? Yet this article takes such a powerful hold when the Turk wins a land that people even submit to it willingly. Therefore let everyone pray who can that this abomination not become lord over us and that we not be punished with this terrible rod of God's anger.

In the second place, the Turk's Koran or creed teaches him to destroy not only the Christian faith, but also the whole temporal government. His Mohammed, as has been said, commands that ruling is to be done by the sword, and in his Koran the sword is the commonest and noblest work. Thus the Turk is really nothing but a murderer or highwayman, as his deeds show before men's eyes. St. Augustine[65] calls other kingdoms, too, a great robbery; Psalm 76 [:4] also calls them "the mountains of prey" because an empire seldom has come into being except by robbery, force, and wrong; or, at the very least, it is often seized and possessed by wicked people without any justice, so that the Scriptures, in Genesis 10 [:9], call the first prince upon earth, Nimrod, a mighty hunter. But never has any kingdom come into being and become so mighty through murder and robbery as that of the Turk; and he murders and robs every day, for robbing and murdering, devouring and destroying more and more of those that are around them, is commanded in their law as a good and divine work; and they do this and think that they are doing God a service. Their government, therefore, is not a godly, regular rulership, like others, for the maintenance of peace, the protection of the good, and the punishment of the wicked, but a rod of anger and a punishment of God upon the unbelieving world, as has been said. The work of murdering and robbing pleases the flesh in any case because it enables men to gain high place and to subject everyone's life and goods to themselves. How much more must the flesh be pleased when this is a commandment, as though God would have it so and is well pleased by it! So it is among the

---

[65] *The City of God* (*De civitate dei*), IV, 4, 6.

Turks that the most highly regarded are those who are diligent to increase the Turkish kingdom and constantly murder and rob those around them.

This second thing must follow from the first,[66] for Christ says in John 8 [:44] that the devil is a liar and murderer. With lies he kills souls and with murder he kills bodies. If he wins with a lie, he does not take a holiday and delay; he follows it up with murder. Thus when the spirit of lies had taken possession of Mohammed, and the devil had murdered men's souls with his Koran and had destroyed the faith of Christians, he had to go on and take the sword and set about to murder their bodies. The Turkish faith, then, has not made its progress by preaching and the working of miracles, but by the sword and by murder, and its success has been due to God's wrath, which ordered that since all the world has a desire for the sword, robbery, and murder, one should come who would give it enough of murder and robbery. As a rule, fanatics, when the spirit of lies has taken possession of them and led them away from the true faith, have not been able to stop there, but have followed the lie with murder and taken up the sword, as a sign that they were children of the father of all lies and murder. Thus we read how the Arians[67] became murderers and how one of the greatest bishops of Alexandria, Lucius by name, drove the orthodox out of the city, and went into the ship and held a naked sword in his own hand until the orthodox were all on board and had to go away.[68] And these tender, holy bishops committed many other murders even at that time, which is almost twelve hundred years ago. Again, in St. Augustine's time, almost eleven hundred years ago, the holy father abundantly shows in his books how many murders the Donatists committed.[69] In such an utterly worldly way did the clergy conduct

---

[66] I.e., the murdering and robbing comes from Turkish doctrine.

[67] The Arians, followers of Arius (ca. 250-336), maintained that the Son was not divine by nature, but was a creature. The issue caused widespread controversy in the early church but despite condemnation of this doctrine by the Council of Nicaea (325), Arianism persisted—particularly among Germanic tribes—until the early sixth century.

[68] These events took place in 374 during the reign of the Arian emperor Valens. The orthodox bishop was Peter.

[69] Cf. Augustine, *Against Gandentius* (*Contra Gandentium*), I, 22. MPL 43, 720.

themselves! They had only the name and guise of bishops among the Christians; but because they had fallen away from the truth and become subject to the spirit of lies, they had to go forward in his service and become wolves and murderers. What was Münzer[70] seeking in our own times, but to become a new Turkish emperor? He was possessed by the spirit of lies and therefore there was no holding him back; he had to take on the other work of the devil, take the sword and murder and rob, as the spirit of murder drove him, and he created a rebellion and such misery.

And what shall I say of the most holy father, the pope? Is it not true that he and his bishops have become worldly lords, and, led by the spirit of lies, have fallen away from the gospel and embraced their own human doctrine, and thus have committed murder down to the present hour? Read the histories and you find that the principal business of popes and bishops has been to set emperors, kings, princes, lands, and people against one another, and they themselves have fought and helped in the work of murder and bloodshed. Why? Because the spirit of lies never acts any other way. After he has made his disciples teachers of lies and deceivers, he has no rest until he makes them murderers, robbers, and bloodhounds. Now who has commanded them to bear the sword, to wage war, and to incite and arouse men to murder and war, when their duty was to attend to preaching and prayer?

They call me and my followers seditious; but when have I ever coveted the sword or urged men to take it, and not rather taught and kept peace and obedience, except when I have instructed and exhorted the regular temporal rulers to do their duty and maintain peace and justice?[71] One knows the tree by its fruits [Matt. 7:16]. I and my followers keep and teach peace; the pope, along with his followers, wages war, commits murder, and robs not only his enemies, but he also burns, condemns, and persecutes the innocent, the pious, the orthodox, as a true Antichrist.[72] And he does this while sitting in the temple of God [II Thess. 2:4], as head of the church;

---

[70] Cf. p. 5, n. 3.
[71] Cf. p. 52.
[72] The term Antichrist is used to designate the prince of Christ's enemies. Cf. I John 2:18, 22; 4:3; II John 7. According to II Thess. 2:3-10 he would appear after great apostasy and set himself up in the sanctuary and claim to be God. Luther had long identified the papacy with the Antichrist.

the Turk does not do that. But just as the pope is the Antichrist, so the Turk is the very devil incarnate. The prayer of Christendom against both is that they shall go down to hell, even though it may take the Last Day to send them there; and I hope that day will not be far off.[73]

Summing up what has been said, where the spirit of lies is, there also is the spirit of murder, though it may not get to work or may be hindered. If it is hindered, it still laughs and is jubilant when murder is done, and at least consents to it, for it thinks murder is right. But good Christians do not rejoice over any murder, not even over the misfortunes of their enemies.[74] Since, then, Mohammed's Koran is such a great spirit of lies that it leaves almost nothing of Christian truth remaining, how could it have any other result than that it should become a great and mighty murderer, liar, and murderer under the appearance of truth and righteousness? Now just as lies destroy the spiritual order of faith and truth, so murder destroys all temporal order which has been instituted by God; for there can be no good, praiseworthy temporal government where murder and robbery are rampant. Because they cannot think more highly of peace than of war and murder or attend to the pursuits of peace, as one can see in soldiers,[75] the Turks do not regard the work of agriculture highly.

The third point is that Mohammed's Koran has no regard for marriage, but permits everyone to take wives as he will. It is customary among the Turks for one man to have ten or twenty wives and to desert or sell any whom he will, so that in Turkey women are held immeasurably cheap and are despised; they are bought and sold like cattle. Although there may be some few who do not take advantage of this law, nevertheless, this is the law and anyone who wants to can follow it. That kind of living is not and cannot be marriage, because none of them takes or has a wife with the intention of staying with her forever, as though the two were one body, as God's word says in Genesis 3 [2:24], "Therefore a man cleaves to his wife and they become one flesh." Thus the marriage of the Turks closely resembles the chaste life soldiers lead with their

---

[73] Cf. p. 18, n. 3.
[74] See Luther's comments in WA 15, 71-72.
[75] Cf. pp. 134-135.

harlots; for the Turks are soldiers and must act like soldiers; Mars and Venus, say the poets, must be together.[76]

These are the three points I wanted to mention. I am sure of them from the Koran of the Turks. I will not bring up what I have heard besides because I cannot be sure about it. Suppose, then, that there are some Christians among the Turks. Suppose that some of them are monks. Suppose that some are honorable laymen. Now supposing all this, what good can there be in the government and the whole Turkish way of life when according to their Koran these three things rule among them, namely, lying, murder, and disregard of marriage, besides the fact that everyone must be silent about Christian truth and dare not rebuke or try to reform these three points, but must look on and consent to them (as I fear), at least to the point of keeping silent? What could be a more horrible, dangerous, terrible imprisonment than life under such a government? As I said, lies destroy the spiritual estate; murder, the temporal; disregard of marriage, the estate of matrimony. Now if you take out of the world *veram religionem, veram politiam, veram oeconomiam,* that is, true spiritual life, true temporal government, and true home life, what is left in the world but flesh, world, and devil? It is like the life of the "good fellows" who live with harlots.

It is said that among themselves the Turks are faithful, friendly, and careful to tell the truth. I believe that and I think that they probably have more fine virtues in them than that. No man is so bad that there is not something good in him. Now and then a woman of the streets has more good qualities than do ten honorable matrons. The devil would have a cloak and be a handsome angel of light, so he hides behind certain works that are works of light. Murderers and robbers are more faithful and friendly to each other than neighbors are, even more so than many Christians. For if the devil keeps the three things—lies, murder, and disregard of marriage—as the real foundation of hell, he can easily tolerate, even help, carnal love and faithfulness being built upon it, as though they were precious gems (though they are nothing but hay and straw), though he knows well that nothing will remain of them in case of fire.[77] On the other

---

[76] Mars was the classical god of war; Venus, the goddess of love. Luther may have had in mind Ovid's *Tristia,* II, 295-298.

[77] Cf. I Cor. 3:11-15.

hand, where there is true faith, true government, true marriage, he strives earnestly to keep a little love and fidelity from appearing and being shown so that he can put the foundation to shame and have it despised.

What is more, when the Turks go into battle their only war cry is "Allah! Allah!" and they shout it till heaven and earth resound. But in the Arabic language[78] Allah means God, and is a corruption of the Hebrew *Eloha*. For they have been taught in the Koran that they shall boast constantly with these words, "There is no God but God." All that is really a device of the devil. For what does it mean to say, "There is no God but God," without distinguishing one God from another? The devil, too, is a god, and they honor him with this word; there is no doubt of that. In just the same way the pope's soldiers cry, *"Ecclesia! Ecclesia!"*[79] To be sure, the devil's *ecclesia!* Therefore I believe that the Turks' Allah does more in war than they themselves. He gives them courage and wiles; he guides sword and fist, horse and man. What do you think, then, of the holy people who can call upon God in battle, and yet destroy Christ and all God's words and works, as you have heard?

It is also part of the Turks' holiness to tolerate no images or pictures, and they are even holier than are our iconoclasts.[80] For our iconoclasts tolerate and are glad to have images on gulden, groschen, rings, and ornaments; but the Turk tolerates none of them and stamps nothing but letters on his coins. He is entirely Münzerian,[81] too, for he exterminates all rulers and tolerates no gradations of government such as princes, counts, lords, nobles, and others. He alone is lord over all in his own land, and what he gives out is only pay, never property or rights of rulership.[82] He is also a papist, for

---

[78] Luther was aware that Arabic was not the language of the Turks. Cf. WA 30[II], 128, n. 2.

[79] Cf. p. 168.

[80] Cf. *Against the Heavenly Prophets in the Matter of Images and Sacraments* (1525). LW 40, 74-223.

[81] Cf. p. 5, n. 3.

[82] Cf. pp. 127-128. The Turkish Sultan, however, invested members of his select troops with small estates upon which they could live as lords. Upon their death the estate reverted to the Sultan. The favored soldiers were known as Timars, and among their ranks were the captured children of Christian parents. See Schwiebert, *Luther and His Times*, p. 62.

he believes that he will become holy and be saved by works. He does not think it a sin to overthrow Christ, lay government waste, and destroy marriage. The pope also works at all these things, though in other ways—with hypocrisy, while the Turk uses force and the sword. In a word, as has been said, the Turk's holiness is the very dregs of all abominations and errors.

I have wanted to tell all this to the first man, namely, Christian,[83] so that he may know and see how much need there is for prayer, and how he must first smite the Turk's Allah, that is, his god the devil, and overcome his power and divinity; otherwise, I fear, the sword will accomplish little. Now this man is not to fight physically with the Turk, as the pope and his followers teach; nor is he to resist the Turk with the fist, but he is to recognize the Turk as God's rod and wrath which Christians must either suffer, if God visits their sins upon them, or fight against and drive away with repentance, tears, and prayer. Let whoever will despise this counsel despise it; I will watch to see what damage he will do the Turk.

The second man who ought to fight against the Turk is Emperor Charles, or whoever may be emperor; for the Turk is attacking his subjects and his empire, and it is his duty, as a regular ruler appointed by God, to defend his own. I repeat it here: I would not urge or bid anyone to fight against the Turk unless the first method, mentioned above, that men had first repented and been reconciled to God, etc., had been followed. If anyone wants to go to war in another way, let him take his chances. It is not proper for me to say anything more about it other than to point out everyone's duty and to instruct his conscience.

I see clearly that kings and princes are taking such a foolish and careless attitude toward the Turk that I fear they underestimate God and the Turk too greatly, or perhaps they do not know that the Turk is such a mighty lord that no kingdom or land, whatever it is, is strong enough to resist him alone, unless God performs a miracle. Now I cannot expect any miracle[84] or special grace of God for Germany unless men amend their ways and honor the word of God

[83] Cf. p. 170.

[84] Luther regarded the lifting of the siege of Vienna in October, 1529, as a miracle. Cf. the letter to Nicholas Amsdorf, October 27, 1529. WA, Br 5, 167.

differently than they have before. But enough has been said about that for those who will listen. Now we want to speak of the emperor.

In the first place, if there is to be war against the Turk, it should be fought at the emperor's command, under his banner, and in his name. Then everyone can be sure in his conscience that he is obeying the ordinance of God, since we know that the emperor is our true overlord and head and that whoever obeys him in such a case obeys God also, whereas he who disobeys him also disobeys God. If he dies in this obedience, he dies in a good state, and if he has previously repented and believes in Christ, he will be saved. I suppose everyone knows these things better than I can teach him, and would to God they knew them as well as they think they do. Yet we will say something more about them.

In the second place, this fighting under the emperor's banner and obedience to him ought to be true and simple. The emperor should seek nothing else than simply to perform the work and duty of his office, which is to protect his subjects; and those under his banner should seek simply to do the work and duty of obedience. By this simplicity you should understand that you are not fighting the Turk for the reasons the emperors and princes have been urged to go to war for, such as the winning of great honor, glory, and wealth, the extension of territory, or wrath and revenge and other such reasons. By waging war for these reasons men seek only their own self-interest, not what is right or to obey, and so we have had no good fortune up to now, either in fighting or planning to fight against the Turk.

Therefore the urging and inciting with which the emperor and the princes have been stirred up to fight against the Turk ought to cease. He has been urged, as head of Christendom and as protector of the church and defender of the faith, to wipe out the Turk's religion, and the urging and exhorting have been based on the wickedness and vice of the Turks. Not so! The emperor is not the head of Christendom or defender of the gospel or the faith. The church and the faith must have a defender other than emperor and kings. They are usually the worst enemies of Christendom and of the faith, as Psalm 2 [:2] says and as the church constantly laments. That kind of urging and exhorting only makes things worse and angers

God deeply because it interferes with his honor and his work, and would ascribe it to men, which is idolatry and blasphemy.

And if the emperor were supposed to destroy the unbelievers and non-Christians, he would have to begin with the pope, bishops, and clergy, and perhaps not spare us or himself; for there is enough horrible idolatry in his own empire to make it unnecessary for him to fight the Turks for this reason. There are entirely too many Turks, Jews, heathen, and non-Christians among us with open false doctrine and with offensive, shameful lives. Let the Turk believe and live as he will, just as one lets the papacy and other false Christians live. The emperor's sword has nothing to do with the faith; it belongs to physical, worldly things, if God is not to become angry with us. If we pervert his order and throw it into confusion, he too becomes perverse and throws us into confusion and all kinds of misfortune, as it is written, "With the crooked thou dost show thyself perverse" [Ps. 18:26]. We can perceive and grasp this through the fortune we have had up to now against the Turk. Think of all the heartbreak and misery that have been caused by the *cruciata*,[85] by the indulgences,[86] and by crusade taxes.[87] With these Christians have been stirred up to take the sword and fight the Turk when they ought to have been fighting the devil and unbelief with the word and with prayer.

Here is what should be done. The emperor and the princes should be exhorted concerning their office and their bounden duty to give serious and constant thought to governing their subjects in peace and to protecting them against the Turk. This would be their duty whether they themselves were Christians or not, though it would be very good if they were Christians. But since it is and remains uncertain whether they are Christians, and it is certain that they are emperors and princes, that is, that they have God's command to protect their subjects and are duty bound to do so, we must let the uncertain go and hold to the certain,[88] urge them with continual preaching and exhortation, and lay it heavily upon their

---

[85] I.e., the Crusades.

[86] Luther probably means the indulgence granted to crusaders by Pope Urban II. Cf. *LW* 44, 144, n. 59.

[87] Cf. Schwiebert, *op. cit.*, pp. 62, 264.

[88] Cf. Thiele, *Luthers Sprichwörtersammlung*, No. 33.

consciences that it is their duty to God not to let their subjects perish so terribly, and that they commit serious sin when they are not mindful of their office and do not use all their power to bring counsel and help to those who should live, with body and goods, under their protection and who are bound to them by oaths of homage.

For I think (so far as I have observed the matter in our diets) that neither emperor nor princes themselves believe that they are emperor and princes. They act as though it were up to them whether to rescue and protect their subjects from the power of the Turk or not; and the princes neither care nor think that they are bound and obligated before God to counsel and help the emperor in this matter with body and goods. Each of them passes it by as though it were no concern of his and as though he were forced neither by command nor necessity, but as though it were left up to him to do it or not. They are just like the common people who do not think they have a responsibility to God and the world when they have bright sons, to send them to school and have them study; but everyone thinks he has the right to raise his son as he pleases regardless of God's word and ordinance. Indeed, the councilmen in the cities and almost all the rulers act in the same way and let the schools go to ruin, as though they had no responsibility for them, and had an indulgence besides. No one remembers that God earnestly commands and desires bright children to be reared to his praise and for his work. This cannot be done without the schools. On the contrary, everyone is in a hurry to have his children make a living, as though God and Christendom needed no pastors, preachers, physicians of souls, and as though the worldly rulers needed no chancellors, counselors, or secretaries—but more of this another time.[89] The pen must remain empress, or God will show us something else.

Emperor, kings, and princes act the same way. They do not stop to think that God's commandment requires them to protect their subjects; they think that it is a matter for them to decide if they get the notion or if they have leisure for it. Dear fellow, let us all do that! Let none of us attend to that which is commanded him

---

[89] See *A Sermon on Keeping Children in School* (1530), in this volume, pp. 207-258.

and which God orders him to do; let all our actions and duties depend on our own free will, and God will give us good grace and fortune, and we shall be plagued by the Turk here and by the devil yonder in eternity.

Perhaps, then, some worthless prattler—I should say a legate—will come from Rome and exhort the estates of the empire and stir them up against the Turk by telling them how the enemy of the Christian faith has done such great harm to Christendom, and that the emperor, as guardian of the church and defender of the faith, should do this and that; as though they themselves were great friends of the Christian faith![90] But I say to him: You are a base-born scoundrel, you impotent chatterer! All you accomplish is to make the emperor feel that he should do a good Christian work, one that he is not commanded to do, and one that is a matter of his own free choice. His conscience is not touched at all by that, and he is not reminded of the duty laid upon him by God, but the whole thing is left to his free choice.

This is how a legate ought to deal with the estates of the empire at the diet. He should hold God's commandment before them and make it an unavoidable issue, and say, "Dear lords, emperor, and princes, if you want to be emperor and princes, then act as emperor and princes, or the Turk will teach you with God's wrath and disfavor. Germany, or the empire, is given and committed to you by God for you to protect, rule, counsel, and help, and you not only should but must do this at the risk of losing your soul's salvation and God's favor and grace. But now it is evident that none of you believes or takes this seriously; you take your office as a jest, as though it were a Shrove Tuesday mummery.[91] You abandon the subjects God has committed to you to wretched harassment, to being taken captive, put to shame, plundered, slain, and sold by the Turk. Are you not aware that since God has committed this office to you, and has even given you money and people for you to do good to them, he will hold you accountable for all the subjects

---

[90] In 1518 Pope Leo X (1513-1521) sent cardinals Allesandro Farnese, Egidio Canisio, Antonio Bibbiena, and Lorenzo Campeggio as papal legates to the imperial court, Spain, France, and England to lay the groundwork for a crusade.
[91] I.e., as though it were part of the masquerading in the customary carnival on Shrove Tuesday, the day before Ash Wednesday, the first day of Lent.

whom you so shamefully deserted while you danced, reveled in pomp, and gambled? If you seriously believed that God appointed and ordained you to be emperor and princes, you would leave your banqueting and rivalry for seats of honor[92] and other unprofitable displays for a while, and give conscientious consideration to how to discharge your office, fulfil God's commandment, and rescue your consciences from all the blood and misery which the Turk inflicts upon your subjects. How can God, or any godly heart, think otherwise of you than that you hate your subjects or have a secret covenant with the Turk or, at least, regard yourselves as neither emperor nor princes, but as dolls and puppets for children to play with? If you seriously regarded yourselves as overlords appointed by God and did not discuss and take counsel about these matters differently than before, your consciences could not possibly give you any peace. In this you see that you are steadily becoming Turks to your own subjects.

"Why, you even take up the case of Luther and discuss in the devil's name whether one can eat meat in the fasting seasons, whether nuns can take husbands, and things of that kind which are not your business to discuss and about which God has given you no commandment. Meanwhile the serious and strict commandment of God, the commandment by which he has appointed you protectors of poor Germany, hangs in the air; and you become murderers, betrayers, and bloodhounds to your own good, faithful, obedient subjects, and abandon them—no, you cast them into the Turk's jaws, as a reward for the bodies and money, wealth and honor that they stake on you and extend to you."

A good orator can see well what I would like to say here if I were skilled in the art of oratory, and what a legate should aim for and expound at the diet, if he would discharge his office honestly and faithfully.

This is why I said above that Charles, or the emperor, should be the man to fight against the Turk, and that the fighting should be done under his banner. "Oh, that is easy! Everyone knew that a long time ago. Luther is not telling us anything new, but only

---

[92] Rivalry for prominent seats played a sorry role at the imperial diets. Cf. *BG* 7, 471, n. 3.

worn-out old stuff." But, my dear fellow, the emperor must truly see himself with other eyes than before, and you must see his banner with other eyes. You and I are talking about the same emperor and the same banner, but you are not talking about the eyes I am talking about. You must see on the banner the commandment of God that says, "Protect the good; punish the wicked." Tell me, how many can read this on the emperor's banner, or really believe it? Do you not think that their consciences would terrify them if they saw this banner and had to admit that they were most guilty before God because of their failure to help and protect their faithful subjects? Dear fellow, a banner is not simply a piece of silk; there are letters on it, and he who reads the letters will lose his taste for luxury and banqueting.

It is not difficult to show that up to now the banner has been regarded as a mere piece of silk, for otherwise the emperor would long ago have unfurled it, the princes would have followed it, and the Turk would not have become so mighty. But because the princes called it the emperor's banner with their lips and were disobedient to it with their fists, and by their deeds treated it as a mere piece of silk, things have come to the state we now see with our own eyes. God grant that all of us are not too late in coming—I with my exhortation and the lords with their banner—and that it may not happen to us as it did to the children of Israel, who would not fight against the Amorites when God commanded them; afterward, when they would have fought, they were beaten because God would not be with them [Deut. 1:19-46]. Nevertheless, no one should doubt that repentance and right conduct always find grace.

So when emperor and princes realize that by God's commandment they owe this protection to their subjects, they should be exhorted not to be presumptuous and undertake this work defiantly, or to rely upon their own might or action; for there are many foolish princes who say, "I have right and authority; therefore I will do it!" Then they pitch in with pride and, boasting of their might, ultimately meet defeat. If they had not felt their power, the matter of right would have little effect on them, as is proved in other cases in which they had little regard for what was right. It is not enough for you to know that God has committed this or that to you; you should do it with fear and humility, for God commands no one to do anything on the basis of his own wisdom or strength. He, too, wants to have a part in it and be feared. He wants to do it through us and wants us to pray to him so that we will not become presumptuous or forget his help, as the Psalter says, "The Lord takes pleasure in those who fear him, and in those who hope in his steadfast love" [Ps. 147:11]. Otherwise we would persuade ourselves that we could do things and did not need God's help, and would claim for ourselves the victory and honor that belong to him.

An emperor or prince ought to learn well that verse of the Psalter, in Psalm 44 [:6-7], "For not in my bow do I trust, nor can my sword save me. But thou hast saved us from our foes and hast put to confusion those who hate us," as well as the rest of what that Psalm says. And Psalm 60 [:10-12], "Thou dost not go forth, O God, with our armies. O grant us help against the foe, for vain is the help of man! With God we shall do valiantly; it is he who will tread down our foes." These and similar words have had to be fulfilled by many kings and great princes from the beginning down to the present day. They have become examples, though they had God's commandment, authority, and right. Emperor and princes, therefore, should not treat these words as a jest. Read the apt illustration given in Judges 20 [:18-25] of how the children of Israel were beaten twice by the Benjaminites, despite the fact that God bade them fight and that they had the best of right. Their boldness and presumption were their downfall, as the text itself says, *Fidentes fortitudine et numero.*[93] It is true that one should have horses and men and weapons and everything that is needed for battle, if they are to be had, so that one does not tempt God. But when one has them, one must not be bold because of it lest God be forgotten or despised, since it is written, "All victory comes from heaven" [I Macc. 3:19].

If these two things are present, God's commandment and our humility, then there is no danger or need so far as this second man, the emperor, is concerned. Then we are strong enough for the whole world and must have good fortune and success. But if we do not have good fortune, it is certainly because one of the two things

---

[93] "Trusting in bravery and numbers." This version is from the Latin text of Judg. 20:22.

is lacking; we are going to war either without God's commandment, or in our own presumption, or the first soldier, Christian, is not there with his prayers.[94] It is not necessary here to warn against seeking honor or booty in war; for he who fights with humility and in obedience to God's command, with his mind fixed solely upon the simple duty of protecting and defending his subjects, will forget about honor and booty; they will come to him without his seeking, more richly and gloriously than he can wish.

At this point someone will say, "Where are we going to find such pious warriors who will act this way?" Answer: The gospel is preached to all the world, and yet very few believe; nevertheless, Christendom[95] believes and abides. I am not writing this instruction with the hope that it will be accepted by all; indeed, most people will laugh and scoff at me. I will be content if I am able to instruct some princes and their subjects with this book, even though their number may be small; numbers do not matter to me; there will be victory and good fortune enough. And would to God that I had instructed only the emperor, or whoever is to conduct the war in his name and at his command; then I would be of good hope. It has often happened, indeed, it usually happens, that God bestows good fortune and success upon a whole land and kingdom through one single man; just as on the other hand he brings a whole land into all sorts of distress and misery through one scoundrel at court, as Solomon says in Ecclesiastes [9:18], "One sinner destroys much good."

We read of Naaman, the captain of the king of Syria, that through this one man God gave the whole land good fortune and success [II Kings 5:1-27]. Through the holy Joseph God gave good fortune to the whole kingdom of Egypt [Gen. 39:5], and in II Kings [3:14] Elisha says to Jehoram, "Were it not that I have regard for Jehoshaphat the king of Judah, I would neither look at you nor see you." Thus the godless kings of Israel and Edom had to be helped for the sake of one godly man, when otherwise they would have been ruined in all kinds of distress. And in the book of Judges one can see the good that God did through Ehud [Judg. 3:15-30], Gid-

---

94 Cf. pp. 172-173.
95 I.e., the totality of Christians.

eon [Judg. 6:11–8:28], Deborah [Judg. 4:4–5:31], Samson [Judg. 13:2–16:31], and other individuals, though the people were not worthy of it. See, on the other hand, what great harm Doeg did at the court of King Saul, I Samuel 22 [:18], and what Absalom accomplished against his father David with the aid and counsel of Ahithophel, II Samuel 16 [:22–17:23].

I say this so that we will not be frightened or moved in any way if the great majority who fight under the emperor's banner are unbelieving and have an un-Christian mind. We must also remember that Abraham, all by himself, was able to do much—Genesis 14 [:17; 18:24-33]. It is also certain that among the Turks, who are the army of the devil, there is not one who is a Christian or who has a humble and right heart. In I Samuel 14 [:6], the godly Jonathan said, "Nothing can hinder the Lord from saving by many or by few," and he himself inflicted a great slaughter on the Philistines such as Saul with his whole army could not do. It does not matter, then, if the entire crowd is not good, provided only that the head and some of the chief men are upright. Of course, it would be good if all were upright, but that is scarcely possible.

Moreover, I hear it said that in Germany there are those who desire the coming of the Turk and his government because they would rather be under him than under the emperor or princes.[96] It would be hard to fight against the Turk with such people. I have no better advice to give against them than that pastors and preachers be exhorted to be diligent in their preaching and faithful in instructing such people, pointing out to them the danger they are in, the wrong they are doing, and that by holding this opinion they make themselves a party to serious and innumerable sins in God's sight. It is dreadful enough to have the Turk as overlord and to endure his government; but willingly to submit oneself to it, or to desire it when one need not and is not compelled—well, the man who does that ought to be shown what kind of sin he is committing and how terrible his conduct is.

In the first place, these people are disloyal and are guilty of perjury to their rulers, to whom they have taken oaths and done homage. In God's sight this is a great sin which does not go un-

---

[96] Cf. p. 157.

punished. The good king Zedekiah perished miserably because of such perjury; he did not keep the oath he gave to the heathen emperor at Babylon [Jer. 21:7]. Such people may think or persuade themselves that it is within their own power and choice to go from one lord to another, as though they were free to do or not to do whatever they pleased, forgetting God's commandment and not remembering their oath, by which they are bound to be obedient until they are compelled by force to abandon that loyalty or are put to death because of it. This is what the peasants wanted to do in the recent rebellion, and this is why they were beaten.[97] For just as a man may not slay himself, but must submit to being slain by the violence of others, so no one should evade his obedience or his oath unless he is released from it by others, either by force or by favor and permission.

This is what the preachers must diligently impress on such people; indeed, their office of preaching compels them to do so, for it is their duty to warn their parishioners and to guard them against sin and harm to their souls. No one who willingly turns from his lord and submits to the Turk can ever remain under the Turk with a good conscience; his own heart will always accuse and rebuke him this way, "See, you were disloyal to your overlord and deprived him of the obedience you owed him, and robbed him of his right to rule you; now, no sin can be forgiven unless stolen goods are restored." But how will you make restitution to your lord when you are under the Turk and cannot make restitution? One of two things, then, must happen. Either you must toil and labor forever, trying to get away from the Turk and back to your overlord; or your conscience must forever suffer compunction, pain, and unrest (God grant that it does not result in despair and everlasting death) because you submitted to the Turk willingly and without necessity, contrary to your sworn duty. In the latter case you must be among the Turks physically, but with your heart and conscience yearn to be over on this side. What have you gained then? Why did you not stay on this side from the first?

In the second place, besides all that, such faithless, disloyal, and perjurious people commit a still more horrible sin. They make

---

[97] Cf. p. 50.

themselves a party to all the abominations and wickedness of the Turks; for he who willingly goes over to the Turks is their comrade and accomplice in all they do. Now we have heard above what kind of man the Turk is, that he is a destroyer, enemy, and blasphemer of our Lord Jesus Christ, a man who instead of the gospel and faith sets up his shameful Mohammed and all kinds of lies, ruins all temporal government and home life or marriage, and his warfare, which is nothing but murder and bloodshed, is a tool of the devil himself. See, then! He who consorts with the Turk has to be a party to this terrible abomination and brings down on his own head all the murder, all the blood the Turk has shed, and all the lies and vices with which he has damaged Christ's kingdom and led souls astray. It is dreadful enough if one is forced against his will to be under this bloodhound and devil and to see, hear, and put up with these abominations, as the godly Lot had to do in Sodom, as St. Peter [II Pet. 2:7-8] writes; it is not necessary to desire or to seek them of one's own accord.

Indeed, a man ought far rather die twice over in war, obedient to his overlord, than, like a poor Lot, have to be brought by force into such Sodoms and Gomorrahs.[98] Still less ought a godly man desire to go there of his own accord, in disobedience and against God's commandment and his own duty. That would mean not only becoming a party to all the wickedness of the Turk and the devil, but strengthening and furthering them; just as Judas not only made himself a party to the wickedness of the Jews against Christ, but strengthened and abetted it; Pilate did not act as wickedly as Judas did, as Christ testifies in John 17 [19:11].

In the third place, the preachers must impress upon the people that if they do go over to the Turks, they will not have bettered themselves and that their hopes and intentions will not be realized. For it is characteristic of the Turk not to let those who are anything or have anything stay in the place where they live, but to put them far back in another land, where they are sold and must be servants. Thus they fulfil the proverbs about "running out of the rain and falling in the water," "lifting the plate and breaking the dish," and

---

[98] Cf. Gen. 13:10-13.

"bad becomes worse."[99] It scarcely serves them wrong. For the Turk is a real warrior who has other ways of treating land and people, both in getting and keeping them, than our emperor, kings, and princes have. He does not trust and believe these disloyal people and he has the force to do as he will; so he does not need these people as do our princes.

The preachers and pastors, I say, must impress this upon such disloyal people, with constant admonition and warning, for it is the truth, and it is needed. But if there are some who despise this exhortation and will not be moved by it, let them go to the devil, as St. Paul did with the Greeks and St. Peter with the Jews;[100] the others should not mind. Indeed, if it were to come to war, I would rather that none of these people were under the emperor's banner, or stayed under it, but were all on the Turk's side. They would be beaten all the sooner and they would do the Turk more harm in battle than good, for they are out of favor with God, the devil, and the world, and they are surely condemned to hell. It is good to fight against such wicked people, for they are plainly and surely damned both by God and the world. There are many depraved, abandoned, and wicked men; but anyone with any sense will certainly heed such exhortation and be moved to remain obedient and not throw his soul so carelessly into hell to the devil, but rather fight with all his might under his overlord, even though he is slain by the Turks in so doing.

But then you say, "If the pope is as bad as the Turk—and you yourself call him Antichrist, together with his clergy and his followers—then the Turk is as godly as the pope, for he acknowledges the four Gospels and Moses, together with the prophets. Ought we not, then, fight the pope as well as the Turk, or, perhaps, rather than the Turk?" Answer: I cannot deny that the Turk esteems the four Gospels as divine and true, as well as the prophets, and that he also speaks very highly of Christ and of his mother. But at the same time, he believes that his Mohammed is superior to Christ and that

---

[99] These expressions are found in Thiele, *Luthers Sprichwörtersammlung*, No. 478; cf. also Nos. 276 and 477.

[100] Cf. I Cor. 1:22-25 and Gal. 2:7-8. It is unlikely that Luther had specific passages in mind. The point is that neither apostle effected the conversion of the entire people to whom his mission was directed.

Christ is not God, as we said above.[101] We Christians acknowledge the Old Testament as divine Scripture, but now that it is fulfilled and is, as St. Peter says in Acts 15 [:10-11], too hard without God's grace, it is abolished and no longer binding upon us. Mohammed treats the gospel the same way. He declares that the gospel is indeed correct, but that it has long since served its purpose and that it is too hard to keep, especially in those points where Christ teaches that one is to leave all for his sake [Matt. 19:29], love God with his whole heart [Matt. 22:37], and the like. This is why God has had to give another new law, one that is not so hard and one which the world can keep. And this law is the Koran. But if anyone asks why the Turk performs no miracles to confirm this new law, he says that that is unnecessary and of no use, for people had many miracles before, when Moses' law and the gospel arose, and did not believe. This is why his Koran does not need to be confirmed by wasted miracles, but by the sword, which is more persuasive than miracles. This is how it has been and still is among the Turks: everything is done with the sword instead of with miracles.

On the other hand, the pope is not much more godly than Mohammed and resembles him extraordinarily; for he, too, praises the gospel and Holy Scripture with his lips, but he holds that many things in it are too hard, and these are the very things Mohammed and the Turks also consider too hard, such as those contained in Matthew 5 [:20-44]. So he interprets them and makes them *consilia,* that is, "counsels," which no one is bound to keep unless he desires to do so, as Paris and other universities, schools, and monasteries have brazenly taught. Therefore, he, too, does not rule with the gospel, or word of God, but has made a new law and Koran, namely, his decretals, and these he enforces with the ban[102] just as the Turk enforces his Koran with the sword. He even calls the ban his spiritual sword, though only the word of God is that and should be called that (Ephesians 6 [:17]). Nevertheless, he also uses the temporal sword when he can, or at least he calls upon it and urges and incites others to use it. And I am confident that if the pope could use the temporal sword as mightily as the Turk, he would do

---

[101] Cf. p. 176.

[102] The sentence of excommunication, which often carried with it a variety of civil punishments and disabilities.

197

so with less goodwill than the Turk, and indeed, he has often tried it.

God visits them with the same plague, too, and smites them with blindness so that it happens to them as St. Paul says in Romans 1 [:28] about the shameful vice of the dumb sins, that God gives them up to a perverse mind because they pervert the word of God. Both the pope and the Turk are so blind and senseless that they commit the dumb sins shamelessly, as an honorable and praiseworthy thing. Since they think lightly of marriage, it serves them right that there are dog-marriages (and would to God they were dog-marriages), indeed, also "Italian marriages" and "Florentine brides"[103] among them; and they think these things good. I hear one horrible thing after another about what an open and glorious Sodom Turkey is, and everybody who has looked around a little in Rome and Italy knows very well how God revenges and punishes the forbidden marriage,[104] so that Sodom and Gommorah, which God overwhelmed in days of old with fire and brimstone [Gen. 19:24], must seem a mere jest and prelude compared with these abominations. On this one account, therefore, I would very much regret the rule of the Turk; indeed, his rule would be intolerable in Germany.

What are we to do, then? Ought we to fight against the pope as well as against the Turk, since the one is as godly as the other? Answer: Treat the one like the other and no one is wronged; like sin should receive like punishment. This is what I mean: If the pope and his followers were to attack the empire with the sword, as the Turk does, he should receive the same treatment as the Turk; and this is what was done to him by the army of Emperor Charles outside of Pavia.[105] God's verdict is, "He that takes the sword shall perish by the sword" [Matt. 26:52]. I do not advise men to wage war against the Turk or the pope because of false belief or evil life, but because of the murder and destruction which he does. The best thing about the papacy is that it does not yet have the sword, as the Turk does; otherwise it would certainly undertake to subject the

---

[103] These expressions were current names attached to perversions and vices usually identified with Italy. Cf. BG 7, 482, n. 3.

[104] I.e., homosexuality.

[105] Cf. p. 90, n. 8.

whole world, although it would accomplish no more than to bring it to faith in the pope's Koran, the decretals. For the pope pays as little heed to the gospel or Christian faith as the Turk, and knows it as little, though he makes a great pretense of Turkish sanctity by fasts (which he himself does not observe); thus they deserve the reputation of being like the Turk, though they are against Christ.

The first man, Sir Christian,[106] has been aroused against the papacy because of its errors and wicked ways, and he attacks it boldly with prayer and the word of God. And he has wounded it, too, so that they feel it and rage. But raging does not help; the axe is laid to the tree and the tree must be uprooted, unless it bears different fruit.[107] I see clearly that they have no intention of reforming, but the further things go, the more stubborn they become, the more they want to have their own way, and the more they boast, "All or nothing, bishop or drudge!" They are so godly I know that rather than reform or turn from their shameful ways (both they themselves and the whole world admit that it is not to be endured) they would rather go over to their comrade and brother, the holy Turk. Oh well! May our heavenly Father soon hear their own prayer and grant that, as they say, they may be "all or nothing, bishop or drudge." Amen! This is what they want. Amen! So be it; let it happen as God pleases!

But you say further, "How can Emperor Charles fight against the Turk now, when he has against him such hindrances and treachery from kings, princes, the Venetians,[108] indeed, from almost everybody?" This is my reply: A man should let lie what he cannot lift.[109] If we can do no more, we must let our Lord Jesus Christ counsel and aid us by his coming, which cannot be far off.[110] For the world has come to its end; the Roman Empire is almost gone; it is torn asunder; it is like the kingdom of the Jews when Christ's birth was near. The Jews had scarcely anything of their kingdom; Herod was

---

106 Cf. p. 170.

107 Cf. Matt. 3:10.

108 The Venetian republic, through the influence of Pope Clement VII, had supported the French king Francis I against the emperor. Along with Francis, Venice broke the terms of the Treaty of Madrid.

109 Cf. Thiele, *Luthers Sprichwörtersammlung*, No. 488.

110 Cf. p. 18, n. 3.

the token of the end.[111] So I think that now that the Roman Empire is almost gone, Christ's coming is at the door, and the Turk is the empire's token of the end, a parting gift to the Roman Empire. And just as Herod and the Jews hated each other, though both stood together against Christ, so Turk and papacy hate each other, but stand together against Christ and his kingdom.

Nevertheless, the emperor should do whatever he can for his subjects against the Turk, so that even though he cannot entirely prevent the abomination, he may nonetheless try to protect and rescue his subjects by checking the Turk and holding him off. The emperor should be moved to do this not only by duty, his office, and God's command, nor only by the un-Christian and vile government the Turk brings, as has been said above,[112] but also by the misery and wretchedness that befalls his subjects. Doubtlessly they know better than I how cruelly the Turk treats those whom he takes captive. He treats them like cattle, dragging, towing, driving those that can move, and killing on the spot those that cannot move, whether they are young or old.

All this and more like it ought to move all the princes, and the whole empire, to forget their own causes and quarrels, or to put them aside for awhile, and earnestly unite to help the wretched so that things may not go as they went with Constantinople[113] and Greece.[114] They quarreled with one another and looked after their own affairs for a long time until the Turk overwhelmed both of them, as he has already come very near doing to us in a similar case. But if this is not to be, and our unrepentant life makes us unworthy of any grace, counsel, or support, we must put up with it and suffer under the devil; but that does not excuse those who could help and do not.

I wish it clearly understood, however, that it was not for nothing that I called Emperor Charles the man who ought to go to war against the Turk.[115] As for other kings, princes, and rulers who despise Emperor Charles, or are not his subjects, or are not obedi-

---

[111] *Die letze*, i.e., a farewell banquet, the end.

[112] Cf. pp. 178-179.

[113] Constantinople fell to the forces of Mohammed II on May 29, 1453.

[114] Mohammed II completed the conquest of Greece in 1461.

[115] Cf. p. 170.

ent, I leave them to take their own chances. They shall do nothing because of my advice or admonition; what I have written here is for Emperor Charles and his subjects; the others do not concern me. I know quite well the pride of some kings and princes who would be glad if it were not Emperor Charles, but they, who were to be the heroes and victors who win honor against the Turk. I grant them the honor, but if they are beaten, it will be their own fault. Why do they not conduct themselves humbly toward the true head and the proper ruler? The rebellion among the peasants was punished, but if the rebellion among the princes and lords were also to be punished, I think that there would be very few princes and lords left.[116] God grant that it may not be the Turk who inflicts the punishment! Amen.

Finally, I would have it understood as my kind and faithful advice that if it comes to war against the Turk, we should arm and prepare ourselves, and not underestimate the Turk and not act as we Germans usually do, and come on the field with twenty or thirty thousand men. And even though good fortune is bestowed upon us and we win a victory, we have no power in reserve,[117] but sit down again and carouse until another danger comes along. And although I am not qualified to give instruction on this point, and they themselves know, or ought to know, more about it than I, nevertheless, when I see people acting so childishly I must think either that the princes and our Germans do not know or believe the strength and power of the Turk, or that they have no serious intention of fighting against the Turk, but just as the pope has robbed Germany of money under the pretense of the Turkish war and by indulgences,[118] so they, too, following the pope's example, would swindle us out of money.

My advice, then, is that we not insufficiently arm ourselves and send our poor Germans off to be slaughtered. If we are not going to make an adequate, honest resistance that will have some reserve power, it would be far better not to begin a war, but to yield lands and people to the Turk in time, without useless bloodshed, rather

---

[116] When the Peasants' War ended in 1525 many peasants were executed; see pp. 59-60.

[117] I.e., manpower in reserve.

[118] Cf. LW 44, 144.

than have him win anyhow in an easy battle and with shameful bloodshed, as happened in Hungary with King Louis.[119] Fighting against the Turk is not like fighting against the king of France, or the Venetians, or the pope; he is a different kind of warrior. The Turk has people and money in abundance; he defeated the Sultan twice in succession,[120] and that took people! Why, dear sir, his people are always under arms so that he can quickly muster three or four hundred thousand men. If we were to cut down a hundred thousand, he would soon be back again with as many men as before. He has reserve power.

So there is no point in trying to meet him with fifty or sixty thousand men unless we have an equal or a greater number in reserve. Just count up the number of lands he controls, dear sir. He has Greece, Asia, Syria, Egypt, Arabia, etc. He has so many lands that if Spain, France, England, Germany, Italy, Bohemia, Hungary, Poland, and Denmark were all counted together, they would not equal the territory he has. Besides, he is master of all of them and commands effective and ready obedience. And, as has been said, they are constantly under arms and are trained in warfare so that he has reserve power and can deliver two, three, four heavy battles, one after another, as he showed against the Sultan. This Gog and Magog[121] is a different kind of majesty than our kings and princes.

I say this because I fear that my Germans do not know it or believe it, and that perhaps they think they are strong enough by themselves and that the Turk is a lord like the king of France, whom they would easily withstand. But I shall be without blame and shall not have wet my tongue and pen with blood if a king takes on the Turk by himself. It is tempting God to set out with a smaller force against a stronger king, as Christ shows in the Gospel of Luke

---

[119] At the battle of Mohacs, August 29, 1526, Louis II of Hungary with thirty thousand troops was opposed by a Turkish army of more than one hundred thousand. It has been estimated that in this engagement the Hungarians lost twenty thousand men, including their king.

[120] The victories of the Ottoman Turks at Aleppo (1516) and Reydaniya (1517) secured their supremacy in the Muslin world. Cf. A. W. Ward *et al.* (eds.), *The Cambridge Modern History* (New York: The Macmillan Company, 1903), I, 90-91.

[121] Cf. Ezek. 38:2.

[14:31], especially since our princes are not the kind of people for whom a divine miracle is to be expected. The king of Bohemia[122] is a mighty prince now, but God forbid that he match himself alone against the Turk! Let him have Emperor Charles as his captain and all the emperor's power behind him. But then, let whoever will not believe this learn from his own experience! I know how powerful the Turk is, unless the historians and geographers—and daily experience, too—lie; I know that they do not lie.

I do not say this to frighten the kings from waging war against the Turk, but to admonish them to make wise and serious preparation, and not to go about this matter so childishly and lethargically, for I would like, if possible, to prevent useless bloodshed and lost wars. The best preparation would be if our princes would wind up their own affairs and put their heads and hearts and hands and feet together and make one body out of the great crowd from which one could make another army if one battle were lost, and not, as before, let individual kings and princes set upon him—yesterday the king of Hungary,[123] today the king of Poland, and tomorrow the king of Bohemia—until the Turk devours them one after another and nothing is accomplished except that our people are betrayed and slaughtered and blood is shed needlessly.

If our kings and princes were to agree and stand by one another and help each other, and the Christian man were to pray for them, I should be undismayed and of good hope. The Turk would stop his raging and find his equal in Emperor Charles. Failing that, if things go as they are going now, and no one is in agreement with another or loyal to another, and everyone wants to be his own man and takes the field with a beggarly array, I must let it go at that. Of course, I will gladly help by praying, but it will be a weak prayer, for because of the childish, presumptuous, and short-sighted way in which such great enterprises are undertaken, I can have little faith that it will be heard, and I know that this is tempting God and that he can have no pleasure in it.

---

[122] Ferdinand of Austria, brother of Emperor Charles V, was elected king of Bohemia in 1526. Luther did not regard him very highly. Cf. *WA* 30^{II}, 146, n. 3.

[123] Cf. p. 202, n. 119.

What do our dear lords do? They treat it as just a joke. It is a fact that the Turk is at our throat,[124] and even if he does not decide to march against us this year, he is still there, always armed and ready to attack us when he will. Meanwhile, our princes consult about how they can harass Luther and the gospel: It is the gospel which is the Turk! Force must be used against it! The gospel must be put to rout! That is what they are doing right now at Spires,[125] where the most important matters are the eating of meat and fish and foolishness like that. May God honor you,[126] you faithless lords of your poor people! What devil commands you to deal so vehemently with spiritual things concerning God and matters of conscience which are not committed to you, and to be so lax and slothful in things that God has committed to you and that concern you and your poor people now in the greatest and most pressing need, and thereby only hinder all those whose intentions are good and who would gladly do their part? Yes, go on singing and hearing the Mass of the Holy Ghost.[127] He is greatly pleased with that and will be very gracious to you disobedient, stubborn fellows because you neglect those things that he has committed to you, and work at what he has forbidden you! Yes, the Evil Spirit may hear you!

With this I have saved my conscience.[128] This book shall be my witness concerning the measure and manner in which I advise war against the Turk. If anyone wishes to proceed otherwise, let him do so, win or lose. I shall neither enjoy his victory nor pay for his defeat, but I shall be innocent of all the blood that will be shed in

---

[124] Cf. p. 157.

[125] The Second Diet of Spires was in session at the time Luther wrote. At this diet Charles V, fresh from his victory over the League of Cognac (an alliance of France, England, the pope, Venice, and Milan), commanded the estates to execute the terms of the Edict of Worms (1521), which, in effect, had been suspended by the First Diet of Spires (1526).

[126] The implication is that Luther cannot honor them.

[127] The Mass of the Holy Ghost is a votive mass, i.e., a mass celebrated not in conformity with the office of the day, but according to the wish (*votum*) of the celebrant, his superior, or of the person for whom the mass is offered. The mass is celebrated on Thursdays. See J. O. O'Connell, *The Celebration of Mass* (London: Burns, Oates & Washbourne, Ltd., Publishers to the Holy See, 1941), I, 63-113.

[128] Cf. Ezek. 3:19; 33:9.

vain. I know that this book will not make the Turk a gracious lord to me should it come to his attention;[129] nevertheless, I have wished to tell my Germans the truth, so far as I know it, and to give faithful counsel and service to the grateful and the ungrateful alike. If it helps, it helps; if it does not, then may our dear Lord Jesus Christ help, and come down from heaven with the Last Judgment and strike down both Turk and pope, together with all tyrants and the godless, and deliver us from all sins and from all evil. Amen.

---

[129] A few years after the publication of this book a member of an ambassadorial party in Turkey reported that the Sultan had inquired about Luther. When told that Luther was forty-eight years old, the Sultan replied, "I wish he were younger; he would find me a gracious lord." Cf. Köstlin, *op. cit.*, I, 283.

A SERMON ON KEEPING CHILDREN IN SCHOOL

1530

Translated by Charles M. Jacobs
Revised by Robert C. Schultz

INTRODUCTION

Education was generally held in contempt and derision by the masses during the early decades of the sixteenth century. To a large extent this negative attitude was fostered by a spirit of materialism which went hand-in-hand with the rapid expansion of trade and commerce. Unless a youth was destined for a learned profession in law, medicine, or theology, parents and children saw little if any value in learning which was not obviously and directly related to the world and work of commerce. Time spent in school, they reasoned, could be spent more profitably in earning a living. Indeed, the spirit of the age was so averse to formal education that the derisive saying was widespread in Germany, "The learned are daft."[1]

But the spirit of materialism was not the sole factor responsible for the anti-education attitude of the masses. A second and perhaps even more significant factor is to be found in the popular reaction to the Reformation. One of the early results of the Reformation movement had been the large-scale abandonment of monasteries and cloisters by monks and nuns won over to the evangelical point of view. For practical, religious, and economic reasons, the secular authorities confiscated the properties and endowments of the abandoned monasteries and cloisters. Although not so intended, these actions of the monastics and of the secular authorities caused the collapse of existing monastic and other church-dominated schools which were staffed by monks and nuns and supported by the endowments of their religious communities.[2]

Further, there were those who interpreted the doctrine of the spiritual priesthood of believers to mean that the ministerial office required no formal education. They held that the inner word, prompted by the Holy Spirit, was all sufficient, and that formal education and academic degrees were dispensable vanities and even offensive to God.[3]

---

[1] *Gelehrte sind verkehrte.* See p. 232. See also *LW* 45, 241-342, and Preserved Smith, *The Life and Letters of Martin Luther* (Boston and New York: Houghton Mifflin Company, 1911), p. 185.

[2] Cf. *LW* 45, 342; Smith, *op. cit.,* pp. 185-186.

[3] *LW* 45, 342.

Most important of all, however, was the common reaction of the masses to the Reformation contention that many of the church's doctrines, teachings, and practices were not only permeated by error, but were actually dangerous to salvation. If such were actually the case, parents reasoned, why should they send their children to schools where such errors were inculcated?[4] Their negative conclusions were reflected in the sharp decline in enrolment at educational institutions, including the University of Wittenberg where Luther was the star of the faculty.[5]

It was under the pressure of this anti-education attitude and the collapse of many schools that Luther, in 1524, issued his appeal *To the Councilmen of All Cities in Germany that They Establish and Maintain Christian Schools.*[6] In this treatise Luther offered the authorities practical advice and replied to current popular arguments against schooling. This appeal had some measure of success, for in that very year the cities of Magdeburg, Nordhausen, Halberstadt, and Gotha took action. Eisleben and Nürnberg followed suit in 1525 and 1526 respectively.[7] Territorial church orders also stressed the matter of providing schools.[8]

Despite these and other efforts, however, little actual progress was made, for the problem of persuading parents to send their children to school and to keep them there still remained. Luther announced his intention of setting himself to this task in the spring of 1529 when he wrote a preface for a book[9] by his friend Justus Menius. The book dealt with the duties of married people and the Christian training of children. In this preface Luther wrote, "Thus, even in worldly government, you can serve your lord or your city better by training children than by building him castles and cities and gathering the treasures of the whole world;

---

[4] *LW* 45, 342.

[5] See p. 234, n. 39.

[6] *LW* 45, 339-378.

[7] *LW* 45, 344.

[8] Schwiebert cites particularly the *Hallische Kirchenordnung* of 1526, the *Braunschweig'sche Kirchenordnung* of 1528, and the *Hamburger Kirchenordnung* of 1529. See Schwiebert, *op. cit.*, pp. 677-678.

[9] The book was entitled *Oeconomia Christiana*. See the text of Luther's preface in WA 30[II], 60-63.

for what good does all that do if there are no learned, wise, and godly people? I shall say nothing of the temporal gain and eternal reward that accrue to you before God and the world, how in this way your child will be even better fed than by raising him in the shameful, despicable, hoggish way you had intended. But I shall deal with this matter more fully another time in a separate book, God willing, in which I shall really go after the shameful, despicable, damnable parents who are no parents at all but despicable hogs and venomous beasts, devouring their own young."

Luther carried out this intention in the summer of 1530. With the diet in session at Augsburg, a period of enforced idleness at the Coburg Castle was imposed upon him. It was there that the sermon began to grow on him.[10] He was already hard at work on the manuscript by July 5 when he remarked both candidly and humorously concerning it in a letter to Melanchthon, "I was never so verbose as I seem now to have become; perhaps it is the garrulity of old age."[11] The manuscript was completed by the middle of July and sent to Nickel Schirlentz in Wittenberg for printing. On August 15 Luther wrote to his wife that if the printing still was not even begun she should "take the manuscript from Schirlentz and give it to George Rau."[12] By August 20 Luther had received at least a portion of the printed text from Schirlentz.[13] On August 24 and 25 he sent his only copies of the full text to Melanchthon and to Lazarus Spengler,[14] to whom—on the suggestion of Veit Dietrich—he had dedicated the work.

Whereas Luther's 1524 appeal *To the Councilmen of All Cities in Germany that They Establish and Maintain Christian Schools* argues for the establishment and maintenance of schools, the present treatise argues for the use of the schools thus established. Together these treatises give a clear conception of Luther's ideas on education.

---

[10] Cf. p. 213.

[11] *WA*, Br 5, 439. At the time Luther was approaching his forty-seventh birthday.

[12] *WA*, Br 5, 546.

[13] *WA*, Br 5, 552.

[14] *WA*, Br 5, 560-561.

The translation by Charles M. Jacobs was based on *CL* 4, 144-178. Our revision was made on the basis of the text, *Eine Predigt, dass man Kinder zur Schulen halten solle,* in *WA* 30ɪɪ, 517-588.

C. M. J.
R. C. S.

A SERMON ON KEEPING
CHILDREN IN SCHOOL

To the honorable and wise Lazarus Spengler, syndic of the city of Nürnberg, my especially dear sir and friend: grace and peace in Christ, our dear Lord and faithful Savior. Amen.

Honorable and wise dear sir and friend, I have composed a sermon[1] to the preachers here and there to the effect that they should exhort people to keep their children in school. It has grown on me to the point where it has almost become a book, though I have forcibly restrained myself to keep it from becoming altogether too big, so full and rich is this subject. I hope that it may do much good, and I have published it under your name[2] with the sole thought that it may thereby receive greater attention and, if worthy, be read by the people of your city. For although I can well believe that your preachers will be diligent enough in this matter—they have been endowed by God with great gifts—to understand and promote the cause without any need, thank God, of admonition or instruction on my part, still it does no harm to have many people agreeing with one another and opposing the devil the more strongly.

For it is hardly likely that in so great a city with such a large population the devil will not try his arts and tempt some to despise the word of God and the schools. This is true particularly because there are many things there (especially trade and commerce)[3] to turn the children away from the schools to the service

---

[1] On the sense in which many of Luther's treatises were and may be called "sermons," see *LW* 51, xiii.

[2] On the suggestion of Veit Dietrich the treatise was dedicated to Lazarus Spengler (1479-1534), a leader of the reform movement in Nürnberg. Spengler first met Luther in 1518 when the Reformer was on his way to Augsburg. His published defense of Luther's doctrines in 1519 led to his being included in the bull *Exsurge, Domine*. Spengler represented Nürnberg at the diets of Worms (1521) and Augsburg (1530). Cf. *LW* 45, 135, n. 7.

[6] On the evils Luther saw in trade and commerce, see his 1524 treatise on *Trade and Usury*. *LW* 45, 231-310.

of Mammon. The devil undoubtedly thinks that if he could cause the word and the schools to be despised in Nürnberg, his purpose would in large measure have been accomplished, for he would have set an example that would carry great weight throughout Germany and be a real blow to the schools in all the other cities. For Nürnberg truly shines throughout all Germany like a sun among the moon and stars, and what is practiced there has a powerful influence on other cities.

But praise and thanks be to God, who has long since countered the devil's intentions and put it into the heart of an honorable and wise council to found and equip such a splendid and excellent school.[4] They spare no expense to find and secure the very finest people, so that it can be said without boasting that no university, not even Paris, has ever been so well provided with teachers. (Everyone who has ever studied in the universities as I have will have to say the same thing, for I know what they are and have learned what they teach; I still know them only too well!)[5] This is indeed a magnificent achievement. It is a credit to your distinguished city and a fitting honor to its widely renowned council. For in this they have shown generous Christian consideration of their subjects, contributing faithfully to their eternal salvation as well as to their temporal well-being and honor. God will assuredly strengthen such a work with ever increasing blessings and grace, though the devil must strive against it for a while since he cannot be happy when so excellent a tabernacle is built to the Lord in this sun.[6] He must assemble clouds and mist and dust, trying in every way to keep such glory from shining too far, or at least to dim its splendor. What else could he do?

For this reason I hope that the citizens will recognize the fidelity and love of their lords, and help earnestly to support this work by keeping their children in school, since without cost to themselves their children are so bountifully and diligently cared

---

[4] In 1526 the city of Nürnberg had Melanchthon dedicate its new school among whose teachers were such distinguished scholars as Joachim Camerarius in Greek and Eobanus Hess in poetry. Cf. WA 30^{II}, 518, nn. 1 and 2.

[5] See Luther's critique of university curriculum in To the Christian Nobility (1520). LW 44, 202-207.

[6] Cf. Mark 9:5-7.

for, with everything provided for them. This will happen only if the preachers get behind it. If they do not urge it, the common man will be beset and overcome by thoughts from Satan, and he will easily give up. Other responsibilities will keep him from thinking the matter through, as a preacher can, and seeing how important it is, how much is to be gained—or lost. This is why we must be patient with such people as long as they are not obdurate or wicked. I know Nürnberg well enough to know that it has, thank God, many fine Christian people who gladly and from the heart do that which they ought to do, provided they know or are told what that is. They have a reputation for this, not only with me, but far and wide, and there is no reason to fear that they will fail in this matter. There may, of course, be an occasional idolater, a servant of Mammon [Matt. 6:24], who will take his son out of school and say, "If my son can read and do arithmetic, that is enough; we now have books in German, etc." Such a person sets a bad example for all the other good citizens. With the best of intentions they imitate him, thinking it the right and only thing to do, without realizing the harm involved. The preachers can be of real help in such a situation.

Every community, and especially a great city, must have in it many kinds of people besides merchants. It must have people who can do more than simply add, subtract, and read German. German books are made primarily for the common man to read at home. But for preaching, governing, and administering justice, in both spiritual and worldly estates, all the learning and languages in the world are too little, to say nothing of German alone. This is particularly true in our day, when we have to do with more than just the neighbor next door. But these idolaters forget all about this matter of governing. They do not realize that without preachers and rulers they could not serve their idol a single hour.

Of course, I can understand that among so many people there may be an occasional idolater who would not care whether honor or shame came to the noble city of Nürnberg, so long as he got his two cents.[7] But then people ought not to care about such a

---

[7] *Pfennig.*

despicable idolater either. They should ignore him and his bad example, figuring that the greater the reputation that comes to our city when our honorable council deals so earnestly and faithfully with the schools, the greater would be the shame if our citizens were to despise the faithfulness and generosity of our lords, and the greater would be their share in the bad example and offense we give to all the other cities, which could then say, "Well, if that is what they do at Nürnberg—and they have fine people there too—why should we do any better?"

You idolater, if you will give no thought to what God and honor require, and will think of nothing but Mammon, God will find others who will give thought. Thank God that I have known several cities where although the council cared nothing for the word or the schools, there were many upright citizens who by daily persistence compelled the council to found schools and churches. God willing, therefore, Nürnberg will not come to such a sorry pass on account of you that the citizens follow your example and despise the schools which an honorable council has faithfully established and maintained at such great cost, while in much smaller cities the citizens have secured schools for themselves, even though their councils thought nothing of them.

But here I am talking on and on, dear sir and friend. I suppose it lies in the nature of these things that there has to be much talk about them. In this case what I have been trying to do is to speak in your name to all the citizens of your city, and I hope that you will not take offense. Indeed, I hope you will continue to push and promote this matter, as you have been doing anyway all along. God knows, I mean it well.

May Christ our Lord strengthen and preserve you until that day when, God willing, we shall see each other with joy and in another form. For he who has given you so much to do for his work and word as you have done till now, will also go on and complete it all. To him be praise and thanks forever. Amen.

Your obedient servant,
MARTIN LUTHER

From Martin Luther to all my dear friends, pastors, and preachers who truly love Christ: Grace and peace in Christ Jesus, our Lord.

My dear sirs and friends, you see with your own eyes how that wretch of a Satan is now attacking us on all sides with force and guile. He is afflicting us in every way he can to destroy the holy gospel and the kingdom of God, or, if he cannot destroy them, at least to hinder them at every turn and prevent them from moving ahead and gaining the upper hand. Among his wiles, one of the very greatest, if not the greatest of all, is this—he deludes and deceives the common people so that they are not willing to keep their children in school or expose them to instruction. He puts into their minds the dastardly notion that because monkery, nunning, and priestcraft no longer hold out the hope they once did,[8] there is therefore no more need for study and for learned men, that instead we need to give thought only to how to make a living and get rich.

This seems to me to be a real masterpiece of the devil's art. He sees that in our time he cannot do what he would like to do; therefore, he intends to have his own way with our offspring. Before our very eyes he is preparing them so that they will learn nothing and know nothing. Then when we are dead, he will have before him a naked, bare, defenseless people with whom he can do as he pleases. For if the Scriptures and learning disappear, what will remain in the German lands but a disorderly and wild crowd of Tartars or Turks,[9] indeed, a pigsty and mob of wild beasts? But he does not let them see this now. He blinds them in masterly fashion so that, when it comes to the point where their own experience compels them to see it, he can laugh up his sleeve at all their weeping and wailing. However much they may wish it, they will then be able to do nothing about it; they will have to admit that things have gone on too long. Then they will be will-

---

[8] Luther makes the same point at the beginning of his 1524 appeal *To the Councilmen of All Cities in Germany that They Establish and Maintain Christian Schools. LW* 45, 348-349.

[9] On the menace to Europe posed by the Turks, see *On War Against the Turk,* in this volume, pp. 155-205.

217

ing to give a hundred gulden for half a scholar, where today they will not give ten gulden for two whole scholars.

And it will serve them right. Because they are not now willing to support and keep the honest, upright, virtuous schoolmasters and teachers offered them by God to raise their children in the fear of God, and in virtue, knowledge, learning, and honor by dint of hard work, diligence, and industry, and at small cost and expense, they will get in their place incompetent substitutes,[10] ignorant louts such as they have had before, who at great cost and expense will teach the children nothing but how to be utter asses, and beyond that will dishonor men's wives and daughters and maidservants, taking over their homes and property, as has happened before. This will be the reward of the great and shameful ingratitude into which the devil is so craftily leading them.

Now because it is a part of our duty as pastors to be on guard against these and other wicked wiles, we must not shut our eyes to a matter of such great importance. On the contrary, we must advise, exhort, admonish, and nag with all our power and diligence and care, so that the common people may not let themselves be so pitifully deceived and deluded by the devil. Therefore let each of us look to himself and remember his office so that we do not go to sleep in this matter and allow the devil to become god and lord. For if we are silent about this and shut our eyes to it, and the young people are neglected and our offspring become Tartars or wild beasts, it will be the fault of our own silence and snoring, and we shall have to render full account for it.

I know very well that many of you, without any exhortation on my part, are acting in this matter and would do so anyway better than I can advise. Moreover, I have already published a message to the councilmen in the cities.[11] Nevertheless, because some may have forgotten this, or would be more persistent as a

---

[10] Luther specifically refers—with customary contempt—to the *Locaten*, classroom helpers and overseers who lacked the educational requirements for a full-fledged teaching position of their own, and *Bachanten*, upperclassmen assigned to supervise classes in some lower grades during the absence of a teacher. MA³ 5, 439, n. 265, l. 8.

[11] See Luther's 1524 treatise *To the Councilmen of All Cities in Germany that They Establish and Maintain Christian Schools*. LW 45, 339-378.

result of my example, I have sent you this sermon of mine, which I have preached more than once to our people. From it you can observe that I am working faithfully with you in this matter, and that we are doing our best everywhere and are guiltless before God in the conduct of our office. The case is truly in our hands because we see that even the clergy, who are called spiritual, appear to take the view that they would let all schools, discipline, and teaching go by the board, or themselves even help to destroy them, simply because they cannot have their own way with them as they once did. This too is the devil's doing, through them. God help us. Amen.

A Sermon on
Keeping Children in School

Dear friends, the common people appear to be quite indifferent to the matter of maintaining the schools. I see them withdrawing their children from instruction and turning them to the making of a living and to caring for their bellies. Besides, they either will not or cannot think what a horrible and un-Christian business this is and what great and murderous harm they are doing everywhere in so serving the devil. For this reason I have undertaken to give you this exhortation, on the chance that there may be some who still have at least a modicum of belief that there is a God in heaven and a hell prepared for unbelievers, and that by this exhortation they might be led to change their minds. (Actually, almost everybody is acting as if there were neither a God in heaven nor a devil in hell.) I propose, therefore, to take up the question of what is at stake in this matter in the way of gains and losses, first those that are spiritual or eternal, and then those that are temporal or worldly.

I hope, indeed, that believers, those who want to be called Christians, know very well that the spiritual estate[12] has been established and instituted by God, not with gold or silver but with the precious blood and bitter death of his only Son, our Lord Jesus Christ [I Pet. 1:18-19]. From his wounds indeed flow the sacra-

---

[12] *Der geistliche stand* refers to the clergy or the ministry.

ments[13] (they used to depict this on broadsides).[14] He paid dearly that men might everywhere have this office of preaching, baptizing, loosing, binding, giving the sacrament, comforting, warning, and exhorting with God's word, and whatever else belongs to the pastoral office. For this office not only helps to further and sustain this temporal life and all the worldly estates, but it also gives eternal life and delivers from sin and death, which is its proper and chief work. Indeed, it is only because of the spiritual estate that the world stands and abides at all; if it were not for this estate, the world would long since have gone down to destruction.

I am not thinking, however, of the spiritual estate as we know it today in the monastic houses and the foundations with their celibate way of life, for it has long since fallen from its glorious beginning and is now nothing more than an estate founded by worldly wisdom for the sake of getting money and revenues.[15] There is nothing spiritual about it except that the clergy are not married (they do not need marriage for they have something else in its place); except for this, everything about it is merely external, temporal, perishable pomp. They give no heed to God's word and the office of preaching—and where the word is not in use the clergy must be bad.

The estate I am thinking of is rather one which has the office of preaching and the service of the word and sacraments and which imparts the Spirit and salvation, blessings that cannot be attained by any amount of pomp and pageantry. It includes the work of pastors, teachers, preachers, lectors, priests (whom men call chaplains), sacristans, schoolmasters, and whatever other work belongs to these offices and persons. This estate the Scriptures

---

[13] In his *Lectures on the Gospel According to St. John* (Tractate 120), Augustine comments on how the Evangelist in John 19:34 significantly says that Jesus' side was not pierced "but 'opened,' that thereby, in a sense, the gate of life might be thrown open, from whence have flowed forth the sacraments of the Church." *PNF*[1] 7, 434.

[14] Some of the one-page tracts or book pages frequently illustrated with woodcuts which Luther may have had in mind are suggested in *WA* 30[II], 527, n. 1, and *MA*[3] 5, 439, n. 266, l. 21. The scene of Christ's blood dripping from his wounded feet into a sacramental chalice at the base of the cross was a common theme in art.

[15] *Zins;* for an explanation of this term, see *LW* 45, 235-238.

highly exalt and praise. St. Paul calls them God's stewards and servants [I Cor. 4:1]; bishops [Acts 20:28]; doctors, prophets [I Cor. 12:28]; also God's ambassadors to reconcile the world to God, II Corinthians 6 [5:20]. Joel calls them saviors.[16] In Psalm 68[17] David calls them kings and princes. Haggai [1:13] calls them angels,[18] and Malachi [2:7] says, "The lips of the priest keep the law, for he is an angel of the Lord of hosts." Christ himself gives them the same name, not only in Matthew 11 [:10] where he calls John the Baptist an angel, but also throughout the entire book of the Revelation to John.

This is why the ancients greatly avoided this estate.[19] Because of its great dignity and honor they so dreaded to take the office upon them that they had to be forced and driven into it. To be sure, there have been many since then who have praised this estate highly, though more because of the saying of mass than because of the preaching. This praise and glorification grew to the point where the office and estate of the priesthood (that is, of the sacrificing of the mass) was placed above Mary and the angels because the angels and Mary could not say mass but a priest could. A new priest and his first mass were glorious, and blessed was the woman who bore a priest [Luke 11:27]. The office of preaching the word, however, which is the highest and chief of all, was not regarded so highly. In a word, a priest was a man who could say mass, even though he could not preach a word and was an unlearned ass. Such in fact is the spiritual estate even to the present day.

Now if it is true and certain that God himself has established

---

[16] *Heilande*, which may have reference to Joel 2:23, where Luther followed the Vulgate (*doctorem justitiae*) in his 1545 German Bible by rendering the ambiguous Hebrew *hammoreh litsedaqah* ("early rain for your vindication" in the RSV) as *Lehrer zur gerechtigkeit* ("teachers unto righteousness"). WA, DB 11ᴵᴵ, 221.

[17] Luther consistently understood the "kings" of Ps. 68:12 as "the host of those who bore the tidings" in the preceding verse. In his German Psalter he translated the verse, "The kings of the armies are friends with one another," and in a marginal gloss he noted that "[kings] are the apostles whose teaching is in harmony." WA, DB 10ᴵ, 321-313.

[18] Etymologically the term "angel" means "messenger." The Hebrew *malak* is translated both ways in German as in English.

[19] Gregory of Nazianzus is an example. Cf. WA 30ᴵᴵ, 529, n. 1.

and instituted the spiritual estate with his own blood and death, we may conclude that he will have it highly honored. He will not allow it to be destroyed or to die out, but will have it maintained until the Last Day. For the gospel and the church must abide until the Last Day, as Christ says in the last chapter of Matthew [28:20], "Lo, I am with you always, to the close of the age." But by whom then shall it be maintained? Oxen and horses, dogs and swine will not do it; neither will wood and stone. We men shall have to do it, for this office is not committed to oxen and horses, but to us men. But where shall we get men for it except from those who have children? If you will not raise your child for this office, and the next man will not, and so on, and no fathers or mothers will give their children to our God for this work, what will become of the spiritual office and estate? The old men now in the office will not live forever. They are dying off every day and there are no others to take their place. What will God finally say to this at last? Do you think he will be pleased that we shamefully despise his office, divinely instituted to his honor and glory and for our salvation and won at such a price—so despise it that we ungratefully let it fade away and die?

He has not given you your children and the means to support them simply so that you may do with them as you please, or train them just to get ahead in the world. You have been earnestly commanded to raise them for God's service, or be completely rooted out—you, your children, and everything else, in which case everything you have done for them is condemned, as the first commandment says, "I visit the iniquities of the fathers upon the children to the third and fourth generation of those who hate me" [Exod. 20:5]. But how will you raise them for God's service if the office of preaching and the spiritual estate have fallen into oblivion?

And it is your fault. You could have done something about it. You could have helped to maintain them if you had allowed your child to study. And where it is possible for you to do this but you fail to do so, where your child has the ability and the desire to learn but you stand in the way, then you—and mark this well!— you are guilty of the harm that is done when the spiritual estate disappears and neither God nor God's word remains in the world.

To the extent that you are able you are bringing about its demise. You refuse to give one child—and would do the same if all the children in the world were yours. So far as you are concerned, the serving of God can just die out altogether.

It does not help your case to say, "My neighbor keeps his son in school, so I don't need to." For your neighbor can say the same thing, and so can all the neighbors. Meanwhile, where is God to get people for his spiritual office? You have someone you could give, but you refuse—as does your neighbor. The office simply goes down to destruction so far as you are concerned. But because you allow the office instituted and established by your God and so dearly won to go to ruin, because you are so horribly ungrateful as to let it be destroyed, you yourself will be accursed. You will have nothing but shame and misery both for yourself and for your children, or be so tormented in other ways that both you and they will be damned, not only here on earth but eternally in hell. This will happen so that you may learn that your children are not so wholly yours that you need give nothing of them to God. He too will have what is rightfully his—and they are more his than yours!

And lest you think I am being too severe with you in this matter, I shall lay before you a partial statement of the gains and losses you are effecting—for who can recount them all?—such that you will have to admit yourself that you indeed belong to the devil and rightly deserve to be damned eternally in hell if you acquiesce in this fault and do not amend your ways. On the other hand, you may rejoice and be glad from the heart if you find that you have been chosen by God to devote your means and labor to raising a son who will be a good Christian pastor, preacher, or schoolmaster, and thereby to raise for God a special servant, yes (as was said above), an angel of God, a true bishop before God, a savior of many people, a king and prince in the kingdom of Christ, a teacher of God's people, a light of the world—indeed, who can recount all the distinction and honor that a good and faithful pastor has in the eyes of God? There is no dearer treasure, no nobler thing on earth or in this life than a good and faithful pastor and preacher.

Just think, whatever good is accomplished by the preaching office and the care of souls is assuredly accomplished by your own son as he faithfully performs this office. For example, each day through him many souls are taught, converted, baptized, and brought to Christ and saved, and redeemed from sin, death, hell, and the devil. Through him they come to everlasting righteousness, to everlasting life and heaven, so that Daniel [12:3] says well that "those who teach others shall shine like the brightness of the firmament; and those who turn many to righteousness shall be like the stars for ever and ever." Because God's word and office, when it proceeds aright, must without ceasing do great things and work actual miracles, so your son must without ceasing do great miracles before God, such as raising the dead, driving out devils, making the blind to see, the deaf to hear, the lepers clean, and the dumb to speak [Matt. 11:5]. Though these things may not happen bodily, they do happen spiritually in the soul, where the miracles are even greater, as Christ says in John 14 [:12], "He who believes in me will also do the works that I do; and greater works than these will he do." If the single believer can accomplish these things working independently with individuals, how much more will the preacher accomplish working publicly with the whole company of people? It is not the man, though, that does it. It is his office, ordained by God for this purpose. That is what does it— that and the word of God which he teaches. He is only the instrument through which it is accomplished.

Now if he accomplishes such great things spiritually, it follows that he also does bodily works and miracles, or at least gets them started. For how does it happen that Christians will rise from the dead at the Last Day, and that all the deaf, blind, lame, and other sufferers of bodily ills must lay aside their ailments? How does it happen that their bodies will not only become healthy, sound, and beautiful, but even shine as bright and fair as the sun [Matt. 13:43], as Christ says? Is it not because here on earth, through God's word, they have been converted, become believers, been baptized and incorporated into Christ? Thus Paul says in Romans 8 [:11] that God will raise up our mortal bodies because of his Spirit which dwells in us. Now how are men helped to this faith and to this beginning of the resurrection of the body except through the office of preaching and the word of God, the office your son performs? Is this not an immeasurably greater and more glorious work and miracle than if he were in a bodily or temporal way to raise the dead again to this life, or help the blind, deaf, dumb, and leprous here in the world, in this transitory life?

If you were sure that your son would accomplish even one of these works in a single human being, that he would make one blind man to see or one dead man to rise, snatch one soul from the devil or rescue one person from hell, or whatever else it might be, ought you not with utmost joy devote all your means to train him for this office and work? Ought you not leap for joy that with your money you are privileged to accomplish something so great in the sight of God? For what are all the foundations and monastic houses of our day with their self-appointed works in comparison with one such pastor, preacher, or schoolmaster? To be sure, they were originally founded long ago by pious kings and lords precisely for this precious work of training such preachers and pastors. But now, sad to say, the devil has brought them to such a wretched state that they have become death traps, the very ramparts of hell, to the hurt and detriment of the church.

Now just look at what your son does—not just one of these works but many, indeed, all of them! And he does them every day. Best of all, he does them in the sight of God who, as we have said, looks upon them so highly and regards them as precious, even though men may not recognize or esteem them. Indeed, if all the world should call your son a heretic, deceiver, liar, and rebel, so much the better. That is a good sign that he is an upright man, like his Lord Christ. For Christ too had to be a rebel, a murderer, and a deceiver, and be condemned and crucified with the murderers. What would it matter to me as a preacher if the world were to call me a devil, so long as I knew that God calls me his angel? Let the world call me a deceiver as much as it pleases, so long as God calls me his faithful servant and steward, the angels call me their comrade, the saints call me their brother, believers call me their father, souls in anguish call me their savior, the ignorant call me their light, and God adds, "Yes, it is so," and the angels and all creatures join in. Ah! How prettily the world, with the devil, has deceived me with its slanders and scoffing! How the dear world has hurt me and gained at my expense!

I have spoken so far about the works and miracles which your son does for individual souls, helping them against sin, death, and the devil. Beyond that, however, he does great and mighty works for the world. He informs and instructs the various estates on how they are to conduct themselves outwardly in their several offices and estates, so that they may do what is right in the sight of God. Every day he can comfort and advise those who are troubled, compose difficulties, relieve troubled consciences, help maintain peace and settle and remove differences, and countless other works of this kind. For a preacher confirms, strengthens, and helps to sustain authority of every kind, and temporal peace generally. He checks the rebellious; teaches obedience, morals, discipline, and honor; instructs fathers, mothers, children, and servants in their duties; in a word, he gives direction to all the temporal estates and offices. Of all the good things a pastor does these are, to be sure, the least. Yet they are so high and noble that the wisest of all the heathen have never known or understood them, much less been able to do them. Indeed, even to the present day no jurist, university, foundation, or monastery knows these works, and they are not taught either in canon law or secular law. For there is no one who regards these offices as God's great gifts, his gracious ordinances. It is only the word of God and the preachers that praise and honor them so highly.

Therefore, to tell the truth, peace, the greatest of earthly goods, in which all other temporal goods are comprised, is really a fruit of true preaching. For where the preaching is right, there war and discord and bloodshed do not come; but where the preaching is not right, it is no wonder that there is war, or at least constant unrest and the desire to fight and to shed blood. We can see even now how the sophists[20] can do nothing but cry bloody murder and spit fire. They shed the blood of innocent priests who get mar-

---

[20] *Sophisten* was Luther's term for the scholastic theologians. Cf. *LW* 45, 200, n. 5.

ried,[21] even though the pope and their own canon law in punishing such clerical marriages at most merely suspend the priest from office,[22] without so much as touching his person or property or Christian honor, much less condemning him to hell or regarding him as a heretic. This the jurists and everybody else will have to concede. It was even made a law at the Diet of Nürnberg.[23] But these blind bloodhounds have given up preaching and betaken themselves to lies, and this is why they cannot desist from murder. The devil their god does the same; according to John 8 [:44] he was "from the beginning" and still is "a liar and a murderer."

A true pastor thus contributes to the well-being of men in body and soul, in property and honor. But beyond that see how he also serves God and what glorious worship and sacrifice he renders. For

---

[21] Georg Winkler, a priest in Halle, was tried by an ecclesiastical court at Aschaffenburg for administering the sacrament in both kinds. It was known at the time that he was also guilty of having taken a wife. He was released by Archbishop Albrecht of Mainz, but on the way home was set upon and murdered on April 23, 1527. Suspicion fixed upon the archbishop as the instigator of the crime. Cf. Luther's letter of sympathy *To the Christians at Halle* in WA 23, 402-430; cf. especially his reference to the archbishop on pp. 407-408.

[22] See Luther's *Articles Against the Whole Synagogue of Satan and All the Gates of Hell*, written about the same time, in which the last ten of forty articles deal specifically with the marriage of priests, the punishment of which is said to be limited to suspension from office (WA 30ᴵᴵ, 423-424). See also the second of Luther's nine articles prepared about the same time for his colleagues at the Diet of Augsburg, in which he makes the same point (WA, Br 5, 431). The applicable canon laws (listed in LW 34, 20, n. 19) had recently been brought to Luther's attention again in a little book written by Lazarus Spengler in which Spengler recounts the instances in which canon law conformed to God's word (the book was published early in 1530 with a preface by Luther; the text of Luther's preface is given in WA 30ᴵᴵ, 219). In 1089 Pope Urban II had prescribed removal from priesthood and benefice for any member of the higher orders of clergy who took a wife; see *Decreti Magistri Gratiani Prima Pars, dist.* XXXII, C. X. *CIC* 1, 120.

[23] The Diet of Nürnberg rejected papal demands for strict enforcement of the Edict of Worms, declaring specifically on March 6, 1523, "Since the extant laws of the temporal authority provide no punishment for priests who marry or for monks and nuns who leave the cloister none shall be inflicted beyond that stipulated in the canon law. The spiritual authorities are not to be hindered but protected in their enforcement of such penalties as may apply, the loss of rights, privileges, benefices, etc. Where such priests, monks, and nuns offend in other ways, however, they are to be punished according to established law." A. Kluckhohn and A. Wrede (eds.), *Deutsche Reichstagsakten unter Karl V* (4 vols.; Gotha: Perthes, 1893-1905), III, 451; and *St. L.* 15, 2145.

by his work and word there are maintained in this world the kingdom of God, the name and honor and glory of God, the true knowledge of God, the right faith and understanding of Christ, the fruits of the suffering and blood and death of Christ, the gifts and works and power of the Holy Spirit, the true and saving use of baptism and the sacrament, the right and pure teaching of the gospel, the right way of disciplining and crucifying the body, and much more. Who could ever adequately praise any one of these things? And what more can still be said? How much he accomplishes by battling against the devil, the wisdom of this world, and the imaginations of the flesh; how many victories he wins; how he puts down error and prevents heresy. For he must strive and fight against the gates of hell [Matt. 16:18] and overcome the devil. This too is not his own doing; it is accomplished by his office and his word. These are the innumerable and unspeakable works and miracles of the preaching office. In a word, if we would praise God to the uttermost, we must praise his word and preaching; for the office and the word are his.

Now even if you were a king, you should not think you are too good to give your son and to train him for this office and work, even at the cost of all that you have. Is not the money and the labor you expend on such a son so highly honored, so gloriously blessed, so profitably invested that it counts in God's sight as better than any kingdom or empire? A man ought to be willing to crawl on his hands and knees to the ends of the earth to be able to invest his money so gloriously well. Yet right there in your own house and on your own lap you have that in which you can make such an investment. Shame, shame, and shame again upon our blind and despicable ingratitude that we should fail to see what extraordinary service we could render to God, indeed, how distinguished we could be in his sight with just a little application of effort and our own money and property.

The sophists accuse us Lutherans of not teaching good works. Isn't that great! They know so much about good works! Are not these things we have been speaking of good works? What are all the works of the foundations and monasteries compared with these glorious miracles? They are like the cawing of jackdaws and ravens, though not as good. For the daws at least like to caw; they do so gladly. But the sophists take no pleasure in their croaking; they caw reluctantly, like the hoopoes and owls. Now if it was formerly the custom to think highly of new priests and their first masses, and if fathers and mothers and all their friends were glad that they had raised a son to be an idle, lazy, useless mass-priest or glutton[24] who puts God to shame with his blasphemous sacrifice of the mass and his wasted prayers and scandalizes and defrauds the world with his unchaste life, how much more should you rejoice if you have raised a son for this office of preaching in which you are sure that he serves God so gloriously, helps men so generously, and smites the devil in such knightly fashion? You have made of your son such a true and excellent sacrifice to God that the very angels must look upon it as a splendid miracle.

You ought also to know the harm that you are doing if you take the opposite course. If God has given you a child who has the ability and the talent for this office, and you do not train him for it but look only to the belly and to temporal livelihood, then take the list of things mentioned above and run over the good works and miracles noted there, and see what a pious hypocrite and unproductive weed[25] you are. For so far as it is up to you, you are depriving God of an angel, a servant, a king and prince in his kingdom; a savior and comforter of men in matters that pertain to body and soul, property and honor; a captain and a knight to fight against the devil. Thus you are making a place for the devil and advancing his kingdom so that he brings more souls into sin, death, and hell every day and keeps them there, and wins victories everywhere; the world remains in heresy, error, contention, war, and strife, and gets worse every day; the kingdom of God goes down to destruction, along with Christian faith, the fruits of the suffering and blood of Christ, the work of the Holy Spirit, the gospel, and all worship of God; and all devil worship and unbelief get the upper hand. All of this need not have happened and could have been prevented, things could even have been improved, if your son had been trained for this work and entered it.

---

[24] *Messpfaffen oder fresspfaffen.*
[25] *Kreutlein;* cf. WA 33, 162, n. 1.

Suppose God were to address you on your deathbed, or at the Last Judgment, and say, "I was hungry, thirsty, a stranger, naked, sick, imprisoned, and you rendered me no service. For in that you have not done it to people on earth and to my kingdom or gospel, but have helped put them down and allowed men's souls to perish, you have done this to me. For you could have helped. I gave you children and material means for this purpose, but you wantonly allowed me and my kingdom and the souls of men to suffer want and pine away—and you thereby served the devil and his kingdom instead of me and my kingdom. Well, let him be your reward. Go with him now into the abyss of hell. You have not helped to build but to weaken and destroy my kingdom in heaven and on earth; but you have helped the devil to build and increase his hell. Live, therefore, in the house that you have built!"[26]

How do you think you will stand then? You will not be tainted by little drops of sin, but inundated by whole cloudbursts of it— you who now give no heed but just go nonchalantly along as if you were doing well in keeping your child from an education. But then you will have to say that you are justly condemned to the abyss of hell as one of the most odious and vile men who ever lived. Indeed, if you were to consider these things even now, while you are living, you would be truly horrified at yourself. For no conscience can bear to be found guilty of even one of the things that have been mentioned; how much less can it bear it if suddenly all these things, more than can be numbered, fall on it all at once? Your heart will then have to cry out that your sins are more than the leaves and the grass, indeed, greater than heaven and earth; and you will say with Manasseh, king of Judah, "The sins I have committed are more in number than the sands of the sea; my transgressions are multiplied" [Pr. of Man. 9]. Even the law of nature tells you that he who is able to prevent injury but does not do so is guilty of the injury because he certainly desired and willed it and would have inflicted it himself if he had had occasion or opportunity. These people, therefore, are certainly no better than the devil himself because they are so angry with both God and the world that they help to ruin both heaven and earth, and serve the devil faithfully. In a word, if we cannot adequately

---

[26] Cf. Matt. 25:42-43.

denounce the devil, neither can we adequately denounce these people who hinder the work and office of God, for they are the devil's servants.

In saying this I do not mean to insist that every man must train his child for this office, for it is not necessary that all boys become pastors, preachers, and schoolmasters. It is well to know that the children of lords and other important people are not to be used for this work, for the world also needs heirs, people without whom the temporal authority would go to pieces.[27] I am speaking of the common people, who used to have their children educated for the sake of the livings and benefices but now keep them away from learning to earn a livelihood. Even though they need no heirs they keep their children out of school, regardless of whether the children have the ability and talent for these offices and could serve God in them without privation or hindrance. Boys of such ability ought to be kept at their studies, especially sons of the poor, for all the endowments and revenues of the foundations and monasteries are earmarked for this purpose. In addition, though, other boys as well ought to study, even those of lesser ability. They ought at least to read, write, and understand Latin, for we need not only highly learned doctors and masters of Holy Scripture but also ordinary pastors who will teach the gospel and the catechism[28] to the young and ignorant, and baptize and administer the sacrament. That they may be incapable of doing battle with heretics is unimportant. For a good building we need not only hewn facings but also backing stone. In like manner we must also have sacristans and other persons who serve and help in relation to the office of preaching and the word of God.

Even though a boy who has studied Latin should afterward learn a trade and become a craftsman, he still stands as a ready reserve in case he should be needed as a pastor or in some other service of the word. Neither will such knowledge hurt his capacity to earn a living. On the contrary, he can rule his house all the better because of it, and besides, he is prepared for the office

---

[27] The temporal government which Luther knew best was the hereditary feudal lordship.

[28] I.e., the Ten Commandments, the Creed, and the Lord's Prayer.

of preacher or pastor if he should be needed there. It is especially easy in our day to train persons for teaching the gospel and the catechism because not only Holy Scripture but also knowledge of all kinds is so abundant,[29] what with so many books, so much reading, and, thank God, so much preaching that one can learn more now in three years than was formerly possible in twenty. Even women[30] and children can now learn from German books and sermons more about God and Christ—I am telling the truth!—than all the universities, foundations, monasteries, the whole papacy, and all the world used to know. Ordinary pastors, however, must be able to use Latin. They cannot do without it any more than scholars can do without Greek and Hebrew,[31] as St. Augustine says[32] and canon law even prescribes.[33]

But you say, "Suppose things turn out badly and my son becomes a heretic or a knave? As they say, 'The learned are daft.' "[34] Well, you have to take that chance. Your diligence and labor will not be lost. God will have regard for your faithful service and count it as though it had turned out well. You simply have to

---

[29] By this time Luther had already published his translation of the New Testament (1522), the Pentateuch (1523), Joshua—Esther (1524), Job—Song of Solomon (1524), Jonah (1526), Habakkuk (1526), Zechariah (1527), and Isaiah (1528). Complete Bibles translated by Protestants had appeared in German in 1529 at Zurich and Worms. Cf. *LW* 35, 227-229.

[30] For instances of Luther's repeated advocacy of education for girls, see *LW* 45, 175, 188-189, 344 n. 12, 368-371, and *LW* 44, 206.

[31] See Luther's fuller argument for the study of classical languages in his 1524 appeal *To the Councilmen of All Cities in Germany. LW* 45, 356-377 *passim.*

[32] "Men who know the Latin language . . . have need of two others in order to understand the Sacred Scriptures. These are Hebrew and Greek, by which they may turn back to the originals if the infinite variances of Latin translators cause any uncertainty." *Christian Instruction* (*De doctrina Christiana*), Book II, chap. 11. *FC* 4, 73; cf. *MPL* 34, 42.

[33] The eleventh canon of the Council of Vienna (1312) directed that in the interests of scriptural exposition and world mission Greek, Hebrew, Syriac, and Arabic be taught at the principal universities of Paris, Oxford, Bologna, and Salamanca, as well as in the curriculum for curial studies—though not general studies—at Rome. Berthold Altaner, "Die Durchführung des Vienner Konzilsbeschlusses über die Errichtung von Lehrstühlen für orientalische Sprachen," *Zeitschrift für Kirchengeschichte*, LII (1933), 227. The text of the decree as altered and promulgated by Pope John XXII on October 25, 1317, is given in *Clementis papae V. Constitutiones*, lib. v, tit. I: *De Magistris, C. I. CIC* 2, 1179.

[34] *Die Gelehrten, die Verkehrten.*

take the chance as you would in any other occupation for which you might train your son. How was it with the good Abraham? His son Ishmael did not turn out well; neither did Isaac's son Esau, or Adam's son Cain. Should Abraham therefore have given up training his son Isaac, or Isaac his son Jacob, or Adam his son Abel for the service of God? How many bad kings and people there were among the holy and chosen nation of Israel! With their heresies and idolatries they brought on all kinds of trouble and killed all the prophets. Ought Levi the priest to have let the whole nation go on that account, and no longer trained anyone for the service of God? How many bad priests and Levites were there among the tribe of Levi, which God himself had chosen for the priesthood? How many people has God on earth who misuse all his kindness and all his creatures? Ought he on that account to desist from his kindness and let no man live? Ought he cease to do good?

Moreover, that you may not worry too much about where your son's living will come from if he gives himself to learning and to this divine office and ministry, God has not left you or forgotten you in this matter either, so you need not worry or lament. He has promised through St. Paul in I Corinthians 9 [:14] that "those who proclaim the gospel should get their living by the gospel"; and Christ himself says in Matthew, "The laborer deserves his wages; eat and drink what they have."[35] Under the Old Testament, so that his office of preaching might not perish, God chose and took the whole tribe of Levi, that is to say, one-twelfth of the whole nation of Israel, and gave them the tithe from the whole nation, besides the first-fruits, all kinds of sacrifices, their own cities and pasture lands,[36] fields and meadows, cattle, and all that goes with them. Under the New Testament, see how in former times emperors, kings, princes, and lords gave to this office rich possessions, which the foundations and monasteries now have in more abundance than even the kings and princes themselves. God will not and cannot fail those who serve him faithfully, for he has bound himself by the promise given in Hebrews 13 [:5], "I will never fail you nor forsake you."

---

[35] Luke 10:7-8; cf. Matt. 10:10.
[36] *Vorstedte;* cf. Num. 35:1-8.

Think, too, how many parishes, pulpits, schools, and sacristan-ships there are. Most of them are sufficiently provided for,[37] and vacancies are occurring every day. What does this mean except that God has provided kitchen and cellar for your son in advance? His living is ready for him before he needs it; he does not have to scrape it together for himself. When I was a young student I heard it said that in Saxony there were (if I remember rightly) about eighteen hundred parishes.[38] If that is true, and every parish required at least two persons, a pastor and a sacristan (except that in the cities there are preachers, chaplains, assistants, schoolmas-ters, and helpers), then in this one principality about four thou-sand educated persons are needed, of whom about one-third die off every ten years. I would wager that in half of Germany today there are not four thousand pupils in the schools. Now I estimate that there are scarcely eight hundred pastors in Saxony; how many will that make for the whole of Germany? I would like to know where we are going to get pastors, schoolmasters, and sacristans three years from now. If we do nothing about this, and if the princes especially do not try to see that the boys' schools and the universities are properly maintained, there will be such a scarcity of men that we shall have to give three or four cities to one pas-tor and ten villages to one chaplain, if indeed we can get even that many men.

The universities at Erfurt, Leipzig, and elsewhere, as well as the boys' schools here and there, are so deserted that it is distress-ing to behold; little Wittenberg now does better than any of them.[39] The foundations and the monasteries, I suppose, will also

---

[37] I.e., by endowments.

[38] If the reference is limited to Electoral Saxony, Luther's memory—or infor-mation—could be wrong, for the 1528-1529 visitation disclosed that apart from Wittenberg there were only one hundred forty-five pastoral positions. C. A. H. Burckhardt, *Geschichte der sächsischen Kirchen- und Schulvisitation* (Leipzig: Grunow, 1879), pp. 30-36.

[39] When Luther entered Erfurt as a student in 1501 the enrolment was about two thousand (Schwiebert, *Luther and His Times*, p. 131), but by 1529 the enrolment had dropped to twenty. The enrolment at Leipzig dropped from a five-year average (1526-1530) of 175 to 93 in 1529. En-rolment at the University of Wittenberg, which was founded later than the universities of Erfurt and Leipzig and had been a much smaller school, dropped from 250 to 173 in the same period. Cf. WA 30^{II}, 550, n. 2.

feel the scarcity, but who cares?[40] Cocky as they are, they are going to have to come down off their high horse[41] and accept—even recruit—people into their chapters whom they formerly would not have looked at twice. Let your boy go on with his studying, therefore, and do not worry; perhaps if the world lasts a while longer[42] and God gives the princes and the cities grace to act, the property of the foundations and monasteries will be restored to the use for which is was originally intended. And why worry anyway about the belly? Christ stands there and says, "Do not be anxious about what you shall eat and drink. Your heavenly Father knows well that you need all this. Seek first the kingdom of God and his righteousness, and all these things shall be yours as well" [Matt 6:31-33]. If anyone does not believe Christ, he can just go on worrying—and die of hunger too!

Although it is true that a few years ago many pastors did suffer great want, and many still do, that is due to the convulsions[43] of our time: people are so wicked, ungrateful, and avaricious that they even persecute the gospel. By this God is trying us to see whether we are upright and sincere. We must think of our time as being like that of the martyrs, for then, too, godly teachers suffered great want and poverty, as Paul himself boasts [II Cor. 11:27], and Christ also prophesied in Matthew 9 [:15], "When the bridegroom is taken away from them, then they will fast." This is the fasting that is true to the gospel. Then, too, whenever God's word has come forth hard times have almost always come with it. In the days of Abraham [Gen. 12:10], Isaac [Gen. 26:1], Jacob and Joseph [Gen. 41:56], Elijah [I Kings 18:2], and

---

[40] *Solten sie ein gut jar haben.* Thiele, *Sprichwörtersammlung*, No. 186; *WA, Br* 5, 370, n. 7; Jacob and Wilhelm Grimm, *Deutsches Wörterbuch*, IV², 2232-2233.

[41] *Nicht so hoch hinaus singen, wie sie es angefangen haben* refers to the embarrassment of the vocalist whose voice must crack before he finishes because he foolishly pitched his song too high at the beginning. Cf. Thiele, *Luthers Sprichwörtersammlung*, No. 159.

[42] See p. 18, n. 3.

[43] The term *paroxysmus*, which recurs in several of Luther's letters during this same period, has reference to that part of Greek drama which is called the epitasis, the extreme or climactic stage which follows the protasis and precedes the catastrophe. *WA, Br* 5, 459, n. 3; cf. also 417, n. 9; 471, n. 1; 473, n. 4.

Elisha [II Kings 4:38] there was, besides the great light of truth, cruel famine. And in the beginning of the gospel there was a great famine throughout the world [Acts 11:28]. This of course has to be blamed on the dear gospel and the word of God, not on the world's former misdeeds and present obstinate ingratitude! Thus did the Jews blame all their misery on the teaching of Jeremiah [Jer. 44:16 ff.]. And the Romans, when they were overthrown by the Goths, knew nothing to blame it on except the fact that they had become Christians. Indeed, it was to refute this charge that St. Augustine wrote a great book, *De civitate dei.*[44]

Well, they can say what they please—the world is still the world. As in those days the liars were exposed and destroyed, so shall it be today, so that Christ and his word may yet abide. He sits exalted and immovable, as it is written, "The Lord said to my Lord, 'Sit at my right hand'" [Ps. 110:1]. There he sits; if anyone is wicked and wants to pull him down, let him do so! But as long as he remains seated there, we too shall remain; and that is that! To put it in a word, your son can easily get as good a living from the preaching office as from a trade—unless of course you are thinking of great wealth and of making your son a great lord in the eyes of the world, such as the bishops and canons are. If that is what you are after, then what I am saying does not concern you. I am speaking here only to believers, who respect and honor the preaching office above all riches as being, next to God himself, the greatest treasure ever given to men. I would have them know how great is the service they can and ought to render God in this matter, as men who would rather participate in this work, even though the material rewards be few, than to have this world's goods and be without this work. Such men will recognize that the soul is more than the belly, and that though the belly be surfeited it will still be obliged to leave everything else behind at death. But those who seek [true] riches will take all their goods with them, leaving nothing behind; that is for sure!

So much then for the first part of this sermon, a brief and cur-

---

[44] Augustine wrote *The City of God* in the years 413-426 to refute the pagan charge that the fall of Rome to Alaric in 410 was due to the abolition of heathen worship. Cf. *LW* 45, 110, n. 68.

sory account of the spiritual gains and losses which accrue from the maintenance and neglect of the schools.

The second part will deal with the temporal or worldly gains and losses. And in the first place, it is true that the office of temporal authority cannot at all be compared with the spiritual office of preaching, as St. Paul calls it [Col. 1:25]; for it is not purchased at so dear a price as the preaching office, by the blood and dying of the Son of God. Neither can it therefore do such great wonders and works as the preaching office. For all the works of this estate belong only to this temporal, transient life. They protect body, wife, child, house, property, and honor, and whatever else pertains to the needs of this life. As far, then, as eternal life surpasses this temporal life, so far does the preaching office exceed the temporal office—even as the substance surpasses the shadow. For worldly lordship is an image, shadow, or figure of the lordship of Christ. The office of preaching—where it exists as God ordained it—brings and bestows eternal righteousness, eternal peace, and eternal life; thus does St. Paul extol it in II Corinthians 4. Worldly government, on the other hand, preserves peace, justice, and life, which is temporal and transient.

Nevertheless, worldly government is a glorious ordinance and splendid gift of God, who has instituted and established it and will have it maintained as something men cannot do without. If there were no worldly government, one man could not stand before another; each would necessarily devour the other, as irrational beasts devour one another. Therefore as it is the function and honor of the office of preaching to make sinners saints, dead men live, damned men saved, and the devil's children God's children, so it is the function and honor of worldly government to make men out of wild beasts and to prevent men from becoming wild beasts. It protects a man's body so that no one may slay it; it protects a man's wife so that no one may seize and defile her; it protects a man's child, his daughter or son, so that no one may carry them away and steal them; it protects a man's house so that no one may break in and wreck things; it protects a man's fields and cattle and all his goods so that no one may attack, steal, plunder, or damage them. Protection of this sort does not exist among the beasts, and if it

237

were not for worldly government there would be none of it among men either; they would surely cease to be men and become mere beasts. Do you not think that if the birds and beasts were to see the worldly government that exists among men they would say—if they could speak—"O men! Compared with us you are not men but gods! What security you have, both you and your possessions, while among us no one is safe from another regarding life, home, or food supply, not even for a moment! Shame upon your ingratitude—you do not even see what a splendid life the God of us all has given you compared with us beasts!"

It is certain, then, that temporal authority is a creation and ordinance of God, and that for us men in this life it is a necessary office and estate which we can no more dispense with than we can dispense with life itself, since without such an office this life cannot continue. That being true, it is easy to understand that God has not commanded and instituted it only to have it destroyed. On the contrary, he wills to have it maintained, as is clearly stated by Paul in Romans 13 [:4], and in I Peter 3 [2:13-14], to protect those who do good and to punish those who do wrong. Now who will maintain this office except us men to whom God has committed it, and who truly need it? The wild beasts will not maintain it, nor will wood and stone. And what men are capable of doing it? Certainly not those who would rule only with the fist, as many now think to do. For if men were to rule solely by the fist, the end result would surely be a bestial kind of existence: whoever could get the better of another would simply toss him into the discard pile. We have enough examples before our eyes to see what the fist can accomplish apart from wisdom or reason.

This is why Solomon says in Proverbs 8 [:14-15] that wisdom, not force, must rule. He speaks of wisdom this way, "I, Wisdom, have counsel and sound wisdom. I have insight, I have strength. By me kings reign, and rulers decree what is just." And Ecclesiastes 10 [9:18, 16] says, "Wisdom is better than weapons of war"; and again, "Wisdom is better than might." All experience proves this and in all the histories we find that force, without reason or wisdom, has never once accomplished anything. Indeed, even murderers and tyrants, if they are not clever enough to adopt for themselves and

238

among themselves some kind of laws and regulations to control and limit the power of the fist (even though these be equally wicked), will not be able to continue; they will fall out among themselves and perish by each other's hand. Briefly, then, it is not the law of the fist but the law of the head that must rule—not force but wisdom or reason—among the wicked as well as among the good.

Accordingly, since the government in our German lands is supposed to be guided by the imperial law of Rome,[45] and this law is our government's wisdom and reason, given it by God, it follows that this government cannot be maintained and will inevitably perish unless this law is maintained. Now who will maintain it? Not fist and weapons; heads and books must do it. Men must learn and know the law and wisdom of our worldly government. It is a fine thing, to be sure, if an emperor, prince, or lord is by nature so wise and able that he can instinctively hit upon what is right, as could two men I knew, Duke Frederick of Saxony[46] and Sir Fabian von Feilitzsch,[47] to speak only of men no longer living. Such rulers are pretty rare birds.[48] It would be dangerous to make an example of them because others may not have this power by nature. In ruling it is better to stick to the written law, which carries with it greater recognition and respect and obviates the need for special gifts or charisms.

Thus the jurists and scholars in this worldly kingdom are the persons who preserve this law, and thereby maintain the worldly kingdom. And just as in the kingdom of Christ, a pious theologian

---

[45] See p. 15, n. 29, and LW 44, 203, n. 219.

[46] Known as Frederick the Wise, the elector of Saxony (1486-1525) remained officially neutral toward the Reformation faith until shortly before his death; he was, however, staunch in his defense of the person of his subject Luther and of Luther's rights to freedom and justice. Cf. LW 36, 227, n. 91.

[47] Fabian von Feilitzsch, counselor at the court of Frederick the Wise, was a defender of the Reformation. He died shortly after Luther had dedicated his 1520 *Defense of All the Articles of Martin Luther Condemned by the Recent Bull of Pope Leo X* (*Assertio omnium articulorum M. Lutheri per bullam Leonis X novissimam damnatorum*) to him; though the treatise had not yet actually been published at the time of Fabian's death, Luther refused to change the dedication, in which he refers to Fabian as a Christian "layman," one of "the new generation of clergy" (*WA* 7, 95). Cf. *MA*³ 5, 441, n. 280, l. 38. See also Luther's later laudatory reference to both Fabian and Frederick in his 1534 *Exposition of Psalm 101* (*LW* 13, 157).

[48] See p. 29, n. 29.

and sincere preacher is called an angel of God, a savior, prophet, priest, servant, and teacher (as has been said above),[49] so a pious jurist and true scholar can be called, in the worldly kingdom of the emperor, a prophet, priest, angel, and savior. Again, just as in the kingdom of Christ a heretic or false preacher is a devil, thief, murderer, and blasphemer, so in the emperor's house or realm a false and faithless jurist is a thief and a knave, a traitor, scoundrel, and devil for the whole empire. Now when I speak of the jurists I mean not only the doctors but the whole profession, including chancellors, clerks, judges, lawyers, notaries, and all who have to do with the legal side of government; also the counselors at the court, for they too work with law and exercise the function of jurists. And just as the word "counselors" is not far from the word "traitors,"[50] so the deeds of the two are not far apart. These bigwigs[51] sometimes "counsel" their lords so effectively that no traitor could do a better job of deceiving them.

You see, then, how much good a pious jurist or legal scholar can produce. Indeed, who can recount it all? For any ordinance and work of God constantly produces so much great fruit that it cannot be counted or comprehended. For one thing, the jurist with his law book (by God's ordinance) maintains and helps to further the whole worldly government—emperor, princes, lords, cities, land, and people, as was said above; for all these must be preserved by wisdom and law. But who is able adequately to praise this work alone? By it you receive protection of life and limb against neighbors, enemies, and murderers. Then, too, you have peace and tranquillity for your wife, daughter, son, house and home, servants, money, property, lands, and everything that you have. For all of this is comprehended in, encompassed by, and hedged about with law. What a great thing this is can never be fully told in any book; for who can adequately describe what an unspeakable blessing peace is, and how much it both gives and saves even in a single year?

---

[49] See pp. 220-221.

[50] An untranslatable play on the words *Rethe* and *Verrether* which has to do with the "advisor" who gives "bad advice."

[51] *Die grossen Hansen;* see LW 36, 246, and LW 45, 121, n. 102.

All these great works your son can do. He can become such a useful person if you will hold him to it and see him educated. And you can have a share in all this, and invest your money that profitably. It ought to be a matter of great honor and satisfaction for you to see your son an angel in the empire and an apostle of the emperor, a cornerstone and bulwark of temporal peace on earth, knowing for a certainty that God so regards it and that it really is true. For although such works do not make men righteous before God or save them, nevertheless, it is a joy and comfort to know that these works please God so very much—and the more so when such a man is a believer and is in the kingdom of Christ, for he thereby thanks God for his benefits, bringing to him the finest thankoffering, the highest service.

You would have to be a gross, ungrateful clod, worthy of being numbered among the beasts, if you should see that your son could become a man to help the emperor preserve his empire, sword, and crown; to help the prince rule his principality; to counsel and help cities and lands; to help protect so many men's bodies, wives, children, property, and honor—and yet would not risk enough on it to let him study and come to such a position. Tell me, what do all the foundations and monasteries do that can begin to compare with this? I would take the work of a faithful, pious jurist and clerk over the holiness of all the priests, monks, and nuns, even the very best. And if these great and good works do not move you, then you ought at least to be moved by the honor and good pleasure of God, knowing that by this means you thank him so gloriously and render him such great service, as has been said. We shamefully despise God when we begrudge our children this glorious and divine work and stick them instead in the exclusive service of the belly and of avarice, having them learn nothing but how to make a living, like hogs wallowing forever with their noses in the dunghill, and never training them for so worthy an estate and office. Certainly we must either be crazy, or without love for our children.

But listen still further. Suppose God means to have his way with you and demands your son for this office! For you surely owe it to your God to help maintain this estate if you can. Yet it cannot possibly be maintained unless people keep their children studying

241

and in school; there is no doubt about that. Indeed, there is need in this office for abler people than are needed in the office of preaching, so it is necessary to get the best boys for this work; for in the preaching office Christ does the whole thing, by his Spirit, but in the worldly kingdom men must act on the basis of reason—wherein the laws also have their origin—for God has subjected temporal rule and all of physical life to reason (Genesis 2 [:15]). He has not sent the Holy Spirit from heaven for this purpose. This is why to govern temporally is harder, because conscience cannot rule; one must act, so to speak, in the dark.

Now if you have a son who is able to learn, and you are in a position to keep him at it, but do not do so, if you go your way without even asking what is to become of worldly government and law and peace, then you are doing all in your power to oppose worldly authority, like the Turks, indeed, like the devil himself. For you are taking from empire, principality, land, and city, a savior, comforter, cornerstone, helper, and deliverer. So far as you are concerned the emperor will lose both sword and crown, the land will lose its peace and tranquillity. And you will be the one who is responsible when—as much as it is up to you—no man will have any security for his person, his wife, child, house, home, and property. You blithely hack them all to pieces,[52] causing men to become mere beasts who devour one another in the end. This is what you assuredly are doing, especially if you knowingly keep your son from this wholesome estate for the sake of the belly. Now are you not a fine, useful man in the world? Every day you use the empire and its peace, and in return, by way of thanks, you rob it of your son and stick him in the service of avarice. In so doing you are striving as best you can to see to it that there will be no one to help maintain the empire and law and peace, and that everything will go down to destruction, even though it is only by this empire that you have and maintain your own life and limb, property and honor.

What do you think you have deserved by this? Are you even worthy to dwell among men? But what will God, who has given you child and property with which to serve him by keeping your

---

[52] *Opffert . . . auff die fleissch banck;* see WA 18, 94, n. 1, LW 40, 110-111, and WA 17¹, 369, n. 1.

son in his service, say to this? Is it not a service of God to help maintain his ordinance of worldly government? Now you neglect that service as if it were no concern of yours, or as if you were more free than other men and did not have to serve God but could do just as you please with your child and property, even though God and both his worldly and spiritual kingdoms should fall into the abyss. Yet at the same time you want to make daily use of the empire's protection, peace, and law; you want to have the preaching office and the word of God ready for you and at your service. You want God to serve you free of charge both with preaching and with worldly government, so that you can just calmly turn your child away from him and teach him to serve Mammon alone. Do you not think that God will some day pronounce a benediction[53] over your avarice and concern for the belly such as will destroy you both here and hereafter together with your child and all that you have? Dear fellow, is not your heart terrified at this abominable abomination—your idolatry, despising of God, and ingratitude, your destruction of both these institutions and ordinances of God, yes, the injury and ruin that you inflict on all men? Well, I have told you and warned you. Now you see to it! Having heard both the gains and the losses that are involved, you can just do as you please: God will reward you accordingly.

I shall say nothing here about the pure pleasure a man gets from having studied, even though he never holds an office of any kind, how at home by himself he can read all kinds of things, talk and associate with educated people, and travel and do business in foreign lands; for there are perhaps very few people who are moved by this pleasure. But since you are so bent on the pursuit of Mammon and the making of a living, see what great wealth God has put at the disposal of the schools and scholars so you will have no need to despise learning and knowledge for fear of attendant poverty. Just look, emperors and kings must have chancellors and clerks, counselors, jurists, and scholars. There is no prince who does not need to have chancellors, jurists, counselors, scholars, and clerks. All the counts, lords, cities, and castles must have syndics, city

---

[53] *Benedicite;* "benediction" is used in the sense of saying the last word or bringing to an end. *MA*³ 5, 441, n. 283, l. 38.

clerks, and other scholars. There is not a nobleman who does not need a clerk. And to speak also about men of ordinary education, there are also the miners, merchants, and businessmen. Just count the number of kings, princes, counts, lords, cities, villages, and other places. Where shall we be getting the educated men three years from now, when here and there the shortage is already beginning to be felt? I really believe that kings will have to become jurists, princes chancellors, counts and lords clerks, and mayors sextons.

Unless something is done about this quickly, we must all become Tartars or Turks—either that or incompetent schoolmasters[54] will become doctors and counselors at court. This is why I hold that there was never a better time to study than right now, not only because knowledge is so abundant and cheap, but also because of the great wealth and honor to which it leads. Those who study in these times will become so highly prized that two princes and three cities will yet compete for one scholar. For whether you look above you or about you, you find that in these next ten years countless offices will be waiting for educated men; yet very few are being trained to fill them. And not only has God appointed such great wealth for schools and scholars, but it is honorable and divine wealth, earned in a divine and honorable estate by many glorious, good, and useful works which please God and are a service to him. The avaricious man, on the contrary, earns his wealth with spite (even though his works are not godless and sinful) and with hateful works, about which he cannot have a glad conscience or say that they are a service of God. For my part, I would rather earn ten gulden by a work that is a service of God, than a thousand gulden by a work that is not a service of God but serves only self and Mammon.

Beyond this honestly gotten wealth, there is also the honor which accrues to them. Chancellors, city clerks, jurists, and the people who hold such offices also sit in high places and help to counsel and rule, as has been said. They are in actual fact lords upon earth, even though they are not that by virtue of their own person, birth, or estate. For Daniel says that he had to do the king's

---

[54] *Locat oder bacchant;* see p. 218, n. 10.

work [Dan. 8:27]. And that is true: a chancellor must go about the work or business of the emperor, king, or prince; a city clerk must do the work of the council or the town. And they do this with God and with honor, to which God adds blessing, good fortune, and success. And when an emperor, king, or prince is not at war but simply goes about the business of ruling in accordance with the law, what is he but a clerk or jurist, so far as his works are concerned? He is dealing with the law, and that is the work of a clerk or jurist. And who actually rules the land and people in time of peace? Is it the fighting men or their officers? I think it is the pen that does it. And what is the avaricious man doing in the meantime with his Mammon? He attains no such honor but defiles himself all the while with his rust-eaten money [Matt. 6:19].

The Emperor Justinian[55] himself declares, *"Oportet maiestatem imperatoriam non solum armis decoratam, sed etiam legibus armatam esse."*[56] "Imperial majesty," he says, "must not only be adorned with arms, but also armed with laws." See how marvelously this emperor turns his words about. He calls the laws his armor and weapons, and he calls arms his decoration and adornment; he would make his clerks his knights and fighting men. That is excellently put, for the laws are indeed the true armor and weapons which maintain and protect land and people, yes, the empire and worldly government itself, as has been sufficiently stated above.[57] Wisdom is indeed better than might [Eccles. 9:16], and pious jurists are the true knights who defend the emperor and the princes. One could cite many passages to this effect from the poets and the histories, but it would take too long. Solomon himself declares in Ecclesiastes 9 [:15] that a poor man by his wisdom delivered a city from a mighty king.

By this I do not mean to say that we should despise, reject, or do away with soldiers, fighting men, and those whose business is war. They too, when they are obedient, help with their fist to main-

---

[55] Justinian, emperor of Rome from 527 to 565, was the great consolidator of Roman law, which was the basis of the German legal system of Luther's day.
[56] The sentence which Luther here quotes almost verbatim is the opening sentence in the Preface to the *Institutes of Justinian* in the *Corpus iuris civilis*.
[57] See pp. 237-240.

tain peace and protect things. Every occupation has its own honor before God, as well as its own requirements and duties. For once, though, I must also praise my own—because my neighbors have fallen out with it and there is danger that it may come into contempt—even as St. Paul also praises his office so constantly that some think he goes too far and is guilty of pride. Whoever wants to praise and honor soldiers and the fist will find ground enough for doing so, as I myself have—I hope—intentionally and extensively done in another little book.[58] For the jurists and pen-pushers do not please me either when they so praise themselves as to despise or ridicule other estates, as if they were everything and no one else in the world amounted to anything except themselves, as the "shavelings" and indeed the whole papacy used to do. All the estates and works of God are to be praised as highly as they can be, and none despised in favor of another. For it is written, *"Confessio et magnificentia opus ejus,"* "What God does is fine and beautiful";[59] and again in Psalm 104 [:31], "God rejoices in his works." These ideas ought to be impressed particularly by the preachers on the people from their youth up, by schoolmasters on their boys, and by parents on their children, so that they may learn well what estates and offices are God's, ordained by God, so that once they know this they will not despise or ridicule or speak evil of any one of them but hold them all in high regard and honor. That will both please God and serve the cause of peace and unity, for God is a great lord and has many kinds of servants.

We find, too, some swaggers who fancy that the name "writer" is scarcely worth either speaking or hearing. Well, do not let that worry you! Remember that these guys occasionally have to have their little jokes; well, let them enjoy it! You are still a writer in the eyes of God and of the world. However much they swagger, you notice that they still pay the highest honor to the quill:[60] they put it atop their hats and helmets as if to confess by this very act that the pen is indeed supreme in the world and that without it they

---

[58] See *Whether Soldiers, Too, Can Be Saved* (1526), in this volume, pp. 87-137.
[59] Luther's free rendering of Ps. 111:3 does not correspond either to that of his earlier or later Psalters (WA, DB 10ˣ, 478-479) or to the Latin of the Vulgate he had just quoted.
[60] *Fedder,* which means both "pen" and "plume."

would be neither equipped for battle nor able to walk about in peace, much less swagger so boldly. For they too must make use of the peace which the emperor's preachers and teachers, that is, the jurists, teach and maintain. You see, therefore, that they put the tool of our trade, the good quill, on top, and rightly so, whereas the tool of their trade, the sword, they gird about their loins where it hangs handsomely for their purposes. On their heads it would not be becoming—there the feather must wave. So if they have sinned against you, this is their penance, and you should forgive them.

But that brings me to this, that there are many bigwigs for whom the business of writing is a hateful thing because they do not know, or do not consider, that it is a divine office and work. They do not see how necessary and useful it is to the world. And if they were to see it—God forbid!—their knowledge in any case would have come too late. This, therefore, is what you ought to do. Pay no attention whatever to them. Instead just look around at such fine, pious noblemen as Count George of Wertheim,[61] Baron Hans von Schwarzenberg,[62] Baron George von Frundsberg[63] and others

---

[61] Count George of Wertheim (1509-1530) was a member of the special commission appointed at the 1521 Diet of Worms to plead with Luther privately and in a friendly way to recant his writings (WA 7, 843-844); Luther names the count himself in reporting the affair on May 3 to Albrecht of Mansfeld (WA, Br 2, 322). The following year the count introduced the Reformation into his territory by asking for and receiving from Luther an evangelical pastor for Wertheim (WA, Br 2, 597, n. 14; EA 4, 3, n. 11). In a Table Talk of 1531 Luther refers to Count George of Wertheim and Duke George of Saxony as illustrative of the "righteous man who perishes" and the "wicked who prolongs his life" in Eccles. 7:15 (WA, TR 1, No. 44).

[62] Baron Johann von Schwarzenberg II (1463-1528), friend of Albrecht Dürer and patron of learning, learned a good deal of what he knew about Luther from his cousin and close friend George of Wertheim, whose daughter married his son Friedrich in 1527. Working in close collaboration with Hans von der Planitz, von Schwarzenberg—who served as imperial chamberlain in 1521—was instrumental in blocking papal efforts to implement the Edict of Worms at the Diet of Nürnberg (see p. xi; see also LW 45, 164, n. 15). As the chief deputy of Margrave George of Brandenburg/Ansbach he was instrumental in establishing the 1528 church visitation which consolidated the Reformation in that area (LW 41, 141, n. 374). See the popularized biography by Johannes von Wagner, Johann von Schwarzenberg (Berlin: Bücherfreunde, 1893), especially pp. 268-269, 293, 298-301, 364, 368; cf. also Willy Scheel, Johann Freiherr von Schwarzenberg (Berlin, 1905).

[63] Baron George von Frundsberg (1473-1527) was a professional soldier who instilled pride of calling into the foot soldiers of the emperor, demonstrated

of blessed memory—not to mention those who are still living—and take comfort in such men. Remember that for the sake of one man, Lot, God honored the whole land of Zoar [Gen. 19:21]; for the sake of a single Naaman, the whole land of Syria [II Kings 5:1]; for the sake of one Joseph, the whole kingdom of Egypt [Gen. 41:53-56]. Why should not you also, for the sake of the many honest noblemen whom you doubtless know, honor all the nobility? And when you look at them you must think that there is not a bad one left. How could it be that untimely fruit should not fall from the fair tree of the nobility, and that some of the fruit should not be wormy and warty? That does not necessarily make the tree bad and worthy of condemnation.

This is how the children of God look at things, for God himself spares the whole human race for the sake of one man, whose name is Jesus Christ; if he were to look at men alone, he would have nothing but wrath. The preaching office and temporal authority of course cannot do this; they cannot ignore or shut their eyes to evil. For they must punish the bad, one with the word, the other with the sword. In saying all this I am speaking to individual Christians. I am saying that they should learn to distinguish between God's work and men's wickedness. In all of God's offices and estates there are many wicked men; but the estate itself is good and remains good no matter how much men misuse it. You find many bad women, many false servants, many unfaithful maids, many despicable officials and counselors; nevertheless, the estates themselves—wife, servant, maid, and all the offices—are God's institution, work, and ordinance. The sun remains good, even though everyone misuses it, one to rob and another to kill, one to do this kind of evil and another that. And who could do any evil at all if he did not have the sun to light his way, the earth to hold him up and nourish him, and the air to keep him alive—in short, God himself to sustain him? The saying remains true, "The whole creation was subjected to futility, but not of its own will" (Romans 8 [:20]).

---

the decisive role of the infantry in military conflict, and insisted on subordination of the military to the duly constituted authority. His acquaintance with both the peasant soldiers and the ruling nobility enabled him to mediate in the Peasants' War and bring peace in Swabia and Salzburg. *Allgemeine Deutsche Biographie*, VIII, 154-159.

Some think that the office of writer is simple and easy, that real work is to ride in armor and suffer heat, cold, dust, thirst, and other discomforts. It is always the same old story: no one sees where the other's shoe pinches; everyone is aware only of his own problems and thinks the other fellow has it made. True, it would be hard for me to ride in armor; but on the other hand I would like to see the horseman who could sit still with me all day and look into a book—even if he had nothing else to care for, write, think about, or read. Ask a chancery clerk, preacher, or speaker whether writing and speaking is work! Ask a schoolmaster whether teaching and training boys is work! The pen is light, that is true. Also there is no tool of any of the trades that is easier to get than the writer's tool, for all that is needed is a goose feather, and you can pick them up anywhere free of charge. But in writing, the best part of the body (which is the head) and the noblest of the members (which is the tongue) and the highest faculty (which is speech) must lay hold and work as never before. In other occupations it is only the fist or the foot or the back or some other such member that has to work; and while they are at it they can sing and jest, which the writer cannot do. They say of writing that "it only takes three fingers to do it"; but the whole body and soul work at it too.

I have heard it said of the noble and illustrious Emperor Maximilian[64] that when bigwigs complained that he was using so many writers in ambassadorial and other posts he said, "What else can I do? You cannot be used, so I have to take writers." He is also supposed to have said, "I can make knights, but I cannot make doctors." I once heard too of a fine nobleman who said, "I want my son to study. It takes no great skill to hang two legs over a horse and become a knight; in fact I taught him that myself already." That was very well put. Once more, I do not want this to be understood as though I were speaking against the knight's estate, or any other estate. I am speaking only against the worthless swaggerers who despise all learning and wisdom and can boast of nothing except wearing armor and hanging two legs over a horse—though they are seldom actually called upon to do so and in return have enough of comfort, pleasure, joy, honor, and wealth the whole year

---

[64] See p. 108, n. 39.

round.[65] It is true, as they say, that learning is easy to carry but armor is heavy. On the other hand, though, the wearing of armor is easily learned whereas learning is not easily acquired, nor easily put to work.

To bring all this talk to an end, we ought thus to know that God is a wonderful lord. His business is to take beggars and make them into lords, even as he makes all things out of nothing, and no one can disrupt him in his work. He has the whole world sing of him, in Psalm 113 [:5-8], "Who is like the Lord our God, who is seated on high, who looks far down? He raises the poor from the dust and lifts the needy from the dunghill, to make them sit with princes, with the princes of his people." Look about you at the courts of all the kings and princes, at the cities and the parishes, and see whether they do not contain many striking examples of the fulfilment of this psalm. There you will find jurists, doctors, counselors, writers, preachers, who for the most part were poor and who have certainly all attended school, and who by means of the pen have risen to where they are lords—as this psalm says—helping to rule land and people like princes. It is not God's will that only those who are born kings, princes, lords, and nobles should exercise rule and lordship. He wills to have his beggars among them also, lest they think it is nobility of birth rather than God alone who makes lords and rulers. They say, and rightly so, that the pope too was once a schoolboy. Therefore do not look down on the fellows who come to your door saying, "Bread for the love of God,"[66] and singing for a morsel of bread; you are listening—as this psalm says—to the singing of great princes and lords. I too was such a crumb collector[67] once, begging from door to door, especially in my beloved city of Eisenach[68]—though afterward my dear father lovingly and faith-

---

[65] Cf. Luther's discussion of military men on p. 128.

[66] *Panem propter deum* was the beggars' cry, the reference to God being intended as an appeal to greater generosity. *MA*³ 5, 442, n. 289, l. 16.

[67] *Partekenhengst*, derived from the Greek term for something given over or laid out (*paratheke*), had reference to the students who sang and begged for alms. *WA* 33ᴵ, 4, n. 7, l. 22.

[68] Prior to enrolling at the University of Erfurt in the spring of 1501, Luther spent four years in the St. George's school at Eisenach, where he enjoyed participating in the popular practice of student begging though he was by no means financially dependent upon it. Schwiebert, *op. cit.*, p. 127.

fully kept me at the University of Erfurt, by his sweat and labor helping me to get where I am.[69] Nevertheless, I was once a crumb collector, and I have come so far by means of the writer's pen—as this psalm says—that I would not now change places with the Turkish sultan, giving up my knowledge for all his wealth. Indeed, I would not exchange what I know for all the wealth in the world multiplied many times over. Without any doubt, I should not have come to this if I had not gone to school and become a writer.

Therefore go ahead and have your son study. And even if he has to beg bread for a time, you are nonetheless giving to our Lord God a fine bit of wood out of which he can carve you a lord. That is the way it will always be: your son and my son,[70] that is, the children of the common people, will necessarily rule the world, both in the spiritual and the worldly estates, as this psalm testifies. For the rich misers cannot and will not do it; they are the Carthusians[71] and monks of Mammon, whom they must serve day and night. The born princes and lords cannot do it alone; they are particularly unable to understand anything at all about the spiritual office. Thus both kinds of government on earth must remain with the middle class of common people, and with their children.

And do not be disturbed because the run-of-the-mill miser despises learning so deeply and says, "Ha, if my son can read and write German and do arithmetic, that is enough. I am going to make a businessman of him." They will soon quiet down; indeed, they will be glad to dig twenty feet into the earth with their bare hands just to get a scholar. For if preaching and law should fail, the businessman will not be a businessman for long; that I know for sure. We theologians and jurists must remain or everything else will go down to destruction with us; you can be sure of that. When the theologians disappear, God's word also disappears, and nothing but heathen remain, indeed, nothing but devils. When the jurists dis-

---

[69] Luther takes the occasion to pay this tribute to his father, who had died less than two months earlier, on May 29, 1530. WA 30ᴵᴵ, 576, n. 3.

[70] At the time Luther had only one son. Of the three sons ultimately born to him and Katherine, Hans (born 1526) became a lawyer and was later employed in the chancellory of Weimar; Martin (born 1531) studied theology but never occupied a pulpit; and Paul (born 1533) became an able and distinguished physician.

[71] I.e., the strictest devotees.

appear, then the law disappears, and peace with it; and nothing but robbery, murder, crime, and violence remain, indeed, nothing but wild beasts. But what earnings and profits the businessman will have when peace is gone, I shall let his ledger tell him; and what good all his wealth will do him when the preaching comes to an end, his conscience will surely show him.

It is particularly vexing that such rude and un-Christian words are spoken by those who claim to be so thoroughly evangelical. They know how to get the better of everyone and shout down their opponents with Scripture; yet they begrudge both God and their own children the honor and the material means that would be involved in sending their children to school so that they may attain to these splendid and divine estates in which they can serve God and the world—even though it is plain and certain that these estates are established and ready and well provided with both wealth and honor. On the contrary, they turn their children away from such estates and push them instead into the service of Mammon, in which nothing is plain and certain, which is necessarily full of danger to body, soul, and property, and which in addition is not and cannot be a service of God.

At this point I should also mention how many educated men are needed in the fields of medicine[72] and the other liberal arts.[73] Of these two needs one could write a huge book and preach for half a year. Where are the preachers, jurists, and physicians to come from, if grammar[74] and other rhetorical arts are not taught? For such teaching is the spring from which they all must flow. To speak of this here in detail would be too big a task. I will simply say briefly that a diligent and upright schoolmaster or teacher, or anyone who faithfully trains and teaches boys, can never be ade-

---

[72] *Ertzney,* i.e., all the medical arts, which in the academic situation of Luther's time were taught in connection with the liberal arts. *MA³* 5, 443, n. 290, l. 28.

[73] The liberal arts were traditionally seven in number. Grammar, rhetoric, and dialectic comprised the trivium of the medieval elementary schools; music, arithmetic, geometry, and astronomy comprised the quadrivium of the secondary schools. *LW* 45, 356, n. 15.

[74] *Grammatica,* the most basic of the liberal arts, included much more than we understand by the term "grammar" today. It included, besides the rules of a language, such things as vocabulary, reading, interpretation, and creative expression. *LW* 45, 376, n. 56.

quately rewarded or repaid with any amount of money, as even the heathen Aristotle says.[75] Nevertheless, this work is as shamefully despised among us as if it amounted to nothing at all. And still we call ourselves Christians! If I could leave the preaching office and my other duties, or had to do so, there is no other office I would rather have than that of schoolmaster or teacher of boys; for I know that next to that of preaching, this is the best, greatest, and most useful office there is. Indeed, I scarcely know which of the two is the better. For it is hard to make old dogs obedient and old rascals pious; yet that is the work at which the preacher must labor, and often in vain. Young saplings are more easily bent and trained, even though some may break in the process. It surely has to be one of the supreme virtues on earth faithfully to train other people's children; for there are very few people, in fact almost none, who will do this for their own.

We can see with our own eyes that the physicians are lords; experience teaches clearly that we cannot do without them. It is not the practice of medicine alone, however, but Scripture too that shows it to be a useful, comforting, and salutary estate, as well as a service acceptable to God, made and founded by him. In Ecclesiasticus 38 [:1-8] almost an entire chapter is devoted to praise of the physicians, "Honor the physician, for one cannot do without him, and the Lord created him; for all healing comes from God. The skill of the physician lifts up his head, and in the presence of great men he is admired. The Lord created medicines from the earth, and a sensible man will not despise them. For as in the time of Moses the bitter water was made sweet with a tree,[76] so it was his will to make known to men thereby what medicine can do. And he gave skill to men that he might be glorified in his marvelous works. For by them the physician can take away all kinds of pain, and make many sweet and good confections, and prepare salves whereby the sick become well; and of these works of his there shall be no end." But I have

---

[75] In his *Large Catechism* of 1529 (I:130) Luther quotes the full Latin proverb, ascribing it to the "wise men of old": *"Deo, parentibus, et magistris non potest satis gratiae rependi."* Cf. WA 30¹, 151; cf. also Theodore G. Tappert (ed.), *The Book of Concord* (Philadelphia: Muhlenberg Press, 1959), p. 383.

[76] Cf. Exod. 15:23-25.

already said too much about this; the preachers will be able to expand upon these points more fully, and show the people better than I can write about it the gains and losses they can effect in this matter for the whole world, and for our descendants.

Here I will leave the matter, faithfully exhorting and urging everyone who can to help in this cause. Only think for yourself how many good things God has given and still gives to you each day free of charge: body and soul, house and home, wife and child, worldly peace, the services and use of all his creatures in heaven and on earth; and besides all this, the gospel and the office of preaching, baptism, the sacrament, and the whole treasure of his Son and his Spirit. And all of this not only without any merit on your part, but also without cost or trouble to you; for you do not now have to support either schools or pastors,[77] as you would be bound to do according to the gospel.[78] Yet you are such an accursed, ungrateful wretch that you will not give a son into training for the maintenance of these gifts of God. You have everything, all of it free of charge; yet you show not a particle of gratitude. Instead you let God's kingdom and the salvation of men's souls go to ruin; you even help to destroy them.

Ought not God to be angry over this? Ought not famine to come? Ought not pestilence, flu,[79] and syphilis[80] find us out? Ought not blind, fierce, and savage tyrants come to power? Ought not war and contention arise? Ought not evil regimes appear in the German lands? Ought not the Turks and Tartars plunder us? Indeed, it would not be surprising if God were to open the doors and windows of hell and pelt and shower us with nothing but devils, or let brimstone and hell-fire rain down from heaven and inundate us one and all in the abyss of hell, like Sodom and Gomorrah [Gen. 19:24]. If Sodom and Gomorrah had had or seen or heard as much as we, they would surely have remained until this day [Matt. 11:23]. For they were not one tenth as wicked as Germany is today, for they did not

---

[77] Cf. p. 214.

[78] See p. 222.

[79] *Schweis*, which probably referred to the so-called "English sweat," an influenza which had reached epidemic proportions just a year earlier. MA³ 5, 443, n. 292, l. 4.

[80] *Frantzosen;* see LW 45, 44, n. 44.

have God's word and the preaching office. We have both, free of charge, yet act like men who want God, his word, and all discipline and honor to go to ruin. Indeed, the fanatics have actually begun to suppress the word of God, and the nobles and the rich too have attacked it to overthrow discipline and honor—so that we may become the kind of people we have deserved to be!

For we have the gospel and the preaching office only by the blood and sweat of our Lord. He won them by his anguished, bloody sweat. He earned them by his blood and cross, and gave them to us. We have them without any cost to ourselves, having done nothing and given nothing for them. Ah, God! How bitter it was for him! Yet how kindly and gladly he did it! How greatly the dear apostles and all the saints suffered that these things might come to us! How many have been put to death for them in our own time!

To boast a bit myself, too, how many times have I had to suffer—and will yet suffer—the pains of death for them, that I might thereby serve my countrymen! But all this is nothing compared with what Christ, God's Son and our dear heart, has given for them. Yet by all this suffering he will have earned from us only this, that some men persecute, condemn, blaspheme, and consign to the devil this dearly-bought office of preaching the gospel, while others keep hands off, supporting neither pastors nor preachers and giving nothing toward their maintenance. Besides this, they turn the children away from this office, so that it will soon go to destruction, and Christ's blood and agony will be in vain. Still, they go their way undisturbed, having no qualms of conscience, no repentance or regret, for this hellish and more than hellish ingratitude, this unspeakable sin and blasphemy. They show neither fear nor awe of God's wrath, neither desire nor love for the dear Savior in return for his bitter pain and agony. Instead, with these terrible abominations they still claim to be evangelicals and Christians!

If this is the way things are to go in the German lands, then I am sorry that I was born a German, or ever wrote or spoke German; and if I could do it with a good conscience, I would give my aid and counsel to have the pope come back to rule over us, and with all his abominations to oppress and shame and ruin us worse than before. Formerly, when people served the devil and put the blood of Christ to shame, all the purses stood wide open. There was no limit to men's giving to churches, schools, and all sorts of abominations. Children could be driven, pushed, and forced into monasteries, churches, foundations, and schools at unspeakable cost—all of which was a total loss. But now when men are to establish real schools and real churches—no, not establish them but just maintain them in a state of good repair, for God has established them and also given enough for their maintenance—and we know that in so doing we keep God's word, honor Christ's blood, and build the true church, now all the purses are fastened shut with iron chains. Nobody can give anything. And besides, we tear the children away. We will not allow them to be supported by the churches (to which we give nothing) and to enter these salvatory offices in which, without any effort on their part, even their temporal needs are met. We will not allow them to serve God and to honor and preserve Christ's blood, but push them instead into the jaws of Mammon while we tread Christ's blood underfoot—and yet are good Christians!

I pray that God will graciously let me die and take me from here, that I may not see the misery that must come over Germany. For I believe that if ten Moseses stood and prayed for us [Exod. 17:11], they would accomplish nothing. I feel, too, when I would pray for my beloved Germany, that my prayer rebounds; it refuses to ascend as when I pray for other things. For it simply must be so: God will save Lot and inundate Sodom [Gen. 19:29]. God grant that in this matter I must be lying, a false prophet! This would be the case if we were to reform and honor our Lord's word and his precious blood and death differently from what we have been doing, and if we were to help and train our young people to fill God's offices, as has been said.

But I hold that it is the duty of the temporal authority to compel its subjects to keep their children in school, especially the promising ones we mentioned above. For it is truly the duty of government to maintain the offices and estates that have been mentioned, so that there will always be preachers, jurists, pastors, writers, physicians, schoolmasters, and the like, for we cannot do without them. If the government can compel such of its subjects as are fit for military service to carry pike and musket, man the ramparts, and do other kinds of work in time of war, how much more can it and should it compel its subjects to keep their children in school. For here there is a worse war on, a war with the very devil, who is out to secretly sap the strength of the cities and principalities, emptying them of their able persons until he has bored out the pith and left only an empty shell of useless people whom he can manipulate and toy with as he will. That is, indeed, to starve out a city or a land and destroy it without a battle, before anyone is even aware of what is going on. The Turk has quite a different approach. He takes every third child in his whole empire and trains it for what he will.[81] How much more ought our lords, then, to take some boys for schooling, since that would not be to take the child away from his parents, but to train him for the benefit of the whole community—and the good of the parents too—and for an office in which enough is given him.

Therefore let everyone be on his guard who can. Let the government see to it that when it discovers a promising boy he is kept in school. If the father is poor, the resources of the church should be used to assist. Let the rich make their wills with this work in view, as some have done who have established scholarship funds. This is the right way to bequeath your money to the church, for this way you do not release departed souls from purgatory[82] but, by maintaining God's offices, you do help the living and those to come who are yet unborn, so that they do not get into purgatory, indeed, so that they are redeemed from hell and go to heaven; and you help the living to enjoy peace and happiness. That would be a praiseworthy Christian testament. God would have delight and pleasure in it, and would bless and honor you in return by giving you pleasure and joy in him.

Well, then, my beloved Germans, I have told you enough.

---

[81] On Luther's knowledge of the Turks, see p. 176, n. 62.

[82] Luther's reinterpretation of the traditional doctrine of purgatory began with the *Ninety-five Theses* of 1517 (*LW* 31, 26-28) and the *Explanations of the Ninety-five Theses* the following year (*LW* 31, 114-118), and led finally to an explicit refutation of the arguments supporting purgatory in his 1530 *Disavowal of Purgatory* (*Widerruf vom Fegefeuer*) (*WA* 30^{II}, 367-390).

You have heard your prophet.[83] God grant that we may obey his word, in praise and thanksgiving to our dear Lord for his precious blood so freely offered for us; and may he preserve us from the abominable sin of ingratitude and forgetfulness of his blessings. Amen.

---

[83] In his *Warning to His Dear Germans* (*Warnung an seine lieben Deutschen*) of less than a year later, Luther refers to himself as "the German prophet" who out of faithfulness is obliged to warn and instruct his people concerning the peril in which they stand; *WA* 30^{II}, 290; cf. *LW* 45, 348.

ON MARRIAGE MATTERS

1530

Translated by Frederick C. Ahrens

INTRODUCTION

As the separation between Catholic and Protestants solidified on the civil and ecclesiastical levels, and as canon law, to which the civil law had subordinated itself on marriage matters, was abandoned by Protestants, Protestant clergy and rulers were in a quandary. What provisions of the canon law and previous practice could be kept with clear conscience and in accord with the gospel? The interests of society and the troubled consciences of believers demanded an answer.

The reason there was confusion among clergy and civil authorities as well as among the masses is not difficult to see. For many centuries the Western church had accepted and conformed to the Roman civil law and custom in problems related to marriage.[1] According to Roman law all that was necessary to constitute a marriage was the formal mutual consent of a man and woman symbolized by the joining of hands in the presence of witnesses. No civil or religious act or ceremony was necessary to confirm the agreement.[2] Even after the collapse of the old empire and the ascendancy of the Roman church with its canon law and sacramental system, an ecclesiastical act was not indispensable. The act of marriage was performed by the man and woman in the verbal pledge, "I take thee to my wife (or husband),"[3] followed by conjugal cohabitation. The validity of such a marriage did not even depend upon the presence of witnesses. To be sure, marriage without a ceremonial act of the church was regarded as irregular, and if the church courts chose to do so, parties to such a marriage could be prosecuted; but the marriage was as valid as if the pope himself had solemnized it.[4]

Over the centuries the old Roman law and practice expanded

---

[1] Paul G. Hansen et al., Engagement and Marriage (St. Louis: Concordia Publishing House, 1959), p. 52.

[2] Ibid.

[3] According to Roman Catholic teaching the bridal couple administer the sacrament of marriage to themselves; the priest is the authorized witness of the church. Cf. The Catholic Encyclopedia, IX (1910), 700.

[4] G. G. Coulton, Medieval Panorama (Cleveland: Meridian, 1955), p. 634.

to accommodate other national customs, particularly those of the Germans. According to German custom, an agreement to marry in the future (i.e., engagement) followed by intercourse constituted a marriage.[5] This accommodation gave rise to a fine distinction between the *sponsalia de futuro* and *sponsalia de praesenti* (a consent to marry in the future and a consent to marry in the present).[6] Gradually, however, this distinction became theoretical rather than functional.

In theory there was no such thing as divorce, for marriage was regarded by the church as indissoluble,[7] and this doctrine was enforced by the state. Nonetheless the church could and did dissolve marriages on the grounds that they were invalid by virtue of certain impediments. Among these impediments were consanguinity, disparity of religion, previous betrothal, ordination, and impotence. The impediment of consanguinity was even extended to include baptismal sponsors and relatives of a deceased fiance.[8]

In the first part of the book Luther develops five points which he supports with arguments drawn from Scripture, law, and common sense: (1) secret engagements should not be made; (2) public engagements take precedence over secret engagements; (3) of two public engagements the first is valid and punishment should be imposed for the second; (4) intercourse with another man or woman after engagement is adultery and should be punished as such; (5) forced engagements, i.e., engagements imposed upon young people against their will and without their consent, are not valid.[9]

In the second part Luther discusses briefly the matter of divorce and impediments to marriage. Throughout the entire book Luther seeks to lay down general principles for evangelical consciences, not laws to be rigidly imposed and observed. His primary

---

[5] Hansen, *op. cit.*, p. 65.

[6] *Ibid.*, p. 61. See also Luther's discussion below, pp. 273-275.

[7] The Council of Florence (1439) declared marriage to be a sacrament, and thus indissoluble.

[8] Luther had discussed these impediments at some length in *The Babylonian Captivity of the Church* (1520). LW 36, 96-105.

[9] Luther deals with this matter at length in *That Parents Should Neither Compel nor Hinder the Marriage of Their Children, and That Children Should Not Become Engaged Without Their Parents' Consent* (1524). LW 45, 379-393.

concern—repeatedly stated—is to aid pastors in ministering to troubled consciences, not to assume the role of legislator.

The date of composition and publication can be fixed with a fair degree of accuracy. In a letter to Justus Menius,[10] an old friend of Luther, dated September 2, 1529, Melanchthon mentioned Luther's intention to write on the subject. It is even possible that Luther had already begun to write at that time,[11] but if so, the writing was interrupted for at least several weeks when Luther journeyed to Marburg to meet with Zwingli.[12] On the basis of a letter from Luther to Nicholas Hausmann[13] on January 3, 1530, it is assumed that the first part was completed by early January, 1530.

The first edition, printed in Wittenberg in 1530, appears to have been exhausted very quickly. Two further editions were published later that same year in Nürnberg. A decade later Joseph Klug of Wittenberg published a new edition, followed in 1541 by two more editions.[14] The translation, the first in English, is based on the text, *Von den Ehesachen*, in WA 30ɪɪɪ, (198) 205-248.

R. C. S.

---

[10] *C. R.* 1, No. 632. Cf. also an undated letter to Spalatin in *C. R.* 1, No. 647.

[11] *MA*³ 5, 433.

[12] *MA*³ 5, 433.

[13] *WA*, Br 5, No. 1515.

[14] *WA*, Br 5, No. 1515.

ON MARRIAGE MATTERS

To the worthy gentlemen, Messrs. N. and N.,[1] pastors and preachers at N., my dear brothers in Christ.

Grace and peace in Christ, our Lord and Savior. You are not the only ones, my dear sirs, who are having a great deal of trouble with marriage matters; others are having the same experience. I myself am greatly plagued by them; I put up a stiff resistance, calling and crying out that these things should be left to the temporal authorities, and as Christ says, "Leave the dead to bury their own dead" [Matt. 8:22]. God grant that they may do this, rightly or wrongly, for we are supposed to be servants of Christ, that is, we are to deal with the gospel and conscience, which gives us more than enough to do against the devil, the world, and the flesh.

No one can deny that marriage is an external, worldly matter, like clothing and food, house and property, subject to temporal authority, as the many imperial laws enacted on the subject prove. Neither do I find any example in the New Testament where Christ or the apostles concerned themselves with such matters, except where they touched upon consciences, as did St. Paul in I Corinthians 7 [:1-24], and especially where unbelievers or non-Christians are concerned, for it is easy to deal with these and all matters among Christians or believers. But with non-Christians, with which the world is filled, you cannot move forward or backward without the sharp edge of the temporal sword. And what use would it be if we Christians set up a lot of laws and decisions, as long as the world is not subject to us and we have no authority over it?

Therefore I simply do not wish to become involved in such matters at all and beg everyone not to bother me with them. If you do not have sovereigns, then you have officials.[2] If they do not render just decisions, what concern is it of mine? They are responsible, they have undertaken the office. I am horrified too by

---

[1] Luther means any minister.

[2] Luther means a judge of the bishop's court, the chief legal officer in a diocese.

the example of the pope, who was the first to get mixed up in this business[3] and has seized such worldly matters as his own to the point where he has become nothing but a worldly lord over emperors and kings. So here too I am afraid that the dog may learn to eat leather by nibbling at his own rags[4] and we too may be misled with good intentions, until finally we fall away from the gospel into purely worldly matters. As soon as we begin to act as judges in marriage matters, the teeth of the millwheel will have snatched us by the sleeve and will carry us away to the point where we must decide the penalty. Once we have to decide the penalty, then we must also render judgment about the body and goods, and by this time we are down under the wheel and drowned in the water of worldly affairs.

Now the whole world knows (praise God) what effort and zeal I have already expended and how hard I am still toiling to see that the two authorities or realms, the temporal and the spiritual, are kept distinct and separate from each other and that each is specifically instructed and restricted to its own task.[5] The papacy has so jumbled these two together and confused them with each other that neither one has kept to its power or force or rights and no one can disentangle them again. This is what I dread, and with God's help I want to avoid it and stay within the charge of my own office, and as I said above, "Leave the dead to bury their own dead; you go and proclaim the kingdom of God," Matthew 9.[6] Now this is to be my answer to you, may you do likewise.

But since you persist so strongly in asking instruction of me, not only for yourselves and your office, but also for your rulers who desire advice from you in these matters, and ask me what I for my part would do if I were asked for advice—especially since your rulers complain that it is burdensome to their consciences to render decisions according to the spiritual or papal laws, which in such cases are unreliable and often run counter to all propriety, reason,

---

[3] Luther may have had in mind Pope Innocent III (1160-1216), who in 1204 excommunicated Alfred IX of Leon for marrying a relative. See also below, p. 270, n. 15.

[4] *Lepplin.* Cf. Thiele, *Luthers Sprichwörtersammlung*, No. 107.

[5] For example, cf. p. 94.

[6] Luke 9:60; cf. Matt. 8:22.

and justice, and since the imperial laws too are ineffective in these matters—I will not withhold my opinion from you. Yet I give it with this condition (which I hereby wish to have stated clearly to you and to everyone), that I want to do this not as a judge, official, or regent, but by way of advice, such as I would in good conscience give as a special service to my good friends. So, if anyone wishes to follow this advice of mine, let him do so on his own responsibility; if he does not know how to carry it out, let him not seek shelter or refuge with me, or complain to me about it. I do not wish to place myself under the restraint of any authority or court, and since I am under none now, I do not wish to be under any in the future. Let whoever is supposed to rule or wants to rule be the ruler; I want to instruct and console consciences, and advise them as much as I can. Whoever wishes to or can comply, let him do so; whoever will not or cannot, let him refrain. This has been my position up to now, and I intend to adhere to it in the future.

Well then, let us in God's name get down to the business at hand and summarize these opinions and this advice of mine in several articles and points, so that they may be understood and retained that much the better.

The First Article

Secret engagements should not be the basis of any marriage whatsoever.

The Second Article

A secret engagement should yield to a public one.

The Third Article

Of two public engagements, the second should yield to the first and be punished.

The Fourth Article

If anyone touches another woman after a public engagement, so to marry her in order thereby to break the first engagement, this action is to be regarded as adultery.

The Fifth Article

Forced engagements should not be valid.

We will let these articles be sufficient for the first part of this little book. Now let us state our reasons for these articles. The reasons for the first article are:

First, the divine law, that because marriage is a public estate which is to be entered into and recognized publicly before the church, it is fitting that it should also be established and begun publicly with witnesses who can testify to it, for God says, "Every word should be confirmed by the evidence of two or three witnesses" [Matt. 18:16]. But where two people become engaged secretly, no one can be sure whether it is true or not, because husband and wife (and likewise bride and bridegroom) are one flesh and one voice, on whose testimony and witness nothing is to be based, nor can such an uncertain marriage be confirmed thereby.

To prevent anyone from wrangling with words here, I define a secret engagement as one which takes place without the knowledge and consent of those who are in authority and have the right and power to establish a marriage, such as, father, mother, and whoever may act in their stead. Even if a thousand witnesses were present at a secret betrothal and it nonetheless took place without the knowledge and consent of the parents, the whole thousand should be reckoned as acting in the darkness and not in the light, as only one voice, and as assisting treacherously in this beginning without the presence of orderly public authority.

Second, we also have here the temporal imperial law which clearly forbids such secret betrothals. Now in our external conduct we are bound to obey the temporal law. We should not cause the imperial laws to yield and subjugate themselves to papal laws because these same papal laws often run counter to public ordinances, reason, and good sense.

Third, this is also confirmed by the ancient canons and by the best points of the canon law,[7] all of which forbid such secret engagements, indeed, even today the pope forbids the making of such engagements. But on the other hand, once they have taken

---

[7] Cf. *Decretalium D. Gregorii Papae IX*, lib. iv, tit. III. *CIC* 2, 679-680.

place he wants them to be kept, to be valid and binding, so he makes them merely a sin of disobedience, thus rewarding them with the joy and satisfaction of those who disobey, so that they achieve their purpose with the sin of disobedience, which is contrary to all that is right and proper.

Fourth, add to this the example of the old law and all the fathers, among whom it was both law and custom that the parents gave their children in marriage by parental authority, as is clearly stated in Exodus 21 [:9], and as the examples of Isaac,[8] Jacob,[9] Joseph,[10] Samson,[11] etc., show.

Fifth, it was also in the natural law among the heathen, and also with the Greeks, who were the wisest people on earth. We read these words in the works of the Greek poet Euripides, "It is my father's business to arrange for my marriage. It is not fitting that I have anything to do with it."[12] St. Ambrose finds this passage very pleasing, liber 1 de Abraham,[13] and he admonishes all women not to betroth themselves or to choose husbands according to the example of Rebecca,[14] but to leave this care and right to their parents.

Sixth, we also have reason and natural common sense. Who would approve my action if after I had reared my daughter with so much expense and effort, care and danger, zeal and toil, and had risked my whole life with body and goods for so many years, she should receive no better care than if she were a cow of mine that had strayed into the forest where any wolf might devour it? Should my child be standing there, unprotected, so that any young rascal who is unknown to me and may even have been my enemy would have free access to steal her from me secretly and take her away without my knowledge or consent? Surely no one would be willing to leave his money and property so unprotected that the first one who came along might take it. Now this rascal is not only

---

[8] Gen. 24:1-10.
[9] Gen. 28:1-5.
[10] Gen. 48:1-7.
[11] Judg. 14:1-3.
[12] Euripides, Andromache, 987-988.
[13] MPL 14, 453.
[14] Cf. Gen. 24:15-50.

taking my money and property, but also my child whom I have reared with great effort, and in addition he gets my money and property along with my daughter. So I am forced to reward him, and for all the wrong he has committed against me I must let him be my heir to the property I have acquired with great toil and effort. This is rewarding evil with honor; this is opening doors and gates and granting an opportunity for damage and destruction.

And although it may occasionally turn out that it is an honest fellow, so that all is well, nevertheless, both the rascal and the honest fellow are given the opportunity and the right to perpetrate such malice against me that I lose everything. I say that every reasonable person must judge this sort of thing to be violence and injustice, and it would all be prevented so easily if secret engagements were forbidden. Then no rascal would dare to win over a good man's child, or presume to become a strange heir to property he has not worked to own, for he would know that it would be wasted effort, even if he had obtained a thousand secret vows.

Seventh, we should be influenced by the great dangers and mischief that have so often resulted from such secret betrothals and still do. Here I want to show what impelled me, even before I had considered these causes, to advise and act against secret engagements. It often happened that a married couple came to me (not counting those who came to others all over the world), one or both of whom had previously become secretly engaged to others, and now there was misery and distress. Then we confessors or theologians were supposed to counsel these captive consciences. But how could we do this? There was the law and custom of the officials which decreed that the first secret betrothal was a true marriage in God's sight, and that the second one was an open act of adultery. So they went ahead and tore up the second marriage and ordered them to keep the first secret betrothal, even if they had ten children together in the second marriage and had joined their inheritance and property into one.[15] They had to separate,

[15] Pope Innocent III had commanded that if a man had become engaged to a woman with whom he had already been intimate, and then married another, he should return to the first woman even if there were children by the second woman. Cf. Hansen et al., Engagement and Marriage, p. 61; cf. also MPL 214, 44.

whether God granted that the first betrothed was present and claimed the woman, or whether he was elsewhere, even though he had married elsewhere and no longer wished to have her. Further, if this engagement was so secret that it could not be attested by a single witness, and the second one was openly confirmed in the church, then they were forced to comply with both: first, they must consider the secret betrothal as the true marriage in their consciences before God, and on the other hand the woman was forced on pain of excommunication and by obedience to share the table and bed of the second man as her true husband, because this marriage was publicly attested, while the former secret engagement no one dared to acknowledge except she herself, and that in her conscience before God. What should a poor conscience do in a case like this? How could the situation be more confused than by such contradictory laws and decisions? If she were to run from the second husband to the first she would be regarded as an adulteress, put under the ban, and deprived of the sacraments and of all her Christian rights. But if she remained with the second man she would again be looked upon as an adulteress before God. So she could not stay in any one place and yet she had to stay there.

Now what kind of real advice do they give to such a conscience? This is what they give: they say she should keep the first engagement, and if she is forced by the ban to stay with the second man, she should suffer this ban as one that did her no harm in the sight of God. If she could not come to the first man in person and was compelled to share the bed of the second one and render to him the conjugal duty, to which he is entitled, she should bear with this, too, and perform her duty with her body, but with her heart she should cling to the first betrothal, and she should demand no conjugal duty from the second husband, for she has no power over his body, but should desire and demand it from the first man. This is called consoling and instructing consciences. These are the fruits of secret engagements and such were the conditions at that time.

My dear fellow, what strange kind of wife is this? She is the second man's wife, but this same second man is not her husband. The first man is not her husband, but she is his wife nevertheless, for as a wife she has the right and power to demand conjugal duty from him, but he does not have to grant it to her, for she does not have to go to him. On the other hand, the second man is her husband, but she is not his wife, for she has neither the right nor the power as a wife to demand conjugal duty from him. I will not mention the danger of forcing a woman into a man's bed to perform the conjugal duty and yet not allowing her to demand it of him. Indeed, it is easy to cut into someone else's hide;[16] it is easy to impose laws upon others which do not affect us.

No doubt there are more such unseemly cases resulting from such unseemly laws and commandments, for what good could result from such crazy, unreasonable, unnatural, and godless laws, when it is so very difficult for good to come from the finest and best of laws? To prevent such dangerous and unseemly horrors I have torn through such commandments and laws and freely advised, as I still do, that secret engagements should be prohibited and rendered void, and then we would be secure and safe from such mischief and countless other similar dangers. And even if no worldly authority wants to follow me in this course, and secret engagements are not publicly condemned and abolished, as would be fitting and proper, I do not care. I will still have consoled and set straight all those whose consciences are so entangled and perplexed by secret engagements because of the pope, bishops, officials, preachers, and confessors, so that they will joyfully and confidently scorn all these papal laws, regard secret betrothals as worthless, and keep to one another in open marriage like true married persons, without any dread or fear of adultery, whether it be in the matter of demanding or performing conjugal duty. If anyone can follow such advice and will do so, well and good; if anyone does not wish to do so, he can leave it. I do not want to drive anyone to compliance by means of laws, nor am I able to do so.

I hope that in this instance the bishops will not accuse me of interfering with or destroying their rule; no, I am not destroying it, nor have I ever done so. On the contrary, I am strengthening and confirming it. I am simply saying, as they command, that in such a case the wife is to stay with the second man on pain of the

---

[16] Cf. Wander (ed.), *Deutsches Sprichwörter Lexikon*, II, "Haut," No. 34.

ban and for the sake of obedience. Indeed, I put it more strongly, under pain of God's displeasure and for the sake of conscience. But when they make the further statement that in God's sight she is the wife of the first man, then I tear it up and destroy it secretly in my conscience, as I have done before, and as I have torn up and destroyed other articles.[17] These things do not come under their jurisdiction; they are mad abuses and accretions which needlessly confuse consciences. Because they are not theologians, but rather people who compel obedience to the law, it behooves the officials and bishops not to dogmatize in matters of conscience. That belongs to us theologians. Let the bishops rule the forum; we theologians will rule the conscience.

However, I do not blame only the pope for this unseemly law concerning secret betrothals, since the unlearned jurists and officials have contributed mightily to it. As soon as they have heard one passage from the laws they immediately become doctors of all doctors, for there is a popular saying current in their laws concerning cases of favoritism,[18] and they say, "*In causis matrimonii semper est iudicandum pro matrimonio*,"[19] that is, in gracious matters one should always prefer to act for rather than against them. Now marriage is a gracious thing, therefore they have taken pains to establish a marriage wherever they have found even a scrap of reason for it, and so the secret betrothal had to be valid and serve as a sufficient reason to establish marriage. But now we have heard what spiteful, hostile, and abominable danger and mischief have arisen from such an untimely and friendly intention: gracious here, friendly there—right and good conscience are much more gracious and better than marriage, and therefore they should act in the interest of right and conscience rather than against them, rather than promoting marriage more.

Likewise they have carried on pure tomfoolery with verbs in the present and future tense; they have broken up many a marriage

---

[17] On December 10, 1520, outside the Elster Gate in Wittenberg, Luther publicly burned the volumes of canon law, papal decretals, and scholastic theology. See *Why the Books of the Pope and His Disciples Were Burned* (1520). *LW* 31, 379-395.

[18] *De favoribilibus.*

[19] In matrimonial matters one should always act in favor of matrimony.

which was valid according to their law and made binding those that were not valid. The words, "I will have you as a wife," or, "I will take you, I will have you," "you shall be mine," and the like they have generally called future verbs and pretended that the man should say, *"accipio te in uxorem,"* "I take you to be my wife," and the wife should likewise say, "I take you to be my husband." They have not seen or noticed that this is not the custom in speaking German when one is speaking in the present, for in German one says in the present, "I will have you," *"ego volo te habere";* this is present tense, not future. Thus no German is speaking of a future betrothal when he says, "I will have you" or "take you," for one does not say, "I am going to have you," as they juggle with *accipiam te.* On the other hand, *accipio te* really means in German, "I will take you" or "have you" and is understood to be present, that the man now is saying "yes" in these words and giving his consent to the bargain.[20]

Indeed, I myself would not know how a boy or girl should or could become engaged in the German language by means of future verbs, for when they become engaged it is by verbs in the present. The common people especially know nothing of such nimble grammar, that *accipio* and *accipiam* are different things. They follow the custom of our language and say, "I will have you," "I will take you," "you shall be mine," etc. They say "yes" now, at this very moment, without further delay or hesitation. I would allow this to be called future tense if a condition, clause, or reservation were added, such as, "I will have you if you will wait a year or two for me"; also, "I will have you if you bring me a dowry of a hundred gulden,"[21] also, "if your parents or mine are willing," and the like. In such words the will is not free to consent to the bargain, but is held back and tied to something that is not within its power, and since the person at the same time admits that he

---

[20] The ceremonial formulas used in betrothal and marriage were discussed at length in the Middle Ages. On the basis of Roman civil law the church held that the formula *accipiam te* constituted an engagement later to be followed by marriage, whereas the formula *accipio te* constituted marriage as a present reality. Luther discusses these formulas in the *Sermon on Marriage* (1519), published by an auditor without the Reformer's knowledge. The text is given in *WA* 9, 213-219.

[21] Cf. p. 131, n. 92.

cannot do it yet and that his will is not free, therefore such a betrothal is not as binding as one with verbs in the present tense.[22]

Whether the one party is nevertheless obliged to keep his bargain with the other if the condition or clause is fulfilled is a question I leave to the jurists to fight out. I maintain that if secret engagement vows had been prohibited, this question would be unnecessary, for in public betrothal of course only verbs in the present have any effect. And if perchance public betrothals did take place by means of future or conditional verbs and the conditions were fulfilled, it is my opinion that one should act in this as in all other contracts where one is obliged to keep faith, unless other grave, important, and valid reasons intervene which would justifiably prevent one from keeping faith before God. But who can enumerate such cases because they are unusual events. To sum up, if secret betrothals were abolished, then I would call the open engagements made by means of present verbs *sponsalia*,[23] disregarding the fact that one usually calls engagements made by verbs in the future *sponsalia*, because one cannot make any definite assumption about such engagements and they are rare cases and unusual events. For according to common custom a public betrothal must take place with present verbs. It seems to me that this would be a great improvement and would prevent many errors. Let whoever will, do this. I am merely advising and making no firm statements, except in so far as consciences need my instruction.

At this point I must now turn to the grounds on which they confirm secret engagements and thus frighten and entangle consciences. They cite Christ's words in Matthew 19 [:6], "What therefore God has joined together, let no man put asunder." Now they say that God has joined together the two people who have secretly become engaged. See how badly they apply this verse, for according to their opinion the meaning of this verse would be that where two people come together, God has joined them. From this it

---

[22] The German auxiliary verbs *sollen* and *wollen* ("shall" and "will") had been used to form the future through the Middle High German period and into Early New High German; *werden* became fairly well established in the fifteenth century in the south in literary works. Cf. George O. Curme, *A Grammar of the German Language* (New York: Macmillan, 1922), p. 284.
[23] Cf. pp. 261-262.

would also follow that the adulterer and the adulteress could not be separated either, for God has joined them together too, since we are well aware that they could not live for one minute without God, let alone come together. So we would have to say that a thief and his theft and a robber and his spoils should not be separated either, for God has joined them together. In this way all evil would go unpunished, and they would finally put the blame on God as Adam did in paradise, when he put the blame on God through Eve, and said, "The woman whom thou gavest to be with me, she gave me the fruit of the tree, and I ate" [Gen. 3:12], as if he were saying, "If you had not given me the woman, I would have remained innocent, punish yourself first," etc.

So here all will depend on a sound knowledge and understanding of what this verse, "What God has joined together," is trying to say. It does not say, "What has joined itself together," but, "What God has joined together." The joining together is easily seen, but men refuse to see that it is to be God who does the joining. As soon as a joining together has come about by the parties' own efforts, they immediately want to hang God's name over it as a cloak to hide their shame, and say that God did it. This is misusing and dishonoring God's name and is contrary to the second commandment. The verse itself clearly indicates that two kinds of joining take place, one by God, the other without God. Joining by God means that which is done by us according to his word and commandment; joining without God means that which is done by ourselves alone without his word and commandment. Now we have taught so often that we should do nothing unless we have the express approval of God's word; God himself has nothing to do with us, nor we with him, except through his word, which is the only means by which we recognize his will, and according to which we have to govern our actions. Whoever has a god but not his word has no god, for the true God has included our life, being, estate, office, speech, action or inaction, suffering, and everything in his word and shown us by example that we must not and shall not seek or know anything apart from his word, even of God himself, for apart from his word he does not wish to be understood, sought, or found through our invention or imagining, as Solomon says, "Whoever searches majesty will be crushed by it."[24] Therefore it behooves us not to do anything or to judge according to the secret counsel and will of his majesty, but to do and judge everything solely according to the open counsel and will of his word.

Now this is our conclusion: What has been joined together by God's word has been joined together by God, and nothing else. Now let the secret betrothals prove that God's word is present and has ordered or commanded them. Tell me, how do you know that God has joined you together? Give us a sign that God has done it and not you yourselves, without God. It is rather much more against God and his word, namely, against the obedience to one's parents which God has openly commanded, and in this same commandment God is present and forbids such engagements and does not join together at all. That which joins itself without God's command is both sinful and wrong and contrary to God and his word. For this reason they cannot cite this verse on their behalf except to their own disgrace and God's dishonor. So we read in Moses, Exodus 21 [22:16-17], that if a man seduces another man's daughter and ravishes her (which certainly does not happen unless they come together, and much too close at that), he could not keep her, even though the law itself awarded her to him, but the father of the girl could separate them and dissolve the marriage, or the father's consent would have to be obtained anew. From this example it is sufficiently clear that this verse, "What God has joined together, let no man put asunder," does not quarrel with our opinion about forbidding secret engagements, for this "Let no man put asunder" falls away if they come together with God.

Christ speaks in the same way in the passage about those who are already living together at home in marriage [Matt. 5: 31-32; 19:3-9] when he says that they are not to divorce one another, and with this passage he sets aside the law of the certificate of divorce, as the text clearly implies. The question arises from the fact that the Jews were divorcing their wives according to the law of Moses [Deut. 24:1-4] whenever they wished, and then they took other wives to themselves. It is about such wanton and unnecessary divorce that they are asking Christ, whether it is

---

[24] Cf. Prov. 25:1-7.

right to divorce wives in this way for all sorts of reasons, for it seems even to them that it is too easy and unjust to obtain a divorce so readily. Concerning this frivolous divorce Christ answers and says that it is wrong, and that Moses had left them this law because of their hardness and stubbornness of heart [Matt. 19:8] so that they would do nothing more terrible and kill their wives. Thereupon he says, "What therefore God has joined together, let no man put asunder." That is, they are not to obtain divorces so frivolously according to the law of Moses, as had been their custom, but just as God has joined them together, they are to stay together until God himself separates them. Hence this passage really applies to those who are already living together in marriage. Here we are dealing with secret betrothals, however, before there is any marriage or coming together, to decide whether this has sufficient power to bind them to come together in the future and for that reason cannot be dissolved or torn asunder.

But suppose you ask, "Now I know how and when God joins a man and a woman together, but how do I know when God puts them asunder?" My reply is this: First, by death, as Paul in Romans 7 [:2] cites God's word and says, "If the husband dies, the wife is discharged from the law concerning her husband." Second, when one party commits adultery, for God's commandment judges and punishes adultery with death [Deut. 22:22]; therefore an adulterer is already divorced from his spouse by God himself and by his word. Such a divorce does not mean that it is done by men, because it does not take place without the word of God. We will say more about this later on; let us now finish this part concerning secret vows.

But to prevent anyone from troubling his conscience because they find themselves together in the married state, having come together through secret vows against their parents' will, and maybe thinking, "O Lord God, what am I to do? I did not come to my spouse through God, but contrary to God and his word, through myself and against my parents' will, and so, sadly, I have had no true marriage up to now, and perhaps will never be able to have one with this spouse, etc."; and this person wanted to obtain a divorce, although reluctantly.

In this case I say: By no means, for those who have come together and are living together in open marriage should remain together and not obtain a divorce on the grounds of a secret betrothal. For what we are writing and advocating here and now concerning secret engagements is not directed against secret engagements that happened long ago in the past, but against future ones, to prevent the countless confusions of conscience which have up until now sprung from these secret engagements. Even though the previous secret engagements have not been right, they still have some justification in the fact that there was a common law, indeed, a common error, custom, and practice which the parents had to give in to and agree to, so that the blame lies not so much with the children as with the clerical tyrants, who by this means robbed fathers and mothers of their parental power and authority and thereby made the children much too free. Since their matrimonial state has now been ratified and it is no longer a secret engagement, they are not to regard this writing as applying to them and are to be content, and pray God for pardon because they have erred and done wrong, for here we are only trying to prevent secret engagements henceforth in the future.

I want this same answer to apply also to those stubborn, rude, evil men and women who would like to separate from each other and seek grounds in this passage, pretending, "I too was not joined to my spouse by God, therefore I want to reform myself and divorce my spouse." No, you shall not find such a cloak for your villainy in God's word; we will take care to prevent that. You know, my dear fellow, that there are two kinds of law: one commands, the other punishes. I will now call them the disciplinary law and the penal law. Whoever does not keep the disciplinary law must suffer the penal law. The disciplinary law states that you shall stay with your wife and preserve your marriage. The penal law states that if you do otherwise, you must neither stay with your wife nor preserve your marriage, but forfeit your head or go into exile.

Likewise, if you have gained your wife sinfully through secret betrothal and now married her openly, then you have acted contrary to the disciplinary law and have fallen into the penal law and must keep what you have gained, whether you like it or not. For you have deprived the daughter of her honor, outraged her parents and relatives, and these things may not be atoned for by discarding her. In doing so you would be committing a much worse offense, against both the child and her parents, and you cannot give her back as you took her. Consider therefore, if you want to repudiate her, then make her again as virtuous as she was before you made a whore of her, or else keep her as punishment and penance, even if they should punish you further for this, as the law of Moses states [Deut. 22:28-29].

It would be useless, dear fellow, if you had stolen a pair of shoes from a shoemaker and afterward wanted to give them back to him when you had torn them. It is against the disciplinary law to steal shoes, and if one can possibly manage to do so, one should return the shoes to the shoemaker unstolen, or at least undamaged. But if it happens that they are stolen, you should not bring the shoes back when they are damaged, but keep them and pay for them, and in addition be punished for your theft. In the same way one should resist and prevent a secret betrothal from becoming a marriage. If this does happen, and the maid becomes a wife, now that she has been defiled and become worthless to others, you should not give her back, but keep her, and in addition you should make amends. A common woman too earns her wages in sin and lewdness, yet she is not obliged to return the wages, and no one can demand this from her. A gambler also obtains money sinfully, but when he has won it he is not required to give it back to the person from whom he won it, for that is the way he wanted it, since he was willing to risk the gamble and try his luck.

Here again someone will say, "Yes, if a rascal sees that he cannot get my daughter with a secret engagement, he will take pains to ravish her secretly and thereby think that she must remain his because her virtue is damaged, or the two might make a bargain that they would both confess to having had carnal knowledge of each other, even though it was not true." I answer: Who can defend himself against all rascals? Take thought to guard your child. If you cannot preserve her honor, how will you prevent a secret engagement? In such cases, the civil authorities should impose punishment on these rascals and violators of virgins, and they would desist. But since punishment is not imposed, as it ought to be, but the maid is even given to him as a reward for his villainy, no one has any right to ask me for advice; let everyone take what comes to him. What advice or help can I give if the authorities do not punish a rascal who steals your money and property and does other harm and violence to you; I must let you accept what has happened to you.

Let this be the final conclusion of this first article: As long as there is in effect no marriage, and no actual injury has been done to the girl and her parents and she is still completely under her parents' control and authority, secret betrothals should be forbidden altogether and not considered a marriage. Let whoever will accept and follow this do so; whoever does not wish to, let him do as he pleases. Unless the preachers and pastors adhere to this teaching as I have stated it, that they consider no secret betrothal binding on the conscience, and unless they can induce the officials or authorities to consider them invalid in public law, then let them continue to do as they are doing now. And if a man or a woman who had been secretly betrothed to one or two people and was now living in open marriage with still another should come with a burdened conscience, you should set their minds at rest and tell them to remain with this other one in good conscience, as they are urged to do by the penal law and God's word (which confirms this law).

The Second Article

From the article above, the second one and the two following ones are clear enough, namely, whenever a dispute arises because a public betrothal is questioned or challenged because of a secret betrothal, as has happened so often before, both in falsehood and in truth, one should henceforth neither see nor hear the secret betrothal and not allow the claim or grant it any validity, but one should go ahead with the public betrothal or wedding without any hesitance, as if there were no obstacle at all, regardless of the fact that the officials and custom have until now held a quite different opinion. It should have no effect either if in the secret betrothal there were gifts from the bridegroom, or if other pledges or agreements were made. If the authorities refuse to do this, however, or the parties themselves do not accept it, then (as we have said) let things go as they will, and let them confuse and intermingle secret and public engagements and cook, brew, boil, and roast them together however they will, but you can remain sure and free in your conscience that secret vows are not valid in the sight of God and do not endanger you if you are afterward publicly united to another person.

But what is one to do if the secret engagement is not merely an engagement, but is followed by a secret lying together? I have stated above that the authorities should impose punishment upon those who secretly steal away someone's child with a betrothal and afterward lie with her. If no punishment is meted out, then one should see to it that he keeps her in marriage and cause the public betrothal to yield to the private one, for much greater injury and dishonor is done to the girl and her parents when she thus remains in shame than to the one who is merely deceived in an engagement and still retains her virginity, and the one who has lain with her has not been able to become publicly betrothed to another, because he has been caught in an unfulfilled obligation, not only with the mere secret engagement but also with the lying together. This is also the judgment of Moses in Deuteronomy 22 [:28-29], "If a man seduces a virgin, he shall make her his wife, and he shall also be punished."

This is to apply if the secret betrothal and the lying together are made known or proven, but if they are not made known or proven, and the man who has lain with her denies it under oath, then we must let the matter rest on his conscience and permit the public betrothal to continue in effect and allow the first girl freedom to marry someone else, even though she knows in her conscience that the man who has lain with her has perjured himself. Knowing this in her conscience, she must allow him to continue as an adulterer in the sight of God, as one who abandons her and divorces her, indeed, as a dead and deceased man from whom she is free and to whom she owes no obligation, through no fault of her own, and let God judge. But if both of them want to swear an oath, then one must consult with the legal experts whether they should be allowed to take an oath or not, or whose oath shall be believed most. This matter is too complicated for me to deal with, and it is not necessary that I do so. Rather, I give this advice, that if one party swears an oath, the second party, although knowing that the former is perjuring himself, should by no means swear an oath, but should leave the matter as it is and commend it to God and be free.

Further, if her seducer later on, when he is living in open marriage with the second woman, begins to feel remorse and is struck by pangs of conscience because he has deceived the poor girl and her parents so wickedly, lied to them, and disgraced them without making any amends, and besides that has denied and dishonored God by his false oath and cleared himself of his vice by using God's name, which is also a great evil—well, this too is one of the fruits of secret engagement and marriage. This man, as we have said above,[25] the officials force to stay with the first woman and at the same time with the second one, but forbid him to demand conjugal rights. Now what good is that kind of advice? To be sure, I wish him this chastisement of remorse, which he well deserves, so that he may be an example to others so that they may learn not to sin against conscience, for such remorse must finally come to him, and the longer it is in coming, the more severe will be its effect when it does appear.

My advice, however, is this: He should make amends to the first woman and be reconciled to her in a Christian way and stay with the second woman, both demanding and granting conjugal rights as befits a true, free married state. Because marriage is a public estate ordained by God and not a shady business to be carried on in dark corners, he who seeks it in corners and dark places or enters into it secretly is a marriage-thief, for he has stolen it and not obtained it honestly from God and through obedience to his word, as is fitting so honorable an estate. Therefore a marriage obtained by treachery and stealth, secretly and dishonestly, should yield to one obtained openly and honestly with God and honor. This is what must and shall be our rule in this matter, that private arrangements must yield to public ones, other things being

---

[25] Cf. pp. 271-272.

equal; that is to say, secret betrothals shall yield to public ones. Likewise, living together in secret shall yield to that which is public. For it would not be right in the sight of God for the second woman who married with God and in obedience to him to be deprived of her marriage and, as it were, punished for her virtue and, at the same time, be made to suffer for another's sin. And on the other hand, it is not right for the first woman who married without God and in disobedience to God to benefit and be rewarded for her vice by ordering another's virtue to be misused for her disobedience. Therefore the second woman is to retain the man in public marriage, solely and freely, and only this marriage shall exist and be valid between the two of them, with no restrictions on either one, for neither temporal nor spiritual authority permits the taking away of the second woman's right to the husband and the tearing up of her marriage without any blame or cause on her part. Therefore the man too shall continue in it.

And even if the man openly admitted this secret marriage and lying together, or brought suit and swore an oath (as he may well do, and which would be a good thing as an example to others, so that no one henceforth would make such sport with conscience), one should still not believe him but, as we have said, should punish him as well, for he cannot prove it; and even if one were to believe his oath, it shall be of no use to him. Marriage which is open, public, and based on God and honor is to maintain its integrity and right against the stolen, treacherous, disobedient marriage hidden in corners, so that henceforth girls and women will beware of lying with a man in secret and not believe the fine words of the seducer so easily and thoughtlessly. For they believe in the words of a man, and so they fare according to the Scripture, "Whoever trusts in men will surely be mistaken," and again, "He who trusts in men will surely come to grief."[26] The woman who is openly betrothed, however, stands and trusts in God, for she has God's word and testimony which one must believe, but the one who is secretly betrothed has no word of God, no witness, but only the fine words and promise of her seducer, who is human and alone, and therefore she deserves to be deceived.

---

[26] Cf. Ps. 146:3; Jer. 17:5-6.

But what if the parents or relatives did not wish to allow the seduced girl to follow her betrayer into marriage—for example, if they were rich and socially prominent and did not wish to give their child to a lowly, insignificant man, but insisted on his immediate punishment, etc.? Answer: If one can bring the authorities to punish him, let it be done. And as I have said above, I would be happy to see this, but if not, I would advise them to give the girl to him and let her follow him, and not allow her to remain suspended in shame and peril. If it happens, however, that she is restrained by force and there is no hope that she will be given to him or follow him, then in my opinion the seducer is not bound if he proves his claim with witnesses, as is proper, and may well marry another, I Corinthians 7 [:15]. But what is the girl to do then? She must do as a captive among the Turks must do and endure this captivity as punishment for her disobedience and for lying with him in secret. And if later on she is given to another man by her parents or relatives, she should endure it, obeying and accepting this as one who had lost her freedom to resist and to refuse among the Turks, just as David's wife Michal had to suffer her father Saul to give her to another man and followed him, until time brought other circumstances [I Sam. 25:44].

On the other hand, if poor parents perhaps would like to see their daughter secretly married to a rich man and have him lie with her, and this happened without any deceit or trickery on the parents' part, purely from the wish and desire of the persons involved, then in my opinion this should be allowed to stand as a marriage, as I have said above, regardless of the fact that the man is rich, for the law is no respecter of persons.[27] If a man and his parents can be happy that he secretly gets the daughter of a richer man according to this law, then he should also be happy to get a poorer man's daughter according to the same law. But if any deceit or trickery is employed by the girl's parents to trap the rich man's son maliciously (such cases cannot be enumerated here, for who could consider all the trickery and deception that is yet to come), then it would be right for them to have to suffer the disgrace

---

[27] Cf. Acts 10:34.

of ridicule, and, as Psalm 7 [:15] says, "fall into the hole they have made."

What would happen, however, if there were a case where two people wished to act according to this opinion and become publicly engaged with a free conscience in this way, one or both of them desiring to give up a previous secret engagement that they had entered into with someone elsewhere? And later on if one or both of them were enticed by evil people or in some other way moved by the devil's temptation or through their own wantonness sought a reason to obtain a divorce and went to another place where secret engagements took precedence over open betrothals, so that one could not compel them by force to keep the open engagement, what is the second party to do then? Should this party follow the first one, or wait and remain as he is, or consider himself unbound and free to unite with another spouse? The answer is as above: Let whoever will not stay go, yet one should be sure to admonish the first party according to Christ's words, Matthew 18 [:15-17], and demand that he appear within a given time with testimony, as is proper. If he refuses to come, then let your judge, or if he refuses, your pastor, pronounce you free and not bound to anyone, and proclaim your right and ability to marry again, according to the rule of St. Paul, I Corinthians 7 [:15], "But if the unbelieving partner desires to separate, let it be so; in such a case the brother or sister is not bound." Whoever can and will (I repeat), let him comply; whoever will not, let him desist.

One should judge similarly if they were already married and one partner would like to leave the other and would either say in earnest, or pretend to do so, "Yes, I am indeed publicly betrothed and joined to you, but now my conscience bothers me because I previously became engaged to someone else. My confessor has advised me to do this, etc." If she is in earnest, let her go ahead. If she will not or cannot remain, although the pope does not allow her this separation, either do it surreptitiously or go to a strange land. If she is not in earnest, however, but only seeks an excuse to leave you, and has until now followed this advice of ours but now wants to follow that of the official[28] again, both from malicious

---

[28] Cf. p. 265, n. 2.

wantonness, and thus separates from you, then give her your bless-ing and say after her, "Go, you whore, go to the devil for all I care." The world is so full of malice that it cannot be fathomed, let alone prevented by laws. So now they are in a predicament. If someone does not like it under the papacy, he comes to us and deceives us; if he does not like it under us, he disgraces us and goes back to the papacy. There he will find protectors, even for all the sins and crimes he has committed while among us.

This is just what some priests' wives[29] have done. When they are tired of one and would like to have another they run off with some fine fellow and pretend that it never was a marriage, that their consciences could not bear it, and now they want to be good girls. Off with you,[30] my pretty darling. We can deceive the world completely with the little word "conscience" as long as Christ is lying in the cradle and is still a child,[31] but once he grows up and comes with his power we will find out who has deceived whom. In the meantime let us be as free as they are and sing, "I feel just as you do, my noble A.[32] Go ahead and trot, you will find your kind yet," etc. After these cases and examples, let whoever will or can judge in other similar cases, for to enumerate all of them is impos-sible.

And wherever so strange or unusual a case occurs, whether it be in this or other articles and matters, that it cannot be decided on the basis of some writing or book, then one should seek the ad-vice and opinion of one or two good, pious men in the case; and after they have given their advice and opinion, their judgment and advice should be followed without any wavering or doubt. For although they may not always meet with the strictest demands[33] of the law, so slight a fault will do no harm, and it is better at last to have peace and quiet with this drawback and less justice than to have to keep on seeking the most pointed and severe justice, with

---

[29] I.e., concubines of priests, often known as priests' whores. Luther felt great concern for those women who were wives in all but name and legal status. Cf. his remarks in *To the Christian Nobility* (1520). *LW* 44, 177.

[30] Cf. Thiele, *Luthers Sprichwörtersammlung*, No. 54.

[31] Cf. WA 30ᴵᴵᴵ, 222, n. 5.

[32] Luther substituted "A" for a crude expression. Cf. WA 30ᴵᴵᴵ, 222, n. 6.

[33] Cf. WA 30ᴵᴵᴵ, 222, n. 7.

endless discord and unrest. It is not necessary for a good marksman always to hit the bull's-eye; one must also concede that he who comes close to it or hits the target[34] is a good shot. All who are wise in the ways of the world admit that there are more and more of these cases and that they are daily increasing, and at a pace faster than one could make laws or rules. Hence they also say, "Strict justice is the greatest injustice,"[35] and Solomon too says, "Be not righteous overmuch; why should you destroy yourself?" [Eccles. 7:16], and again, "Pressing the nose produces blood" [Prov. 30:33].

So, even if these pious men should err a little in such confused cases, God will be satisfied with their error, because their intentions are sincere and true, and they are not seeking advantage for themselves or knowingly speaking against the established laws, and he will bury it all in the Lord's Prayer when we say, "Forgive us our trespasses." In the same way every government must often make mistakes and cannot help it, but nonetheless does not give up its office or despair of it on that account. This life is too sinful and too blind! Even though we do our best, we make mistakes in many things which we must commend to God and say with King David in Psalm 19 [:12], "Who can discern his errors? Cleanse thou me from hidden faults," etc., and James 3 [:2], "For we all make many mistakes," etc., so that God may find an opportunity to forgive our errors and sins and to show us his mercy.

Yet no tyrant or villain is to understand this to mean that I am allowing him the freedom to render an opinion in any matter according to his own pleasure or fancy and contrary to public law or truth. I am speaking here of pious men; not of public, indisputable law, but of obscure, confused cases which cannot be decided by means of indisputable public laws and where there is a lack of laws and books, so that we can put an end to these cases and satisfy people in their consciences and not leave them forever dangling in doubt because of questionable law. Peace is certainly worth more than all law, and peace is not made for the sake of the law; rather the law is made for the sake of peace. Therefore, if

---

[34] Cf. Thiele, *Luthers Sprichwörtersammlung*, Nos. 2, 330.
[35] Cf. Thiele, *Luthers Sprichwörtersammlung*, No. 234.

one must yield, then the law ought to yield to peace and not peace to the law. Now if we can have peace without legal squabbling, then let the quarrelsome law go, and the error will do no harm to the law, but rather will it be the great virtue of peace.

However all this may be, if it should become the custom and practice that secret engagements were invalid for everyone, though some mischief would remain (for no law or doctrine ever became so perfect that it was not often weakened by abuse and malice, as the saying is, *"Inventa lege inventa est fraus in legem,"* "When a law is found, an error is found in the law")[36]—nevertheless, untold error and confusion will be averted which otherwise would get the upper hand everywhere, and in many cases one would be able to arrive at a point where pastors, judges, and also the parties themselves[37] would have so much more peace and quiet, and less burdened consciences and trouble as well.

The Third Article

Of two public engagements the second should yield to the first and be punished.

In John 3 [:29] John the Baptist says, "He who has the bride is the bridegroom." Now because the first betrothed man has the bride and is the bridegroom, she cannot afterward become engaged to anyone else, nor can the bridegroom become engaged to another woman. So it is that in Deuteronomy 22 [:23-24] Moses calls a betrothed virgin a married woman, when he says, "If there is a betrothed virgin and a man meets her in the city and lies with her, then you shall stone them to death with stones, the young woman because she did not cry for help and the man because he violated his neighbor's wife." There you see that the Scriptures call a betrothed bride a married woman. Likewise in Matthew 2 [1:20] the angel said to Joseph when Mary was betrothed to him, "Joseph, son of David, do not fear to take Mary your wife. . . ." Therefore this article is sufficiently certain: when two people are publicly

---

[36] Cf. p. 104, n. 20.

[37] I.e., those troubled in conscience about having been party to a secret engagement.

betrothed and this same betrothal is adhered to, neither can leave the other during his lifetime.

But now, as we have heard above, there is such widespread confusion in marriage matters with cases that come about contrary to established laws and articles that there is a very common saying, "He who is lucky takes home the bride."[38] This is as if to say that who is to get the bride is not a matter of law but of luck, that it does not depend on the law but on luck, and not every dancer gets the prize.[39] It is also true that the cases vary a great deal, and the laws governing secret betrothal have been so peculiar that many a man has had to allow his bride to be taken out of his arms, and neither betrothal nor witnesses nor publishing the bans[40] has been of any use.

This is how it is in a case like this: If it is merely a betrothal, one can soon decide that no subsequent betrothal shall be valid, for it is a true marriage in the sight of God and of the world. But what if someone becomes publicly engaged to a person and meanwhile keeps silent about the fact that he has previously been secretly engaged to another, and has even lain with her and made her pregnant? He is a scoundrel. In such a case I would render this decision: If the secret engagement and lying together are known or proven, then in such a case the scoundrel shall first be punished for so deceiving and humiliating the maid and her parents or the widow and her relatives with a public betrothal; and after he has been punished, the second betrothal, which has not yet been consummated, shall yield to the secret one, which has been consummated, as we have said above.

At this point, however, someone might object, "You said before that where there is a public betrothal it is to be considered a true marriage, and that the betrothed woman shall be called a married woman, as you have proved from Moses and Matthew 2.

---

[38] Cf. Thiele, *Luthers Sprichwörtersammlung*, No. 145.

[39] A German proverb, *"Hilfft nichts darumb tantzen,"* not cited by Wander or Thiele. Cf. WA 30ᴵᴵᴵ, 224, n. 2.

[40] The practice of publishing marriage bans originated during the Middle Ages. The purpose was to make public announcement of a couple's intention to wed, ask prayers for the couple, and to give opportunity for just cause to be shown why the couple might not be joined in matrimony.

How can you now justify the advice that a secret engagement followed by lying together is to constitute a marriage? In that way marriage by public betrothal would be torn asunder." My reply is this: One must deal prudently with the laws of Moses, for his rule in marriage matters is of a completely different character than ours, especially in two respects. The first is that a man could have two or more lawful wives, and so he states that if a man had already become betrothed to one woman publicly and thus entered into a true marriage, even having taken the bride to his house, and it happened that he had lain with another woman before or during the time when the secret betrothal existed, or even if he lay with her after the public wedding, he could keep the woman with whom he had lain together with his public bride or wife. But such a thing is quite out of order among us, since a man is permitted to have only one wife. This is why Moses' law cannot be valid simply and completely in all respects with us. We have to take into consideration the character and ways of our land when we want to make or apply laws and rules, because our rules and laws are based on the character of our land and its ways and not on those of the land of Moses, just as Moses' laws are based on the ways and character of his people and not those of ours.

Second, among the people of Moses no great importance was attached to whether anyone had lain with the girl, especially in anticipation of a coming marriage, for she could still get married without any difficulty and was in no danger. Furthermore, the fruit of the womb was valued so highly among them and was such a precious thing that people regarded physical virginity or honor as very little in comparison. This is not the case with us, however; but on the contrary, among us womanly honor is regarded as more important than any fruit of the womb, and a girl who has lain with someone can hardly maintain her reputation, and there is great danger that she may even become a common woman. This is why we must conduct ourselves according to this state of affairs and can no longer call it the law of Moses if we accept it in one thing where it serves our purpose and disregard it in another. Moses can do both: he can judge that the publicly betrothed girl is a married woman who cannot be discarded by any means, and at the same time he can declare that the one with whom the same man has lain is an honorable woman and can give her in marriage to him. We do, however, follow Moses to the extent that we declare that the publicly betrothed woman is a wedded wife, but because we cannot give to him the one with whom he has lain, as Moses does, we must find a way here that can be accepted by our people, and that will not permit the honor and reputation of which the girl was deprived, which we consider her greatest treasure, to remain imperiled.

Therefore it has been my wish to give this advice: Where the public betrothal is still pure and there has been no lying together, and where there has been a previous secret betrothal with lying together, which is known, sworn to, and proven, the publicly betrothed girl shall yield, as is reasonable, in view of the fact that she still retains the treasure of her honor intact and hence still has a good chance to marry. But according to the ways of our land, the girl who has lain with the man and forfeited her greatest treasure probably cannot get married, as she might easily have done under Moses. This seems right and proper to me, as long as the authorities impose no punishment upon those who secretly lie with virgins and violate them. But if punishment were imposed, that would soon take care of this case and many others too. I do not consider it good that such things should go unpunished, since it is a terrible and disgraceful thing to break up a public betrothal and to leave in shame the one with whom a man has secretly lain. Both the man and the woman who have lain together deserve at least to be expelled from the country for a time, so that the scandal might thereby be atoned for and made good and others would be given an example to fear.

But if anyone were to pretend that injustice and damage are done to the publicly betrothed bride if she is separated because the man has previously lain with the first woman, the answer should be this: She nonetheless retains her highest treasure, her honor; and her innocence too is to be highly regarded and praised, because she is deceived and must suffer this separation without deserving it. She should take into consideration what she would do if her betrothed sweetheart had previously become engaged to another woman or had become publicly engaged to someone else-where—then she would still have to be separated and suffer all this. If in addition her deceiver is punished, her innocence becomes all the more worthy of respect, and this deception turns out to her best advantage.

But that other poor girl now is left with nothing, and the punishment does not restore her honor, and a woman who has lost her honor is quite worthless because we do not regard the fruit of the womb as highly as the Jews. Yet this lying together in secret in anticipation of betrothal cannot be reckoned as whoredom, for it takes place in the name and with the intention of marriage, which spirit, intention, or name whoredom does not have. Therefore there is a great difference between whoredom and lying together in secret with the intention of betrothed marriage. Indeed, no Christian or honest man would do otherwise if he had gone so far that he would make the mistake of lying secretly with a girl on the promise of betrothal, if he thought that he would have to keep her and disavow all public betrothals subsequently entered upon.

However, I have written this article as a warning which any-one may regard as he pleases, for I have learned from experience what a coarse rabble there is in the world. Loose fellows are wandering around and running through the land from one place to the other, and wherever one of them sees a wench that takes his fancy he starts getting hot and right away he tries to see how he can get her, goes ahead and gets engaged again, and thus wants to forget and abandon the first engagement that he entered into else-where with another woman. And what is worse, they go ahead and have their wedding—some even get married in several places and so carry on a great and shameful scandal in the name and under the appearance of marriage.

This is where the pastors should be careful to warn their people and point out this danger, namely, that no citizen or peasant should give his child in marriage to a strange fellow or man, and that the authorities, too, should not permit such a marriage. The pastor should not publish the bans, marry, or bestow his blessing upon any of these people, but if they are strangers, men or women, they should be required to furnish adequate testimonials of their character, both written and oral, so that one may be certain what kind of people they are, whether they are single or married, honest or dishonest, as do some craftsmen who demand letters of recommendation from their fellow craftsmen, and as the monks used to do who would not accept anyone unless they knew that he was free and not obligated to anyone by betrothal, debt, or servitude. How much more should one demand such recommendations from strange men or women who wish to enter into matrimony! It is certainly a matter of importance for every person to see what kind of spouse he is getting and to whom he is giving his child or relative. It is also up to the council and the community to see what kind of male or female citizen and member they are getting in their community.

For we learn from experience, as has been said, that rascals and wenches run here and there, taking wives and husbands merely to perpetrate their skulduggery, and afterward steal all they can and run off. They treat marriage as the Tartars and gypsies do,[41] who continually celebrate weddings and baptisms wherever they go, so that a girl may well be a bride ten times and a child be baptized ten times. I know a village not far from here—I will not mention the name of the region (I do not want to mention it for the sake of its reputation)—where, when our gospel[42] came, we found thirty-two couples living together out of wedlock, where either the husband or the wife was a fugitive. I did not think that there were many more than thirty-two houses or inhabitants in the place. The good bishops, officials, and authorities had so managed and looked after things that in this hiding place there were gathered together all those who had been driven out of or had run away from other places. But now, praise God, the gospel has swept away this scandal so cleanly that no open adultery, whoredom, or illicit cohabitation is any longer tolerated anywhere. And yet the poor gospel must be called a heresy from which no good comes!

In this article, too, there are many kinds of cases which cannot all be enumerated, and which must be left to the counsel and

---

[41] See Luther's remarks about marriage among the Turks, pp. 181-182.
[42] I.e., the Reformation movement.

judgment of pious people, as was noted above. Let me give one example: Suppose a man had children by the second woman and lived in the same house with her for a long time, and they kept a common table, etc. Answer: This changes nothing. Because he was publicly betrothed to the first woman and is her lawful husband, he cannot keep the second woman and her children, and, as the canon law says, it is all the more scandalous that they have lived together so long in adultery and their souls have lain in the bonds of the devil, provided that both knew of the public betrothal to the first woman. For if one party did not know about it, then that one is innocent of adultery and has been deceived, although he was negligent in that he did not make inquiries beforehand and make certain that his spouse had no ties elsewhere. So now he must accept this separation and disgrace as penance, and must be an example and a warning to himself and all others that no one should become engaged unless he has certain knowledge that his spouse is free and single.

But now what if the first betrothed, when she saw that her husband had left her and was living with another, also went ahead and took another man, with whom she now also has children and property in common? Answer: This too is wrong, and she too is to be separated from the second man, for she made herself a judge and proclaimed herself free and unattached and let the first man go without demanding or entreating under the law, as a pious wife ought to do, so that by her silence she has consented, as it were, to the first man's adultery or illicit cohabitation, and added her own in the bargain. Therefore in such cases one should first resort to the law and raise an objection to the man's betrothal to the second woman, or even after the wedding demand to have him back. If he then ran away or could not be restrained by the law, then she should have herself declared free and in God's name also marry again.

But what if the first betrothed was so angry that she refused to take the man back, even if he was willing to leave the other woman and return? Answer: The authorities should insist that she do this and take the man back. But if she refuses to take him back she is to be driven out and remain single forever, as long as the man lives, I Corinthians 7 [:11]. And after punishment has been imposed, the man is to stay with the second woman, and henceforth their lying together is to be reckoned as a lying together before public betrothal because the first woman was given an opportunity to have the first public betrothal reinstated and she still refuses, thereby annulling it as far as she is concerned and depriving herself of any right to it. But if the authorities compel her, and she much rather prefers to run away or quit the country, then let her go, and, as has been said, let the man remain with the second woman. What I have said concerning the woman in this case against the man, I also want to apply to the man against the woman, and our ground remains I Corinthians 7 [:15], "But if the unbelieving partner desires to separate, let it be so; in such a case the brother or sister is not bound."

The same answer is to be given if it happened that disunity and enmity arose between the engaged persons so that no one could reconcile them and one left the other, pretending to have a legitimate reason and took another spouse and lived with the latter. Answer: This is all wrong, for no one is to be his own judge and grant himself a divorce. He should first have summoned his bride before the authorities and had them compel her and, if she then refused, have her remain unmarried forever (as we have said above), have himself declared a single man, and only then go to the second woman.

Yes, but what if he does not know where his first betrothed is because he left her behind in another country when he moved away, and does not know whether she is dead or joined to another or still single? Answer: Then you can consider and look into the matter, investigate and make inquiries in the places adjacent to where you took your leave of her, and in the meantime make no move as far as the second woman is concerned. What if a man had diligently made inquiries for a year or half a year (according to the time imposed upon him) and was unable to learn anything of the first woman? Here my opinion is (but it is subject to correction by wise people) that he should serve notice on her by means of public notices and from the pulpit for a definite period of time. And if she did not come then, he should stay with the other woman, under protection of the law against the first woman in the event that she did come back.

Again, what if someone believed and was persuaded by convincing evidence and proofs that his betrothed had died, and she afterward came back and found another woman with him? Answer: He is to take back the first one and let the other one go. What if she simply refuses to return to him and, in short, will not have him? Well then, let the authorities know this and compel her to return to you, and if she refuses, have yourself declared free and your marriage with the other woman confirmed because it is not your fault. You were willing to take her back and you have sinned unwillingly through a well-founded but false assumption. She is obliged to forgive you for this assumption. If she refuses, it is just the same as if she were now running away from you and wantonly leaving you. On this basis anyone can judge other cases, and wise, pious people will indeed judge correctly.

The Fourth Article

If anyone touches another woman after a public engagement, so to marry her in order thereby to break the first engagement, this action is to be regarded as adultery.

This article, too, is clear. Even the papal laws have not permitted such lying together to be valid over public betrothals, not even against secret betrothals, but have ruled in all such cases that they confirm the first betrothal, whether it be secret or public, as a marriage, and do not regard a subsequent lying together as a betrothal[43] constituting a marriage. However, it is necessary not to allow such a lying together to go unnoticed, but point out that it is such grave and serious adultery that in the law of Moses it was punished by death.[44] Therefore pastors should diligently warn and point out how grave this adultery is, for it is to be feared that no one has a very serious regard for marriage if he has so little love for his bride that even during and before the wedding he separates his love and his body from the bride, when love for the bride

---

[43] I.e., as an act of betrothal.
[44] Deut. 22:23-25.

297

should reasonably and naturally drive away all other evil love of the flesh. He must be a vicious person and a loose, evil man, not worthy to live, let alone have a marriage.

Since we have heard above that a girl who has been publicly betrothed is considered a wedded wife,[45] and this public betrothal, if it is pure and free from any lying together with other girls beforehand, forms a true, honest marriage, then the man also is certainly a true husband. And because it is not proper among us to have more than a single wife, who is one's only wedded wife, the man is no longer master of his body and cannot touch another woman without committing adultery. Likewise there is also a great difference between lying together before public betrothal and lying together after public betrothal. For prior to the public betrothal the man is still single and free, and does not commit adultery by lying with the woman to whom he is secretly betrothed, but after the public betrothal he is no longer single; he is a bridegroom and a husband. If it is a true marriage, however, then the canon law that permits such a betrothed man or woman to leave the other party and run off to a convent should not be permitted or be valid. For the party is now a wedded spouse and has no power to become a monastic or remain a virgin without the other's consent, and just as the pope permits and orders that a wedded wife may demand that her husband be released to her from the monastery, so he should not have permitted and ordered the bride and bridegroom to run away from each other into the monastic life. It is just as much a marriage after the public betrothal as after the wedding. And if one were to pretend that because a public betrothal may be broken by a previous lying together, as has been said, therefore a marriage does not hold as firmly before the wedding as after the wedding—this is not always true. One can just as well find cases which tear a marriage asunder after the wedding as before; the one is like the other.

But this point is no longer very important for us, because monastic life as it formerly prevailed is now condemned,[46] so that,

---

[45] Cf. p. 283.

[46] One of the most significant social results of the Reformation was the wholesale abandoning of monastic and conventual life. Cf. LW 44, 247, n. 12.

God willing, no marriage may henceforth be prevented by it. But if someone nevertheless wishes to remain chaste after his public betrothal and will not be persuaded to take his spouse, I would not allow this in any other way than St. Paul does in I Corinthians 7 [:11], where he admonishes the wife to be reconciled to her husband or remain single, and thus leaves her to her bad conscience. And I would judge that this partner should remain single, not for chastity's sake, but because she will not be persuaded to go with her husband, and that she be called the unreconciled bride. Chastity is not chosen for the sake of merit or high repute, but that one may have more peace and opportunity to devote to God's word and prayer and have fewer cares with children and the household, as St. Paul recommends [I Cor. 7:32-35]. If this is not what is sought in chastity, but a holy estate,[47] or if one would like to be free of a betrothed spouse—both of these are to be repudiated and are nothing more than seeking one's own wilfulness and advantage. In short, I do not wish hereby to declare her conscience free or safe; let her risk such chastity on her own responsibility. For because it has come to the point where she has publicly given herself in marriage, it is safer for her to keep the promise that she has given; God has no need for her offering of chastity for any reason.

Many strange cases are included in this article; the first among them is what happened to the holy patriarch Jacob when his father-in-law Laban gave him his other daughter Leah instead of Rachel [Gen. 29:21-30] (who was his true bride and betrothed wife). Did either Jacob or Leah sin here? Answer: Neither one of them sinned because each one believed in his heart and conscience that he was with his married spouse. Jacob thought that it was his Rachel, and Leah thought that she had to take Jacob at her father's bidding. In the same way it has also happened that a man has committed adultery with his own wife, when he had secretly arranged a meeting with another woman and his wife had secretly come to the same place, etc. Now according to the strict interpretation of the law the holy Jacob would not have been obliged to keep Leah, but he did so as a pious man; since he had touched

---

[47] I.e., a supposed higher righteousness.

her he did not want to leave her, especially because it was the custom of the land at that time to have more than one wife. But if such a case happened now, that another person were brought in to him, which (in my opinion) will not very likely happen, he should keep the first betrothed and dismiss the one with whom he has lain because he has been deceived and cannot keep both of them. He has not lain with her willingly, as does the man who knowingly lies with the woman for the sake of a secret betrothal. If he did it knowingly, then it would be adultery, as we have said.

Again, if someone discovered that his publicly betrothed bride was unchaste because another had lain with her first, and he found this out before or after the wedding, could he leave her and take another? To be sure, in the law of Moses [Deut. 22:20-21] such a woman is stoned and burned, so it is clear that this is a complete separation. The pope allows him to separate her from his bed and board, but does not allow him to take another wife. But our opinion is that because separation from bed and board is a true divorce, not a scrap of marriage remains (for what kind of a marriage is it to be separated in bed and board, other than a painted or illusory marriage?). So he may well take another wife, and there is no command of God that would enjoin him to remain unmarried or keep the unchaste woman. It is true, however, that if he is a good man, he may let himself be persuaded to accept damages for it and keep her in the hope that in the future she might conduct herself honorably; this would be a good deed and better than being divorced. If he is that pious, he may do as Joseph did in Matthew 2 [1:19], when he wanted to divorce Mary quietly so as not to put her to shame, and for this reason he is praised as being a just man.

This is the statement I want to have made if the bride is convicted of being unchaste. To pay attention to evil suspicion or wicked fancy or even evil tongues which secretly slander such a girl is contrary to God and right. Satan himself has deprived many a person of marriage through such wicked fancies and evil tongues, or where he could not prevent the marriage, he has embittered and ruined it with the darkest kinds of suspicion. This is what you should do to protect yourself against this shameful evil and devil's trick: if someone comes to you and reports that your bride or wife is not chaste and boasts how he has seen and heard it and is sure of all this, etc., then take him at his word and say, "Will you stick to your word and openly state and testify to this in court (if I accuse her)?" If he refuses to do this and pretends that he wants to warn you secretly in a friendly and confidential way, then you may firmly believe and have no doubt that the devil himself has sent him to you, and that he is lying like a rascal and a fool, even if it were your father, mother, brother, or sister. Mark this too: he wants to warn you and advise you in secret, after it happened. Why did he not do it before? And since he refuses to testify publicly so that you could get free of her, his poisonous warning and counsel is equivalent to this: he sees you caught fast and does not want to help you get free by testifying publicly, but wants to embitter your heart in secret and cause eternal hatred and unrest in you against your bride. In this way you see that he is lying when he says that he wants to warn you and is doing it in your best interests. This is a devil's trick, as I have said.

So then, tell him that he should in God's name keep his mouth shut, which he has opened in the name of the devil, or you will take him to court where he must either prove his statement or be punished as a vile and vicious slanderer. What you have to do when this kind of thing happens is to put the best interpretation on it; this is godly and right, especially where one cannot or will not publicly testify to the contrary. What matter was ever so good that in secret it could not be made into the most horrible thing? If one were to believe such treacherous tongues, however, nothing, not even God and justice, would remain, either in heaven or on earth. But if you want to believe him, your reward will be that you will never have any peace in your marriage or betrothal. If you believe this you will be doing just what the devil wants, for he is an enemy of marriage and an unclean spirit of whoredom, so he does not want a man to marry, or fills the marriage with unrest when a man does take a wife.

The preachers and pastors ought to be diligent to prevent and thwart these secret tricks of the devil and they ought to denounce them and resist them and warn the people against them. And if it did happen that such slanderous reports were made about a girl to her bridegroom, she should take great pains to turn her bridegroom from this devilish poison and convince him of its falseness, and roundly denounce to him the devil's messengers who were the source of the report as rascals, villains, poisonous evil worms. Or, if they were good friends of his, she should denounce them as mad fools and stupid persons.

I personally know of four or five fine maidens who enjoyed the reputation of being honorable and virtuous and did not have a single flaw of character, but as soon as they became engaged, the devil's tongue came to the bridegrooms or their good comrades. One had seen and heard this, the other that, and it all had to be true, true, true, although it was twice foully invented and three times a lie. So I finally had to make this proverb for myself: Surely no good child ever becomes a married woman without first becoming a whore. I saw that although they were pious and pure as far as their bodies were concerned, these stinkmouths had to make them out to be whores.

The poor women have nothing more precious or noble than their honor, and this the devil must by no means let them retain. He is called *diabolus* or *diabel*, that is, a slanderer or blasphemer, and that he is and remains; fortunate is he who knows or believes this. This is why I praise this proverb against this devilish business, "One should praise women, whether it be true or false; they have need of it."[48] And again, "Many a man speaks ill of women, who does not know what his mother did,"[49] for among women are included all our mothers, sisters, wives, daughters, aunts, and relatives, and their honor is our honor, and their shame is our shame. Enough of this for now.

Again, suppose that someone becomes engaged to a woman who is a bondwoman, or that a nobleman becomes engaged to one who is not noble, or that a man becomes engaged to a woman who is a leper, or deaf or blind or has some loathsome or incurable disease. Can he, too, take another wife? Answer: If he knew about it and became engaged to her nevertheless, he is to keep

48 Thiele, *Luthers Sprichwörtersammlung*, No. 11.
49 *Ibid.*

her, as he wanted. Likewise, if one or two such defects should strike a person after the betrothal, the parties shall not separate, but shall suffer what God has inflicted upon them and bear it together. But if one was not aware of any defect and was deceived, it is dangerous to give an answer, for if a man later on discovers such a defect, with which he certainly would not have accepted her if he had known of it previously, it is proper for him to be free to leave her, for he never agreed to take her with this condition.

But who will prevent evil persons from seeking reasons to separate if they have regrets and think they can make a better match? The one party will pretend: I would not have taken her if I had known of the defect, and yet he is lying, for in his passion he did not notice the defect which he now sees. The other party, however, will deny this and claim to have been without defect and to have received it only after the betrothal or marriage. This is how it goes in a world filled with lying and deception where everyone seeks his own interest, advantage, or caprice. Such people who have no fear of God or conscience I turn away from me and send to the judge, and from the judge to the hangman, so that there they may be bound or loosed with oaths or other legal means as best they can. I am writing here for pious, good consciences, where one of these has found some great, permanent defect in his betrothed, with which he would never have knowingly accepted her; he has been deceived and ought to be free to marry another. The canon laws even state that *error* and *conditio dirimunt contractam*,[50] but because that same law allows divorce to the masses in general only on condition that no one may remarry, we consider such a divorce to be worthless, indeed, pure deception dangerous to the soul and the conscience. Therefore if anyone wishes to make use of this law, let him do so; we do not wish to use it according to our conscience, for it is utterly useless for dealing thoroughly and conclusively with marriage matters.

And although the latter party deserves to be at a disadvantage because he failed to inquire diligently about this defect in advance and the blame must thus be laid on his lack of foresight,

---

[50] Error and condition break the contract.

it shall be of even less help to the former that he knowingly deceived his neighbor and allowed him to misplace his trust so dangerously and unwisely. Who would not excuse a bridegroom for this lack of foresight on his part in view of his genuine love and praiseworthy ardor? Indeed, who would not much rather praise his hearty good confidence and trust in not asking questions? And the former party's disloyalty and misdeed is all the more despicable for not warning the latter and even helping him to stumble and fall. And even if someone would gladly search out all defects, it is not the custom of the land; and if it were the custom, no one would be anxious to reveal his defects, especially secret ones such as leprosy, to his own disadvantage, but would deny having them and cover them up and adorn them and make them as small and insignificant as he possibly could.

Whatever additional cases come up I commend (as I said above) to pious, God-fearing men to decide as best they can, whether they do so by civil law or by canon law wherever it is good, for in most every case the latter judges as though its master[51] had not been married and had not thought of becoming so, and thus it does not concern itself very much with how married people fare through its judgment, which, however, the civil laws do not do either.

The Fifth Article

Forced engagements should not be valid.

The whole world is unanimous in this article, for God has created man and woman so that they are to come together with pleasure, willingly and gladly with all their hearts. And bridal love or the will to marry is a natural thing, implanted and inspired by God. This is the reason bridal love is so highly praised in the Scriptures and is often cited as an example of Christ and his church.[52] Therefore parents sin against God and nature when they force their children into marriage or to take a spouse for whom they have no desire. We read in Genesis, chapter 24 [:58],

---

[51] I.e., the author of the law or laws in question. MA³ 5, 436, note to p. 244.
[52] Cf. Eph. 5:21-27.

that when Rebecca's relatives betrothed her, they demanded and inquired of her whether she would have Isaac, and they thought it right to have the girl's prior consent. The Holy Spirit did not cause such an example to be written down in vain; he wished by this to confirm the natural law, which he created in such a way that marriage partners are to be joined together without force or compulsion, but willingly and with pleasure.

Our daily experience teaches and shows us what kind of mischief has resulted from forced marriage. Indeed, so much grace is required for marriage to be successful against the devil, the flesh, and the world even when it is begun amiably with God's blessing and commandment, obediently and with pleasure, that one would not dare to begin it contrary to God's law and with animosity and ill will, thus painting the devil over the door when he comes by himself.[53] And it is a strange thing for someone to want to have a bride when he knows that she does not want or care to have him, and for parents to be so foolish as to force their children into eternal animosity and aversion. Dumb animals would not do it, and even if God and nature had not already commanded that marriage should be without compulsion, a fatherly or motherly heart should still not allow children to enter into anything other than that which takes place agreeably and with pleasure. But Mammon and the belly are mighty gods, and this is why pastors should diligently urge this point and frighten the people away from such compulsion.

It may well be that until now neither children nor parents have known that it is a sin against God and nature to force anyone into marriage, and so the parents have had no scruples about compulsion and did not regard it as a sin, but found satisfaction in it as if they had done a good deed and it were completely within their power to do this with their children. No, my dear fellow, no one should allow you to have this power, but should deny it to you and take it from you by God's word and commandment, so that you may know that you have no such power over your child. This power of compulsion is not a paternal power, but an unpaternal, tyrannical, criminal power, not much better than if

---

[53] Cf. Thiele, *Luthers Sprichwörtersammlung*, No. 356.

a thief or robber took away your property or kept it from you by force. And the authorities should not permit any father to do this. Instead the authorities should punish him and force him to stay within the limits of his paternal power and not allow him to go further than a father ought to. It would be a horrible sin if someone wantonly murdered his child or made him blind or lame, but how much better do you think you are doing when you force your child into a marriage for which he has no wish or desire, even though it might be that your child would rather be dead? Take care that you do not become a murderer of your own child by striving against the nature and essence of marriage, which is ordered by God, and fall into a grievous, damnable, mortal sin.

Yes, the crude masses have been quick to learn this from the gospel: that paternal power is to be feared and that children are not to become secretly engaged. In this matter they can accept the gospel and go ahead and misuse it; it has to serve as a cloak for their shame, and they want to make of paternal might a criminal might, and they do this as freely and unscrupulously as if they had earned indulgence by it. Yes, my dear fellow, if you want to accept the gospel when it gives you power over your child and demands filial obedience to you, then you should also accept it when it commands you to treat your child in a paternal way and forbids you to use your power shamefully and criminally in this matter, since the salvation of your child is in danger, for you cannot give your child the desire and love for his spouse that he should have according to the commandment of God, who desires that husband and wife shall love one another. If you now can make a big thing out of the sin of filial disobedience on the basis of the gospel, then one can also make a big thing out of your unpaternal crime on the same basis, and if filial disobedience is a sin, then your unpaternal criminal power is two sins. So that you may know that you are to be regarded as tyrants who keep or force their children away from the Christian faith, according to which they are not obliged to be obedient, but are free and are to be disobedient, Christ says, "He who loves father and mother more than me is not worthy of me" [Matt. 10:37]. How a pastor may further emphasize and elaborate upon this!

What if a child has already been forced into marriage? Shall this be and remain a marriage? Answer: Yes, it is a marriage and shall remain one, for although she was forced into it, she still consented to this coercion by her action, accepted it, and followed it, so that her husband has publicly acquired conjugal rights over her, which no one can now take from him. When she feels that she is being coerced, she should do something about it in time, resist, and not accept it, call upon some good friends, and if that were of no avail she should appeal to the authorities or complain to the pastor or give public, verbal testimony that she did not want to do it, and thus cry out openly against the compulsion. For these four means, namely, calling upon good friends, appealing to the authorities, complaining to the pastor, and protesting openly, should be powerful enough to prevent a forced marriage. Indeed, the authorities with the law or the pastor with good counsel can probably do it alone.

If the girl remains silent during her public betrothal, however, and leaves these means untried, then she is to keep the promise she has made and afterward keep silent and not complain or pretend that she was forced. One is not to believe her if she does complain. "Yes," you say, "Who knew that one could resist force by these means?" Answer: Learn it now, anyone who can or will. Why haven't your preachers or judges taught you this? And why did you not seek advice from your pastor? People no longer want to have preachers or pastors; they do not heed them or need them and they act as if they could do all things and well live without them. Well then, people will have to suffer the consequences of this and take it as their reward and spare us the complaint and howling. That is the way you wanted it, it serves you right! Why does God provide you with parents, pastors, and authorities if you do not need them?

However, if a case could be found where a child was closely guarded and could not gain access to these means and was betrothed without her co-operation through intermediaries who married her off by force, and she could afterward furnish witnesses that she had not given her consent, I would pronounce her free, even after the consummation. The same thing happens to her as

307

when a girl's honor is taken away by force, which is called rape, and is not to be considered a marriage. All those who abet this and aid in it are guilty of violence and the rape of her honor. But if one can persuade her to let it pass, and she is willing to stay with the man, as she would have to do in Turkey, it is so much the better, and it now becomes a true marriage through her consent, as the Romans write that their ancestors' wives, robbed from the Sabines,[54] did, and as the maidens who were carried off at Shiloh did in the last chapter of Judges [21:23], although this was for a different reason, for they were not carried off wantonly but out of great need, as the text there states [vs. 7].

Further, one also finds people so crude that they simply will not give their daughters in marriage, even when the child is willing. To that extent there is a marriage which would be honorable and beneficial to her, but the father puffs up his belly like a crude peasant[55] and even wants to use the gospel to justify his caprice and contend that the child must be obedient to him. He is unwilling, however, because he can use her at home instead of a maid and is seeking to use his child for his own advantage. This is not forcing into marriage, but away from it; and yet they have no conscience about such unpaternal malice, just as if they were doing right by it. Perhaps it was these great louts who first gave the canon law cause to sanction secret engagements! Before I would tolerate such peasant caprice with paternal power on the part of these rude louts, I would rather advise their children and tell them to get engaged without the consent of such fathers. For paternal power is not given to the fathers by God for their caprice or to do harm to their children, but to further and help them. And anyone who uses paternal power in any other way or to the disadvantage of his children forfeits it thereby and is not to be considered a father, but an enemy and destroyer of his own children.

It is my advice, then, that if the father or father's deputy refuses to give a child in marriage, and if good friends, the pas-

---

[54] The allusion is to the ancient legend that the first citizens of Rome secured wives by abducting the Sabine women.
[55] Cf. Thiele, *Luthers Sprichwörtersammlung*, No. 266.

308

tor, or the authorities recognize that the marriage is honorable and advantageous for the child and that the child's parents or their deputies are seeking their own advantage or caprice, then the authorities shall adopt the child in the father's stead, as they do with abandoned children and orphans, and compel the father. And if he refuses to comply, they shall seize him by the neck and throw him into jail, and thus deprive him of all paternal power and, in addition, punish him as a public enemy, not only an enemy of his child and of God, but as an enemy of the discipline and honor of all and the good and improvement of the entire community. For thereby he is hindering and preventing the citizenry and the community with all his might from growing and is causing it to decrease rather than increase and is robbing the city of a citizen. If the authorities refuse to do this, then let the pastor counsel and help with good friends, as much as he can, and give to the child, as one deserted by her father and prevented by him, the free right before God to become engaged in good conscience, and confirm this marriage for the reason that paternal power is not created by God to be free wantonness but is an obligation first of all to serve the children with advice and help for their benefit and honor and with all diligence to further and seek the improvement and increase of the community. And the pastors are publicly to point out most emphatically the malice of these crude people as most shameful, so that they will have some conscience about it. And even if they do not fear God, they must still be ashamed before men and obey the authorities.

The same applies, too, when it happens that a child resists her father and wants to use the gospel for her own caprice, because she knows and relies on the fact that she cannot be forced, but must be left to her own will, perhaps because she is attached to someone by a foolish love and therefore rejects a marriage which would be praiseworthy and honorable for her in the opinion of good friends, and even in the opinion of the pastor and the authorities. Here indeed the father should be given the power to punish the child, for because the marriage is honorable and advisable for the child according to the opinion of pious, good people, and no malice or caprice but true paternal loyalty is felt on the father's part, the child, if she has no other reason than her foolish young love which she bestows on another, should fittingly abandon this love and render filial obedience to this loyal, paternal advice. And she ought to know that if she does not do so, she is not free to resist this paternal will without sin, but is in danger of violating the fourth commandment. For Christian freedom is not given to anyone to be used for his own pleasure and caprice and to the harm, injury, and vexation of others, but only for the need and danger of the conscience, so that each may serve the other and benefit him.

But because the world is filled with cunning and deceit and a child may easily make excuses and pretend that she is not doing this out of caprice or foolish love, but cannot or is not able to love this one or that one, well then, we must let the fathers use their common sense and understanding and decide how to deal with such children. But the preachers likewise are to be diligent in informing the young people and must hold their conscience to filial obedience by pointing out the position in which they find themselves and that they are unjustly excusing themselves, that they are twice sinning against paternal authority, both with disobedience and deception. This will do them no good later on, and it is to be feared that they will receive as punishment an unhappy marriage or a short life. They should be careful not to trifle in these matters, for it is certain that they will not deceive the father but themselves, for God will surely discover their lying and deception. If the fact that I preferred something else and did not want to give it up were any kind of sufficient reason, then there would be no obedience left, either in heaven or on earth. Abraham, too, loved his son Isaac, yet he had to give him up and surrender him [Gen. 22:2]. Let this be enough for the time being on the five articles.

The Second Part

Necessity demands that we also say something about divorce and other subjects, such as degrees of kinship and the like. We have heard above that death is the only reason for dissolving a marriage. And because God has commanded in the law of Moses that adulterers should be stoned [Deut. 22:22-24], it is certain that adultery also dissolves a marriage, because by it the adulterer is sentenced and condemned to death, and also because Christ, in Matthew 19 [:9], when he forbids married people to divorce each other, excepts adultery and says, "Whoever divorces his wife, except for unchastity, and marries another, commits adultery." This verse is also confirmed by Joseph in Matthew 2 [1:19], when he wanted to leave Mary because he considered her an adulteress, and yet he is praised by the evangelist as a pious man. Now he certainly would not be a pious man if he wanted to leave Mary unless he had the power and right to do so.

Accordingly I cannot and may not deny that where one spouse commits adultery and it can be publicly proven, the other partner is free and can obtain a divorce and marry another man. However, it is a great deal better to reconcile them and keep them together if it is possible. But if the innocent partner does not wish to do this, then let him in God's name exercise his right. And above all, this separation is not to take place on one's own authority, but it is to be declared through the advice and judgment of the pastor or authorities, unless like Joseph one wanted to go away secretly and leave the country. Otherwise, if he wishes to stay, he is to obtain a public divorce.

But in order that such divorces may be as few in number as possible, one should not permit the one partner to remarry immediately, but he should wait at least a year or six months. Otherwise it would have the evil appearance that he was happy and pleased that his spouse had committed adultery and was joyfully seizing the opportunity to get rid of this one and quickly take another and so practice his wantonness under the cloak of the law. For such villainy indicates that he is leaving the adulteress not out of disgust for adultery, but out of envy and hate toward his spouse and out of desire and passion for another, and so is eagerly seeking another woman.

Second, the pastors should diligently see to it that the guilty partner (if the authorities do not punish him) shall humble himself before the innocent one and beg forgiveness. When this has been done, they are confidently to entreat the innocent partner with the Scriptures, where God commands us to forgive, and on this basis press hard upon his conscience and point out what a grave sin it is not to forgive his spouse (if the latter remains unpunished and has not been expelled by the authorities) and take her back in the hope that she will mend her ways. For it can very easily happen to all of us that we fall, and who is without sin? [John 8:7]. And how would we have our neighbor act toward us if we had fallen? So we too are to act toward others and be strong, continuing to practice Christian love and the duty we have to forgive another if he mends his ways, and thus aid in restraining the law of divorce as much as we can. If that does not help, well, then let the law take its course.

In addition there is another case, namely, when one spouse runs away from the other, etc. May this one in turn marry still another? Here my answer is this: Where it happens that one spouse knowingly and deliberately leaves the other, such as merchants or those required to go to war, or for any other reason of necessity, and both of them agree to this—here the other partner shall wait and not marry again until there is certain and trustworthy evidence that the spouse is dead, even if the pope in his decretals decrees and permits more than I do.[56] Inasmuch as the wife consents to this journey of her husband and enters into this risk, she is to adhere to it, especially if it takes place for the sake of goods, as may happen with merchants. If for the sake of goods she can consent to her husband's making dangerous trips, let her have the same danger if it comes; why does she not keep him at home with less goods and be content in her poverty?

But if he is such a villain, and I have found many in my time, who takes a wife and stays with her for a while, spends a lot of money and lives well, then runs away without her knowledge and consent, secretly and treacherously, leaves her pregnant or with children, sends her nothing, writes her nothing, offers her nothing, pursues his villainy, and then returns in one, two, three, four, five, or six years and relies on her having to take him back when he

---

[56] *Decretalium D. Gregorii Papae IX*, lib. iv, tit. I, C. XIX. *CIC* 2, 668.

comes, and on the city and house being open to him,[57] then it would be high time and necessary for the authorities to issue a stern decree and take severe measures. And if a villain were to undertake such an action or trick, he should be forbidden to enter the country, and if he were ever caught, he should be given his deserts as befits a villain. Such a villain shows his contempt for matrimony and the laws of the city. He does not consider his wife as his wedded wife, nor his children as his lawful children, for he withholds from them the duty, food, service, provision, etc., that he owes them, against their knowledge and consent. And he is acting contrary to the nature and character of marriage, which is and imposes a way of life, an estate in which a man and a woman are joined together and stay together and live and reside together until death, as the temporal laws also state: *Individuam consuetudinem vitae*, etc.,[58] and they are not to be apart or live apart without mutual consent or unavoidable necessity.

And in addition he withholds his person and services from the authorities and the community as a faithless, disobedient person, contrary to his oath,[59] and uses the city, his wife, house, and property like a robber and a thief when he comes running back, and no one would or should have any use for him. There is no villain whom I would rather have hanged or beheaded than this scoundrel. And if I were asked to, or had I the time for it, I would paint or portray such a villain and make it very clear that no adulterer should be compared with him. Therefore, I have advised and still advise (if one wants to do it at all) that if there is such a villain in a village or city who has been absent like this for a year or half a year, the pastor or the authorities are to counsel and help the wife to seek the villain wherever she can or expects to find him and demand his appearance within a given time. If he does not come, public notices are to be posted on the church or city hall summoning him publicly with the threat that he will be banished and his wife declared free. If he still does not come, then he is

---

[57] I.e., without fear of prosecution or exile.

[58] *Individuam consuetudinem vitae continens*, i.e., maintaining an undivided relationship for life. Luther may be alluding to the legislation known as *Institutio de putria potestate*. MA³ 5, 437, note to p. 252.

[59] I.e., an oath of fealty.

never to come any more.[60] His villainy has been so common, and in addition has gone unpunished, that it is beyond description, and it cannot be tolerated by any authority, either spiritual or temporal.

Such and similar mischief all results from the fact that no one has either preached or heard what marriage is. No one has looked upon marriage as a work or estate which God has commanded and placed under worldly authority, and therefore everyone has treated it as a free man does his own property, with which he can do as he wishes, without any qualms of conscience. No, my dear fellow, if you are bound to a wife, then you are no longer a free man; God compels and orders you to stay with your wife and children, to provide for them and rear them, and then to obey your authorities and help and advise your neighbors. Such good, noble works you want to leave undone, and instead, just like a villain, you want to take advantage of all the good and profit that marriage as an estate has and brings with it. Yes, my dear fellow, one would have to let Master Hans on the gallows[61] show you that it does not pay to inflict nothing but harm and damage and take nothing but profit and goods from everyone in return.

But if sometimes one party runs away from the other out of anger or rage, it is quite a different matter, and there is not this secret, treacherous running away. Here we can see what to do from St. Paul, I Corinthians 7 [:11], namely, they are to be reconciled or, if the reconciliation does not succeed, remain single. There may well be a case where they are better off separated than together, otherwise St. Paul would not have permitted them to remain single if they did not wish to be reconciled. And who can enumerate all the cases like these or make laws to deal with them? Sensible people must be the judges here.

But what if the man or woman was publicly disciplined or banished from the land? Shall the other party go along, or remain behind and remarry? Answer: They are to bear such misfortune together and not separate on that account. For just as they have become one flesh [Matt. 19:5], they must also remain one flesh, come honor or shame, prosperity or poverty, for we read in Mat-

---

[60] I.e., he is banished.
[61] I.e., the hangman.

thew 18 [:25] that the servant who owed his lord ten thousand talents was not only to be sold himself, but also his wife and children, etc. Thus a woman must share both the benefits and losses of her husband. There are many more cases, such as where one fears poison or murder, or where a wife was forced by her husband to steal or commit a shameful offense. But in such cases the authorities and sensible people can be of help, for no one can be forced to sin. On the other hand, a spouse must run the risk of poison or murder, especially where it is undertaken secretly. Open undertakings can be prevented and deterred by the authorities or friends.

Concerning kinship or degrees of kinship,[62] my advice would be to leave this up to the temporal laws; or if, according to the canon law, one wishes to consider the third and fourth degree as prohibited also, let it be so. For as far as the lawless, crude, savage people who despise the gospel and misuse it to their caprice are concerned, I would make them go into the fifth or the sixth or the seventh degree, for they deserve neither comfort nor freedom. Let whatever will, happen to them. One should see to it, however, that those who have gone or still go into the third or fourth degree should not have cause to be troubled in their consciences before God. Especially when otherwise they are good, pious, sensible people, and because it is not forbidden in the imperial law or the Scriptures, and it is evident that the pope and the clergy themselves do not hold to the prohibition of the third and fourth degree, but accept money and sell both the third and fourth degree and the second as well.[63] If Mammon can accomplish this without God's word, then God's word can do it without Mammon!

Accordingly, although the second degree is forbidden in the temporal law, namely, that one may not take his brother's or sister's daughter in marriage, yet if it had happened, as has often been the case with some great kings through papal dispensation, and it still could happen that a Jew and his wife became Christians and she was related to him in the second degree, which is not

---

[62] Cf. Luther's treatise *The Persons Related by Consanguinity and Affinity who Are Forbidden to Marry According to the Scriptures, Leviticus 18* (1522). *LW* 45, 3-9.
[63] Cf. *LW* 44, 183-184.

forbidden in the law of Moses, just as Abraham and Nahor took the daughter of their brother Haran, Genesis 12 [11:29], then one should let this marriage stand and not dissolve it, as the imperial laws in such a case also permit and advise. For although it is a marriage entered into in disobedience of the temporal law, nonetheless, because it has now been consummated and is not contrary to God's word, and the wife would lose her honor and become worthless, it is to remain a marriage out of mercy and to prevent greater calamity. I say this for the sake of consciences which perhaps would not be satisfied that the pope had given permission or sold it for money. What degrees or persons are forbidden in the temporal law, however, I will leave to the jurists and those learned in the law to teach; I am writing more for the sake of consciences than for the sake of laws.

Now perhaps a clever jurist will argue that the imperial laws have yielded to the canon law in this point, and therefore it is of no use if one wants to conform to the temporal law because the latter now considers itself inferior to the canon law, and that we must concur with him in this. I answer: I know all too well, unfortunately, that the emperors have indeed in many respects subjugated themselves and their law to the pope and the canon law, but how willingly they did this, how pleasing it was to God, and how well it turned out we are shown all too convincingly by the ceaseless, horrible bloodshed which the pope has caused thereby, and in addition by the unceasing, eternal hate, envy, discord, and other untold horrors which have in the past raged between popes and emperors, and which may never cease to the inexpressible, insuperable harm of Christianity throughout the world. It is said, "Render unto Caesar the things that are Caesar's, and to God the things that are God's" [Matt. 22:21]. Now inasmuch as the imperial law has concerned itself with marriage as a temporal affair and codified and interpreted it, my dear pope should rather have left it at that and not interfered in another's office that was not committed to him, for that is the same thing as taking it by force and robbery.

If I were a servant and my master were about to undertake a great risk to his person and property and place himself in jeopardy,

I certainly would not always follow him. I would hold back if he would not follow or obey the command not to do such things. So it is in this matter: if the emperor were about to surrender a great deal and even subject himself completely to the pope, to the point where the pope would completely control my person and property too, we do not have to follow the emperor, for then the imperial rule would be without effect everywhere, whereas it is supposed to be above all government on earth. The same is true here: Because this point is codified and interpreted in the imperial law, one should be governed by it, as was done in times past when there were pious Christians just as there are now, regardless of what that mighty robber and huntsman, the pope, later snatched for himself and brought under himself, or that the emperor has subjugated himself. I say this for the sake of guiding the consciences of men. Whoever wants to go along with the emperor and be under the pope, let him go ahead; I refuse to consent to such papal robbery and imperial subjugation and will not be a party to the fruits borne of such robbery and subjugation, namely, all this blood, murder, hate, discord, and destruction of Christianity until the Last Judgment, as was said above.

It is indeed true that no better rule ever came upon the earth to plague the desperate evil world than the rule of the Turks[64] and of the pope, and no better rule could come for this purpose unless it were the immediate rule of the devil himself, for the world does not deserve to have one line of good, useful law or to see a pious sovereign, but it should have only evil, destructive laws and only tyrants and bloodthirsty rulers. These belong in the world, for the world cannot tolerate good laws and pious people. So I am hardly concerned, as long as I can instruct and console consciences, that the pope, the Turk, and the devil tread evil rogues under foot. Let them judge rightly or wrongly as God wills; they do no harm to good consciences who have the right instruction and understanding, and externally we can well endure such a plague beside the world.

Here I want to close and leave this matter for now, and, as I did above, advise my dear brothers, the pastors and clergy, to

---

[64] Cf. pp. 178-179.

refuse to deal with marriage matters as worldly affairs covered by temporal laws and to divest themselves of them as much as they can. Let the authorities and officials deal with them, except where their pastoral advice is needed in matters of conscience, as for example when some marriage matters should come up in which the officials and jurists had entangled and confused the consciences, or else perhaps a marriage had been consummated contrary to law, so that the clergy should exercise their office in such a case and comfort consciences and not leave them stuck fast in doubt and error.

For whenever such a case or error or doubt comes up, where the conscience could not be aided unless the law or statute were repealed, and yet this same law cannot be publicly repealed because it is universal, one should, before God and secretly in one's conscience, respect the conscience more than the law. And if conscience or law has to yield and give way, then it is the law which is to yield and give way, so that the conscience may be clear and free. The law is a temporal thing which must ultimately perish, but the conscience is an eternal thing which never dies. It would not be right to kill or ensnare an eternal thing for a transient thing to remain and be free. Rather, the opposite should be true; a transitory thing should perish rather than an eternal one be destroyed. It is better to strangle a sparrow so that a human being may survive than to strangle a human being so that a sparrow may survive.[65] The law exists for the sake of the conscience, not the conscience for the sake of the law. If one cannot help both at the same time, then help the conscience and oppose the law.

I am saying this because I have often heard confessors complain that marriage matters, of such a nature that they were impossible to decide, have come before them and they said, "We must commend these matters to the unfathomable goodness of God." I have also seen how much the doctors, especially Gerson,[66] had to deal with *perplexis conscientiis,* confused consciences. All this comes from commingling spiritual and temporal law and regarding

---

[65] Cf. Matt. 10:31.

[66] John Gerson (1363-1429) was a prominent medieval theologian and conciliarist. As a moral theologian he held to the doctrine that the sinfulness or goodness of an act depended solely on the will of God.

the external transitory laws as equal to the internal, eternal laws. One is not well learned in the law, however, if one confuses consciences by them; laws are supposed to instil fear and punish, prevent and forbid, not to confuse and ensnare. But where they do confuse they are certainly no longer laws, or else they are not rightly understood. Therefore, if you find that a confusion of conscience is about to arise over the law, then tear through the law confidently like a millstone through a spiderweb,[67] and act as if this law had never been born. And if you cannot tear it up outwardly before the world, then let it go and tear it up in your conscience. It is better to leave the body and one's property confused in the law than the conscience and the soul.

And one should especially observe this rule or method *in preteritis,* that is, when a thing has happened, and say, "What has happened, has happened; gone is gone; who can gather it together again as it was before, when it has been spilled?"[68] See to it that it does not happen again, and forgive and forget what has happened to spare consciences. An intelligent physician does well when he spares the medicine as long as a man is healthy, but if a man is sick and he wants at first to leave him unattended to save medicine, he is a fool. So here, too, whoever wishes to restore the law which has been transgressed to its entirety, so that he would rather let consciences choke on it before he would omit one bit of the law—he is the biggest fool on earth; that was the practice of the monks and clergy under the papacy. To learn or know laws is no great art, but to use the laws correctly and keep them within their goals and province requires that one use restraint, and that is an art.

I should probably also have treated the canon law or the pope's decretals in this work, but the canon law is thrown together in so disorderly a fashion, often contradictory, and gathered together out of circular letters of the pope which have been issued at many times and for many reasons, that it would be too great an effort for me and would lead to a great disputation which I could not cover in many pages, as has happened to the jurists and still

---

[67] Wander (ed.), *Deutsches Sprichwörter Lexikon,* IV, "*Spinne,*" No. 1.
[68] *Ibid.,* IV, "*Verschütten,*" No. 1.

happens daily, when they are to abridge it and compare it. It is true that there are many good decisions and verdicts in it, but some are just so-so. Many think that Angelus has abridged it in his *Summa*.[69] Let them be of this opinion; I would not like it if I had to follow Angelus in every point. Therefore my advice is this: Let the temporal laws apply here, but in conscience our canon shall be this: Because public betrothals take precedence over secret and private ones, so also prior lying together takes precedence over future betrothals, other things being equal.[70]

---

[69] Angelus di Chivasso (1411-1495), whose *Summa angelica de casibus conscientiae* was a popular guide for confessors, had listed the questions of conscience in alphabetical order. See the treatment of this book by Johannes Dietterle in *Zeitschrift für Kirchengeschichte*, XXVII (1906), 296-310.

[70] *Quod publica sponsalia preiudicent clandestina et privatis, sic ante copulata carne preiudicent sponsalibus futuris caeteris paribus.*

INDEXES

INDEX OF NAMES AND SUBJECTS

Abbots, 5
Abel, 233
Abimelech, 41
Abomination, 177-178, 184, 195, 198, 200, 243, 255-256
Abraham, 39, 97-98, 173, 193, 233, 235, 310, 316
Absalom, 41, 102, 193
Abstinence from wine, 177
Academic degrees, 209
Accipio and *accipiam*, 274 n. 20
Adam, 233, 276
  the old, 132, 169
Adoption, 309
Adrian VI, pope, XI, XII
Adulterer, adulteress, 98, 271, 276, 282, 311, 313
Adultery, 77, 262, 267, 270, 272, 278, 294-295, 297-300, 311
Advice, 267, 271, 283
Aequitas, 102
Aesop, 111 n. 44, 112 n. 45
Agag, 66
Agricola, John, 111 n. 43
Agriculture, 131 n. 91, 181
  occupation of, 128
Ahab, 66, 120, 131, 172
Ahithophel, 193
Ai, men of, 125
Alaric, 236 n. 44
Albrecht, count of Mansfeld, 47, 247 n. 61
Albrecht of Brandenberg, archbishop of Mainz, 90 n. 11, 227 n. 21
Aleppo, battle of, 202 n. 120
Alexander, Roman emperor, 105 n. 26
Alexander the Great, 107 n. 31
Alexandria, bishop of, 179 n. 68
Alfred IX of Leon, 266 n. 3
Allah, 183-184
Alliance between Denmark and Hanseatic League, 113 n. 52
Alliances between German rulers, 90 n. 12
Amalek, 66

Amaziah, 120
Ambrose, St., 269
Amends, making, 280, 283
Amorites, 120, 190
Amputation, 96-97
Amsdorf, Nicholas, 184 n. 84
Amulets, 135 n. 99
Anabaptists, 5 n. 4, 90 n. 13
Anarchy, XII
Anathema, 147 n. 13
Angels, 176, 221 n. 18, 225, 229, 240
  of God, 223, 225, 240
Angelus di Chivasso, 320 n. 69
Annas, servants of, 102
Annates, 164 n. 16
Anthony, St., 117 n. 60
Antichrists, 8-9, 180 n. 72, 181, 196
Apostasy, 180 n. 72
Apostles, 149, 151, 177, 196 n. 100, 255, 265
  and disciples, 51
  time of, 95, 163
Apostolic poverty, 5
Apostolici regiminis (decree), 177 n. 64
Appenzell, 106 n. 28
Arabia, 202
Arabic, 183 n. 78, 232 n. 33
Arbitration, 42, 75 n. 30
Arians (Arius), 179 nn. 67, 68
Aristotle, 111 n. 44, 253
Arithmetic, 215, 251, 252 n. 73
Armor, 245, 249-250
Arms, bearing, XIII, 89, 245
Army, armies, 94, 168, 191
  Christian, 167
  emperor's, 89 n. 2
Arson, 8, 70
Articles, of the king of Denmark, 113 n. 49
Asa, 173
Asia, 202
Assyria, 41
Assyrians, 107 n. 30, 110
Astronomy, 252 n. 73
Augsburg, 213 n. 2

Diet of (1530), 211, 213 n. 2, 227 n. 22
Reformation in, 39 n. 50
Augsburg Confession, 6 n. 8
Augustine, St., 164 n. 12, 178 n. 65, 179 n. 69, 220 n. 13, 232 n. 32, 236 n. 44
Aunts, 302
Authorities, xii, 27, 32, 50, 99, 101, 127, 210, 281-282, 285, 292-297, 306-307, 309, 311-312, 315
    civil, 21 n. 9, 261, 280
    governing, 25, 50-51, 61, 134
    secular, 209
    spiritual, 227 n. 23
    worldly, 272
Authority, 25 ff., 31, 74, 126-127, 190, 226, 267-268
    from God, of God (*see* God, authority from, of)
    human, 100
    of man over animals, 13
    one's own, 311
    parental, 268-269, 279, 281
    public, 268
    secular, 209
    spiritual, 227 n. 23, 266, 284, 314
    temporal, 52, 227 n. 23, 231, 237-238, 248, 256, 265-266, 284, 314
    worldly, 242, 314
Azariah, 120

Babylon, 194
Bachanten, 218 n. 10, 244 n. 54
Bamberg, 72 n. 25
Ban, 197 n. 102, 271, 273
    Luther under, 162
Banishment, 313, 314 n. 60
Banner
    of cross, 168-169
    emperor's, 185, 189-190, 196
Bans, publishing, 290 n. 40, 293
Baptism, 51, 177, 227, 254
    office of, 220, 231
    repeated, celebration of, 294
    sponsors in, 262
Baptized souls, 224
Battle, 133, 135
Battle cries, 130
Beasts (wild), 211, 217-218, 237-238, 242, 252
Beggar, parable of, 111 n. 44
Beggars, 250-251
Belgrade, 157

Believers, xiv, 170, 219, 224-225, 236, 261, 265
    in God, 122, 135
Bells, use of, 175 n. 58
Belly, 235-236, 241-242, 305
Benediction, 243 n. 53
Benjaminites, 191
Betrothals, engagements, 262, 267-310 *passim*
    act of, 297 n. 43
    forced, 262, 268, 304-310
    formulas, 274 n. 20
    future, promise of, 274, 293, 320
    in land of Moses, 291-292
    public, 262, 267, 271, 275, 281-304 *passim*, 307, 320
    repeated, 293
    secret, 220, 262, 267-288 *passim*, 289 n. 37, 290 ff., 297, 300, 306, 308, 320
    validity of, 262, 273
Betrothed
    bride, 289, 291-292, 295, 298, 300 (*see also* Bride)
    fiance, deceased, 262
    first, 270-271, 289, 295-296, 300
    man, 287
    missing, 297-298
    persons, 296, 298, 303
    publicly, 289-290
    secretly, 281, 284
    sweetheart, 292
    virgin, 289
Bibbiena, Antonio, cardinal, 188 n. 90
Bibles, German Protestant, 232 n. 29
Biblical texts, 143 n. 14
Billichkeit, 102 n. 17
Binding and loosing, office of, 220
Birds, 13, 238
    hunting, 39
Bishops, 5, 19, 116, 149, 164 nn. 15, 16, 165-166, 168-169, 173, 179-180, 186, 199, 221, 236, 272-273, 294
    let rule forum, 273
    true, 223
Blasphemers, 34, 51-52, 66, 74, 162, 195, 302
Blaspheming God, 48, 50, 147
Blasphemy, 19, 148, 174, 178, 186, 240, 255
Blessings, 72, 220
    bestowing on marriage, 293
    of God, 214, 245, 305

horse and rider, 135
temporal, 100
those who insult us, 29
Blind, 198, 306
making to see, 224-225
woman, 302
Blood, 42, 189 (*see also* Christ, blood of)
Bloodhounds, 68-69, 74, 180, 189, 227
Bloodshed, 27, 40, 42, 49, 54, 63, 82-83, 129, 157, 180, 195, 201-203, 226, 326
Blood-tithe, 11 n. 23
Body, 39, 51, 74, 96-97, 108, 130, 132, 150, 166, 179, 187, 224, 237, 249, 297, 319
disciplining and crucifying, 228
and goods, 187, 266, 269
living, 146 n. 9
and property, 127
and soul, 23, 25, 32, 42-43, 48 ff., 53, 117, 136, 227, 249, 252, 254
Bohemia, 202, 203 n. 122
Bondswoman, 302
Booty, 133
Bowing and kneeling, 174
Boys, education of, 231, 234, 246
promising, 257
Braunschweig, 59-60, 130
Braunschweig'sche Kirchenordnung, 210 n. 8
Bread, earning, 134
Bridal couple, 261 n. 3
Bridal love, 304
Bride, 290-291, 296-297, 305 (*see also* Betrothed)
and bridegroom, 268, 289
publicly betrothed, 292
unchaste, 300-301
unreconciled, 299
Bridegroom, 235, 282, 298, 302, 304 (*see also* Betrothed)
Broadsides, 220 n. 14
Bull's eye, 288
Businessmen, 244, 251-252

Caesar, rendering unto, 50-51, 134, 316
Caesarini, Julian, cardinal, 167 n. 28
Cain, 233
Call for a Crusade Against the Turks . . ., 157 n. 4
Callings, 166
Camerarius, Joachim, 6 n. 8, 214 n. 4

Campeggio, Lorenzo, cardinal, xii, 188 n. 90
Canaanites, 120, 125
Canisio, Egidio, cardinal, 188 n. 90
Canon law, xiv, 168, 226, 227 nn. 22, 23, 232 n. 33, 261, 268, 273 n. 17, 295, 298, 303-304, 308, 316
burned by Luther, 273 n. 17
Canons, 166, 236, 268, 320
Caprice, 309-310
Captives (*see* Turk, captive among, Christians among)
Cardinals, 164, 169
Carnal knowledge, 280
Carnal life of Turks, 175-176
Carthusians, 251 n. 71
Casimir, margrave of Brandenburg, 47 n. 2, 72 n. 26
Castles, 47, 50, 243
Castration, 148 n. 20
Catechism, 231-232
Catholic
leagues and alliances, xiii
opponents of Luther, 59
princes, 59, 90 n. 9
and Protestants, 261
rulers, xiii, 90
rulers, German, xii
side, ii
Cattle-tithe, 11 n. 23
Celibate life, 220
Ceremonial formulas and laws, 146, 274 n. 20
Chaeronea, battle of, 107 n. 31
Chancelors, 187, 240, 243 ff.
Chancery clerk, 249
Chanclor, 85 n. 53
Chaplains, 220, 234
Chapters, 174, 176, 235
Character testimonials, 293-294
Charles V, emperor, xi, xiii, 89 n. 2, 90 nn. 8, 9, 106 n. 29, 120 n. 67, 168 ff., 184, 189, 198-201, 202 n. 122, 204 n. 125
Chastity, 149, 299
Chastity, poverty, and obedience, 146 n. 6, 147
Cheek, turning the other, 164
Children, 76, 97, 112, 222-223, 226, 252-253, 255-256, 299, 305-309, 313-314 (*see also* Sons, Daughters)
abandoned, 309
Christian training of, 210

education of (*see* Education)
forced into marriage, 304
of God, 237, 248
keeping in school, 213-258 *passim*
and parents, 114, 209, 246
protection of, 237
raising, 218
by second woman, 295
of unbelief, 153
Christ, 9, 25, 27, 29-32, 39, 49, 64,
    81-84, 97, 99, 101-102, 145, 149,
    151, 165, 169, 173, 176-177, 184,
    195 ff., 199-200, 213, 216-217,
    224, 232, 235, 265
belief, believers in, 31, 150, 185
birth of, 36, 199
blood and agony of, 255
blood and dying, 237
blood of, 12, 135, 219, 220 n. 14,
    228-229, 256
as a child, 135 n. 98, 287
and the church, 304
coming of, 200
commands, 50, 175
confessing, 175
crucified, 255
death of, 177, 219, 228
denying, 76, 150
destroying, 183
doctrine of, 30, 165
enemies of, 30, 165, 176-177, 180
    n. 72
example of, 30
faith in, of, 95, 175
fulfils law, 145-146
gospel of, 30, 36, 175
injuring, 175
king, 177
kingdom of (*see* Kingdom, of
    Christ)
kingship of, 81, 97, 166
law of, 27-28, 30
Lord, 175, 177, 195, 204, 219, 237
Lord and servant, 39
love of, 217
man, 248
Master, 51
Messiah, 9
mother of, 196
name of, 29, 32, 48, 165
office of (prophet), 176-177
pain and agony of, 255
passion of, 30, 134, 142
peace of, 16

people of, 165
praise of, 177
preaching of, 30
prophesied, 235
Redeemer, 12, 177
righteousness in, 64
Savior, 176-177, 255
sayings of, 69 n. 21, 130, 136, 145-
    146, 153, 164, 179, 202, 222,
    224, 233, 265
servants of, 265
side of, pierced, 220 n. 13
Son of God, 135, 176-177, 219,
    254-255
Spirit of, 166, 242
suffering of, 228-229
Supreme Lord, 28
taking property of, 29-30
teaching of, 37-38, 51, 67-68, 111,
    114, 197
testifies, 195
understanding of, 228
"wanton against," 150
word of, 26, 63, 69, 175
word of, perverted, 164
words of, 9, 275, 286
work of, 166
wounds of, 219
Christendom, xiii, 158, 171, 181, 185,
    187-188, 192, 316
Christian, 27, 30-31, 37, 39-40, 52,
    76, 78, 95, 98, 122, 159, 164 ff.,
    168, 193, 197
advice, 43
agreement, 13
army, 167
attitude, 135
bearing arms, 90 n. 13
beliefs, believers, 170, 177
cause, 7
consideration, 13, 214
custom, 132
death, 81
doctrine, 164, 177
duty of, 61, 70, 164
faith, 89, 95, 136, 175, 178, 188,
    199, 306
freedom, 39, 141, 310
heart, 133, 177
honor, 227
law, 8, 25-26, 28-31
life, 177
love, 96, 145, 312
the man, 203, 293

manner, 98
matters, 12, 40
means, 43
name of, 28, 30-33, 36, 40-43, 130
pastor, 223
people, 215
power, 170
preacher, 83, 168, 223
reader, 8, 10
rights, 271
rulers, 32, 83
school (Eisleben), 47
schoolmaster, 223
sense, 38
"Sir Christian," 170, 184, 192, 199
spirit, 17
teacher, 98, 129
testament, 257
thing to do, 96
training of children, 210
truth, 181-182
way, 8-9, 38, 83, 283
weapons, 170
word, 236
work, 96, 188
Christian Association of Peasants, 7 n.
    14, 24, 27-28, 50 n. 7, 70 n. 24
"Christian brethren" (see Christian
    Association of Peasants)
Christian II, king of Denmark, 106 n.
    29, 107 n. 34, 113 n. 50, 115
Christianity, 317
conversion to, 175 n. 58
Christians, 27 ff., 31-32, 34-37, 40, 43,
    70, 79, 81, 83, 89, 99, 107, 122,
    145-146, 150, 161, 163-164, 166,
    169-170, 173, 175 ff., 180, 182,
    184, 186, 219, 224, 236, 248,
    253, 255-256, 265, 315
    army of, 165, 168
    baptized, 51
    body of, 170
    faith of, 179
    false, 186
    fine, 51
    good, 181
    pious, 54-55, 317
    sincere, XIII
    totality of, 192 n. 95
    true, 12, 17, 165
    under Turkish rule, 175 n. 58, 183
        n. 82
Christopher, St., 135 n. 98
Church, XIV, 18 n. 3, 159, 163, 166,
    168, 171-172, 185, 188, 222, 225,
    262, 268, 271, 304, 313
    army of, 168
    ceremonial act of, 261
    courts, 261
    and Crusades, XIII
    doctrine of, 16, 210
    enemies of, 168
    financial institutions of, 5
    giving money to, 256-257
    head of, 180
    institutional, 5
    papal, XIII
    practices, 16, 209
    provost, 11 n. 20
    reform, XI, 5-6, 142
    resources, 257
    of Rome (see Roman church)
Church-dominated schools, 209
Churches, 47, 216, 256
    endowed, 142
    territorial, XIII
Cicero, 100 n. 9, 110 n. 42, 124 n. 80
Circumcision, 145
Cities, 210, 215, 234-235, 240, 243-
    245, 250, 257, 309, 313
Citizens, 116, 294, 309
    of Nürnberg, 216
City council, 214, 216, 245, 294
Civil authorities (see Authority,
    Authorities)
Civil law, 261, 304
Clement VII, pope, XII n. 4, 169 n. 34,
    199 n. 108
Clementis papae V. Constitutiones,
    232 n. 33
Clerical tyrants, 279
Clergy, 81, 112, 159, 163 n. 11, 166,
    179, 186, 196, 219 n. 12, 220,
    261, 315, 317, 319
    Protestant, 261
    spiritual class, 163
Clerks, 240-241, 243 ff.
Cloister schools, pope's, 164
Cloistered life, 141
Cloisters, 109
Clothing and food, 265
Coburg Castle, 211
Cochlaeus, John, 60 n. 7
Cognac, League of, 204 n. 125
Comforting, office of, 220
Commandments, 178, 272
    of God (see God, commandments
    of, Ten Commandments)

of men, 10
of worldly rulers, 98
Commission
  arbitration, 8
  to interpret divine law, 7
Common fields, 15
Common man, 215
Common people, 18 n. 3, 19, 21, 187, 217 ff., 231, 251, 274
Common sense, 262, 268-269, 310
Common table, 295
Common woman, 280, 291
Community, 13, 15, 38, 78, 126 n. 82, 131, 215, 294, 309, 313
  chooses pastor, 11, 37
  laws of, 9 n. 17
  power of, 10
Compulsion, 305, 307
Concubines, priests', 287 n. 29
Conditional verbs, 275
Confessing Christ, 175
Confession of sins, 172
Confessors, 270, 272, 286, 318, 320 n. 69
Confidence, 123
Confiscation of properties, 209
Conjugal cohabitation, 261
  duty, 271 ff.
  rights, 283, 306
"Conrad," 85 n. 52
Consanguinity, 262, 310, 315-316
Consciences, 17, 33, 40, 43, 52, 83, 89, 93, 105, 112, 114-115, 117, 119, 121, 129, 163, 169, 184, 187-190, 194, 204, 226, 242, 261, 265-266, 271 ff., 275, 278, 281-284, 286 ff., 299, 303, 308 ff., 312, 316-320
  bad, 113, 299
  burdened, 281, 289
  captive, 270
  clear, 159
  confusion of, 279, 318-319
  entangling, 275
  eternal thing, 318
  evangelical, 262
  good, 42, 54, 130, 134-135, 164, 267, 281, 309, 317
  good and bad, 23, 53, 93-94
  innocent, 162
  matters of, 273, 318
  of men, 317
  pious, 303
  poor, 271
  qualms of, 255, 314
  teaching, 39
  troubled, xiv, 261, 263, 289 n. 37, 315
Consent (to marriage)
  father's, 277, 308
  girl's, 305
  mutual, 261-262
  parental, 268
  of partner, 298
Constantinople, fall of, 157, 200 n. 113
Consumers, 128
Consummation, 290, 307, 318
Content and form of life, 141
Convents, 47, 141, 143, 298
Conventual orders, 141-142, 145
Conversion to Christianity, 175 n. 58
Converted souls, 224
Corinthians, 29, 64
Corvee (free labor), 13 n. 28
Council, general, demand for, xi
Councilmen, 42, 187, 218 n. 11
Counselors, 127, 240, 243-244, 250
Counsels (consilia), 197
Counts, 116, 126, 183
  and lords, 42, 127, 243-244
Courage, 119, 167
Court trial, 81
Courts of law, 127, 267, 301
  royal, 250
Craftsman, 131, 231
  letters recommending, 294
Creation, 248
Creatures, 225, 254
Creed, 136, 171, 231 n. 28
Crimes, 48, 77, 252
Criminal power, 306
Crops, damaged by game, 12
Cross, 29-30, 32, 35, 220 n. 14, 255
Crucifix, 168
Crude people, 309
Cruelty of rulers, 61, 82
Crumb collector, 250 n. 67, 251
Crusaders, 186 n. 86
Crusades, 159, 186, 188 n. 90
  against the Turks, call for, xiii, 157 n. 4, 162
  taxes, 186 n. 87
Custom
  Christian, 132
  German, 262
  of the land, 291-292, 304
  Roman, 261

Damnation, 20, 223
Daniel, 43, 224, 244
Danube, 157
Daredevils, 94
Daughters, 231, 269-270, 277, 280-
    282, 302, 305-310
  of rich and poor, 285
  seduced, 269-270, 280-281, 301
David, 83, 97-98, 102, 112, 172-173,
    193, 221, 285, 288-289
Dead
  let bury their dead, 265-266
  raising the, 224-225
Deaf
  making to hear, 224-225
  woman, 302
Death, 54, 70, 77-78, 126, 194, 224,
    226, 229, 278, 310
  in body and soul, 49-50, 52
  Christian, 81
  natural, 104
  pains of, 255
  penalty, punishment, 48, 53, 59 n.
    5, 101, 211, 255, 278, 297
  peril of, 77, 93, 133-134
  tax, 15 n. 30, 22, 39
  traps, 225
Deborah, 193
Debtors, 153
Decretalium D. Gregorii Papae IX,
    268 n. 7, 312 n. 56
Decretals, pope's, 176, 197, 199, 273
    n. 17, 319
Decreti Magistri Gratiani Prima Pars,
    227 n. 22
Defense of empire, duty of, xiii
Degrees, academic, 209
Denmark, 106 n. 29, 107-108, 113
    n. 49, 114-115, 202
  king of, 113 n. 50
  rebellion in, 106-107
Desires, base, evil, 153-154
Devil (evil spirit), 9, 18 n. 3, 21, 24,
    28, 33, 41-42, 49, 51-55, 63,
    67-68, 70, 77, 79, 84, 117-118,
    121, 129, 134, 150, 162, 165,
    167-168, 170-171, 175, 177, 179-
    184, 186, 188-189, 195-196, 200,
    204, 213-214, 218-219, 223-229,
    240, 242, 251, 254-256, 265, 287,
    295, 301, 305, 317 (see also
    Satan)
  army of, 193
  art of, 217
  candles for, 66-67
  children of, 237
  driving out, 224
  kingdom of, 230
  messengers of, 302
  painting, over the door, 305
  servants of, 170, 174, 231
  is slanderer, 302
  spirit of lies, 179 ff.
  spirit of murder, 180-181
  temptation of, 286
  tongue of, 302
  trick of, 301
  war with, 257
Diabolus, diabel, 302
Dialectic, 252 n. 73
Dienstgelt, 127
Dietrich, Veit, 211, 213 n. 2
Diets, imperial, xi, 167 n. 23, 187-
    188, 189 n. 92
Dionysius of Syracuse, 110 n. 41
Disciples, 51, 63, 102
Discipline, 219, 255, 309
Discord, 316
Disease, 302
Disobedience, 115, 285, 310
  sin of, 269
Disparity of religion (impediment),
    262
Dispensation, papal, 315
Divine law, 7, 24-27, 28 n. 26 (see
    also God, law of)
"Divine right," 9 n. 17, 12 n. 25, 25
Divorce, 262, 277 ff., 282, 286, 296,
    300, 303, 310 ff.
Doctors, 95 ff., 221, 240, 244, 249-
    250, 273
Doctrine
  of Christ, 30, 165
  Christian, 164, 177
  false (pope's), 164
  of works, 177
Doeg, 193
Dog-marriages, 198
Donatists, 179 n. 69
Dowry, 274
Dürer, Albrecht, 247 n. 62
Dumb, making speak, 224-225

"Ecclesia," 168, 183
Ecclesiastes, Luther's work on, 100 n.
    10
Ecclesiastical institutions, 6
Eck, John, 5 n. 4

Economic injustices, 22
Edom, kings of, 192
Educated men, 215, 244, 252
Education, xiv, 209 ff., 230 ff., 253
  for girls, 231 n. 30, 232
  held in contempt, 209-211
  necessity of in government, 237-250
Egypt, 120, 157, 192, 202, 248
Ehud, 192
Eisenach, 250 n. 68
Eisleben, 47, 210
Elijah, 235
  prayer of, 33, 173
Elisha, 192, 236
  prayer of, 173
Ell, 105 n. 27
Eloha, 183
Emperors, 18 n. 3, 33, 50-51, 91, 114
  ff., 125-128, 130, 133, 159, 167
  ff., 180, 184-193, 196, 200, 233,
  239-242, 245, 248 n. 63, 316-317
  and kings, 243, 266
  Roman, 104, 105 n. 26
Empire, 184, 198, 228, 241 ff.
  estates of, 188
  old, 261
Endowments, 209, 234 n. 37, 254 n. 77
Enduring all things, 164
Enemies, 80 n. 42, 115, 132
  of children, 309
  of Christ (*see* Christ, enemies of)
  of God, 115, 309
  public, 309
  underestimating, 123-124
Engaged persons (*see* Betrothed)
Engagement (*see* Betrothal)
England, 202, 204 n. 125
Ephraim, 120
Epieikeia, 102
Epilepsy, 117 n. 60
Equals against equals in war, 103,
  115, 118, 121, 136
Erasmus, Desiderius, xi, 18 n. 3
Erfurt, 47
  university, 234 n. 39, 250 n. 68,
  251
Eric, duke of Braunschweig/Calenberg, 90
Erlau, bishop of, 167 n. 27
Ernst, duke of Braunschweig-Lüneburg, 89

Error, 19, 289, 318
Error and *conditio*, 303 n. 50
Ertzney, 252 n. 72
Esau, 233
Estates of empire, 188
Eternal life, 99, 237 (*see also* Life,
  everlasting)
Eunuchs, 149, 153
Euripides, 269 n. 12
Europe, xiii, 5, 157
Europeans, 157
Evangelical, 64, 252
  appearance, 36
  point of view, 109
  preaching, 142
  princes, 90
  rulers, 90
  sympathies, 52 n. 11
  teaching and practice, xiii
  way, 38
Evangelicals, 34, 37, 255
  of South Germany, xii
Evangelists, 37, 39, 311
Eve, 276
Evil, 26, 28, 31-32, 34, 74, 78, 82,
  99-100, 171, 248, 276
  desires, 153-154
  lusts, 151
  people, persons, 286, 303
  punishing, 95
  resisting, 164 ff.
  root of, 154
  spirit, 41, 204
  spirits, 24
  thoughts, 130-131, 149
  tongues, 300
Evildoers, 98
Exhortation, 186
  to soldiers, 132-133, 135
Exhorting, office of, 220
Exile, 279
Expulsion, 292
Exsurge, Domine (bull), 162 n. 5, 213
  n. 2
Ezekiel, 173

Fables, 111 n. 44, 112 n. 45
Fair wage, 14
Faith, 83, 135-136, 150, 172, 174-175, 177, 181, 185-186, 195, 224
  alone, 83
  breaking, 150
  in, of Christ, 95, 175
  Christian (*see* Christian, faith)

of Christians, 179
defender of, 185, 188
keeping, 275
right, true, 10, 158 n. 9, 179, 183, 228
Turkish (*see* Turks, faith of)
Famine, 235-236, 254
Fanatics, 70, 179, 255
Farmers, 128
Farnese, Allesandro, cardinal, 188 **n.** 90
Fasting, 167, 174, 177, 189, 199, 235
Father (of family), 110, 222, 269, 306, 309
and daughter, 151-152, 308, 310
leaving, for God, 131
loving, 306
and mother, 222, 226, 229, 268, 301
Fathers (patriarchs), 98, 269
Favoritism, 273 n. 18
Feilitzsch, Fabian von, 239 n. 47
Ferdinand of Austria, king of Bohemia, 203 n. 122
Feudal
oath, 113 n. 48
rents, 128
society, 5
structures, 127 n. 85
system, 50 n. 6
Fiance (*see* Betrothed)
Fief, 127-128, 130
Fifth Lateran Council, 177 n. 64
Fighting men, 245
Filial obedience, 277, 306, 310
Fire, 50, 78, 182
and brimstone, 198
First fruits, 233
Fish, 12-13
eating, 204
freedom to catch, 39
Flattery of princes, 115, 117 (*see also* Luther, flatterer of princes)
Flesh, 77, 153, 178, 182, 228, 265, 305
and blood, 10, 41, 52, 165 168
killing, 150
love of, 298
lusts of, 150, 154
man of, 64 n. 3
one, 181, 314
one voice, 268
resisting, 153
self-will of, 12
Flood, 24, 171

Florence, Council of (1438), 262 n. 7
"Florentine brides," 198 n. 103
Flu, 254 n. 79
Fools, 65, 122 n. 76, 167
Force, 7, 61, 76, 305, 307, 316
and violence, 40
Forced engagement (*see* Betrothal, forced)
Forced marriage, 304-307
Foresight, lack of, 303-304
Forests, 13, 39
Forgiveness, 69, 312
of sins, 161, 177
Forster, Johann, 142 n. 8
Fortune, 124-125
Foundations (ecclesiastical), 82, 220, 225-226, 228, 231-235, 241, 256
France, 130, 202, 204 n. 125
king of, 113, 168, 202
Francis I, king of France, 90 n. 8, 120 n. 67, 168, 199 n. 108
Franconia, 6, 47
nobles of, 116
peasants of, 19 n. 5, 72 n. 27
princedoms of, 72 n. 26
Frank, Sebastian, 129 n. 87
Frankenhausen, battle of, 5 n. 3, 59
Fraud, 103-104
Frederick I, king of Denmark, 106 n. 29, 113 n. 49
Frederick the Wise, elector of Saxony, XII, 47, 60, 89 n. 1, 90 n, 10, 106 n. 29, 119 n. 66, 163, 239 nn. 46, 47
"Free brethren," 83
Freedom
of belief, 175
of a Christian, 39, 141, 310
Frogs and the Stork, The, 112 n. 45
Fruit of the womb, 291, 293
Frundsberg, George von, baron, 247 n. 63
Fugitive, 294
Future tense, 273-274, 275 n. 22

Galatians, 40
Galba, Roman emperor, 105
Gambler, 280
Gelehrte sind verkehrte, 209 n. 1
Geographers, 203
Geometry, 252 n. 73
George, count of Wertheim, 247 n. 61
George, duke of Saxony, 20 n. 6, 90

n. 10, 247 n. 61
George, margrave of Brandenburg/-
    Ansbach, 247 n. 62
George, St., 135 n. 97
German
    books in, 215, 232
    lands, 217, 239, 254-255
    language, 215
    national front, XI
    peasantry, 47
    people, populace, 129 n. 87, 161
    reading and writing, 215, 251, 255
    speaking, 274
"German prophet" (Luther), 258 n.
    83
Germans, 79, 101, 127 n. 84, 128,
    136-137, 161, 176, 201-202, 205,
    257, 262
Germany, XI, 22, 52, 78-79, 116, 164,
    184, 188-189, 193, 198, 201-202,
    209, 214, 234, 254, 256
    destruction, disaster in, 8, 19 ff.,
        40, 42
    Southern, 106 n. 28
Gerson, John, 318 n. 66
Geyer, Florian, 47 n. 2
Gideon, 130, 192
Gifts of the bridegroom, 282
Girl, seduced, 281-285
Girls, education of, 232 n. 30
Giving in marriage, 269, 292-293, 308
Glory
    of God, 228
    winning of in war, 185
Glutton, 229
God
    ambassadors of, 221
    angel of, 223, 225, 240
    angering, 174, 186
    angry, 42, 254
    answer to, XIII
    appoints rulers (see Rulers, ap-
        pointed by God)
    authority from, 30, 126-127, 266
    authority of, 26, 66, 108, 126-127,
        191
    believing in, 122, 135
    blaming, 276
    blaspheming, 48, 50, 147
    blessings of, 214, 245, 305
    calling upon, 34, 77, 183
    children of, 237, 248
    command of, 26, 49, 53, 73, 98,
        108, 114 ff., 121, 125, 134, 186-

187, 190 ff., 200, 277, 300, 305,
    312, 314
    commandments of, 12, 76-77, 122,
        187-192, 194-195, 276-279, 305-
        306 (see also Ten Command-
        ments)
    commending to, 283, 288
    commission from, 170, 188 ff.
    condemnation of, 167 n. 25
    creatures of, 12-13, 233, 238, 304
    decree of, 70, 104, 110, 168
    defying, 134
    denying, 77
    despising, 133, 147, 185, 241, 243
    dishonoring of, 277, 283
    disobedience to, 168, 284
    displeasure of, 273
    duty to, 84, 129, 187
    enemies of, 115, 309
    estates of, 246, 248
    example of, 276
    the Father, 51, 67, 177, 136
    Father in heaven, heavenly, 51,
        135, 199, 235
    favor of, 94, 188, 196
    fearing, 21, 64, 80, 123, 125, 130,
        133, 218, 303, 309
    fist of, 133
    gifts of, 141, 213, 226, 237, 239,
        253-254
    glory of, 228
    goodness of, 133, 318
    grace of (see Grace, of God)
    hand of, 95, 112, 159, 170, 174,
        177
    in hands of, 33, 125, 136
    help of, 34, 130, 191, 266
    honor to, 132-133, 148, 186, 228,
        241
    inspiration of, 304
    institutions of, 25, 91, 95-96, 118,
        243, 248, 256
    joins together, 126, 275-279
    judge, 41, 53, 74, 97, 114, 282
    judgment of, 41, 96-97, 108, 113,
        131, 134, 173-174
    justice of, 28, 97
    keeps word, 41
    kingdom of (see Kingdom of God)
    law of, 25-26, 113, 305 (see also
        Divine law)
    love of, 12, 250
    loving, 197
    majesty of, 9, 277

mercy of, 10, 66, 71, 79, 123-124, 135
minister of, 52
miracles of, 30, 184
name of, 24-25, 33, 50, 84, 129, 136, 267, 276, 283, 295, 301
obedience to, 98, 283-284
offenses against, 16
offices of, 224, 246, 248, 256-257
ordinances of, 26, 99, 104, 108, 122, 126, 129, 132, 185 ff., 226, 237-238, 240, 243, 248, 283, 306
people of, 120, 223
persecutors of, 43
pleasing, 55, 84, 132, 141, 172, 241, 244, 246, 316
praise of, 78, 148, 294
praying to, 16, 33-34, 228
promise of, 33, 133, 173, 233
punishment of, 21, 68, 110, 116, 121, 171, 178, 198
rebelling against, 61
reconciliation to, 184, 221
remembering, 123
repenting before, 42
resisting, 132, 158, 162
responsibility to, 187
righteousness before, 95
righteousness of, 66, 146, 191
rod of (God's anger), 68, 70, 158-159, 162, 170, 174, 178, 184
sacrifice to, 148, 229
Savior, 34, 176
servants of, 52, 68, 73, 114, 221, 225, 246
serving, service to, xiv, 81, 98, 129-130, 133, 151, 163, 166, 178, 222, 227 ff., 231, 233, 236, 243-244, 252-253, 256
sin against, 23, 304
Son of (see Son of God)
spear of, 133
Spirit, 102, 224
stewards of, 221
strength from, 32
subjects of, 91
sword of (see Sword of God)
tempting, 172, 191, 202-203
testimony of, 284
thanking, 75, 79, 241
titles of, 24
treason against, 114
true, 176, 276
trust in, 91, 234

trust in false, 135
vengeance of, 19-20, 25, 107-108, 113
verdict of, 43, 198
victory from, 91, 93
vows to, 148, 152-153
weapons of, 171
will of, 18 n. 3, 21, 33-34, 52, 66, 75, 132, 134-135, 153-154, 250, 317-318
word of, 6-7, 9, 12, 14-15, 18, 20, 24 ff., 53, 61, 65 ff., 76, 98-99, 115, 119, 136, 141, 148, 161, 165, 173-175, 183-184, 186-187, 197 ff., 209, 213, 220, 222, 224, 226, 228, 231, 235-236, 243, 248, 251, 255-256, 276 ff., 281, 283-284, 299, 305, 315-316
works of, 96, 183, 186, 228, 231, 240, 246, 248
worship of, 148, 229
wrath of, 18-19, 21-22, 24, 29, 40-43, 52-53, 61, 66, 68-70, 72, 79, 99, 115, 153, 168, 170-171, 174, 179, 184, 188, 255
God, false, 124
God of war, 169
Godfathers, 137
God-fearing men, 304
Godly calling, 100
Gog and Magog, 202
Gold and silver, 219
Good, the, 66, 70, 90
protecting, 95
Good sense, 268
Good works, 130, 135, 178
Goods, 29, 129, 312
protection of, 237
"Goods of the church," 169
Gordian, Roman emperor, 105 n. 26
Gospel, xiii, 8, 9 n. 17, 10, 12, 19, 20 n. 8, 22, 25-26, 28, 30-31, 33, 35-37, 39-40, 47 n. 2, 48-52, 64, 70, 78-79, 81, 82 n. 45, 130, 136, 145, 161-162, 166, 172, 177, 180, 185, 192, 195, 197, 199, 204, 216, 222, 228 ff., 232-233, 235-236, 254-255, 261, 265-266, 306, 308-309, 315
Christ's, 30, 36, 175
fruit of, 161
John's, 135 n. 99
Luther's, 21, 30
opposition to, 18 n. 3

our (Reformation), 294
persecution and suppression of, 31, 41-42, 104-105, 115, 169
preaching of, XI, 22-23
Gospels, four, 196
Gotha, 210
Goths, 107, 110, 236
Governing authorities, 25, 50-51, 61, 134
Government, 27, 48, 65, 75, 99, 107, 112, 178, 182 ff., 256-257, 288, 317
duty of, XIII
of Germany, German lands, 22, 239
head of, 80
legitimate, 91
spiritual, 99
temporal, 95, 104, 163, 166, 178, 181-182, 195, 231 n. 27, 242
true, 183
Turk's, 175, 178, 193, 200
two kinds of (see Kingdoms, two, doctrine of)
worldly, 18, 99, 118, 210, 237 ff., 242-243, 245
Grace, 42, 69, 72, 74, 83-84, 177, 190, 200, 305
day of, 53
double, 102
of God, 10, 33, 53, 79, 94-95, 110, 123-124, 133-134, 137, 197, 214, 235
of the Lord, 79
Grammar, grammatica, 252 n. 74
Greece, conquest of, 200 n. 114, 202
Greed, for honor and money, 132
Greedy men, 130-131
Greek drama, 235 n. 43
Greek language, 102, 232 nn. 32, 33
Greeks, 104, 107 n. 31, 108, 110, 123, 196, 269
Gregory of Nazianzus, 221 n. 19
Grimmenthal, 142 n. 11
Groschen, 183
Grosswardein, bishop of, 167 n. 27
Guilty partner, 311-312
Gulden, 131 n. 92, 183, 274
Gypsies, 294

Haggai, 221
Halberstadt, 210
Halle, 227 n. 21
Hallische Kirchenordnung, 210 n. 8
Hamburger Kirchenordnung, 210 n. 8

Hands, joining, 261
Hangman, 68, 303, 314 n. 61
Hannah, 148 n. 17, 153
Hannibal, 119 n. 64, 124
"Hans on the gallows," 314 n. 61
Hanseatic League, 113 nn. 51, 52, 114-115
Hapsburgs, 106 n. 28
Haran, 316
Hardheadedness, 19
Harlots, soldiers', 182
Harz Mountains, 121 n. 69
Hate, 316
Hausmann, Nicholas, 158 n. 12, 159, 263
Head, best part of body, 249
forfeiting, 279
Headsman, 66
Heart
Christian, 133, 177
hardness of, 278
human, 133
Heathen, 27 ff., 32, 34-35, 76, 81, 104, 106, 110, 122 ff., 150, 154, 163, 186, 226, 251, 269
beliefs, 177
custom, 132
pious, 29
poets, 41
rulers, 32
worship, 236 n. 44
Heaven, 36, 54, 66, 70, 81 ff., 191, 224, 254, 257
and earth, 230, 254, 301, 310
Hebrew, 183, 232 nn. 32, 33
Heilande, 221 n. 16
Heir, 270
Hell, 19, 36, 40, 51, 54-55, 66, 70, 132, 134, 161, 181-182, 219, 223 ff., 229-230, 254, 257
doors and windows of, 254
fire, 84, 254
gates of, 228
Henneberg, 141 n. 3, 142 nn. 5, 9
count of, 142 n. 9
monasteries, 143
Henry, duke of Braunschweig/Wolfenbüttel, 90 n. 9
Hereditary lord or prince, 131
Heresy, 228-229, 233, 294
Heretical ideas, 5
Heretics, 90 n. 8, 225, 227, 231-232, 240
Heriot (death tax), 15 n. 30

Herod, 51, 199-200
Hess, Eobanus, 214 n. 4
Hesse, 59, 90
Hezekiah, 173
Highway robbery, 39
Highwaymen and murderers, 178
Historians, 203
Histories, 238, 245
History, 41, 124
Holdings, unproductive, 14
Holiness, 173
  of Turks, 183
Holy estate, 299
Holy Ghost, 161, 177
Holy Spirit, 41, 150, 153, 209, 220,
  228-229, 242, 305
  Spirit of Christ, 166, 242
  Spirit of the Father, 136
  Spirit of God, 102, 224, 254
Homage, 193
Home life, true, 182
  destroyed by Turk, 195
Homosexuality, 198 n. 104
Honest man, 270, 293
Honor, 15, 77, 117, 132, 185, 226,
  237, 244, 246, 255, 309
  greed for, 132-133
  temporal, 132
  womanly, 280, 291 ff., 302, 308,
  316
Horses, 94, 136, 191
House
  and home, 254
  and property, 265, 313
  protection of, 237
Household, head of, 102-103
Hübmaier, Balthasar, 5 n. 4, 6 n. 7
Human doctrine, 180
Human ordinance and authority, 100
Human race, whole, 248
Humanists, xi, 18 n. 3
Humanity, 42
Humility, 64
Hungarians, 158 n. 9, 167, 202 n. 119
Hungary, 166, 167 nn. 28, 29, 202 n.
  119, 203 n. 123
Hunt, freedom to, 12, 39
Husband, 269, 298, 307, 315
  lawful, 295
  and wife, 141, 151-152, 268, 271-
  272, 274, 278, 294, 299, 306, 312
Hushai the Archite, 102
Hussites, rebellion of, xii
Hutten, Ulrich von, 158 n. 7

Hypocrisy, hypocrites, 148, 184, 229

Iconoclasts, 183 n. 80
Idolater, idolatry, 186, 215-216, 233,
  243
Ignorance, 78, 225
Illicit cohabitation, 294-295 (see also
  Lying together)
Images, 183
Immorality, 153-154
Immortality of the soul, 177 n. 64
Impediments to marriage, 262 n. 8,
  281, 315-316 (see also Consan-
  guinity)
Imperial army, 120 n. 68
Imperial law, 40, 265-268, 315 ff.
Imperial majesty, 245
Impotence, 262
Impurity, 153
*Individuam consuetudinem vitae con-
  tinens*, 313 n. 58
Indulgences, 90 n. 11, 164, 186 n. 86,
  187, 201, 306
Infantry, 248 n. 63
Ingolstadt, battle of, 47 n. 2
Ingratitude, 171, 243, 255, 258
Iniquities of fathers, 222
Injustice, 7, 27-28, 30 ff., 35, 42, 61,
  100-101, 106, 108, 114, 118, 270,
  292
Innocence, 292-293
Innocent, the, 72, 78, 101, 180
Innocent partner, 311-312
Innocent III, pope, 266 n. 3, 270 n.
  15
Inquiry, regarding absent betrothed,
  296
Institutio de putria potestate, 313 n.
  58
Insurrection, xii, 8, 61, 76, 142
Intention of marriage, 293
Intercourse, 262
Isaac, 233, 235, 269, 305, 310
Isaiah, 38
Ishmael, 233
Israel, 41
  children of, 9, 35, 125, 171, 190-
  192
  chosen nation of, 233
  house of, 174
  kings of, 97, 192
  people of, 104, 120
  priests of, 233
  tribes of, 151

Italian campaign, 89 n. 2
Italian marriages, 198 n. 103
Italy, 107 n. 32, 198 n. 103, 202

Jackdaws, 228
Jacob, 233, 235, 269, 299
Jail, 309
Jailers, 127
James, St., 33, 173-174
Jehoram, 192
Jehoshophat, 173, 192
Jephthah, 120
Jeremiah, 43, 79, 171, 176, 236
Jerusalem, 148, 171
Jesias, 173
Jews, 20, 27, 64, 79, 81, 94, 97, 104,
    107, 110, 130, 145-146, 150, 177,
    186, 195-196, 199-200, 236, 277,
    293, 315
  beliefs of, 177
  kingdom of, 199
Joachim of Brandenberg, 90
Joash, 173 n. 53
Job, 43, 78
Joel, 221
John, elector of Saxony, 89 n. 1, 93
    n. 1, 143
John, St., 33
  Gospel of, 135 n. 99
John the Baptist, 97-98, 129, 145,
    221, 289
John XXII, pope, 232 n. 33
Jonah, 120, 176
Jonathan, 193
Joseph, 120, 192, 235, 248, 269, 311
Joseph and Mary, 289, 300
Josephus, Flavius, 111 n. 44
Joshua, 97-98
Josiah, 120, 173 n. 53
Judah
  king of, 120, 192
  kingdom of, 41
  people of, 104, 171, 195
Judas, 101-102
Judge, 50, 80, 94 n. 2, 136, 267, 286,
    303
  making one's self, 27, 41, 107-108,
    113, 295, 297
  office of, 94, 166
  trial, 94 n. 2
Judges, 97, 102, 107, 113-114, 126-
    127, 240, 266, 289, 307, 314
Judgment, 25, 52 n. 10, 64, 66, 70,
    80, 114, 304 (see also God,

judgment of)
  of marriage matters, 287
  of Moses, 282
  of Paul, 25, 50
  of pious men, 287, 295
  rendering, 266
Judgment Day (see Last Day, Last
    Judgment)
Julian, cardinal (see Caesarini, Julian)
Julius II, pope, 168 n. 33, 169
Jurists, 226-227, 239 ff., 243 ff., 247,
    250-251, 256, 273, 275, 316, 318-
    319
Justice, 100-103, 105, 113-114, 123,
    127, 131, 178, 180, 215, 237,
    267, 287, 301
  and injustice, 40, 114, 288
Justification by faith, 60, 83
Justinian, emperor, 245 nn. 55, 56
Juvenal, Satires, 41 n. 54

Kappel, battle of, 107 n. 33
Karlstadt, Andrew Bodenstein, XI, 19
    n. 5, 21 n. 9, 106 n. 29, 146
Killing, 95-96
Kingdom, 171, 228
  of Christ, 30, 39, 177, 195, 200,
    223, 239 ff.
  devil's, 230
  everlasting, 54
  of God, 18 n. 3, 69 ff., 217, 228
    ff., 235, 254, 266
  of heaven, 83, 153
  spiritual, 39, 243
  worldly, external, 18, 39, 41, 54, 69
    ff., 239-240, 242-243
Kingdoms, two, doctrine of, 69-70,
    99, 178, 251
Kings, 20, 105, 113, 127-128, 167,
    187, 199, 223, 228, 243-245, 266,
    315 (see also Rulers)
  fearing, 65-66
  of Israel and Judah, 104
  and lords, 225
  obeying, 107
  and princes, 98, 163, 169, 180,
    184, 196, 200, 202 f., 233, 250
  of Ps. 68:12, 221 n. 17
  work of, 244-245
Kingship
  of Christ, 81, 97, 166
  of this world, 81, 97
Kinship, degrees of (see Consanguin-
    ity)

Kitzingen, 72 n. 26
Klug, Joseph, 263
"Knightlets," 82 n. 13, 101-102, 116
Knights, 245, 249
Knowledge, abundant and cheap, 244
Korah, 41
Koran, 176 n. 62, 178-179, 181 ff., 197, 199
Kram, Assa von, 89 n. 2, 90 n. 12, 93, 137

Laban, 299
Labor, free, 13 n. 28, 39
Laborer, deserves wage, 14, 129, 233
Ladislaus III (see Lassla)
Lame, 224, 306
Landlords, 47
Languages, 215
Lassla (Ladislaus III), king of Bohemia and Hungary, 167 n. 27
Last Day, 51, 54 n. 12, 181, 222, 224, 235
Last Judgment, 165, 174, 177, 205, 230, 317
Latin, 231, 232 n. 32
Law, laws, 31, 64, 70, 100-103, 113-114, 240, 245, 251, 262, 265, 272, 277, 287, 289-290, 295, 297, 303, 307, 311-314, 317 ff.
  ancient, written, 14
  canon (see Canon law)
  of Christ, 27-28, 30
  Christian (see Christian, law)
  civil, 261, 304
  common, 27, 279
  of the community, 9 n. 17
  and custom, 261, 270
  disciplinary, 279
  divine, 7, 24-27, 28 n. 26, 82 n. 45, 268
  error in, 289 n. 36
  established, 288
  exceptions to, 100
  feudal, 101 n. 6
  of the first, 239
  Germanic, 82 n. 45
  of God, 25-26, 113, 305
  good, 317
  Greek, 104
  human, 43
  imperial, 40, 265-268, 315 ff.
  of the land, 34, 113
  legal squabbling, 289
  loopholes in, 104 n. 20
  of love, 131
  martial, military, 95, 102
  of Moses (see Moses, law of)
  natural, 25, 27, 28 n. 26, 29, 34, 108, 110, 114, 230, 269, 305
  new, 197
  no respecter of persons, 285 n. 27
  old, 269
  Old Testament, 146
  and order, 18 n. 3, 27, 75, 166, 181
  papal, 166, 266, 268, 272, 297
  profession of, 209
  and the prophets, 145-146
  Roman, 15 n. 29, 82 n. 45, 101 n. 16, 239, 245 n. 55, 261, 274 n. 20
  secular, 226
  spiritual, 266, 318
  strictest demands of, 287 n. 33
  temporal, 268, 313, 315-316, 318, 320
  Turkish, 178, 181
  universally binding, 159
  of this world, 51
  written, 239
Lawyers, 8, 39, 127, 240, 283 (see also Jurists)
Laymen, 182
  religious societies for, 142
Leah, 299
Learned men, 163, 217
  are daft, 209 n. 1, 232 n. 34
Learning, 209, 215, 217, 250
Lectors, 220
Legal means, 303
Legate, papal, 188 n. 90, 189
Legislator, 263
Legitimacy, 90
Leipzig, university, 234 n. 39
Leo X, pope, xi, 162 n. 5, 164, 166, 188 n. 90
Lepers, leprosy, 224-225, 302, 304
Lese maiestatis, crimen, 101 n. 16, 133 n. 94
Letter kills, 145
Letters of recommendation, 294
Levi, Levites, 233
Liar, 179, 181, 225, 227, 236 (see also Lying)
Liberal arts, 252 nn. 72, 73
Liberty, 28
Life
  eternal, 99, 237

everlasting, 166, 177, 181, 224, 237
physical, 242
religious, 141
risking, 269
secular, 141
Litany, 172
Living together
in secret, 284
out of wedlock, 294
Lombard invasion, 107 n. 32
Lord, lords, 18 n. 3, 20-21, 28, 39,
40-43, 74-75, 81, 91, 101-102,
104-105, 116, 118, 126, 128-131,
135, 176, 183, 201, 204, 210,
214, 216, 225, 233, 239-240, 250
(see also Overlord, Princes, and
lords)
and peasant, agreement of, 14
pious, 84
and prince, 121-122
temporal and spiritual, 8, 11, 13
worldly, 180, 266
Lord, 153, 191, 236, 253 (see also
Christ)
blessings of, 258
blood and cross, sweat of, 256
blood and death of, 256, 258
command of, 151
day of, 174
fearing, 65-66
grace of, 79
hand of, 78
our neighbor, 12
presence of, 148 n. 17
vows to, 152
word of, 256
Lord's Prayer, 33-34, 136, 231 n. 28,
288
Lord's Supper, 12 (see also Sacrament)
Lot, 195, 248, 256
Lotzer, Sebastian, 6 n. 7, 7 n. 14
Louis II, king of Bohemia and Hungary, 90, 157, 167 n. 29, 202 n.
119
Love, 9, 69, 183
brotherly, 13-17
of Christ, 217
Christian, 96, 145, 312
fleshly (carnal), 134, 182
foolish, 309-310
of God, 12, 250
law of, way of, 131
Lower classes, xi

Lucius, bishop of Alexandria, 169
Lübeck, Lübeckers, 113 ff.
"Lüneburg!" 130
Lust, 77, 84, 153-154
of the eyes, 154
of the flesh, 150, 154
Luther, Hans, 251 n. 70
Luther, Katherine, 211, 251 n. 70
Luther, Martin
blamed for defeat at Mohacs, 158
blamed for peasants' rebellion, 161
n. 3
break with Erasmus and humanists,
XI
burned canon law, 273 n. 17
called names, 175
case of, 189
a clergyman and minister, 81
coat of arms, 64 n. 7
critics of, 61
defends self, 31
denounces pilgrimages, 142 n. 11
doctrines and teachings of, 5, 108,
110, 162, 213 n. 2
excommunication of, XI
family of, 141 n. 3, 251 n. 70
father of, 250, 251 n. 69
flatterer of princes, 40, 60, 115,
117, 163
friends of, XII, 60, 141
foes, enemies of, XII, 20 n. 6, 21, 95
gospel of, 21, 30
harassed by princes, 203
journey to Augsburg and Worms,
312 n. 2
journey to Thuringia, 6, 47, 49 n.
3, 72 n. 28
opponents of, XI-XII, 59, 61
position on peasants, XII-XIII
possessions, list of, 11 n. 21
preaching of, 48
reform inaugurated by, XI, 157
sermons, 213 n. 1
sorry born a German, 255-256
spirit of, 63
as a student, 234 n. 39, 250 n. 68
Sultan's inquiry about, 205 n. 129
supporters of, 18 n. 3
wedding of, 61 n. 15
Luther's works
Admonition to Peace, XII, text 3-43,
43 n. 59, 49 n. 1, 59 n. 6, 60-61,
65 n. 12, 75 nn. 30, 31
Admonition to Pray Against the

Turk (1541), 137 n. 104

Against the Heavenly Prophets in the Matter of Images and Sacraments (1525), 146 n. 4, 183 n. 80

Against the Robbing and Murdering Hordes of Peasants (1525), XII, 43 n. 59, text 45-55, 59 n. 4, 60 n. 7, 61, 72 n. 28

An Answer to Several Questions on Monastic Vows (1526), XIII, text 139-154

Antwort auf etliche Fragen . . ., 143

Army Sermon Against the Turk (1529), 137 n. 104, 175 n. 59

Articles Against the Whole Synagogue of Satan . . ., 227 n. 22

Assertio Omnium Articulorum, 238 n. 47

Babylonian Captivity of the Church (1520), 262 n. 8

Bible translations, 232 n. 29

Brother Richard's Refutation of the Koran, Translated into German by Dr. Martin Luther (1542), 176 n. 62

Defense of All the Articles of Martin Luther . . . (1520), 239 n. 47

Disavowal of Purgatory (1530), 257 n. 82

Ein Sendbrief von dem harten Büchlein wider die Bauern, 61

Eine Predigt, dass man Kinder zur Schulen halten solle, 212

Ermahnung zum Frieden auf die zwölf Artikel der Bauernschaft in Schwaben, 8

Explanations of the Ninety-five Theses (1518), 158, 162 n. 6, 157 n. 82

Exposition of Psalm 101 (1534), 239 n. 47

Fables, translated, 112 n. 45

Heerpredigt wider den Türken, 137 n. 104, 175 n. 59

The Judgment of Martin Luther on Monastic Vows (1521), 141, 145 n. 1

Large Catechism (1529), 253 n. 75

Letter accompanying *An Answer to Several Questions*, May 18, 1526, 143 n. 15

Letter to Luther's father, 141 n. 4

Letter to Luther's wife, August 15, 1530, 211

Letter to Melanchthon, July 5, 1530, 211

Letter to Nicholas Amsdorf, October 27, 1529, 184 n. 84

Letter to Nicholas Hausmann, August 5, 1528, 158

Letter to Nicholas Hausmann, February 3, 1529, 159 n. 14

Letter to Nicholas Hausmann, January 3, 1530, 263 n. 13

Ninety-five Theses (1517), XI, 90 n. 11, 257 n. 82

Ob Kriegesleute auch in seligem Stande sein Können, 91

On Marriage Matters (1530), XIV, text 259-320

On the Bondage of the Will (1525), XI

On War Against the Turk (1529), XIII, 137 n. 104, text 155-205, 217 n. 9

An Open Letter on the Harsh Book Against the Peasants (1525), XII, text 57-85

Pentecost sermons at Wittenberg (1525), 60 n. 14

The Persons Related by Consanguinity who Are Forbidden to Marry . . ., 315 n. 62

Preface to Justus Menius' *Oeconomia Christiana* (1529), 210 n. 9

The Right and Power of a Christian Congregation . . . (1523), 37 n. 43

A Sermon on Keeping Children in School (1530), XIII-XIV, 187 n. 89, text 207-258

Sermon on Marriage (1519), 274 n. 20

Sermon on the Unrighteous Mammon, 83 n. 49

Table Talk of 1531, 247 n. 61

Temporal Authority: To What Extent It Should Be Obeyed (1523), 31, 95, 99, 115 n. 55, 136, 163, 166

That Parents Should Neither Compel Nor Hinder the Marriage of Their Children . . . (1524), 262 n. 9

To the Christian Nobility of the German Nation . . . (1520), 22 n. 12, 131 n. 91, 164 n. 14, 214

n. 5, 287 n. 29
To the Councilmen of All Cities in Germany that They Establish and Maintain Christian Schools (1524), 210-211, 217 n. 8, 218 n. 11, 232 n. 31
Trade and Usury (1524), 213 n. 3
Vermähnung sum Gebet wider den Türken, 137 n. 104
Vom Kriege wider den Türken, 159
Von dem Ehesachen, 263
Von Leibaygenschaft Oder Knechthait, wie sich Herren und aygen leut christlich halten sollend, 39 n. 50
Warning to His Dear Germans, 258 n. 83
Warnung an seine lieben Deutschen, 258 n. 83
Whether Soldiers, Too, Can Be Saved (1526), XIII, text 87-137, 158, 165-166, 246 n. 58
Why the Books of the Pope and His Disciples Were Burned (1520), 273 n. 17
Wider die räuberischen und mörderischen Rotten der Bauern, 48
Widerlegung des Alkoran Bruder Richardi; verdeutscht durch Dr. M. Luther, 176 n. 62
Widerruf vom Fegefeuer, 257 n. 82
Luther, Martin, Jr., 251 n. 70
Luther, Paul, 251 n. 70
Lutheran elector, 142
Lutheran doctrine, 90 n. 9
  heresy, 90
  teaching, 20
Lutherans, XII, 20 n. 6, 228
Lying, 182, 301, 303, 310 (*see also* Liar)
Lying together (secret), 282, 284-285, 290-291, 293, 296 ff., 320

Mad dog, 48, 50, 73
Madman, 105
Madrid, treaty of, 159 n. 108
Magdeburg, 210
Magic spells, 135
Magistrates, XIV
Maid, 308
  and mistress, 114
  and parents, 290
Majesty, 277 (*see also Lese maiestatis*)

divine, 133
  imperial, 245
Malachi, 221
Malchus, 29
Malefactor, 172
Malice, 287, 308-309
Mammon, 130, 216, 243 ff., 256, 305, 315
  monks of, 251
  service of, 214-215
Man, men, 104, 130, 238, 248
  heeding, 77
  and wife, 152
  will of (*see* Will, of man)
  and woman, 261, 292, 296, 304, 313
Manasseh, 172, 230
Mangelt, 127
Manpower reserve, 201-202
Mansfeld, 48, 63, 121 n. 69
  counts of, 70
Mantz, Felix, 90 n. 13
Marburg, XII, 263
Margareta, daughter of Count Wilhelm, 143 n. 12
Marksman, 288
Marriage, 198, 220, 261-262, 265-320
  passim (*see also* Betrothal, Betrothed)
  act in favor of, 273 n. 19
  act of, 261
  anticipation of, 291
  arranged by father, 269
  bans, 290 n. 40, 293
  betrothed virgin, 289-290
  ceremony, 261
  clerical, 227
  confusion in, 290
  deception in, 285, 292-293, 303, 310
  defects in partner, 302-304
  definition of, 291
  deputy for father in, 308-309
  destroyed by Turks, 183, 195
  disregard of, 182
  dissolution of, 262, 277, 311, 316
  dog-, Italian, 198 n. 103
  duties in, 210
  entering, 294, 313
  estate of, 182, 268, 278, 283, 314
  formulas, 274 n. 20
  German customs of, 262
  giving in, 269, 292-293, 308
  guilty partner, 311-312

honorable, 309
illusory, 300
impediments, 262 n. 8, 281, 315-316 (*see also* Consanguinity)
indissoluable, 262 n. 7
intention of, 295
keeping in, 282
Moses' rule of, 291
mutual consent, 261-262
obstacles to, 281
obtained by stealth, 283
partners, 305
prevented by monastic life, 298-299
of priests, 227 n. 22
problems, xiv, 261, 270 ff.
public, 283
regard for, 297
remarriage, 295, 311-312, 314
repeated, 295
a sacrament, 262 n. 7
secret, 283 ff.
and strangers, 293-294
thief, 283
true, 183, 270, 278, 290, 291, 298, 308
Turks', 181-182, 294 n. 41
unhappy, 310
validity, 261, 273-274, 281
Mars, god of war, 182 n. 76
Martyrs, 40, 48, 53-54, 81, 149
Mary, Virgin, 176-177, 221, 289, 300, 311
devotion to, 141
Mass, 209-210, 303
celebrating, 172
endowing, 163 n. 7
first, 229
hearing, 163
of the Holy Ghost, 204 n. 127
sacrifice of, 221, 229
saying, 167, 221
Materialism, 209
Mayors, 244
Maximilian, emperor, 108 n. 39, 116, 168, 249 n. 64
Meat, eating, 189, 204
Medicine, 209, 252-253, 319
Medieval piety, 141
Medieval society, 89
Meditation and reflection, 89-90
Melanchthon, Philip, 6 n. 8, 47, 210, 214 n. 4, 263
Members (of the body), 246
Memmingen, 6 n. 7

Menius, Justus, 210 n. 9, 263
Mercenaries, 127 n. 84, 134
Merchants, 215, 244, 312
Mercy, 65-75, 83 (*see also* God, mercy of)
Merit, one's own, 95, 173, 254
Messiah, 9
Michal, 285
Midianites, 130
Milan, 204 n. 125
Military law, 95, 102
Military profession, 90, 93, 97-98, 100, 128 n. 86, 129, 257
Millenium, 5
Ministers, 265 n. 1
of the word, 81
Ministry, divine office, 209, 233
Miracles, 179, 184 n. 84, 197, 203, 224 ff., 228-229
Misers, 251
Mob, 27, 105-106, 112
Möhra, 141 n. 3
Mohacs, battle of, 90, 157, 158 n. 9, 167 n. 29, 202 n. 119
Mohammed, 175-179, 181, 195 ff.
Mohammed II, sultan, 200 nn. 113, 114
Monasteries, 47, 50, 82, 141, 142 n. 9, 148-151, 174, 176, 197, 209, 220, 225, 226, 228, 231-235, 241, 256, 298
abandonment of, 209
Monasticism
life in, 141, 145, 298 n. 46
orders, 141-142, 145
rule, 150
schools, 209
system of, 141
vows of (*see* Vows, monastic)
Money
and property, 228, 269, 281
and revenues, 200 n. 15
Monkery, 217
Monks, xiii, 19, 147, 149, 163, 182, 209, 294, 298, 319
holy people, 177
and nuns, 143, 147, 209, 227 n. 23, 241
Moses, 35, 51, 94, 97-98, 131, 147-148, 151-152, 196, 253, 277, 282, 289-290, 292
land of, in contrast to Germany, 291
law of, 70, 145 ff., 197, 277-278,

280, 291, 297, 300, 311, 316
Mothers, 302
Mühlhausen, 5 n. 3, 49, 84
Mühlpfort, Hermann, 60 n. 9
Müller, Caspar, 60, 61 n. 15, 63, 85
    nn. 52, 53
Münzer, Thomas, xi, 5 n. 3, 19 n. 5,
    21 n. 9, 49 n. 5, 59 n. 1, 64 n. 5,
    72 n. 28, 121 n. 70, 180, 183
    widow of, 84
Murder, 8, 24, 48-49, 53, 70, 81, 129,
    178, 179 n. 66, 182, 227, 252,
    315
    prophets, 20
    and bloodshed, 27, 195
Murderers, 50, 52, 68, 70-71, 74, 80,
    82, 98, 178, 180-181, 189, 225,
    227, 238, 240, 306
    of the saints of Christ, 43, 182, 240
Music, 252 n. 73

Naaman, 192, 248
Nahor, 316
Natural law (see Law, natural)
Nature, 305
Nazirites, 177
Neighbor, 55, 78, 121, 129, 141, 182,
    215, 223, 240, 246, 312
    needy, 169
    offenses against, 16
    our Lord, Christ, 12, 151
    wife of, 289
New Testament, 10, 26, 98, 146, 149,
    172, 233, 265
Nicaea, Council of, 179 n. 67
Nimrod, 178
Noah, 43
Nobility, 42, 101 n. 15, 113 n. 49,
    248, 250
Nobleman, 244, 248-249, 302
Nobles, 59, 101, 116, 125 ff., 183,
    250, 255
    and princes, 116-117
Non-Christians, 186, 265
Nordhausen, 48
Notaries, 240
Nürnberg, 210, 213 n. 2, 214 ff., 263
    city council of, 214, 216
    Diet of (1523, 1524), xi, 167, 227
    n. 23, 247 n. 62
    reform in, 213 n. 2
    school, 214 n. 4
Nuns, 143 n. 12 (see also Monks, and
    nuns)

nunning, 217
taking husbands, 189

Oaths, 50, 146, 151-152, 303
    false, 283
    of fealty, 313 n. 59
    feudal, 50 n. 6, 113 n. 48
    of homage, 187, 193-194
    of king or lord, 113
    of loyalty, peasant's, 48
    swearing, 282 ff.
Obedience, 95, 98-99, 103, 126, 129,
    180, 185, 194, 226
    to God, 98, 283-284
    to parents, 277, 306, 310
    to worldly ordinances, 98
Obligation, unfulfilled, 282
Odenwald peasants, 47 n. 3, 72 n.
    127
Office
    divine, 94, 95, 166, 243
    temporal, 166, 226, 237
Officials, 244, 265 n. 2, 267, 272-273,
    283, 286, 294, 318
Old Testament, 10, 26, 97, 107, 146,
    148, 172, 197, 233
    laws of, 146 n. 3
Oratory, art of, 189
Order (see Law, and order)
Orders, conventual, monastic, 141-142
Ordinances
    divine (see God, ordinances of)
    human, 100
    worldly, 98
Ordination, 262
Ornaments, 183
Orphans, 309 (see also Widows, and
    orphans)
Orthodox, 179-180
Ottoman Turks, 202 n. 120
Outlaws, 50
Overlord, 112 ff., 116, 126-127, 189,
    194
    at war with subjects, 91
Ovid, 182 n. 76

Pallium, 164 n. 15
Papacy, xi, 164 n. 16, 166, 180 n. 72,
    186, 198 ff., 232, 246, 266, 287,
    319
Papal church, xiii
    laws of, 268, 272
    robbery, 317
Papists, 163, 167, 177, 183

Parents, xiv, 257, 269, 279, 304-305
  authority of (see Authority,
    parental)
  and children, 141, 209
  consent of, 268, 278
  and daughter, 281, 290
  poor, 285
  of seduced girl, 285
Paris, university, 197, 214
Parishes, 78, 234, 250
  priest, 10 n. 19
  property of, 11 n. 20
Parlements, 113
Paroxysmus, 235 n. 43
Parties to agreement, 289 n. 37
Passion of Christ, 30, 134, 142
Passions (see Lust)
Pastors, xiv, 11, 158, 166, 171, 174,
    187, 193, 196, 218, 223, 225 ff.,
    229, 231-232, 234-235, 254,
    256, 281, 289, 293, 297, 301,
    305-309, 311, 313
  advice of, 318
  to be chosen by community, 10, 22,
    37-38
  duties of, 10
  office of, 220, 225-226, 232
Patriarchs, biblical, 39, 98 n. 6
Paul, St., 25, 29, 32, 39, 51, 64, 66,
    68, 73-74, 98-99, 107, 118, 126-
    127, 131-132, 150, 175, 196, 198,
    221, 224, 233, 235, 237-238, 246,
    265, 278, 286, 299, 314
  judgment of, 25, 50
Pavia, battle of, 120 n. 67, 168, 198
Peace, 9, 27, 75, 90, 96-97, 100, 110,
    118-119, 121-122, 181, 226, 240-
    243, 246-247, 252, 254, 288
  keeping, 72-73, 95, 180
Peasants, 7-8, 12 n. 5, 13 n. 28, 14,
    20-23, 51 n. 9, 52-55, 65, 67-79
    passim, 82 n. 45, 84, 100
  in arms, 7
  atrocities of, 59
  become lords, 84
  brigades, 47
  cause of, 54, 59
  "Conrad," 85 n. 52
  crude, 7, 308
  defeated, 57, 97 n. 5
  German, 5 n. 1, 47
  grievances of, xii, 17
  and lords, 13-14
  rebellious, xiii, 9, 47, 59, 61, 101

n. 14, 105, 116 (see also Rebels)
  recent rebellion of, xii, 5, 18 n. 3,
    100, 110, 125, 194, 201
  robbing and murdering, 45, 47-55,
    59
  in Swabia, 17
  sympathizers, 70
  Twelve Articles (see Twelve
    Articles)
Peasants' War (1525), xii, 5-6, 91, 95
    n. 4, 97 n. 5, 121 n. 71, 142 n.
    11, 161 n. 3, 201 n. 116, 247 n.
    63
Pen, the, 187, 245, 246-247, 249 ff.
  pen-pushers, 246
Penal law, 279, 281
Penance, 295
Penitence, 42
Perjury, 193-194, 283
Persecution, 37, 105, 173
Persia, 41, 157
Persians, 107
Persons
  and property, 317
  respecting, 132
Pertinax, Roman emperor, 105 n. 26
Perversions, 198 n. 103
Pestilence, 254
Peter, bishop of Alexandria, 179 n. 68
Peter, St., 29-30, 51, 73, 98, 102, 166,
    172, 195 ff.
Phaedrus, 112 n. 45
Pharaoh, 9, 35
Pharisees, 63
Philip, king of Macedonians, 107 n.
    31
Philip of Hesse, 161 n. 1, 162
Philistines, 193
Physicians, 97, 252-253, 256, 319
Piety, medieval, 141
Pilate, 51, 81, 97, 166, 195
Pilgrimage, places of, 142 nn. 6, 9, 11
Pious men, people, 163, 180, 287-288,
    299, 304, 309, 311, 315
  wife, 295
Plagues, 78, 80, 198
Planitz, Hans von der, 247 n. 62
Plundering, 48
Poets, 41, 182, 245
Poison, 315
Poland, 202-203
Polygamy, 181, 291, 300
Pomp and show, 172, 220
Poor, 11, 38, 43, 104, 245

are blessed, 83
oppression of, 41-42
parents, 285
Pope, 163 ff., 180, 183-184, 186, 196
 ff., 201, 204 n. 125, 205, 227,
 250, 255, 261, 266, 268, 272-273,
 286, 298, 300, 312, 315 ff., 319
 army of, 168
 banner of, 169
 crown of, 82
 decretals, 176, 199
 and emperor, 31, 33
 opposes gospel, 18 n. 3
 robbery of, 164
Popularity, 94
Possessions, 74
Power, 32
 paternal, 305-306, 308-309
 and wealth, 35
Praise and thanksgiving, 258
Prayer, 33, 54-55, 79, 149, 159, 163,
 165, 167, 172 n. 47, 173 ff., 180,
 184, 186-187, 199, 203, 256
 against the Turks, 175
 of Christendom, 181
 of the righteous man, 33, 52, 171,
 174
Preachers, 24, 28, 36, 74, 78, 97, 99,
 130, 171, 174, 193 ff., 213, 215,
 220, 223-226, 231-232, 234, 246-
 247, 249-250, 252 ff., 256, 272,
 301, 307, 310
 Christian, 83, 168, 223
 lying, 38
 stupid, 161
Preaching, 48, 142, 165, 167, 174-175,
 179-180, 186, 221, 251-252
 Christ's, 30
 of the gospel, xi, 22-23, 169, 255
 office of, 194, 196, 220, 222 ff.,
 226-229, 231, 233, 236-237, 242-
 243, 248, 253 ff.
Present tense, 273, 275
Pride, 123, 201
Priestcraft, 217
Priesthood, 145, 221, 233
 of believers, 209
Priests, 19, 163, 167, 220, 240-241,
 261 n. 3
 army of, 167
 married, 226, 227 n. 23
 mother of, 221
 new, 229
 Old Testament, 147, 221

wives (whores) of, 287 n. 29
Princes, 7-8, 19, 23, 40, 54, 60, 73,
 102, 105, 116, 122, 125 ff., 132,
 163, 165-167, 169, 171, 183, 185-
 190, 193, 196, 199 ff., 203-204,
 223, 233, 235, 240-241, 243-245
 and lords, 7, 19, 23, 52, 67, 71, 75,
 105, 115, 117, 132, 162-163,
 250-251
 and nobles, rebellious, 116
 office of, God-given, 61
 (see also Kings, and princes)
Principalities, 257
Prison, 68
Prisoners, 39, 175 n. 59
Processions, 172 n. 47
Promise, 307
Property, 26, 39, 51, 74, 101, 108,
 127, 237, 242, 252, 306, 314,
 316, 319
 of Christ, 235
 common (to man and wife), 295
 dedicated to the Lord, 147 n. 12
 expropriated, 13
 and honor, 227
 owner, 37
 under the Turks, 183
Prophecies, 157
Prophets, 39, 145-146, 173, 196, 221,
 233, 240
 chosen, 6
 of discord, 35
 false, 19, 21, 28-29, 38, 40
 German (Luther), 258 n. 83
 of murder, 6, 20 n. 8, 28, 33, 54
 office of (Christ's), 176
Propriety, 266
Prosperity, 75
Protestants, xiv, 232 n. 29, 261
 cause of, 161 n. 1
 clergy, 261
 counteralliances, xiii
 princes, xiii, 59, 106 n. 29
 rulers, 161 n. 1, 261
Proverbs, 195-196, 302
Psalms, Psalter, 34, 148, 191
Publican, 172
Pulpits, 78, 234
Punishment, 25, 27, 52-53, 68 ff., 73-
 74, 77-78, 82, 85, 95, 98-99, 102-
 103, 109-110, 114-115, 118, 126,
 198, 248, 282, 284, 292, 296
 by death (see Death, penalty,
 punishment)

of God (*see* God, punishment of)
office of, 80
power of, 309
rascals, punish each other, 32, 41, 94, 116, 165
temporal, 48
Purgatory, 54
Luther's doctrine of, 257 n. 82

Quill, 264 n. 60, 247
Quirinus, St., 117 n. 60

Rabble, 75, 293
Rachel, 299
Rain, 28, 169, 195
Ramah, 148
Ramoth, 120
Rape, 308
of Sabine women, 308 n. 54
Rau, George, 211
Ravens, 229
Reason, 177, 237, 239, 242, 266, 268-269
Reasonable person, 270
Rebecca, 269
Rebellion, 19-22, 25, 31, 41-42, 48, 50, 55, 72, 75, 81-82, 91, 101, 108, 116, 161 (*see also* Peasants, recent rebellion of, Peasants' War)
inciting, 20 nn. 7, 8
of princes and lords, 201
spirit of, 33
Rebels, 35, 41, 47, 50, 59, 65-66, 68, 71, 80-83, 101-102, 225-226 (*see also* Peasants, rebellious)
against God and state, 61
fellow-travelers with, 65
Reconciliation, of man and wife, 283, 296, 311, 314
Redeeming from sin and death, 166
Reformation, xi, 5 n. 1, 18 n. 3, 89, 90 n. 10, 106 n. 29, 209-210, 239 n. 47, 247 nn. 61, 62, 298 n. 46
in Augsburg, 39 n. 50
faith, 239 n. 46
in Henneberg, 141, 142 nn. 5-8
Lutheran, xi-xii
movement, 294 n. 42
Regent, 267
Relatives (of bride), 290, 302
Relics, veneration of, 141
Religious societies for laymen, 142

Remarriage, 295, 311-312, 314
Remorse, 283
Rents, 14, 39
Repentance, 159, 171-172, 174, 184, 255
before God, 42
Reputation, 302
Resurrection
of the body, 224
of the dead, 177
Revelation to John, 221
Revenge, 165, 185
Revolt, revolution, xii, 48, 76 (*see also* Rebellion)
Reward for villainy, 281
Rewarding evil with honor, 270
Reydaniya, battle of, 202 n. 120
Rhegius, Urbanus, 39 n. 50
Rhetorical arts, 252 n. 73
Rhine, on fire, 83 n. 48
Rhodes, Isle of, 157, 166 n. 21
Rich, 100, 255, 257
son of, 285
Riches, 94, 236
Ridicule, 286
Righteous, 70, 73, 174, 286
before God, 95
Righteousness, 95, 99, 153, 224
in Christ, 64
earthly, 64
external, 95
higher, 299 n. 47
instruments of, 153
temporal, both kinds of, 100
Rights, 67, 125-126, 132, 134, 165, 190
Robbers, 26, 37-38, 42, 52, 68, 74, 182, 276, 306, 313
Robbery, robbing, 19, 27, 38-39, 48-49, 70, 72, 95 ff., 170, 178, 179 n. 66, 181, 252
by popes, 164, 317
Rod, 65 n. 11 (*see also* God, rod of)
Roman Catholic teaching, 261 n. 3
Roman church, 261
knavery, 164
spiritual benefits of, 5
and state, xii
teachings, 209
territorial, orders, 210
true, 256
visitation (1528), 247 n. 62
Western, 261
Roman Empire, 41, 104, 105, 107,

119, 127, 199
civil law and custom, 261, 274 n.
20 (see also Law, Roman)
emperors, 127
Romans, 104, 107-108, 110, 119 n.
64, 123-124, 127, 198, 236, 308
n. 54
Rome, 106 n. 29, 164 n. 15, 169, 188,
198
church of (see Roman church)
fall of, 236 n. 44
imperial law of, 239
sack of, 120 n. 68
Rothenburg, 47 n. 2
Ruehel, Johann, 48, 59 n. 5, 60 n. 10
Rulers, xiii, 12, 17, 22, 26, 32, 34, 36,
38, 40, 47-48, 50, 52 n. 10, 53,
59, 61, 64-65, 68 ff., 76, 83, 91,
95, 100, 101 nn. 14, 16, 103, 106
ff., 110, 113-114, 117, 125-126,
130-131, 135, 161, 163, 169, 175,
183-184, 187, 193, 200, 215, 238,
250, 265-267 (see also Kings,
Authority, temporal)
appointed by God, 25, 27, 91, 110,
114
biblical, 98 n. 2
Christian, 32, 83
cruelty of, 61, 82
duty of, 83
evangelical, 90
foreign, 110
luxury and extravagance of, 23
temporal, 19, 114, 163, 180
wicked, 104, 110
worldly, 25, 31, 98-99, 112, 166
Rulership rights, Turk's, 183 n. 82

Sabine women, 308 n. 54
Sacrament (Lord's Supper), 12, 117,
228, 254
administering, 231
in both kinds, 227 n. 21
Sacrament of marriage, 262 n. 7
Sacramental system, 261
Sacraments, 219-220, 271
Sacrifice, 67, 227, 233
to God, 229
of the mass, 221, 229
of thanksgiving, 148, 153
Sacristans, 220, 231, 234
St. Gallen, city and monastery, 106
n. 28
Saints, 23, 34, 135, 141, 172, 174,

225, 255
calling on, 172
of Christ, 43, 182, 240
living, 142
praise of, 177
Salvation, 36, 136, 170, 175, 210,
220, 222
of child, 306
by faith alone, 83
false ideas of, 141
of God, 148
of souls, 108, 188, 254
through Christ, 141
through works, 83, 141
Salzburg, 248 n. 63
Salzungen, 47
Samaria, 107 n. 30
Samson, 83, 193, 269
Samuel, 83, 97, 148 n. 17, 153
Sanctification, 153-154
Satan, 24, 150, 215, 217, 300 (see
also Devil)
Saul, 66, 112 ,131, 193, 285
Savior, 176-177, 255 (see also Christ)
Saviors, 221 n. 16, 223, 240
Saxony, 59, 239
Ducal, 90
Electoral, 89-90, 142, 234 n. 38
Scandinavia, 106 n. 29
Schirlentz, Nickel, 211
Schmid, Ulrich, 6 n. 7
Scholars, 111, 172, 218, 239-240, 243
Scholarship funds, 257
Scholastic theologians, 226 n. 20
Scholastic theology, 273 n. 17
Schoolmasters, 218, 220, 225, 231,
234, 244, 246, 249, 252, 253, 256
Schools, 197, 209-210, 213-214, 216,
219, 234, 243-244, 254
church-dominated, 209
Eisenach, 250
Eisleben, 47
keeping children in, 209 ff., 213-
214, 217 ff., 223, 231, 250, 252,
256
maintenance of, 256
neglect of, 236-237
Nürnberg, 213-216
spiritual gains and losses from, 219-
237
temporal gains and losses from,
237-258
Schwarzenberg, Hans von, baron, 247
Scripture, 6-7, 10-11, 13, 15 ff., 33-

34, 38, 40-41, 70, 73, 77, 84, 98, 120, 141, 148, 150, 153, 167-168, 171, 173, 178, 197, 217, 220, 231-232, 252-253, 262, 284, 289, 304, 312, 315
Seats of honor, 189 n. 92
Secretaries, 187
Security, 242
Sedition, 22
Seducer, seduction, 280-285
Self-defense, 91, 120-121
Selfish purposes, 18
Self-will, 12, 69, 84
Serfdom, serfs, 12 n. 25, 39, 51 n. 9
Sermon, 172, 236
  Luther's use of word, 213 n. 1
Servants, 39, 240
  of Christ, 265
  of the Lord, 80
  and master, 114, 316
Sextons, 244
Shame and peril, 285
"Shavelings," 246
Sheba, 41
Shepherd, good, 146
Shiloh, 308
Shrines, 142-143
Shrove Tuesday mummery, 188
Sick man, 39
Signs, apocalyptic, 18 n. 3
  and wonders, 19, 26, 35, 43
Silence, 122 n. 78
Simeon, 64
Sin, 20, 22, 42, 50, 53, 77, 109, 115, 130, 135, 153, 158, 162, 165, 171, 193-194, 198, 226, 229-230, 255, 305-306, 310, 312, 315
  against conscience, 283
  against God, 42
  against God and man, 23, 49
  against God and nature, 304-305
  and death, 220
  of ingratitude, 258
  mortal, 306
  redemption from, 166, 224
Sinners, 132, 172, 237
Sisters, 302
Slander, slanderer, 300 ff.
Slaves, 39
Society, xiv, 261
Sodom, 24, 195, 198, 256
  and Gomorrah, 171, 173, 195, 254
Soldiers, 93, 98, 124, 127 n. 84, 128-129, 136, 168-169, 181 (see also

Military Profession)
  good, 134
  lives of, 181
  office, profession of, 89, 91, 94-97, 129
  real, 119
  serving two lords, 131
  superstitious, 135 n. 97
Solomon, 65, 72, 100, 107, 128, 131, 152, 192, 238, 245, 276, 288
Son of God, 51, 135, 176-177, 219, 254-255
Sons, educating, 222, 224-225, 228-229, 233-236, 241-242, 249, 251
Sophists, 226 n. 20, 228-229
Soul, 81 n. 44, 108, 146 n. 8, 236, 303, 319
Souls, 8, 23, 54, 67, 91, 93, 165, 179, 195, 224, 230
Spain, 202
Spalatin, George, 61, 263 n. 10
Spear of God, 133
Spears, 136
Speech, 249
Spells, magic, 135
Spengler, Lazarus, 211, 213 n. 2, 227 n. 22
Spires, diets of (1526, 1529), xiii, 167 n. 23, 204 n. 125
Spiritual, estate, 99, 176, 181-182, 215, 219 n. 12, 220 ff.
Spiritual office, 165, 222, 237, 251
Spouse, 294, 299, 306, 311-312, 315
Stewards of God, 221
Stiefel, Michael, 89 n. 7
Storch, Nicholas, 19 n. 5
Subjects (of rulers), 99, 114, 116, 126, 186-190
  and lords, 39
  and rulers, 91, 107, 115
  Turk's, 200
  tyrants, 110-111
  warring with overlords, 103, 106, 125 ff.
Suffering, 29, 40
Suleiman the Magnificent, 157, 161 n. 2
Sultan, 118, 183 n. 82, 202 n. 120, 205 n. 129, 251
Superstitions, 135
Supreme Judge, 74
Suspicion, 300
Swabia, 6, 17, 248 n. 63
Swabian League, 7 n. 12, 59

Swiss, Switzerland, XII, 106 n. 28,
    107 n. 32, 108
  rebellion of, 107
Sword, 19, 25, 34, 41, 52, 61, 66, 68,
    70, 73-74, 76, 80, 84, 95-99,
    112, 118, 121-122, 126, 136,
    165-166, 168, 178-179, 184, 186,
    197-198, 247-248
  divine institution, 90
  emperor's, 186
  glorification of, 176-177
  of God, 97, 130, 171
  office of, God-given, XIII, 53
  perishing by, 25, 30, 41
  Peter's, 29-30
  spiritual, 197
  temporal, 71, 73, 95, 161, 165, 167,
    197, 265
Syndics, 243
Syphilis, 254 n. 80
Syracuse, 110 n. 41
Syria, 157, 202, 232, 248
  king of, 66, 192
Syrians, 120

Tabernacle to the Lord, 214
Tartars, 107, 217 n. 9, 218, 244, 254
Taxes
  death, 15 n. 30, 22, 39
  rates, confiscatory, 23
  war, 11 n. 21
Teachers, 97, 218 n. 11, 220, 240,
    247, 252 (see also Schoolmasters)
  Christian, 98, 129
  false, 19, 112
  of God's people, 223
  office of, 75, 253
Temple, 148 n. 17
  of God, 180
  services, 146
Temporal estate, 176, 182, 215, 220,
    226
Temptation, 149
  of the devil, 286
Ten Commandments, 231 n. 28
  First, 222
  Second, 22, 33, 276
  Fourth, 310
Tenses, present and future, 273 ff.
Terence, 100 n. 9
Territory, extension of, 185
Testimonials, 293
Testimony, public, 301, 307
Theft, 38, 276

Theocracy, 6
Theologians, 251, 270, 273
  pious, 239-240
  scholastic, 226 n. 20
Theology, 209
  scholastic, 273 n. 17
Thief, 71, 74, 98, 240, 276, 306, 313
Thiele, 35 n. 39, 51 n. 8, 64 n. 7, 67
    n. 15, 78 n. 40, 80 n. 42, 103 n.
    18, 109 n. 40, 112 n. 46, 117 nn.
    59, 61, 62, 118 n. 63, 164 n. 13,
    177 n. 63, 186 n. 88, 196 n. 99,
    199 n. 109, 235 nn. 40, 41, 266
    n. 4, 287 n. 30, 288 nn. 34, 35,
    290 nn. 38, 39, 302 nn. 48, 49,
    305 n. 83, 308 n. 55
Thuringia, 6, 47, 59
  peasants of, 72 n. 28
Timars, 183 n. 82
Tithes, 10-11, 22, 38
  in kind, 10 n. 19
  Old Testament, 233
  selling of, 11 n. 22
  "small," 11 n. 23
Titus, 99
Tongue, 249
Tonsures and cowls, 163
Tools, 249
Torgau, 89 n. 5, 90
Trade, 134, 236
  and commerce, 209, 213 n. 3
Traitors, 80, 240
Trasimeno, Lake, 119 n. 64
Treason, against God, 114
Tree, fruit of, 180, 199
Trust in men, God, 284
Truth, 180-181, 236
Turk, Turks, XIII, 18 n. 3, 27, 81, 90
    n. 8, 127, 136 n. 101, 161-205
    passim, 242, 244, 254, 257, 285,
    308
  advance of, 161 n. 2
  army, 202 n. 119
  atrocities, 157 n. 5
  captive among, 285
  carnal life of, 175-176
  chapters and monasteries among,
    176
  Christians among, 175 n. 58, 182
  conquests of, 157
  creed of, 178
  crusade against, 162
  faith of, 177, 179 n. 66, 185-186
  god of, the devil, 170, 183, 188

government of, 175, 178, 193, 200
holiness of, 183-184
kingdom of, 179
language of, 183 n. 2
lies about, 176
literature about, 158 n. 7
Luther's knowledge of, 257 n. 81
marriage among, 181
menace of, xiii, 18 n. 3, 157-158,
   217 n. 8
power of, 187, 201, 203
prayer against, 174-175
sanctity of, 199
servant of the devil, 181
sultan (see Sultan)
rule of, 194, 317
victories of, 202 n. 120
war against, 11 n. 21, 135, 137 n.
   104, 158, 161-205 passim
way of life, 182
wickedness and vice of, 185, 195
Turkey, 175, 198, 205 n. 129
Turkish Book, 157 n. 5
Twelve Articles, 6 n. 7, 7 n. 10, text
   8-16, 17, 18 n. 3, 22-23, 34, 37-
   43, 49 nn. 2, 4, 51 n. 9, 104 n.
   23
Two kingdoms, doctrine of (see Kingdoms, two, doctrine of)
Tyrannicide, 104
Tyranny, 42, 106, 109
Tyrants, 20, 31, 41, 43, 84, 104-116
   passim, 125, 127, 169, 173, 205,
   238, 254, 288, 306
   clerical, 279
   prayer for, 111, 113

Unbelief, unbelievers, 186, 219, 265
Unbelieving partner, 286, 296
Unchastity, 300-302, 311
Unity, 9
Universities, 226, 232, 234
   curriculum, 214 n. 5
   pope's, 164, 197
Urban II, pope, 186 n. 6, 227 n. 22

Valens, Roman emperor, 179 n. 68
Valentin, Veit, 6 n. 7
Varna, battle of, 167 nn. 27, 28
Veneration of relics, 141
Venetians, 120, 199 n. 108
Vengeance, 27, 110, 114
   God's, 25, 28 ff., 73, 107-108, 113
Venice, 204 n. 125

Venus, goddess of love, 182 n. 76
Vespers, 172
Vice, 198 n. 103
Victory, from God, 133
Vienna
   Council of (1312), 232 n. 33
   march on, 161 n. 2
   siege of, 184 n. 84
Village, 244, 294
Villains, villainy, 288, 302, 311, 313-
   314
Violators of virgins, 281
Violence, 48, 61, 157, 252, 270, 281,
   308
Virginity, 282, 291
Virgins, 281-282, 292, 298
   betrothed, 289
Virtue, 102, 284
Vitus, St., 117 n. 60
Vows
   monastic, 141 ff., 145-154 passim
   Luther's views on, 146 n. 7
   Moses' laws about, 146 n. 7, 148,
   151-152
   Old Testament, 152 n. 34, 153
   perpetual, eternal, 141, 147-148
Vulgate, 148 n. 8

Wages
   of laborer, 14, 127-130, 233
   of soldier, 131 ff.
Waldshut, 5 n. 4
Wander, Karl F. W., 21 n. 11, 25 n.
   20, 26 n. 23, 28 n. 25, 29 n. 29,
   32 n. 34, 64 n. 7, 65 n. 11, 68 n.
   16, 69 n. 18, 76 n. 35, 78 n. 38,
   83 n. 48, 84 n. 50, 104 n. 20,
   108 n. 37, 121 n. 70, 122 nn. 73-
   78, 123 n. 79, 125 n. 81, 169 n.
   36, 172 n. 45, 272 n. 16, 290 n.
   39, 319 nn. 67, 68
Wantonness, 72, 150, 153, 286-287,
   309, 311
Warfare, 89-90, 159, 195
Wars, 8, 78, 89 ff., 95-98, 103, 109,
   118-123, 125, 127, 130, 132-135,
   159, 164 ff., 168, 180-181, 185,
   192, 201, 257
   against the Turk (see Turk, war
   against)
   cries, 183
   and discord and bloodshed, 226
   "over empty nut," 122 n. 74
   tax, 11 n. 21

three types of, 91, 103
weapons of, 238, 245
with the very devil, 257
Wartburg, 19 n. 5
Wealth, 129-130, 132, 185, 243-244, 251
Wedding, 281, 293, 295, 298, 300
public, 291
repeated celebration of, 294
Weimar, 72 n. 28
Wenches, 293-294
Wertheim, George, count of, 247 nn. 61, 62
West, 157
Whore, whoredom, 287, 293-294, 301-302
Why the Turks Defeated the Hungarians, 158 n. 9
Wicked, the, 66, 70-71, 73
Wickedness, 68, 81, 248
Widow, 150, 153
and orphans, 15, 42, 50, 78, 101
prayer of, 111
and relatives, 290
Wife, 313-316
and children, 71, 117, 254, 315
and husband (*see* Husband, and wife)
lawful, 302
one, single, 291, 298, 300
priests', 287 n. 29
protecting, 237
reconciling, 299
taking, 154
of Turks, 181
two or more, 287, 291
wedded, 292, 298, 313
Wilhelm VI, count of Henneberg, 141, 142 nn. 9, 11
Will of man, 76-77
bondage of, 18 n. 3
to marry, 304
not free, 274
Wills, made by the rich, 257
Wine, abstinence from, 177
Winkler, Georg, 227 n. 21
Wisdom, 102, 238 ff., 245
of the world, 228
Wise Men, 36
Witnesses, 261 n. 3, 268, 271, 284, 290, 307
Wittenberg, 48, 89, 106 n. 29, 143, 211, 234 n. 38, 263
Reformation, XI

riots, 19 n. 5, 21 n. 9
university, 19 n. 5, 210, 234 n. 39
Woman, women, 42, 271, 276, 315
and children, 71
common, 280, 291
education of (*see* Education, for girls)
first and second betrothed, 295 ff.
honorable, 292
of soldiers, 133
of the streets, 182
Womb, fruit of, 291
Woodcuts, 220 n. 14
Word and sacraments, service of, 220
Word of God (*see* God, word of)
Works, 83, 226
bodily, and miracles, 224
our own, 95
Turks' doctrine of, 177, 184
World, 27, 35, 77, 166, 171, 176, 179, 182, 196, 211, 225, 236, 246-247, 254, 265, 305, 317
end of, 18 n. 3, 55
love of, 154
secular, 141
Worms
Diet of, 142, 213 n. 2, 227 n. 23, 247 n. 61
Edict of, XI, XIII, 204 n. 125, 247 n. 62
printing of Bibles in, 239 n. 29
Worship, 227
of the devil, 229
of God, 148, 229
heathen, 236 n. 44
Writers, writing, 246-252, 256
Württemberg, peasant movement in, 85 n. 52
Würzburg, 47 n. 2

Zedekiah, 194
Zimri, 41
Zins, 220 n. 15
Zoar, 248
Zurich
Anabaptists, 90 n. 13
peasants, 106 n. 28
Zwickau, 158 n. 12
mayor of, 60 n. 9
prophets, 19 n. 5, 21 n. 9, 158 n. 12
Zwilling, Gabriel, 89 n. 5
Zwingli, Ulrich, 5 n. 4, 263
Zwinglian Reformation, XII

INDEX TO SCRIPTURE PASSAGES

Genesis
1 — 11, 13, 51
1:11-12 — 12
2 — 51
2:15 — 242
2:24 — 181
3:12 — 276
7:1-24 — 171
7:17-24 — 24
10:9 — 178
11:29 — 316
12:10 — 235
13:10-13 — 195 n. 98
14 — 10
14:17 — 193
17:23 — 39
18:22-23 — 174 n. 55
18:24-33 — 193
19:21 — 248
19:24 — 198, 254
19:24-28 — 24, 171
19:29 — 256
22:2 — 310
24:1-10 — 269 n. 8
24:15-50 — 269 n. 14
24:58 — 304
26:1 — 235
28:1-5 — 269 n. 9
29:21-30 — 299
39:5 — 192
41:53-56 — 248
41:56 — 235
48:1-7 — 269 n. 10

Exodus
3 — 9
3:7-8 — 9
6:5-7 — 35
14 — 9
15:23-25 — 253
17:11 — 256
21:9 — 269
21:14 — 70
22:16-17 — 277
22:28 — 107
31 — 10 n. 18

Leviticus
26:36 — 22

27 — 147 n. 11
27:16-24 — 147 n. 12

Numbers
6:1-21 — 177
14:40-45 — 120
16:31-35 — 41
21:21-30 — 120
30 — 151
30:1-2 — 151
30:2 — 146 n. 7, 152
30:3-5 — 151
30:6-8 — 151
30:9 — 151
30:10-15 — 152
30:16 — 152
35:1-8 — 233 n. 86

Deuteronomy
1:19-46 — 190
2:26-37 — 120
5:11 — 24, 33
6 — 12
10 — 10
12 — 10
17 — 10
18 — 10, 15
22:20-21 — 300
22:22 — 278
22:22-24 — 311
22:23-24 — 289
22:23-25 — 297 n. 44
22:28-29 — 280, 282
23:21-23 — 152
24:1-4 — 277
25 — 11
28:20, 25 — 94
32:21 — 64
32:35 — 25

Joshua
7:1-5 — 125

Judges
3:15-30 — 192
4:4—5:31 — 193
6:11—8:28 — 193
7:20 — 130
9:22-57 — 41

12:1-6 — 120
13:2—16:31 — 193
14:1-3 — 269 n. 11
20:18-25 — 191
20:22 — 191 n. 93
21:7 — 308
21:23 — 308
21:25 — 75 n. 34

I Samuel
1:22-28 — 148, 153
2:30 — 133
12:15 — 168 n. 31
14:6 — 193
15:4-24 — 66
15:34 — 148
22:18 — 193
24:1-7 — 112 n. 47
25:44 — 285
26:6-12 — 112 n. 47

II Samuel
15:32-37 — 102
16:16-19 — 102
16:22—17:23 — 193
18:14-15 — 41
20:22 — 41
24:10 — 172 n. 38,
    173 n. 49

I Kings
3:6-10 — 173 n. 50
15:25-29 — 104 n. 22
16:8-10 — 104 n. 22
16:18 — 41
18:2 — 235
20:42 — 66
21:27-29 — 172 n. 39
22:2-40 — 120

II Kings
3:14 — 192
4:1-7 — 173 n. 48
4:38 — 236
5:1 — 248
5:1-27 — 192
9:27-28 — 104 n. 22
14:8-14 — 120
17:6 — 107 n. 30

351

19:14-19 — 173 n. 54
23:29 — 120

II Chronicles
14:11-12 — 173 n. 51
20:5-12 — 173 n. 52
24:2 — 173 n. 53
33:10-13 — 172 n. 40
34:33 — 173 n. 53

Job
2:10 — 78, 79 n. 41
12:21 — 19 n. 4
34:30 — 109

Psalms
2:2 — 185
3:6 — 24
7:12-13 — 171
7:15 — 286
7:16 — 43 n. 59
18:26 — 64, 186
19:12 — 288
44:6-7 — 191
46:5 — 10
50:14 — 148, 153
50:15 — 34
50:23 — 149
60:10-12 — 191
66:13-14 — 153
68:12 — 221 n. 17
68:30 — 118, 120
76:4 — 178
76:11 — 153
90:8 — 22
91:15 — 34
104:31 — 246
107:40 — 19, 22
109 — 10
109:17 — 72
110:1 — 236
111:3 — 246 n. 59
113:5-8 — 250
121:1 — 33 n. 36
146:3 — 284 n. 26
147:10 — 170
147:11 — 191

Proverbs
3:9 — 38
8:14-15 — 238
20:25 — 148, 152
24:21 — 107 n. 36
24:21-22 — 65, 66

25:1-7 — 277 n. 24
26:27 — 103 n. 19
30:21-22 — 72
30:33 — 288

Ecclesiastes
5:4 — 148
5:4-5 — 152
5:8-9 — 128
7:15 — 247 n. 61
7:16 — 100, 288
9:15 — 245
9:16 — 238, 245
9:18 — 192, 238
10:1 — 100
10:14 — 65 n. 8
10:20 — 107 n. 36

Isaiah
10 — 14
10:5 — 170
11 — 15
14:5-6 — 70
53 — 12
55:11 — 136, 174
58:1 — 49
61:8 — 38

Jeremiah
15:1 — 43 n. 58
17:5-6 — 284 n. 26
18:7-8 — 171
18:9-11 — 171
21:7 — 194
26 — 14
44:16 ff. — 236

Lamentations
3:22 — 78 n. 41

Ezekiel
2:7 — 49
3:19 — 204
13:5 — 174
14:14 — 43 n. 58
22:30-31 — 174
33:9 — 204
38:2 — 202 n. 121

Daniel
8:27 — 245
12:3 — 224

Joel
2:23 — 221 n. 16

Haggai
1:13 — 221

Malachi
2:7 — 221

Matthew
1:19 — 300, 311
1:20 — 289
2 — 290
2:9 — 36
3:10 — 199 n. 107
3:11 — 75
4 — 12
5 — 11, 12
5:3, 11-12 — 83
5:17 — 145
5:20-44 — 197
5:29-30 — 74
5:31-32 — 277
5:39 — 165
5:39-41 — 28, 164
5:39-42 — 99
5:44 — 29
5:45 — 169
6:9 — 33
6:10, 13 — 34
6:19 — 245
6:22-23 — 73, 74 n. 29
6:24 — 130 n. 90, 215
6:31-33 — 235
7:1 — 49, 107, 113
7:3 — 26
7:3-5 — 109
7:12 — 111, 114
7:16 — 180
8 — 15
8:22 — 265, 266 n. 6
9:13 — 67
9:15 — 235
10 — 11, 14
102:10 — 129, 130 n. 89,
    233 n. 35
10:23 — 37, 105
10:31 — 318 n. 65
10:32 — 175 n. 58
10:37 — 306
11:5 — 224
11:10 — 221
11:13 — 145
11:23 — 254
12:34 — 65
13:43 — 224
15:12-14 — 63

16:18 — **228**
17:5 — 51
18:15-17 — 286
18:16 — 268
18:25 — 315
19:3-9 — 277
19:5 — 314
19:6 — 275
19:8 — 278
19:9 — 311
19:12 — 149, 153
19:29 — 130, 197
22:13 — 84
22:21 — 134, 316
22:37 — 197
23 — 15
23:34 — 37
24 — 18 n. 3
25:31-45 — 12 n. 26
25:34-36 — 83
25:42-43 — 230 n. 26
26:49 — 102
26:52 — 25, 30, 41, 166,
  198
28:20 — 222

Mark
4:15 — 9 n. 16
9:5-7 — 214 n. 6
9:23 — 136
13 — 18 n. 3
14:72 — 172 n. 41

Luke
1:52 — 23
2:34-35 — 64
3 — 14
3:14 — 97, 129
4 — 12
6 — 11, 15
6:36 — 67
9:60 — 266 n. 6
10:7 — 129 n. 88
10:7-8 — 233 n. 35
10:28 — 151
11:27 — 221
14:31 — 202-203
15:7 — 172 n. 44
18 — 9
18:10-14 — 172 n. 43
19:10 — 67
19:11 — 195
20:25 — 50, 51
21 — 18 n. 3

22:55 — 102
23:34 — 30
23:40-42 — 172 n. 42

John
1:1-14 — 135 n. 99
3:12 — 63
3:17 — 166
3:29 — 289
6 — 10, 11
6:15 — 166
6:35 — 175 n. 60
8:7 — 312
8:44 — 49, 81 n. 43, 179,
  227
10:11 — 146
13 — 12
14:12 — 224
14:14 — 33
18:10 — 29
18:36 — 81, 97, 166
19:11 — 195
19:15 — 20
21:15-19 — 172 n. 41

Acts
4:32-37 — 51
5 — 12
5:29 — 77, 130
10:9-13 — 12
10:34 — 285 n. 27
11:28 — 236
14 — 10
15:10-11 — 197
20:28 — 221

Romans
1 — 9
1:28 — 198
3:8 — 26
3:21 — 146
6:12-13, 19 — 153
7:2 — 278
8 — 9
8:11 — 224
8:12-13 — 150, 153
8:13 — 150
8:20 — 248
10 — 13
10:4 — 145
10:9 — 175
11 — 9
12:4 — 166
12:19 — 25 n. 22, 28, 29,
  107, 113

13 — 12
13:1 — 25, 50, 51, 55, 96,
  125, 134
13:1-4 — 95, 98
13:1-5 — 99
13:1-7 — 103
13:2 — 25, 50, 55, 66, 127
13:3-4 — 70, 74
13:4 — 25, 52, 53, 66, 68,
  73, 99, 118, 121, 238

I Corinthians
1:22-25 — 196 n. 100
3:11-15 — 182 n. 77
4:1 — 221
4:8 — 64
4:11 — 37
6:1-2 — 29
6:1-8 — 31
7:1-24 — 265
7:11 — 296, 299, 314
7:15 — 285, 286, 296
7:21-24 — 39 n. 48
7:32-35 — 299
9 — 11
9:7 — 131
9:14 — 130 n. 89, 233
10:30 — 12
12:14-26 — 166
12:28 — 221
13:4-7 — 131
14:40 — 166
15:24 — 127

II Corinthians
2:16 — 162
3:7, 6 — 145
4 — 237
5:20 — 221
10:4 — 32
11:20 — 29
11:27 — 235
12:9 — 32

Galatians
1:6 — 40 n. 52
1:9 — 147 n. 13
2 — 10
2:7-8 — 196 n. 100
2:19 — 145
3:28 — 39 n. 49
5:3 — 145
5:13 — 39 n. 49
6:7 — 82, 117

Ephesians
2:2 — 52
4:6 — 163
5:21-27 — 304 n. 52
6 — 14
6:5-9 — 39 n. 48
6:12 — 52, 168
6:17 — 197

Colossians
1:25 — 237
2:16-19 — 12
3:5-6 — 150, 153
3:22-25 — 39 n. 48

I Thessalonians
4:3-5 — 153

II Thessalonians
2:3-10 — 180 n. 72
2:4 — 180

I Timothy
2:1-2 — 107
3 — 10
4:3-5 — 12
4:10 — 34
5 — 11
5:11-12 — 150, 153
5:15 — 150
6:1-2 — 39 n. 48

6:10 — 154

II Timothy
2:26 — 77

Titus
1 — 10
1:12 — 84
2:9-10 — 39 n. 48
3:1 — 99

Hebrews
10:28 — 70
13:5 — 29, 233

James
3:2 — 288
5:16 — 174
5:16-17 — 33
5:17 — 173

I Peter
1 — 12
1:18-19 — 219
2 — 12
2:13 — 51
2:13-14 — 95, 98, 238
2:14 — 25, 70 n. 23, 73
2:16 — 32 n. 33, 36 n. 42
2:18 — 28
2:23 — 30
5:10 — 30 n. 30

II Peter
2:7-8 — 195

I John
2:15-17 — 154
2:18 — 8, 180
2:22 — 180
4:1 — 24
4:3 — 180
5:14 — 33

II John
7 — 180

APOCRYPHA
Wisdom of Solomon
6 — 12

Ecclesiasticus (Sirach)
18:30 — 153
27:25 — 67 n. 15
33:24 — 76 n. 35
38:1-8 — 253

Prayer of Manasseh
9 — 230

I Maccabees
3:19 — 191
5:55-60 — 120

Type used in this book
Body, 10 on 13 Caledonia
Display, Bulmer and Caledonia
Paper: Standard White Antique